The North Runner

A CONDENSATION OF THE BOOK BY

R. D. Lawrence

ILLUSTRATED BY JIM SHARPE

PUBLISHED BY ANDRÉ DEUTSCH

This is a true story, powerfully written out of deep personal experience. A story of nature untouched by civilization, and of an unexpected love.

R. D. Lawrence's search for inner peace and a new beginning had taken him to the frozen hinterlands of Canada. Alone there, and unsure of himself, he was faced one day by a brutally mistreated wolf dog, as untamed as the north itself.

A strange friendship sprang up between man and beast as together they struggled to survive, and learned from each other the true nature of interdependence.

Finally, for both of them, a long-closed door was opened, leading them through to a wider trust. Their wounds healed, their emotions tempered in the cold fire of the north, they could rejoin their fellows.

Chapter 1

THE yellow eyes bored into mine as the lips parted, wrinkled, and drew back into a silent snarl, showing the great fangs and the moist cavern of the mouth. He was without a doubt the most ill kept, the most beaten up, and the *biggest* sled dog that I had ever seen. His entire bearing bristled with threat, but it was the almond-shaped wolf eyes that most clearly signaled his aggressiveness; this dog was wild, and would not hesitate to go for the throat. He stood, his great paws planted on the bottom of the truck box, holding my eyes where another dog would have averted his glance. While we stared at each other, Alfred, the Ojibway Indian who hoped to sell the wolf dog to me, hovered nearby, a stout club in his hand.

I needed a lead dog for my team, but this monster spelled trouble, a creature more wolf than dog who had learned early to hate man. No, he wasn't for me. I had noted the heavy chain which secured him in the back of the pickup truck, the open cut on his left shoulder. I paused to have a closer look, being careful not to get within reach of those strong white teeth. There was something about the animal that touched me. Half starved and evidently brutalized since puppyhood, the dog yet had dignity, and the strength of him showed in every line.

We faced each other for some time in mutual appraisal. Then I

9

spoke to him as though he were another person. "You're a wild-looking dog, but I think I like the looks of you."

At the sound of my voice the dog pricked up his ears and raised his tail slightly; it seemed to me there was the merest nuance of a wag in the movement. I fervently hoped so, because by now I was determined to buy him, albeit against my better judgment. I turned to Alfred, prepared to drive a hard bargain.

"He's not pretty, that's for sure . . . and he looks as though he'd rather tear my throat out than lift his leg—"

"He's a good dog, pulls good," Alfred interrupted. "You carry a club, he's okay. He knows what a club's for, that dog."

"How much?" I asked bluntly.

Alfred, whom I had helped out of a bind in early summer and who had since become a friend, was anxious to turn the dog into cash money. "Would fifteen dollars be too much?" he asked.

I offered him twenty dollars, but I attached one condition: he was to remove the dog from the truck and lead him to an unused shed on my property. It was obvious that a club would be needed to get him there, and the dog was used to such treatment from the Indian. I hoped that if he never saw a club in my hand, I could win him over more quickly.

Alfred walked to the running board of the old truck, brandishing the club and mouthing curses. A moment later he was over the side and into the truck box, always keeping the weapon ready.

The animal backed up warily and snarled. He never took his eyes off the Indian. Alfred unfastened the chain that secured the dog to the truck, threatening all the time with the club, and then started pulling the animal toward the lowered tailgate. The captive moved forward, resisting enough to show he was acting under duress.

Alfred had already told me that the dog was nearly three years old. His grandmother had mated with a timber wolf. One of her litter, who was to become the big dog's father, was bred to another half wolf. The lupine heritage showed in the dog's size, looks, and the way that he moved, fluidly, catlike. Until I actually saw him, I suspected the Ojibway had been exaggerating in the hope of arousing my interest. I knew now that he had underplayed the dog's wolfishness for fear I might not want him.

10

Alfred got the animal to the very edge of the tailgate, jumped to the ground, and pulled the dog with him, turning quickly to threaten even more vigorously with the club. In the shed, I watched to make sure he fastened the animal securely to a stout wooden upright. Then we went out and closed the door. As we walked away, I could hear the prisoner lunging at his chain.

The Indian was anxious to leave and spend some of his wealth. This suited me; I wanted to feed the dog and spend a little time with him. If ever an animal needed a friend, it was this one.

My three other dogs were loose in the hay barn, and they knew instantly that a stranger had arrived, no doubt hearing his growls and certainly scenting his formidable rankness. As I waved Alfred off, the ruckus from the barn was clamorous; the males howled, and the collie bitch barked hysterically. They would not be pacified until I gave them an extra feed of dog meal.

After peace was restored, the new dog's rations were prepared: raw moose-meat scraps, a couple of big marrow bones, some dog meal, and a liberal helping of gravy from cooked moose offal. I also mixed in a larger-than-prescribed dosage of worm powder, for the newcomer would be full of parasites.

When I entered the shed, the wolf dog was lying down, broad head resting on his front paws, his ears pricked forward, and his eyes focused on the door; he didn't move until his keen nose picked up the smell of the food. With nostrils twitching, he jumped to his feet, warily expectant. I walked forward at an easy pace, stopped half a yard from him, and lowered the dish to the floor. As the food slid toward him, his entire body quivered. The poor beast was starving!

Ravenous he was, yet he did not attack the food as a house dog would have done. Instead, he sniffed at it suspiciously for several seconds, drooling continuously; then he picked up one of the bones and retreated to a corner. There he dropped it, smelled it again, licked it, and then padded back to the dish. He ignored me, except for a fast glance or two, just to make sure no hostile moves were made while he bent his muzzle to the feast.

Watching him, I wondered how long it would be before he trusted me enough to let me treat his injuries. They certainly needed attention. A scabbed place on his leg appeared to be

11

festering, and the deep, angry-looking cut on his shoulder needed some quick first aid. His coat was filthy and no doubt full of fleas and ticks. Once I got him cleaned up and fed plenty of nourishing food, he would be a great lead dog. But it would take time.

When he had almost finished the meal, I went to get a pail of water. I returned to find him chewing on the first moose bone. He looked up when I entered but continued his attack. I put the water down, then went to get the dish. He had moved it deeper inside the circumference of the chain, and it was now about five feet from where he was feeding. I bent down, about to grasp the pan with my left hand. He was unbelievably fast! Before my fingers touched the dish, his teeth fastened on the heel of my hand, and I actually heard his two tusks click inside my flesh. I couldn't believe it was happening, and because of this I didn't panic. I think it was my passivity more than anything else that made him let go without ripping and taking another slash. When he freed his hold, he backed up, growling, believing, no doubt, that he was now going to get a thorough clubbing.

For the next few moments my actions were governed by some subconscious feeling that it was vitally important not to show hostility or fear. Instead of backing off, as sanity dictated, I got up, stepped forward, and looked full into his eyes.

"That's the last time you're going to bite me, you hear!" I spoke gruffly, but I didn't raise my voice. He stood as before, eyeing me fixedly. I picked up the dish and left.

In the house, I washed the wounds and poured strong iodine over each fang hole. I had an urge to cut a club and go beat the hell out of the dog, but the ugly desire faded as the pain subsided. When I had regained my composure, I went to the larder, cut three pieces of moose meat, and took them back to the shed.

The dog was lying down again. Holding the meat in my right hand, I moved to within six feet of him, talking softly. He stayed where he was, but he watched me alertly. I extended the bitten hand and held it palm outward, almost like a peace sign.

"Do you see that?" I made my voice gruff again.

His expression didn't change. He looked at my hand, sniffed at it, but soon swiveled his eyes back to mine. He had evidently picked up the scent of the moose meat, for he looked at my other

12

hand expectantly, ears stiffly alert. He got onto all fours and took a step toward me. I switched to gentle talk. It was hard not to back away. I tossed him the three pieces of meat at once. He snapped up one in midair. When he had finished eating, he turned and went to lie down in his corner, the first time that he had fully exposed his back in my presence. Resting his head on the floor between his front paws, he licked his lips a couple of times, yawned, and closed his eyes. I uttered a few more quiet words, and he half opened his eyes to watch me leave the shed.

ALFRED brought the dog to my homestead on November 12, 1955, almost eleven months after I had arrived in the northern Ontario backwoods and eighteen months from the date I had landed in Canada from England. During the first half year of my life in the New World, events had quickly become routine once the bloom of strange surroundings had worn off. One crisp autumn evening I suddenly realized that the real purpose of my departure from Europe had not been achieved. I had simply exchanged metropolitan London for metropolitan Toronto. But my inner restlessness, the extreme distaste for crowds, continued to irritate the tender places I carried somewhere inside my head. There was no peace in Toronto, and peace was what I wanted.

In the summer of 1936, when I was not yet fourteen years old, the Civil War in Spain had found me in a camp for boys on the shores of the Mediterranean. A little more than three years later, when I was still a teenager, World War II arrived to give me a new uniform, a new cause, and final proof that mankind had gone quite mad. Afterward, limping from a shrapnel injury, I tried to settle in London. I got a job as a reporter, grubbed through the city streets on assignments, wrote pointless articles, and at last decided that a new start in a new land had to be made. In 1954 I shook the soot of London from my heels.

Now the less black, but equally abrasive, atmosphere of Toronto had to be dusted off. That evening I returned to my lodgings, packed my few belongings in the car, and set out for the North. Three days and twelve hundred eventful, fascinating miles later found me parked tight against a four-foot snowbank, reading a crudely lettered FOR SALE sign posted on the fence post of a deserted log house. This was it, I decided, the place I had been looking for. It was two hundred acres, forty of them cleared, the rest forested, mingling with thousands of miles of Ontario wilderness. The nearest human was more than a mile away, the nearest town, population nine hundred, was twenty-seven; no telephones, no power lines, but unlimited peace.

There was no address on the sign, but inquiries at a general store in a hamlet four miles away elicited the name and address of the owner. Soon eight hundred dollars changed hands over a couple of signatures in a law office, and before Christmas I was settled on the old homestead.

Winter came and with it logging and hunting for my food and days of wandering through the white-topped land. There were dawns the like of which I had never experienced, and nights of sound, nightmare-free slumber. The wilderness exerts enormous influence on a man alone, freshly arrived from civilization. Some cannot take the solitude, the absence of comfort. The city is too much with them, and they don't last. There are also those who go too far the other way, becoming misanthropes. But between the quitters and the lone stayers, there are those in whom the wilderness acts as a catalyst. They begin to form new values, and to realize that nature is an endlessly patient teacher. This is how the wilderness affected me.

And then came Sussie, a bitch dog, gaunt, starving, a waif of the North, mostly collie. She arrived at the back door and scratched, whining. When I opened it, she entered as though she belonged there. After she had eaten, she curled up by the fire, thumped her matted tail twice in gratitude, and fell into a deep sleep, from which she didn't awaken for four hours. She was my first dog, and a good companion.

Next I bought Rocky, a malamute. He was a true dog of the North, lean, wolfish, eighty-five pounds of sled-puller who more than repaid me the thirty-five dollars he cost. Then I acquired the sled, a heavy U.S. Army war surplus vehicle. Its weight required a third dog, and so Sooner was added. I had hoped he would be the leader; he was older, seemed wiser than Rocky, if not quite as big. But it turned out he would sooner eat than pull, thus his name. All in all, it was an indifferent collection, and that was why, at the end of the next summer, I began looking for a suitable team leader.

The night of the big dog's arrival, I was not at all sure I had found what I was looking for. Washing up one-handed after supper, feeling the throb of the bite, I was most conscious of the work that lay ahead: the winter fuel to cut, a henhouse to build, then a winter of cutting logs to sell to the distant city paper mill. This was my only immediate source of revenue, and it was already half committed to pay for traplines, which I hoped would furnish spring and summer income after the furs were marketed. To this had been added the need to tame the wild dog.

After the dishes were done, I sat for a time sipping coffee and debating my next moves. It was then the idea came. Why not spend the night with him in the shed? With the remaining coffee in a thermos, a paper bag of oatmeal cookies I had baked, my sleeping bag, and a kerosene lantern, I went to the shed.

In the yellow glow of the light the big dog looked more savage than usual, but he did not show actual hostility when I entered. His ears moved at the sound of my voice, and his eyes were fixed on me as I unrolled the sleeping bag just out of his reach. Sitting on the bedroll, back against the wall, I poured a cup of coffee and munched a cookie, now and then speaking to the dog. He couldn't make out what was going on. This was most likely the first time that a human had lain close to him. I threw him a cookie; he smelled it and ate it, rising to come forward even as he was swallowing. He ate three more while I finished the coffee.

For about an hour I sat propped against the wall, puffing silently on my pipe, feeling that I no longer needed to resort to speech. Somehow we had become attuned to each other. Occasionally the yellow eyes would swivel to my face, but their expression was no longer hostile. The November night got chilly, crystaled by the first frosts of the dying year. To keep warm, I slid into the bag. When my eyes got heavy, I shuffled down, burrowing like some animal in its den, concealing even my head.

I THOUGHT at first I had been awakened by a dream. Befuddled as I was with sleep, the sensation of someone shaking my shoulder was strong, but I knew I was alone with the dog. Yet even as I stuck my head out of the sleeping bag, my shoulder was shaken again. I was unprepared for what met my gaze. The furred legs and chest of the dog were very close to me, and when I looked up, it was to see his massive head. His jaws couldn't reach me, for he was at the extent of his chain, but his paws could. As I moved, he lifted one front foot and pawed again, and he was whining! Evidently I had turned over in my sleep, moving, bag and all, a lot closer to him than I would have dared to get while awake.

It must be remembered that I had just come from a deep sleep, that this enormous creature had bitten through my hand not long ago. Reflex made me roll away too quickly, causing him to jump back and snarl. Clearly he had interpreted my sudden move as an act of aggression. He did not seem to be as hostile as yesterday, but he wouldn't respond after I had gathered my wits and walked toward him, talking quietly. Standing close to the wall, he snarled deeply. I was angry with myself for missing the opportunity to win the dog's trust, and I felt it would be better to go have breakfast and return later with food for him. Perhaps then I could make up the lost ground.

It was full daylight when I came back, carrying a dish of meat and dog chow. He rose, already sniffing the aroma of the food, and half wagging his tail as though he were embarrassed at showing emotion. I walked up to him, put the dish down, and left silently.

The other dogs had to be fed, the cow milked, and the chickens inspected and counted. There was a hungry bobcat nearby who had already tried to get his talons in the red rooster. While I was feeding the dog team, I got an idea. When chores were done, I would take Sussie from the barn to the shed and let her and the newcomer become acquainted, for male dogs will not attack a female. After that I would fuss over her, allowing the big dog to see how she trusted me and delighted in being caressed.

Milking the cow and thinking about the scheme, I suddenly realized that the new dog had no name. Presently the white, frothy milk suggested one. I thought of snow, and mountains in the Far North, and although I had not been to the Yukon Territory, the photographs I had seen came to mind. Yukon . . . the name suited him; he was as wild as the North and as rugged as the mountains.

Sometime later I called Sussie, stopped Rocky and Sooner from

sneaking out of the barn behind her, and led the collie to the shed. Sniffing intently while I opened the door, she eagerly popped into the building. By the time I followed, the two were nose to nose, Sussie showing in her stance that she wasn't going to fall all over this scruffy stranger, but coy enough to invite his attention. Yukon was holding himself tall, tail up high, wagging vigorously, ears forward, and (I swear to it!) an inane smile on his face. He didn't glance in my direction, but now pranced as well as his chain would allow, darting forward only to be brought up short. Sussie, the flirt, backed away, wagging her tail sedately. Yukon whined, straining at the chain until he actually coughed.

Stepping back to the far wall, I called Sussie. As always, she came; I spoke to her affectionately, rubbing her belly, while I talked as much for Yukon's benefit as for hers.

Sussie loved every second of the act, but the big lummox sounded as though he was going to choke himself. He coughed and spluttered, jumping against the chain, pleading with the collie to come back to him. What I did next made me feel a little guilty, but I sensed it to be the right move.

Still caressing Sussie, I took her outside, carefully placing us at an angle that allowed Yukon to witness events. I invited her to play, and she ran around me in circles, barking ecstatically and coming in every now and then for more patting. Then Yukon started to howl, the song of the wolf, beginning deep, rising slowly, and fading into a contralto moan. Sussie halted in her tracks, then scampered into the shed. In the meantime, Rocky and Sooner picked up the big dog's howl, and soon Sussie joined in. The concert continued for several minutes.

Yukon and Sussie fell silent. Now she moved close to the other dog and allowed herself to be well and truly sniffed. When I went inside, Yukon was much too busy to devote any attention to me, but when I called Sussie again, he repeated his previous antics. A little at a time I edged closer to him, Sussie at my side. The last step had to be taken, the one that would put me in range of the dog's fangs. Suddenly the big head was under my left hand while Sussie's smaller and finer pate was under my right. My fingers caressed both dogs, but my eyes were glued on Yukon. Right then I knew I had nothing more to fear from him.

Chapter 2

BECAUSE there was so much of the wolf in Yukon, it was he who first taught me about his kin, especially about the strong relationships that exist in the pack. For the wolf, the pack is paramount, its rules are inflexible, but good for all. It inspires deep loyalties and fierce, unselfish love. Of course, members of a pack sometimes compete for position, but whether they win or lose, the fighting is nearly bloodless and rarely leads to killing. The loser does not lose in the sense that humans view the term, but simply returns to his place within the pack's hierarchy, without shame or ostracism.

Until the morning when Yukon put his massive head under my hand, the dog had never acknowledged any leadership but his own. He viewed me as he did all humans, as a threat, and he was determined not to capitulate, taking his lumps, licking his wounds, waiting for the moment when he could either escape or kill. Then he was confronted with kindness, and he was confused. Anger and brutality he could deal with, but this was something quite beyond his understanding.

If I am accurate in this assessment, the contest for leadership was probably won during that first night, when I talked to him and shared the cookies with him. No doubt he then became lonely when I slipped all the way down into the sleeping bag, and it was probably for this reason that he pawed me. What followed reawakened his hostility. But when Sussie came in, showed her trust in me, Yukon voluntarily joined our "pack," electing me its leader.

While stroking the two dogs, I was at first conscious of little else but the pleasure of gaining Yukon's friendship. When my fingers began to encounter the wood ticks, some of them as big and as black as ripe grapes, I was reminded of the dog's distress and the need to care for him. Now I faced a major decision. I *had* to accept the dog's trust without concern for my safety. Anything less would be quickly detected by him.

I squatted between the two dogs, leaned my head against Yukon's vermin-infested face, and slid my arm around his shoulders. He pushed hard against me. Sussie, a bit jealous, licked my face. I judged it was time to stand. Talking softly, caressing each animal, I undid the chain from the wooden upright and moved to the door. Yukon walked next to me, never once tugging at the chain. Sussie trotted beside him. I took them both to the house.

Yukon hesitated for just an instant at the open door of my dwelling, but followed Sussie inside. I closed the door and called Sussie, who had immediately gone to sniff at the cast iron cooking range. Then I took off Yukon's heavy leather collar and went into the living room.

Both dogs ran in after me. Yukon suddenly became aware that the collar was missing from his neck. After such long use, it had worn the hair off almost to the skin. He began to roll on the floor, kicking his legs in the air. Sussie thought this was a fine game. She jumped over him, barking. The two dashed at full speed between the kitchen and the living room. Now and then Sussie knocked into a chair, but Yukon avoided every obstacle with his remarkable catlike grace.

Not very long after that, I set about attending to the big dog's needs, feeling confident he would now allow me to do so.

While I prepared both medication and bug treatment, Yukon lay on the floor, watching me, thumping his tail occasionally. He showed little interest when he saw me approaching with a bowl of antiseptic and a roll of cotton. His keen nose told him that the bowl did not contain food.

As luck would have it, the open cut on his shoulder was uppermost. I sat beside him and spoke softly, stroked his head, then ran my hand over his massive chest and continued toward the cut. The big head raised itself, but the dog was merely interested, watchful. I touched the edges of the nasty wound gently, pushing the lips together. At that, Yukon licked my hand, then licked the wound. I applied some antiseptic to the cut. Again Yukon licked, but the acrid taste made him stop at once. After that he remained docile while I bathed his wounds again and again.

The ticks came next. He was full of them. In the backwoods where these unpleasant beasts are found, practically everybody has a pet method for removing them. But the best way of all is to choke them out. The brutes are air breathing and must suck in oxygen. Anoint them liberally with butter, Vaseline, dubbin, or axle grease and they back out, gasping for air within a minute or two. Butter wouldn't do to rub on Yukon; he would simply lick it off. However, I had a jar of greasy, medicated ointment which would work admirably.

This time Yukon objected to his treatment. He growled half-heartedly and showed his teeth, but I ignored him. I *knew* he wouldn't bite. It was rather wonderful; yesterday he would have torn me to pieces; today he protested but did not attempt to snap. I was at once elated and moved by his acceptance of me.

When the last tick had been anointed, I gave him a good grooming. He loved every minute of it, even suffering his tail to be combed and brushed, and exhibiting considerable curiosity over the great tangled balls of old fur that littered the floor. Then I stepped back to appreciate the results of my labors.

He was no longer the same dog! Yukon's once dirty, tangled fur was sleek, glossy, and fluffed out. His mane, a thick roach of black hair that began atop his shoulder blades and extended along the neck, stood out magnificently. The white on his chest was almost milky; his tail looked twice its former size. He advanced toward me, holding his head high, his slant eyes full of *joie de vivre*.

He came up to me, rose lightly on his hind legs, and put one great front paw on each of my shoulders. Slap! His long pink tongue splashed against my chin and traveled upward to end wetly at my hairline.

For the next week Yukon remained in the house, when he wasn't out with me and Sussie. I wondered how he would react when the time came to put him in the barn with the other dogs, but the thought caused me no great concern. As it turned out, keeping him with me continuously during those first days was, I believe, largely responsible for the strong bonds that were to grow between us. We did all things together, and it was amazing to note how quickly he staked his claim to the homestead. When a woodpecker came to chisel into a dead tamarack behind the barn, Yukon's one ambition was to chase that bird into the next county.

The day he was properly introduced to the other dogs, my participation was confined to opening the barn door. I was thrust aside as he dashed in with tail held high. I followed, but found myself ignored. In the center of the barn stood Yukon, virile, keenly alert, his tail arranged in the tight spiral that reflected superiority and advertised his desire to respond to any challenge.

The other three faced the newcomer. Sussie was wagging her tail, confirming her earlier allegiance to Yukon. Sooner, the smallest of the three males, stood with drooping tail and ears back. His easygoing nature wanted no part of a leadership trial.

Rocky was a different kind of dog. Chunky and well muscled, he was used to dominating the others. He was not about to allow a newcomer to strip him of his power. Sussie and Sooner edged away from the "center ring." The rivals took up a stance some distance apart, lips peeled back, hackles raised. I stood stock-still, worried. There was no doubt who the victor would be. Even though he was not in prime condition, the wolf dog was a fearful creature that outweighed Rocky by a good twenty pounds.

Would Yukon kill Rocky if he weren't stopped? Could I stop him? I decided that I would have to do something. Then it was too late. Even as Rocky took one step forward, Yukon surged swiftly ahead and smashed his big chest into Rocky's right shoulder, a tremendous, battering blow that flung the malamute up against the barn wall with a loud thump. It was simple, but effective, calculated to end the fight before it began.

But Rocky was not going to relinquish his leadership quite so easily. Snarling viciously, he jumped to his feet and rushed at Yukon, seeking to fasten his teeth on the big dog's throat. He came close, but when his jaws snapped shut, the bite managed only to clip a tuft of hair from the wolf dog's shoulder. Then Yukon ducked under the other's jaws and reared upward suddenly, throwing Rocky back off his feet. By the time he hit the floor Yukon was already straddling him, reaching with those enormously powerful jaws to take hold of the other dog's neck. He held on, growling deeply, pinning Rocky down.

At first Rocky growled back, but when he could not break the hold on his neck, his growls became hysterical yelps. In the end the malamute ceased to struggle and became silent.

I realized that Yukon did not intend to kill. This astounded me at the time, for I was not then aware of the built-in, inhibitory factors that prevent animals of the same species from destroying each other, natural safeguards programmed into every species with the exception of our own.

Yukon released his hold slowly and shifted his position, no longer astride his opponent. He, too, stopped growling, but he kept his head down, jaws open, and eyes fixed on the other's face. At this, Rocky lifted his back leg: a canine sign of surrender. He made doubly sure that the new leader would understand this when he turned and offered his throat as a target, the supreme gesture of surrender. Yukon was appeased. Without more ado, he cast one long and challenging glance around the barn and walked to Sooner, who was doing his best to hide between my legs.

Satisfied, Yukon then turned to Sussie, and the two spent some moments licking each other and wagging their tails before the new leader walked casually to me and nuzzled my hand.

"Okay, you're the boss now. How about a *walk?*" I stressed the last word, knowing that they all recognized its meaning. A second or two later I was surrounded by a press of dogs, and Yukon lost some of his dignity as he led the pack to the door.

After that day, I started training the dogs to work together as a team. Northern sled dogs are veritable "muscle machines," bred for generations for endurance and a will to work. Typically, they have fairly short, erect ears; long, bushy tails; and a double layer of warm fur. Roughly speaking, there are three distinct breeds: the Alaskan malamute, the Eskimo husky, and the Siberian husky. Malamutes and Eskimo dogs are big, weighing between eighty and ninety-five pounds. The Siberian dogs are smaller, varying between forty-five and sixty pounds. All three breeds have the stamina, keen intellect, and super senses of the wolf coupled with the muscular body of the larger domestic dogs. A good sled dog can pull twice its own weight. Yukon, for instance, could pull me *and* an additional two hundred pounds.

After chores each day, the dogs were lead-trained for an hour, rewarded with a tidbit afterward, and allowed to frisk. When the play period ended, Sussie, Sooner, and Rocky were returned to the hay barn, while Yukon came into the house with me. He was still receiving preferential treatment, even against the advice of the local sages, who believed that working dogs become spoiled if they are shown affection. I did not then, and do not now, share this view. But today I can be more positive that love, openly shown, produces far better results than the whip.

In any event, Yukon did not go into the barn, not just yet.

Chapter 3

IT HAD become my habit, before Yukon's arrival, to spend a good part of each day walking the wilderness, clearing trails, and marking future trap locations, leaving traps in strategic areas of the line. Now I began taking Yukon with me on these journeys, keeping him on a lead for fear that he would scent something interesting and take off, but releasing him near home so he could have a final run before nighttime. It was while we were on one of these walks that the incident with the bull moose occurred.

It may be that in its madness the moose was simply running in the wrong direction, but sight of the phantasmagoric creature charging directly at me was too much for a nervous system that had for some time been calmly relaxed. I stood as though rooted in the ground, staring at the grotesque, staggering giant.

Forgotten was the Lee-Enfield rifle hanging from its sling over my shoulder; forgotten, too, was the dog straining against his lead. In my mind there was room only for the ragged and emaciated animal that continued to run toward me, eyes showing white, head held high and tilted backward. Sick though it obviously was, it could yet smash its way through the first-growth spruce and snap the younger trees like so many dry sticks.

Now it was no more than twenty feet away, traveling with enough speed to be on top of me within a few seconds. And I just stood there, stunned into immobility.

Yukon, fortunately, was made of sterner stuff. He lunged forward, pulling the lead out of my hand and emitting one deep growl. Then, in silence, he leaped for the moose. High into the air he went, body stretched out fully, every line of him charged with feral menace. They came together, and Yukon's hunting fangs closed on the nose of the crazed animal. Dog and moose went down in a melee of thrashing limbs.

At last I came out of my spell. It took but a split second to remove the rifle from my shoulder, but now I couldn't shoot without hitting the dog. His initial nose hold was shaken loose by the fall, but he instantly secured a fresh grip on the bull's neck, preventing the animal from regaining its feet. The frantic beast kicked wildly.

24

I began to worry about Yukon. The legs of the moose were lethal weapons. One kick, and the dog would be severely injured.

I tried to call him off, but even if he heard, he was too close to the primeval to respond. I stood almost on top of the struggling animals, trying to get a clear shot. Then, heaving mightily, the bull shook his head. Yukon was flung clear.

He was leaping back to attack when I poked the rifle forward and fired. The moose dropped as though poleaxed, shot through the brain. Yukon, already launched into space, sailed over the carcass to land several yards away. He came tearing back to worry his fallen adversary.

Injudiciously I moved forward to pick up his lead. The legs of the moose kicked violently, powered by the last contractions of the nervous system. One of the pointed hoofs grazed my left thigh, scraping off a round patch of skin and throwing me backward. But Yukon, elastic as a rubber band, dodged out of the way.

Give that dog credit! Instead of returning to the dead animal, he came to me, to lick my face and dance around me as I stood up. After taking hold of his lead again, I led him away and tied him to a tree, despite his tugs and yelps of protest. As the victorious hunter, he wanted to return to his prey and take a snack from its body. This I would not allow. The moose had obviously been ill and could not be utilized as food for the dogs or myself.

I walked back to the dead beast and examined it with care. It was woefully thin, its dark coat dry and ragged, the hair actually scraped away in many places. One antler had been snapped off, leaving about three inches of jagged stump. This was clear evidence that the animal must have charged into trees or rocks while in the grip of its suffering. The body and legs were badly lacerated. It was a pitiful sight; I was glad the bullet had quickly ended its tortures.

Wondering about the cause of the animal's distress, I recalled having been told by a neighbor that moose sometimes poison themselves by eating a species of vetch. This plant, also known as locoweed, eventually led to the blind staggers, a term that, when I remembered the bull's behavior, was certainly apt enough.

Nevertheless, I bent to have a closer look. This sort of puzzle fascinated me. I had studied biology in England and still kept up

25

an abiding interest in it. Now I couldn't get rid of the presentiment that the bull's condition was not due to locoweed but to a disease of some kind—a virus or bacteria, perhaps a parasitic infestation. If any of these were responsible, the moose could become a source of infection for a variety of animals. I could not in all conscience walk away knowing that other creatures would eat the tainted meat, not after seeing how the moose had been tortured by the mysterious ailment. I decided I would burn the carcass.

But first I had to take Yukon home. Also, I needed some containers to hold the tissue samples I intended to take from the dead animal. Later I would examine them under the battered old microscope I had brought with me from England.

The part of the wilderness where the bull lay was about three miles from home. More than two hours had elapsed by the time I returned there from the cabin, carrying with me a bow saw, glass jars to hold the samples, and a case of dissecting tools. Working steadily, I cut enough firewood to cover the moose. Then I took tissue samples from the muscles, gut, spinal cord, and brain. Afterward I stacked the wood around the carcass and watched over the macabre bonfire until the flames died down.

Dusk was settling like a vast shroud over the wilderness by the time I got back home, to find Yukon amusing himself by chewing the legs of the kitchen table. Fortunately he was not single-minded about it. He had sampled every leg in several places instead of concentrating on one particular support. In this way the table continued to stand, even if all its limbs showed the ravages of the dog's powerful teeth.

"Hey! You great bum! What d'you think—"

Yukon, not a bit abashed, was instantly on his feet. He dashed at me, bowing and wagging his tail at the same time, then raised himself on his hind legs, the better to hit me in the mouth with a wet, sawdust-laden tongue. My irritation vanished instantly, and even though I would have preferred a different kind of greeting, I could only feel happy that he was here to welcome me.

To show my appreciation, I punched him, a light blow I knew would precipitate a mock battle. He tried to dodge, failed, and turned swiftly to slam into me with his chest. Then he grabbed my pant leg and pulled me around the kitchen, growling ferociously.

26

This play ritual had developed within a few days of our friendship and by now had become habit for both of us. During those times when he knocked me down, which he did often, he would grab whatever part of my clothing his reaching mouth first touched, then let go when I threw my arms around him and wrestled him down beside me. This was almost his favorite sport. He would struggle powerfully, using his back legs to kick and his body, so full of steely muscles, to force me to let go.

That evening I was tired and acknowledged defeat by venting a series of low wolf howls. This always stopped Yukon immediately. He would back off, sit looking rather worried, and gaze deeply into my eyes. If I persisted, he showed signs of acute distress and would begin to howl himself. Then I would immediately open my arms wide and call him to me. He would come and I would put my head against his shaggy coat and we would both enjoy a good love. But I did not persist that night. Instead, I spoke the magic word, "supper." While he was eating, I left the house to take care of the rest of my oddly assorted family.

The next day, still intensely curious, I determined to study the tissue samples I had taken from the sick moose. My microscope revealed nothing abnormal in the muscle tissue, but the first slice of brain tissue gave me a surprise. There, under the lens, were the unmistakable shapes of no fewer than seven tiny roundworms! I had never heard of such a thing. Roundworms in the gut of an animal were common, but in the *brain?*

I spent that afternoon and evening going over my fairly extensive biology literature. Not a single reference to brain worms could I find. The closest I was able to come was an organism called *Pneumostrongylus,* which parasitizes the lungs of wild and domestic animals.

Was it possible, I wondered, that *Pneumostrongylus* had in some way deviated from the lungs into the brain of the moose? If this was so, it would account for the animal's condition, its staggering gait and crazed behavior.

Ten years later I was to learn that my seemingly wild guess had been very close to the mark. Research in Ontario revealed that *Pneumostrongylus* was, indeed, responsible for the blind staggers! Poison vetch was not implicated at all.

27

AFTER THE MOOSE affair, Yukon and I spent several peaceful days walking the trapline, carrying supplies and tools. The weather became colder and the skies were cloudy, but the snow held off, unusual in a country where the first flakes not infrequently come by mid-September. Daily I expected to wake up to a whitened forest, and looked forward to the quiet time when the dead leaves are decently buried and lie silent underfoot.

As that particular autumn was about to disappear forever, I found myself at the crossroads of a friendship that was to become so deep and abiding that it had the power to change my life. I would not have thought it possible that a ragged, seemingly vicious animal could exert such influence on a human. And yet, had I given it enough reflection, I might have recognized that the symbiosis of man and dog, ripening as it had done during unknown ages, does indeed have the power to affect the future of a man, especially under conditions such as Yukon and I were to share in the years to come. Together we traveled the wilderness, and we gave each other strength, friendship, and a kind of love that really cannot be described.

Yukon now carried his share of the load, for I had made him a backpack out of old horse harness straps and heavy canvas. The finished product was hardly aesthetic, but it was practical and durable. And with Yukon's first load it became evident that he derived a sense of purpose from working, as though he *knew* he was doing something useful and necessary.

Back home that first evening, he refused to allow the pack to be taken off, playfully avoiding my attempts to do so. I let him keep it on and decided he might enjoy showing it off to the other dogs. His willingness to carry a load could even be a good example for Rocky and Sooner, neither of whom had backpacked.

When we entered the barn, Sussie welcomed Yukon in her usual way, showed little interest in his satchels, and came to me to be petted. Sooner, always eager to investigate anything that might contain food, forgot pack ritual and pushed forward to sniff the canvas and leather. When Yukon snarled angrily, Sooner quickly realized his error and backed up frantically.

Now Rocky arrived. Intrigued by the newness strapped to Yukon's back, he, too, forgot his manners. He approached arrogantly and extended none of the ritual courtesies. Yukon's mane erected fully, and his growl was heavy with menace. Rocky ignored the warning signs, and a fight ensued instantly. Yukon surged forward, fastened his teeth in Rocky's right shoulder, and shook him with such strength that the malamute was thrown across the barn. When Rocky launched himself again at his attacker, Yukon seized the other dog by the muzzle, twisted viciously, and pinned him to the ground. Poor Rocky quickly capitulated.

The fight couldn't have lasted for more than ten seconds, but it left Rocky with some bad gashes on his shoulder and a slit in one of his ears. Yukon, of course, came off lightly.

But responsibility for the fight was mine. By allowing Yukon to spend so much time away from his teammates, I had not given the dogs a chance to establish pack routines. It was as important for Yukon to become accustomed to leading as it was for Rocky and the others to become used to being led. Henceforth, Yukon would have to spend more time in the barn. That very night he slept with the rest of the team.

The next morning I realized I would have to do something about my depleted meat supply. So, after chores were completed, Yukon and I started off, the dog's pouches stuffed full of traps. I intended to set these out; then I would do a little hunting. One good-sized moose would keep my larder stocked for the winter.

As we traveled through the forest, distributing the traps, I kept a sharp lookout for signs, but not a trace of the animals did we find. By the time we got home I knew I must scout farther afield, among the spruces and beaver ponds, where the moose were sure to be. The job of bringing home six hundred pounds of meat would be made harder because of distance. One reason I was looking forward to the snow was the opportunity it presented to use sled and dogs to haul back meat.

By early December I still had not managed to shoot a moose, and I was worried. As the weather became colder and the snow refused to fall, the moose were retreating into their hiding places, leaving hardly any tracks on the frozen ground. Day after day I set out at first light, alone now because Yukon would have been a hindrance—or so I thought then. Returning at dusk empty-handed and dispirited, I would sit down to a dish of beans laced with a meager amount of bacon. What game was left in the larder was needed for the dogs.

It was not only the lack of hunting success that bothered me. It was a question of time. There was the trapline to run, and I had a contract to cut and deliver fifty cords of spruce pulpwood to a mill some seventy miles to the south. The deadline was January 31, less than two months away. Since this was the only source of grocery money during the winter, I wasn't anxious to fall down on the job. Here, too, I needed the dogs and sled for hauling. And still the snow kept away.

THE calm before the storm is not a cliché in the North. Usually snow arrives in stealth and in the dead of night, bringing as a companion the big cold. At one moment it seems that the usual background sounds of the wilderness are present; at the next, the land becomes utterly still. The animals, magnificently primitive and sensitive, notice the change of tempo and respond to it by gradually quieting even the slight noises that they make. By the time the full calm settles over the wilderness it is as though all life has vanished, leaving only the silently moving aurora that reflects itself endlessly on each particle of frost and creates uncountable, tiny frost stars. And the mercury keeps dropping.

The calm arrived sometime between the supper hour and bedtime at the end of one of those days of abortive hunting. Just before sitting down to my dull supper, I went outside for some firewood. The mercury reading was twenty degrees below zero Celsius. After supper I washed up and sat beside the heater with a book for a couple of hours, then got up to go out for more logs.

The change of temperature struck me as soon as I opened the door. Out on the porch, I felt the intense stillness and saw the blue-green lights rippling in a firmament peppered with bright stars. I watched the spectacle for some moments, never tiring of this display of northern lights. Then I went to look at the thermometer. The mercury was now forty-six degrees below zero Celsius, or, for those accustomed to Fahrenheit, fifty-one degrees below zero. I couldn't believe it; it seemed so *uncold* (one can never say "warm" when describing a night of northern winter).

Keewatin came that night, bringing rising temperatures and

driving endless fat snowflakes before him. *Keewatin*, the north wind of the Cree, spawns the blizzard and may blow for four or five days without cessation. Piles of snow pack into every nook and cranny of the forest, even where the spruces and cedars press close together and try to stop the whirling flakes from settling at their skirts. These places are reserved for the wild ones that must endure the storm curled up under the boughs, there to stay until *Keewatin* loses his anger and retreats whence he has come.

The next morning the temperature was up to ten degrees below zero Celsius, but I had to go outside to see the thermometer because the snow was compacted against the windows. As I stood in the porch doorway and looked across the clearing, my eyes couldn't penetrate the wall of moving white that lay between the house and the forest. Never had I imagined such snow! The whole world was wrapped in white. After hurrying to the barn, I fed the chickens, then, as a treat, led the dogs to the house for breakfast. All was well while they were eating, but as soon as the meal was done, their energies uncoiled and they dashed wildly through the entire house. In the end I had to return them to the barn before sitting down to my own food.

The blizzard continued for two days. The flakes kept coming down, but were blown upward instantly, creating a storm within a storm. Twice I went outside to the clearing after giving the dogs their morning feed. Each time I returned quickly, fleeing to the shelter of the house almost blind and on the threshold of fear lest I should become lost only yards from home, a very real possibility. After the second try, I gave up, and contented myself with watching through the window and reading Thoreau's *Walden*.

In late afternoon of the second day the force of *Keewatin* slackened. The wind had blown itself out by evening, leaving behind a snowy rear guard that continued until sometime after midnight. I went to bed, but my sleep was restless. I awoke at first light, got dressed, and went outside. The snowshoes had been hanging on the porch since last March. I put them on.

Now the walking was silent, the webs sinking four or five inches into snow that was two feet deep. But the forest was a place of sounds again. The nasal, shrill call of a pileated woodpecker issued from the woods. I spotted it, flying with its jerky wing-folding

31

movement across the small clearing. Chickadees twittered softly as they searched for dormant insects.

A soft breeze tousled the treetops, dislodging cascades of snow that came hissing down. Soon the sun rose full over the trees, and the wilderness was bathed in golden light. Content, I spent some time tramping down a good trail between barn and house, my marching accompanied by the howls of the dogs, who wanted to be free to join me. I got their breakfasts ready, and while they were eating, the hens were fed, three frozen eggs were collected, and I went back to cook my own food. An hour later I was off, rifle hanging from the shoulder, in quest of moose and followed by a chorus of reproachful howls.

I do not enjoy killing. Today I don't hunt and haven't done so since I found myself able to afford to buy meat that was killed and butchered by someone else. Killing is a barbarous, bloody business, an essentially ugly act. For this reason, when I hunted, I made myself very single-minded. My mind was locked against the beauty of the wild and concentrated solely on tracking, stalking, and testing the wind.

I was successful that day, but six hours were to pass between the sighting of fresh moose tracks and the final squeezing of the trigger. It took another hour before the animal was slit open and its entrails were removed and burned so they would not release their parasites into the systems of the scavengers. When all things were done, the carcass was hoisted off the ground for safekeeping, with a light set of tackle brought for the purpose. There followed a two-hour tramp home, a footrace against darkness, after which the dogs were hitched to the sled, with Yukon leading them over snow for the first time.

A wild and silent journey ensued. I stood on the ends of the runners, feeling the wind slice my face, listening to the whisper of the runners sliding over the snow. Can there be a more exhilarating experience? It was full dark when we got home with more than six hundred pounds of meat, a big hide, and a grotesque head from which the antlers had been shed.

We dined regally that night. The dogs got a great helping of cooked liver, lungs, and heart mixed with a double handful of chow; I sat down to a huge, tender steak of tamarack beef.

Chapter 4

IT WAS the last day of the old year. As I stood outside the cabin, scanning the forest, the depression I had felt on rising at four forty-five in the cold darkness of my bedroom vanished. No matter what my mood, the wilderness was always able to tranquilize my mind. From the barn came the sounds of the dogs; they knew I was up. A few birds chirped softly, sleepy notes uttered halfheartedly. Mostly the land was wrapped in preday silence.

For several months now it had become my habit to spend a few minutes each morning contemplating the wilderness. I tried to absorb the mood and the feel of the land. After that, I was ready to face the day.

On that December 31 I had wakened to discover that the heater had gone out during the night. The outside temperature was twenty-five degrees below zero; the room temperature was ten degrees warmer. This is not a good way to wake up. Later, after the fire was going, I went to get some water from the well. The rope broke, and the pail plunged into the cistern twenty feet below. It took fifteen minutes to fish it out. The cold crept almost to my very bones. Depression set in, and the temptation to return to bed was well-nigh irresistible. Hot coffee helped a little, and last night's decision to spend the day cutting pulpwood enlisted my sense of duty. But now the promise of one more day surrounded by the magic of nature restored my equanimity.

Work recently had been divided between logging and trapping. But the night before, when I added up the results of my cutting operations, it became obvious that I was going to have to devote a month to logging if I was to meet the January deadline. So I decided that I would cut one more cord before the end of the year, spend New Year's Day pulling the traps, then concentrate on the pulpwood until my quota was reached.

The cutting site was four miles from the home clearing. I usually walked to it, not only because I enjoyed the hour's stroll, but also because I felt it was unfair to have the dogs transport me over such a short distance and then keep them tied up all day while I worked. If there was a load to be carried, the dogs came along; otherwise, they were better off loose in the barn.

When my contemplative time was over that morning, I fed the animals. Then I set out on snowshoes. Visibility was reasonably good in the open, but inside the forest, the world was toned a somber gray. The evening before, a strong wind had risen and the crystalline snow had drifted, leaving dunes several feet high. The trail was filled in, and walking was erratic and difficult. I reached the logging site, bathed in perspiration and already regretting the decision to work.

It was now as light as it was going to get. The sun was concealed by the overcast, but it didn't look as if it was going to snow. There was no wind, and the temperature was rising. For two hours I worked methodically, finally getting nicely into stride and feeling pleased with my accomplishments. But *pride goeth before destruction.* I swung the axe to notch a spruce, and the blade flicked against a nearby branch, deflecting the stroke. Instead of biting into the wood with the steel, I hit the trunk with the handle, snapping it as though it were a carrot. I should have called it quits, but I had become stubborn. Alternately running and walking, I made it back to the homestead, got a spare axe, harnessed the team to the sled this time, and set off anew.

The dogs were well rested, as impatient as thoroughbreds at the starting gate. Standing on the ends of the runners, I let Yukon set the pace, watching as the team worked up to that fluid, mile-consuming gallop that whisks the sled atop the hard snow. When the journey ended, I was disappointed that it was over so soon; so were the dogs. They were still raring to go.

Determined to make up for lost time, I attacked the job vigorously. The dogs were unharnessed and their leads tied to trees. They curled up in the snow, their bushy tails arranged so that each black nose was covered. Soon I became engrossed in my work, and I lost track of time. During the late afternoon I did notice a brisk wind, knifing through the trees and driving a sleety snow before it. But I dismissed it in my eagerness to tackle a new stand of timber.

I don't know how long it was before Yukon drew my attention to the storm by yelping at me loudly, the kind of high-pitched intense cry he reserved for matters of note. I looked up to see him lunging at his lead. The other dogs were also getting to their feet, watching their leader and signaling their own uneasiness. Before I had time to wonder about their restlessness, the driven snow struck my face with the sting of ground glass. As I swiveled to shield my cheeks and wipe the moisture from my streaming eyes, I knew I was witnessing the birth of a blizzard.

It didn't occur to me that we were in danger. Even if conditions doubled our return time, we could still get back in about half an hour. In any event, I thought, as I got ready to leave, most of the way back was through thick evergreens that would shelter us even if the blizzard became fierce.

As soon as I had turned the sled around, facing toward home, Yukon began to dance, anxious to get going. By the time Sooner, Rocky, and Sussie were hitched, the big dog was almost frantic to take his place. I paid little attention to his behavior because he was always eager to travel. It didn't take long to harness the dogs, but before I was ready to set out, the blizzard enveloped us.

The wind increased suddenly, driving great dancing flakes at an impossible angle through a forest that was now cloaked in a moving white shroud. It seemed unbelievable that wind and snow could combine so quickly to obliterate the outlines of trees only a few yards away. I knew the trail would soon be filled in completely. Instead of riding the runners as first planned, I would have to go ahead of the dogs and break trail. I hurried, and as a result I fumbled when I tied Yukon to my waist with the lead rope. No more than a few seconds could have been squandered, but my anxiety rose out of all proportion to the loss of time.

In this particular section of the forest, only one species of tree grew, black spruce, miles of them topping a rugged muskeg bog. Such forests are labyrinthine. The trees stand close together, putting a roof over the land through which the sunlight cannot penetrate. It is never difficult for an inexperienced woodsman to get turned around in these forests on dull summer days. In winter it is usually easy enough to return home following one's back trails. But in a blizzard these can't be relied on.

I had finally realized what could happen if I missed my way, and I began to worry. Dusk was descending quickly, the blanketing snow adding to the murk. By the time we left the small clearing, the pathway home was already indistinct. If this was not enough, Yukon was acting up, pulling away to the left, jerking the line around my waist. I was losing patience with him. I had plenty to worry about without his nonsense. Our route home would take us directly into the teeth of the blizzard, and the trail was already full of new snow, piled in mounds, like the sands of the Sahara.

Traveling head-on into a howling gale makes heavy demands upon the body and the mind. The snow rasps the exposed parts of the face and bruises the eyes, making the tears flow. While part of the mind tries to deal with the physical, another part dwells on fear, fanning the imagination until the bowels churn and the mouth becomes dry and sour.

Within minutes I had to stop to rip my handkerchief into three strips. I knotted the strips together and fastened them around my hood, under the chin, to protect myself from the wind. I looked at the dogs. They were burred white, crusted by snow. They had lain down when the sled stopped, averting their faces from the blizzard's punch, but jumped up quickly when it was time to go.

A while later I found myself sobbing for breath; my body was clammy cold in places and uncomfortably hot in others. The last of the light had vanished. I had made up my mind to stop again for a rest, but at that moment we came to a bend in the trail that I could not recall. Negotiating this, we were brought to an abrupt halt by a tangle of deadfall timber. Even in the darkness I could see that this untidy barrier had been there a long time. I was lost. Somehow we had passed the proper trail, turning instead into a wide game track that now ended. My stomach went spastic; my heart beat alarmingly. How had I missed the way so soon? Where? I had this great urge to rush blindly ahead, to beat the bushes in frenzy until I found the lost pathway.

Panic is difficult to subdue; it washes over the brain like some great cold wave. I remember getting the irrational feeling that I had always stood in that cold, shrieking vortex. Warmth, comfort, security—I had never really experienced any of these things. The storm, the darkness, and the fear were the ghastly realities.

I stood there witless for an interminable time. Then Yukon was beside me; his big head was pressed against my thigh, and he nudged me several times. How can I explain the sudden surge of relief that filled me when that wonderful dog came to tell me that

I was not alone? He gave me heart. I know that he sensed my fear. He was always able to read my emotions. I went down on my haunches and hugged him, resting my head on his ice-covered shoulder. Who knows how long we remained there? I do know that Yukon helped me regain my reason. If I stayed calm, and with his help, things would turn out all right.

Our only hope of getting out of the mess was to retrace our route to the logging site. But first the sled had to be turned in the narrow trail. I unhitched the dogs, working as quickly as possible, but severely hindered by the storm. Then I manhandled the sled around, and as soon as the dogs were hitched again we set off, with me going slowly ahead of the team, trying to pick up our old trail.

An hour later I was still hopelessly lost. At first I had been able to discern our tracks, but as it became darker and darker, my only guides were the vague outlines of trees, which seemed to be pressing closer together. I stopped often, bending down and feeling with unmittened hand, trying to detect the hard ridges left by the sled runners under the newly drifted snow. Yukon continued to be balky, pulling in an unsettling way. He was probably as upset by the storm as I was, I thought, no longer annoyed with him.

When the trail became so narrow that there was hardly room for the sled to pass, I knew I had missed the way back to the logging strip. I had no idea where we were, and I was exhausted. My legs felt like rubber, and my heart was beating at an alarming rate. I knew that if I didn't rest soon, I would collapse. I couldn't turn back for the simple reason that I didn't know rear from front. There was no point in leading the team to nowhere.

Strangely enough, now that we were squarely up against it, my mind was calm. It became clear that my physical condition was of paramount importance. I couldn't afford to collapse. At the same time, the dogs appeared to be in good condition, actually eager to get going. I decided to ride the runners and let the dogs go ahead, knowing that their natural instincts would make them avoid collisions.

That's when Yukon took over. He suddenly charged left, ignoring the drag exerted by the foot brake I automatically pressed down into the snow. There was no stopping him, and on the theory that he couldn't do any worse than I had done, I let him go. Besides, there seemed to be such purpose in his actions that I began to hope. Did he know the way back? What mysterious senses did he have that might enable him to find his way home through this stormy darkness across totally strange country?

Now that I had nothing to do, my imagination started to get active again. I had experienced fear often enough to know how easily it can create havoc, particularly when its owner is physically inactive. But constructive thought will maintain reason; this was one of the few beneficial lessons I had learned during the years of war in Europe.

That night in the Ontario backwoods I kept steady at first by trying to find a pattern in the storm, then by willing my eyes to see through the darkness and the swirling snow, seeking to identify the trees and to pick out landmarks. Peering into the forest, I began to feel exhilarated. I actually chuckled to myself at one point when I remembered how desirable adventure seems to be to those who are comfortably bored in a civilized environment. The fact is that adventure is something nasty happening to *somebody else*.

After that I watched the dogs, whose outlines were easy to detect. Yukon, naturally, was taking the brunt of the pull, breaking trail for the others. Suddenly, against all logic, I became convinced that he knew exactly where he was going. *I* was lost, but that half-wild dog was not. His fine homing equipment was serving him as efficiently as it served his wolf kin. Tail up and head held high, he churned through the snow tirelessly. I marveled at his stamina.

That night Yukon guided us back as surely as if he had been tied to the homestead by some invisible thread. When we came out of the forest into our own clearing, I jumped off the sled, stumbling in the deep snow. Recovering, I ran awkwardly behind the team, floundering occasionally, but so elated that I felt impelled to give physical vent to my emotions.

Crossing the opening took only minutes, yet it was here that the fullness of the blizzard hit us, making me realize just how stiff and cold I really was. The wind was like ice; the thick snow struck my exposed face like chips of splintered quartz. It was as well that the distance across the clearing was short, else I don't believe I would have made it.

By the time I unhitched the dogs and brought them their dinner, I was near the end of my endurance. The dogs, however, didn't seem to be unduly affected by their experience. Inside the barn they clustered expectantly, tails wagging furiously as they sniffed the aroma of the food. I put down their dishes, then crossed the shrieking space between house and barn, entered, and slammed the door. At last I was able to relax.

I dined late that night, but I sat down to a feast all the same: roasted grouse, rice mixed with dried apricots, carrots fried in bacon fat. At midnight I poured a stiff drink of whiskey and drank a toast to the new year. What would it bring? I wondered.

ALL the trees were dressed. The new leaves, each still wrinkled and tender, glowed in the sunlight, mixing their lemon-yellow and saffron hues with the fresh green of the conifers. The forest was a sleek, well-tended wild garden relaxing in the sun after a long, hard winter. Wherever Yukon and I walked in this new land we found the sights and sounds of spring: soft clean air, straight new shoots, small eggs artfully hidden in apple-green grasses. I did not really appreciate the rejuvenating properties of spring until I weathered my first winter in the north woods.

On that particular morning in early May, Yukon and I were enjoying the new season, taking our individual pleasures. Yukon, running free now, was busy with one of those fascinating smells that dogs so delight in. We wandered aimlessly through the forest cloisters. Aromatic cedars closed around us, and beneath them snowshoe hare scampered, slightly demented by the breeding lust.

Presently we came to the open space I had been aiming for, a shallow ridge of pre-Cambrian granite, dotted with blueberry bushes and pale green lichens. When we arrived, it was already noon and time to eat. I sat down, stretched my legs, and slipped off the packsack. Yukon wagged his tail, waiting expectantly for the bone he always received before I ate my sandwiches.

As I munched contentedly, I scanned the countryside. Despite paying lip service to December 31, I was now taking the measure of a year from spring to spring. From this standpoint, the old year had been a good one. It had brought a variety of hardships and uncertainties. But it had also taught me much and made me realize that I knew so very little. Many of my old, urban values had tumbled. Things that had been taken for granted had either become luxuries or were discarded altogether. The moment I went to live in the backwoods, electricity and plumbing vanished, along with theaters, libraries, and the telephone. The list was long, but the only things I missed were libraries, theaters, and, most of all, an easily procured hot bath.

On the other hand, satisfaction followed the accomplishment of relatively simple, but important, tasks. Rudimentary things were appreciated. A week-old newspaper was read slowly from first page to last, then saved to be recycled in some other way. A trip to the nearest town was the ·highlight of each month, a one-day gala affair when seldom seen friends were greeted over a glass of beer. Driving my aging Chevrolet slowly over the rutted road, to conserve precious gasoline, made one sigh with pleasure and feel that life was *good*.

Then came Yukon. He changed my life by giving me love, companionship, and knowledge that I could not have gained without him. I looked at him now. He had finished his bone, and he lay, head on front paws, watching me. When our eyes met, he wagged his tail. He was at peace.

But, suddenly, I found that I was not. Despite my general contentment, there remained one concern that had begun to nag me.

It was thinking about the fur that did it. I had worked hard tending the trapline, visiting each set daily and removing promptly the unfortunates who had stepped into its steel jaws. Soon the fur sale would start, and bundles of hides would go under the hammer so that buyers from "the outside" could compete for them. Thinking about the killing I had done, I realized that this was the hub of my concern. It confused me because I viewed myself as a selfishly unsentimental person. Yet I was forced to admit that each day it became harder to set the traps, to scrape fat and flesh from the pelts, to carve the bleeding meat.

I tried to argue against myself. I needed money, more than I could earn logging. Trapping seemed to be the only other way of earning a living. I wasn't taking that many animals. Such logic couldn't change the feeling. I knew that I couldn't continue to destroy life simply for the sake of its coat.

That afternoon, with Yukon at my side, I started pulling traps. Afterward, instead of carting them back to the homestead so that I could sell them, I dumped them into the lake. Thinking about this final act on the way home, I became confused all over again, but I put my mind on other matters.

Of late I had been too busy to do any writing. Now I could devote a part of each day to my typewriter. That was my long-term plan. More immediately I proposed to buy a horse to help me expand the logging operations. I would also buy a hundred more chicks and "grow" eggs, add half a dozen piglets and "grow" pork.

A week later six hoglets were purchased, and a five-year-old dapple-gray gelding arrived. Not long after this I got a summer contract from the pulp mill to cut and peel twenty-five cords of balsam. For a month I kept busy, refusing to debate the trapline matter any further.

Then, in the second week of June, Yukon had a fight with a bear. It happened at twilight.

I was sitting at my typewriter. Yukon was lying against the kitchen door. Suddenly he sprang to his feet, thumped the door with one paw, and looked at me. I understood that something unusual was going on outside, an event that he felt must be investigated. When I took hold of his collar and opened the door, he immediately dragged me toward the pigpen. Within it I had constructed a small log house. On top of the roof stood a large bear, tearing off the tar paper, trying to get at the hoglets.

Without stopping to think, I released the eager dog. "Go get it!" I urged him. The bear heard us. It stood upright, then whirled around and scrambled off the roof almost at the same time that the streaking dog reached it. Yukon swerved away from the pigpen, caught up to the bear, and charged into it. I raced back to the house to get the rifle. When I ran outside again, the two had disappeared, but crashing sounds were coming from the northwest.

No dog is a match for an adult bear. Even timber wolves avoid them unless their young are threatened. Together, a pack can usually manage to drive a bear away, although some of their number may be killed. The bear usually escapes unscathed.

As I ran toward the fast-fading sounds, I knew that Yukon would chase the marauder until it either treed or turned at bay. I stood little chance of finding them unless the bear stopped quickly. I was too worried about Yukon to consider what my own danger might be. In daylight a Lee-Enfield bullet will stop a bear if the rifleman knows how to handle the gun. But inside a nearly darkened wilderness the rifle sights are invisible. One must shoot almost by instinct. A wounding shot at short range might make a bear charge, maddened by pain. But I wasn't debating these things as I stumbled through the gloomy forest, calling Yukon's name.

When it was too dark to search without light, I returned home to plan my next moves. I didn't intend to give up the search.

I exchanged the rifle for my twelve-gauge shotgun, loaded it with buckshot, and clamped the flashlight on top of the barrel. Then I got a lead for Rocky and set out anew, hoping that he would be able to pick up Yukon's trail. We moved through the darkened forest, while I kept coaxing the malamute to "seek."

It was a grim course over which I was dragged that night. I was scratched by branches and shrubs. My clothes were torn, and my right eye was almost put out by a spruce twig. But only later did I notice the cuts and scratches. Adrenaline kept me going long past the point of exhaustion. During the first hours I whistled and called almost continuously; then my lips couldn't obey anymore. I fired the shotgun, hoping that the irresistible sound would bring Yukon back. And then it was dawn.

I didn't want to, but it was necessary to go back home. In my haste and anxiety I had neglected to feed the other dogs. Worry killed my own appetite, but they would be starving. I also needed a rest. Then, as I started to pull Rocky off the trail, he fought the lead, continuing in the same direction. My hope was forlorn, but I decided to let him go on for another half hour.

A few minutes later Rocky found the place where Yukon and the bear had fought. A grassy area had been beaten down by the action. There were tufts of shaggy black bear fur scattered around. And there was blood; in some places just a few drops, in others big smears, as if a wounded body had rolled on the grasses. I searched for tracks on my hands and knees, and learned that the fight had broken off. The bear had run again, pursued by Yukon. Who had lost the blood? Once more Rocky was put on the tracks. The trail led to a small beaver pond, and ended. Rocky couldn't pick it up again. It seemed the bear had taken to the water and Yukon had followed. Where was he now?

For three days Rocky and I searched. On the evening of the third day I gave up. Either Yukon had been killed or he had run so far into the wild that he would not return. Yukon was gone.

AT FOURTEEN, when the Civil War in Spain came to upset the tenor of my youth, I somehow learned to cope with the loss of relatives and friends. In my late teens and twenties, during World War II, this emotional shield was made stronger. By my early thirties I rather boasted that death could not affect me; I was no longer vulnerable because I thought I knew how to live within myself. Friends were enjoyed in the present and dismissed. Romance was an interesting exercise of the moment, quickly disposed of when it ended. In a vague sort of way I had become incapable of really caring for others; it didn't bother me. Indeed, I preferred it that way. But recently, subtle changes in my emotions made me occasionally uneasy.

Sitting in the living room thinking about Yukon, I became fully aware that a change had come over me. I had become deeply and emotionally involved for the first time in my adult life—with a dog! I immediately rejected the concept. It was nonsense. I was tired from the days of frantic search. I would feel different tomorrow. I found the bottle of whiskey. There was about a third left. I drank. Two hours later the bottle was empty and I was angry, terribly angry. I wanted to smash things. I paced about, kicking at anything that got in the way. I knew I was drunk; yet I was sober. I heard the dogs howling, and rushed outside to tell them to shut up. I had not done that before. The dogs were silent. Back in the house, I stumbled upstairs and went to bed fully clothed. Without knowing why, feeling utterly unmanned and ashamed, I cried.

When I woke up the next morning nursing a deserved headache, I realized that I could not escape reality. Yukon was gone, but I could not dismiss the hurt of his going. I cared. Somehow this made me feel better. It did not minimize the grief, but it allowed me to accept it. I took the dogs their breakfast. They greeted me effusively, but although I patted each, I could not stay to play with them. I was too depressed.

Thinking to take my mind off my problems, I made a shopping list and drove to town, changed my mind, and drove instead to visit Old Alec, a Swedish octogenarian whom I had met soon after arriving in the backwoods. Sitting in his small, neat log cabin, playing chess and drinking aquavit, I told him about Yukon. In the end, he summed up my problem.

"You are in love, Ron. Not yust wit' a dog, wit' life. Yesuss, tho'! You sure did take a long time to love! You're lucky you love somethin' beside yourself, that's good. Yah. . . ." He poured me another drink, filled his own glass, and set up the chess pieces.

When I got home at dusk, I knew that the wilderness, and especially Yukon, had combined to make a considerable breach in my old defenses. I had become involved with a life other than my own for the first time in many years. I knew I would never forget Yukon, but I hoped that the sadness generated by his disappearance would not take too long to become bearable.

When the other dogs had finished their suppers that night, I led them all to the house, feeling somewhat guilty because I had neglected them. During the play that followed I discovered that I cared for all of them more than I would have admitted a few days before, but not in the same way I cared for Yukon.

After returning the dogs to the barn, I found my copy of Steinbeck's *Sweet Thursday* in the cabin and began to read it once more, knowing it almost by heart, but never tiring of it. When something scratched against the living-room window, I was so engrossed that I almost didn't bother to glance up. Then, when I saw what was out there, the sudden rush of gladness that filled me was beyond description.

Standing with both front paws on the windowsill, his face blurred in the yellow light, was Yukon. But even as I jumped to my feet and moved toward the doorway, the gladness changed to deep concern as I saw the bloody look of him. His entire head seemed to be plastered in old gore, and one corner of his mouth sagged dreadfully. His lips, on the left side, were slit beyond his jawbone.

I opened the door and he rushed at me, whining his gladness, pushing against me. His matted tail wagged furiously. I wanted to examine his wounds, but I couldn't help hugging him, and it seemed that he was just as determined to make a fuss over me. He was filthy and bedraggled. He was thin, but he was back! Nothing else mattered.

WHAT actually happened between Yukon and the bear remains a mystery to this day. I could only guess as to the cause of the wound that began at the very corner of his mouth and continued for three inches, slitting open the side of his face so that his left cheek gaped and exposed all his molars. The injury could not have been made by a bite, but it *could* have been made by a claw at the end of a great swinging paw.

The nearest veterinarian was more than seventy miles away, but I would have driven ten times that distance if need be. I knew that it was too late to stitch the edges of the wound together. If anything could be done, Yukon would have to be anesthetized and the dead tissue snipped off down to new flesh that could be drawn together and stitched.

The vet confirmed this, adding that if this was done, it would distort Yukon's mouth and cause more discomfort than if it was left to heal by itself. He would always have a lopsided face, but this would be better than mouth distortion.

Chapter 5

SHE knew I was going to kill her. Her eyes said so for those few seconds during which I aimed directly at her forehead. Then came the sharp crack, and Sussie was dead. My eyes were closed when I lowered the gun, but I had to open them to make sure that she was past feeling the agonies of the bear trap that had crushed her.

When I looked, her accusing eyes were closed. The powerful trap, set by an unknown, lay a few feet away from her mutilated body, its big steel fangs bloody. On the grass, a carmine pool was even now coagulating. Sussie had been in the trap a long time.

The September sun was not yet above the trees when I turned my back on the dog and set out for the homestead, about a mile south of the abandoned farm where the bear trap had been set. But even across that distance, I could still hear the dogs howling in the barn.

It was their howling that had wakened me before daylight that morning, a continuous farrago of distress that caused me to jump out of bed, dress in haste, and go outside. As I walked toward the hay barn, I heard the distant, agonized yelping from due north. It was faint, almost drowned by the voices of the other dogs, but I knew at once that Sussie was in some kind of trouble.

Four weeks earlier she had given birth to pups, Yukon's children. In her desire for privacy, she had crawled under the barn floor from the outside, finding a secure den in which to nurse her little ones. Because of this, I allowed her to run free, but she showed no desire to leave the farmyard. I didn't know how many young ones she had delivered; the only way to get at them would have been to cut through the log floor. But I often listened to their mewling voices while squatting above them on the barn floor, interested and amused by Yukon,. who stood guard over that particular place. The big dog spent practically all his time sitting there, listening to them, his ears moving stiffly at every sound they made. Now and then he would whine softly, as though talking to them.

A week or so after Sussie gave birth, Yukon tried to crawl into the den. His once loving mate growled so furiously that the impatient father backed out. Nevertheless, like all wolves, he was a concerned and solicitous father. Despite the fact that Sussie was fed regularly and given extra rations, Yukon no longer ate the bones that I gave him but would take them to the den entrance and leave them there for Sussie, a bit of self-sacrifice that I found endearing. And Sussie collected Yukon's offerings every day.

As nearly as I could judge, she became pregnant soon after Yukon's recovery from his face wound, sometime in June. My first awareness of her condition came when I noticed that Yukon was becoming exceedingly jealous of the other males, warning them away every time they went near her. One day I saw that Sussie was decidedly heavier around the belly. I called her to me to feel her bulge, and Yukon came too, pushing my hand away with a rough cast of his nose, telling me to keep my hands to myself. I respected him and obeyed. Then, in mid-July, when she was obviously heavy with her young, disaster struck the homestead.

The weather had been stiflingly hot all day. There was no wind, the sky was overcast, and the humidity uncomfortably high. I had taken the horse and a flatbed wagon and spent the morning cutting cedar fence posts in the bush. Despite the insecticide I sprayed on the horse's coat, the flies and mosquitoes were vicious. The horse kept stamping and shaking his head, his tail swishing constantly. I was only a little better off than he was. The discomfort caused by the protective mixture of lard and roofing tar smeared on my body was almost as great as the pests.

By noon the horse and I both had had enough. I finished loading the cut poles, and we returned home. Later, after I wiped myself clean, I rubbed down the horse and led him to the water trough. We were on the way back to the barn when one of my neighbors arrived, driving his team. The man had come to inquire about a stray heifer. Because my horse was acting up in the presence of the strange team, I tied him to a tree while I talked to the neighbor. A little while later the man drove off, and I remembered a stew I had put on the stove. I hurried back to take it off the heat before it burned.

Never dreaming that the gelding would come to harm during a few extra minutes, I stopped to fill and light my pipe. That was when I heard a noise like the rumble of an express train. Curious, I went to a window.

A purple-black curtain filled the western sky. The trees were leaning toward me, as though some giant invisible force were attempting to knock them all down. At first I couldn't understand what was happening, but when I actually saw treetops snapped off and flung upward as the great roaring got louder, I knew it had to be a tornado. And it was coming fast. Mesmerized, I watched for a few minutes before I remembered the horse.

I dashed outside. It was as though a huge and powerful hand had hit me. One second I was running on the ground, the next I was swept off my feet and slammed against the well. I tried to get up, felt a stabbing pain in my side. I had broken a rib.

The great roaring vortex was trying to sweep me away. I clung to the well, making myself as small as possible, feeling the monster wind suck at me. What a noise! A madness of savage sound. Sweeping through the forest, it plucked demented chords from the trees and drew harpy screams from the branches. The house screened me from most of the debris. But even so, I was hit several times by flying branches, and my right hand was cut by a cedar shingle that came spinning down like a well-aimed Frisbee.

In the wake of the twister came the rain, warm, heavy drops that pummeled the ground and rattled roofs. The afternoon was dark, like late evening. There was no wind now, but the departing roar of the racing tornado continued to dominate all other sounds.

I made to get up and fell down again, unable to stifle a cry of pain. Gingerly feeling my right side, I discovered that three ribs were broken, not one. Holding my right arm tight against my body and moving slowly, I managed to gain my feet. I took several shallow, cautious breaths. My side hurt like hell, but the pain was more superficial than internal. This suggested that the bones were cracked rather than broken. The homestead was suddenly a place of quiet. It amazed me that such an intensely violent storm could come and go so quickly; it had lasted not much more than ten minutes. It also had killed my horse.

The gelding, crazy with fear, had wound himself around and around the tree to which he had been tied. He had strangled himself. His eyes protruded frightfully; his mouth was grinning horribly; his head, held by the rope, was twisted upward at an impossible angle. I couldn't help staring at the unfortunate beast until my stomach churned, and then I drew my belt knife and cut the noose. The rope was so tight that I had to saw the knot.

My mind was a little foggy now. I was in shock, not knowing what to do and unable to think. The barking of the dogs, still in the hay barn, penetrated my consciousness. I went and petted them, each movement producing a stab of pain in my side. When they were settled, I returned to the house. Working slowly and painfully in front of a mirror, I strapped up the ribs. They felt better at once. When I was dressed again, I walked to my neighbor's place, about a mile away, to find that he had come off lucky and was already clearing up the mess. He loaned me his horses and a towing chain with which to drag the gray into the forest. It was night before I got home after taking back the neighbor's horses.

The unusual tornado marked the beginning of a bad time, a period of depression, poverty, and mental anguish that came close to bringing an end to my life in the wilderness. No sooner were my ribs mended than, in August, disaster struck again. This time it hit the chickens, which had appeared to be doing well and were already of respectable size. Going to feed them one morning, I found twenty-three of them dead and a large number of the others squatting listlessly. Later I learned that chicken cholera was the villain, but by then a hundred pullets had died of the virulent sickness.

Not long after this second blow, Sussie gave birth to her pups and had to be allowed to run free. Perhaps if my economic position had not been so bleak, I might have paused long enough to take the pups out from under the barn and settle them and their mother in a more suitable place. As it was, the loss of the poultry coming so soon on top of the death of the horse kept me fully occupied with financial survival. It was while I was in this state of mind that Sussie stepped into the bear trap.

I have no idea why she wandered away from her young, and I never did find out who had set that trap and abandoned it. After she had been buried, I picked up the trap and dropped it into the lake. By its condition I judged it had been set for at least a year. Some irresponsible fool had put it out and either forgotten it or was too idle to retrieve it.

Late that day I cut through the barn floor and got the pups. There were three of them, but the runt of the litter was dead. This may have been the reason why Sussie wandered away. The two survivors were in good shape and looked just like their father, without a trace of the collie line. They were dark gray, roly-poly, fluffy wolf pups with perky ears and great big paws.

I attempted to raise them on canned milk and Pablum, but they died. First one, then the other, within two days. Now, after having raised hundreds of orphaned young animals, I know what went wrong. The formula was too rich; it gave them dysentery.

There followed a time of bitter depression. I tried to get rid of my black mood by working furiously and for long hours. The dogs were fed, but neglected emotionally and left locked in the barn. They couldn't understand my change of attitude and tried to get close to me. Finally it was Yukon who made me aware that I was being foolish and grossly unfair.

It was about a month after the pups died. The land was snow-covered, and the cold was starting to bear down hard at night. I was late returning home, so it was already nine o'clock when I prepared supper for the dogs. On the way to the barn with the food pot I paused a moment to look at the sky. There was an early moon, and the stars were out in their millions. I noticed all this, but I wasn't gladdened by the spectacle.

When I put the dishes in front of the dogs, Yukon wouldn't eat. It was the first time since he had come to the homestead that he refused food. When Rocky finished, he edged toward his leader's dish and began to eat. The big dog took no notice. I chased Rocky away and put the food under Yukon's nose. He didn't glance down. Instead, he whined loudly, rose on his hind legs, and licked my cheek. My mood of self-pity could not continue in the face of the dog's distress and affection. All at once I was filled with contrition. I opened my arms wide, and Yukon came into them. Rocky and Sooner rushed up also. The three dogs mobbed me as of old, whining and licking and pushing against me with unabashed joy.

I took them outside, and we ran over the snowy clearing, playing our games. I felt very guilty for having neglected my friends. During this moonlit romp it occurred to me that Yukon must have gone through a bewildering time because of Sussie's death, wondering what had become of his mate. Wolves' emotions may differ from humans', but they have the capacity for love and for sorrow. I felt guiltier than ever. I had withdrawn from Yukon when he needed me.

The next day I hitched the three dogs to the sled and we went for a fast, long run, not returning until dusk. It did us all good. The dogs were stale from inactivity and tired when we got home, but they really enjoyed the workout. They devoured the extra-big meal that I gave them. While I was eating my own supper that evening, Yukon lay sprawled under the table, his big head resting on my feet, drooling as usual. He slept beside my bed that night.

Chapter 6

AGAINST the indigo of the big sky, individual white clouds scudded slowly toward the northeast like the sails of an armada of galleons. The rolling prairie spread itself under the golden sun until it became smudged at the circular horizon. It was a warm May day

on the Saskatchewan plains. Yukon stood at my side. Early yesterday morning we had left the homestead, forced to pull up stakes
because of my refusal to earn a living as a trapper.

Now I stood leaning against the car, scanning our immediate
vicinity. Bumblebees filled the air with their husky droning and
led my gaze to a cluster of blue-violet alfalfa blossoms. The song
of a meadowlark drew my eyes down the road. The bird was
perched on a stalk of chicory, but as I lifted the field glasses, movement in the sky made me look up. A hawk that was new to me
hovered with fast-beating wings some distance to the south.

Anxious to identify it, I went to the car to get Peterson's *Field
Guide to Western Birds.* That was when Yukon found a hole at
the bottom of the tall, chain link fence that was strung parallel
to the road. The dog crawled through quickly and dashed away, to
disappear over the brow of one of those undulating rises so typical of the southern plains. I called him, and when he didn't respond, I whistled. Eventually I decided to go after him, sure that
he was trespassing on private land.

The fence was strong and high, unlike any cattle fence that I had
seen. Driving south from Moose Jaw, we had passed an air force
base. Now I wondered if this section of prairie was also part of
the military establishment and thus definitely out-of-bounds. I
scaled the wire and went to find Yukon. When I was fifty or sixty
paces from the fence, he appeared suddenly on the hillock. He
was running fast, a good deal faster than he had gone. In a moment
the reason for his hurry became awesomely evident.

Spread out in ragged formation, looking as mean and formidable
as any group of animals I have ever seen, seven buffalo cows
charged over the rise in pursuit of Yukon, who, when he saw me
standing openmouthed, changed direction slightly and aimed himself at me. The seven enraged cows also altered course. That was
my first experience with the North American bison outside a zoo.

Yukon passed me at full speed and darted through the hole in
the fence, which was large enough for him but much too small for
me. I became the sole target of the angry bison. Never has a fence
seemed so unattainable. I ran at top speed, very conscious of the
thunder-hoofed beasts that pursued me. It is a curious fact that of
all the animals, only men and apes waste time looking back when

they are escaping. But perhaps that quick look over my shoulder saved me. When I saw, ten yards at my heels, that cluster of big heads with their black, stubby, curved horns, I was able to increase my speed considerably. Yukon, very brave now that he was safe, was pacing up and down outside the fence, woofing and yelping, showing a machismo that had been quite absent when the cows were on *his* heels. I like to think that he would have come to my rescue but I shall never know, because I reached the fence, clutched wildly at the links, and skinned up it. I didn't stop to look around again until I was inside the car.

The big cows stood beside the fence, puffing a little but otherwise appearing no more dangerous than domestic Herefords. Yukon sauntered over to the car, as though the entire episode were quite beneath his dignity. But he wasn't fooling me! He had met his match! That was the first and the last time I saw him run away from anything, but run he definitely did.

Following the disasters at the homestead, already narrated, a combination of events during autumn and winter had made it impossible for me to continue living in the backwoods. Not long after the tragedy of Sussie, I shipped the pigs to the stockyards in Winnipeg just when the bottom dropped out of the hog market. Then, after filling the pulpwood contract, I discovered that the mill had cut back production and was not issuing any more orders from independent cutters. I tried to find buyers for cedar fence posts, but had no luck. With less than six hundred dollars and no prospects, the outlook was bleak. I would be broke by summer. I knew I could no longer remain on the homestead.

One morning in March, after returning from town, where I had bought a daily newspaper, I saw an advertisement for a city editor on a newspaper in a small British Columbia community. On the spur of the moment I replied, and got the job. The starting date was mid-June.

I was going to have to dispose of the dogs.

Seeking a good home for them, I visited Old Alec, and he told me of a friend in Ontario, a man I will call Bill, who ran a sort of dog haven. I drove over to see this man and found an excellent home for Rocky and Sooner. But not for Yukon; nothing would have then induced me to part with the wolf dog.

Soon afterward the two dogs went to live with Bill, and Yukon and I were left alone on the homestead. Since there was now nothing to do, we spent weeks roaming the wilderness, hunting a little for food. Despite concerns for the future, these were idyllic times, and I loathed giving them up when April approached an end.

Now the house was cleaned, a few things were sold, and I loaded the car with tools and personal possessions. Finally my red chestnut canoe was hoisted onto the roof rack and tied down. With a heavy heart, yet with a feeling of excitement, I set off, Yukon sitting tall beside me on the front seat. We would have to cross four Canadian provinces before reaching our destination.

The incident with the bison cows happened after we had been on the road a few days. We had stopped for lunch and a short cat-nap in the province of Saskatchewan. I had no idea there was a herd of buffalo in the area and only later learned that the animals were the responsibility of the Saskatchewan government's wildlife department. It is quite likely that I would have driven past them if Yukon hadn't gone to investigate.

The cows soon tired of standing beside the fence, and turned around to walk almost sedately away over the hillock. Very much interested in these strange bovines, I left Yukon in the car and walked some distance along the road. Then I stopped, looked around to make sure I was unobserved, and climbed the fence again.

Field glasses around my neck, I walked cautiously over the prairie. In a little while I saw the herd's calves, six of them, playing friskily in a slight depression. The cows were there also. One was feeding her calf, two others were lying down; the rest were gazing into space in that wool-gathering way characteristic of the bison. Some distance away two bulls stood solitarily, evidently unperturbed by the recent excitement.

Emboldened, I dared to go closer, ready to bolt at the first hostile move from any of the big beasts. About fifty paces from the nearest cow, I stopped. She fixed her eyes on me but remained unconcerned, chewing the cud with a slow sideways motion of her jaws. It was difficult to reconcile this now peaceful scene with the angry charge that had taken place ten minutes earlier.

Squatting in the thick grass, focusing the glasses on first one, then another huge animal, I marveled at their grotesque, but efficient, architecture, so well designed to withstand the fierce northern winters. Slim in the hips and heavy and well furred on the head and shoulders, the bison were like wedges that forever presented their thick ends to the wind, even now, on this spring day.

Looking at the little herd, I felt a sense of regret that I had come to North America too late to see these animals as they once were. Audubon estimated that one billion bison roamed the plains of North America before the coming of Western man; this was perhaps an exaggeration, but there is no gainsaying the fact that millions of buffalo once wandered over the Great Plains. Belatedly, in 1902, the governments of the United States and Canada began a conservation project. Fortunately it worked, and it seems that today the buffalo are safe from extinction.

These things were much in my mind as I watched the bison. Whether it was because of this line of thought or for some other reason, I suddenly felt a powerful sense of purpose, a calling if you will. I knew that I was now committed to the study of nature, to the observation of the thousands of life forms to be found in the wilderness. And I knew that the years on the homestead had been but an apprenticeship, a time of learning and of trial.

Hunkering there on the Saskatchewan plains, I was filled with a sense of wonderment at the manner in which my life had been influenced. It seemed hardly believable that the experiences of my past could have somehow prepared me for the life I was certain I was going to follow. Even now, so many years later, I cannot quite understand how it all came about. But I know that I have deviated only circumstantially and for relatively short periods from the resolution I made that spring afternoon.

MAJESTIC and beautiful, the Rocky Mountains pressed closely on the narrow highway that threaded its way up their sides, then plunged downward to become lost within the forests that covered a distant valley. The plains had impressed us with their big skies and feeling of space; the foothills of Alberta had offered pastoral serenity mixed with glimpses of rugged wilderness. But the world that spread before us now dwarfed anything yet encountered during our wandering.

Journeying up toward the Crowsnest Pass, Canada's first over-land doorway to the West, I had been struck by the scenery, but because the climb was steep and I was unaccustomed to mountain driving, I was unable to devote proper attention to the country. As a result, when we reached the summit, the sudden, bursting panorama was astonishing. Seeing a small rest area off the highway, I drove onto it and parked. When Yukon and I got out, we were rather like children given the freedom of a candy store. We didn't know what to sample first.

The dog ran up a gentle slope, sniffing with wild urgency at the rocks, bushes, and grasses. I went up after him, and turned to find that I had an almost uninterrupted view of the land below. About a mile away was a smallish lake, its waters aquamarine and sparkling. On the far shore was a flat area big enough for our tent. Even before I lowered my glasses, I was visualizing our trip across the lake in the canoe, making a fast camp, and fresh trout for supper, roasted over a bed of slow coals! I called Yukon, patted his head, and pointed to the lake.

"See that water? We're going to spend the night there. Maybe even a few days. And we're going to get some nice, fat trout!" For a reply, Yukon wagged his tail, bowed, and yawned.

I scrambled down from the Crowsnest Pass viewpoint and led the dog back to the car. It was the first week in June, and I calculated we had traveled two thousand miles since leaving the homestead. Soon I would be anchored to a news desk again. I tried not to think of this as we descended the western flanks of the Rockies and headed for our last carefree campground.

Our three days by the water were memorable, despite my mood. The lake was clear and cold, the trout were hungry, and eagles came to do a little fishing of their own.

A narrow gravel lane had led us off the highway almost to the edge of the water. I took down the canoe, packed the tent and other supplies in it, and pushed it into the water. Yukon sat bolt upright in the bow, like an overlarge, misplaced figurehead. It took half an hour to cross the lake, fifteen minutes to set up camp, and about three more minutes to relaunch the canoe and paddle out again, fly rod ready, Yukon once more in his place.

Four beautiful rainbow trout quickly accepted the dry mosquito fly that is my favorite artificial insect. Here was supper for both of us. So the rod was put away, and as the sun disappeared with the characteristic speed it displays in the mountains, I paddled around the lake. I love an evening jaunt over dead-still silvery water; it allows me to dream my dreams uninterrupted.

The trout were delicious! I roasted mine slowly. Yukon ate his raw and *in toto*. That night, lying in the sleeping bag with the big dog stretched out beside me, I was soon asleep. But not for very long! I awoke to the howling of a wolf right beside my ear. It was Yukon. When I managed to shut him up, I heard the reason for his call. Distant, but clear in the crisp night air, a pack of timber wolves were singing their ageless songs. My companion just naturally answered them. It was wonderful.

Two mornings later we were again riding down the western slope of the Rockies. We stopped only briefly after that, and before long we reached our destination in southeastern British Columbia, arriving five days before I was due to start work. Our trip had taken six weeks, and funds were down to fifty-seven dollars; payday was nineteen days away. In the meantime, we had to find somewhere to live, somewhere cheap, preferably with room enough for Yukon to run.

Fortunately the community was surrounded by wilderness. I found what I wanted seven miles east of town in an area nestled between two mountains, accessible by a narrow track. Examining the place, I discovered the remains of an old log cabin, not an unusual sight in a country once overrun with prospectors.

It took me a couple of hours to set up, for this was to be a semi-permanent camp with a rock fireplace, a twenty- by fourteen-foot canvas fly projecting from the tent doorway, and a rack between two trees for the canoe to rest upside down. In addition, because Yukon would have to stay tied up while I was working, I pounded into the ground a steel anchor pin that would allow him to reach the canvas shelter while he was confined by his chain. Even so, I knew he wasn't going to be happy. But he was going to have to endure it, just as I had to suffer the tedium of editing a small, banal newspaper.

When I accepted the job, I had done so with every intention of holding it for an indeterminate time. Now, confronted by the daily routines of an *inside* job, I realized I had no stomach for that kind of thing. I had always avoided a desk like the plague, preferring to work as a reporter and even accepting lower pay to do it. Reporting allowed me to write—my only love—and kept me outdoors on assignments. But I was in no position to be choosy.

By the end of my second week I was bored to distraction and frustrated beyond concept. I was determined to stay only until I had accumulated enough money to take care of our needs for at least one year of wilderness wandering. My target figure was three thousand dollars. Finding that my employer was perennially shorthanded, I volunteered for as much paid overtime as I could get. I free-lanced, writing for several wire services and a variety of general interest publications. To save as much as possible, I avoided socializing with other people. My newspaper colleagues believed that I was some sort of misanthrope, not without reason, I suppose.

By the third week of July I was lucky enough to rent an abandoned cabin several miles out of town. The place was run-down, but cheap at thirty dollars a month, and located beside a lake. There was no electricity, of course, and no plumbing, but there was a good well and a shed, where I found rolls of wire fencing with which to make an enclosure for Yukon. Adding to the sylvan setting were several wild cherry trees and nine overgrown apple trees. Within forty yards from our own little beach, rainbow trout and kokanee, a species of delicious small landlocked salmon, assured us of a constant supply of protein.

Yukon and I met a new kind of cold that year, less severe, tempered by frequent periods of thaw. We enjoyed the newness of that winter, but neither of us was content being restricted by daily routines. The weeks passed too slowly. We became more restless, and didn't even seem to get the same enjoyment from our weekend outings.

By the end of February, having saved $3,213.55, I gave notice to the newspaper. We would leave in two weeks' time, weather or no weather. Those last days were the hardest to endure! Every morning I ticked off another day on the calendar; every evening I did a little more packing.

Then, at last, it was time to go.

58

Chapter 7

BESIDE me, Yukon was curled up on the seat, licking his paw and paying no attention to the scenery picked out by the full moon. It was about an hour before dawn. The moonlight cast arborescent shadows on the snow. The highway was empty of other traffic. We didn't know where we were going, and we didn't care. It was enough that we were headed north; beyond this we were content to follow the road, stopping when and where we wanted. Time didn't matter, nor the season. There were no deadlines of any kind to meet and no specific goals.

By the morning of our third day on the road Yukon and I found ourselves within four miles of British Columbia's Cariboo region, where winter was still resisting spring. It was not severely cold, but the snow was deep, the waterways frozen.

I consulted a map for the first time since we had started on our journey, and selected a goal at random. The survey map showed a large area of wilderness on the edge of the Fraser Plateau, north of a gravel road that begins at Williams Lake and goes west to Bella Coola, near the Pacific shores. Somewhere in that region I thought I could find a sheltered campsite where we could spend a month or so wilderness watching while waiting for the spring breakup. We started out again and drove over fifty-six miles before entering Williams Lake, and picking up the Bella Coola road. Less than an hour later we arrived at a community called Riske Creek. It was midmorning. I liked the area, and decided to look for what we wanted there.

Riske Creek was small in those days, not much more than a cluster of log and frame houses built haphazardly on both sides of the roadway. An old-fashioned general store did double duty as a trading post. In between bargaining bouts with his Chilotin Indian customers, the trader, an old-timer in the region, advised me of a logging road that wound northward a few miles west of the creek. There, he said, I would find plenty of good camping places.

As it turned out, the road was narrow and uneven. After seven miles it became virtually impassable, clogged with heavy snow that hid a treacherous bottom. I was relieved to find a turnaround where the ground was rocky and not likely to become a bog later on, when the big melt arrived. After I had shoveled the snow to accommodate the car and tent, we made camp. We would use this as a base until we found a more permanent campsite.

We slept well and snug that night, not awakening until the sun was up. We had breakfast outside the tent, before a crackling fire, entertained by the antics of five gray jays who were begging food from me, quite unafraid of Yukon. He mostly ignored the birds until one, bolder than the rest, landed on my shoulder. Suddenly I was struck violently in the back with enough force to knock me off my stool.

Unknown to me, Yukon had been unable to control his jealousy when he saw my hand reach up with food for the bird.

The startled jay squawked loudly as it flew away. No less startled, and trying in a confused way to understand what had happened, I was about to pick myself up when Yukon came to apologize, making me aware that *he* had been the culprit. He intended to lick my face, but I reacted by angrily lashing out with open hand. For the first time in our relationship I struck him in anger. He backed up, whined, looked at me searchingly, and turned swiftly, running into the forest. He refused to come back when I called to him.

Now it was my turn to be contrite, especially when I recalled a few occasions when I had accidentally hurt him. His reactions had always been controlled. He had growled and snapped, but always pulled his bite, following it up swiftly with some manifestation of friendship.

Two hours later he was still away. Was it possible that one hasty slap could have endangered our relationship? I tried to put this thought out of my mind. But at the same time I was acutely aware of Yukon's sensitivity. Knowing him as I did, I could understand his hurt. He had given me his complete trust, something he had never offered to any man. It was not impossible that he might now feel betrayed, and might again become the antisocial beast I had first seen in Alfred's pickup truck. Confused and upset as he was, there was also a chance that he would try to return to the homestead, more than two thousand miles away. A number of equally depressing imaginings caused the morning to pass unpleasantly.

When he hadn't come back by noon, I couldn't stand it any

longer. I would follow his spoor. I put food in a small packsack, strapped on the snowshoes, and left.

At first his trail was easy to follow. He had gone almost due west. But after half an hour his tracks became blurred in a more open area full of snowshoe hare trails. He had evidently done some hunting here as he worked his way toward a forest of hemlocks and cedars. Within the umbrellalike shelter made by a large cedar I found the remains of a recent kill he had made. From the tree, the dog's tracks continued in a westerly direction.

I whistled and listened for him, but the only sound audible above the usual forest noises was a faint, continuous susurrus that I felt sure was made by running water. Yukon's tracks appeared to lead toward this sound, and as I followed I began to feel more confident, believing he would return to the campsite after his run. It wasn't a matter of logic; it was a conviction stemming from my faith in the dog and our relationship. One hasty blow could not possibly unravel the bonds that held us together.

I wasn't concerned about his getting lost. Yet I was not wholly relaxed. The grizzly bears would be getting restless in their dens about now, and it wouldn't do for Yukon to blunder into some cave following a bear's scent. Also, I was concerned because the ice covering the waterways was weakening, becoming treacherous. Immersion in water a degree or two above freezing will kill a mammal (man included) in three to five minutes.

Presently I noted that the dog had lengthened his stride at a place where the grade dropped gently and the evergreens began to thin out. The rushing sound was loud now. Squeezing through a thick stand of cedars, I broke out into a meadowland which ended abruptly at the banks of a creek. The water rushed over a rocky ledge and plunged into a wide pool. It was this sound that I had been hearing all along. Looking around, I saw that the warm March sunshine had melted most of the snow in the little clearing, which was remarkably dry except for a few boggy areas.

This place was a natural sun trap and an ideal campground. Here Yukon and I could spend our time in comfort.

Only then did I realize that I had quite forgotten the dog's absence while contemplating the beautiful clearing.

"Where the heck are you, Yukon?" I said, practically a plea.

All at once I got the feeling that I was being watched. I turned and searched the forest behind me, twice. Nothing was to be seen. I was imagining things. I started back, but before I had gone a dozen paces, Yukon's *wooo . . . woooing* call made me turn around. It was then he came to me, rushing up madly, making his plaintive howl-bark, and wagging his tail furiously. He was so enthusiastic that he knocked me flat on my back in the snow, then stood on my chest with his front paws and began to lick my face all over. I viewed this action with mixed feelings because his jaws and chin were all bloody from his hunt. We made our peace, though, apologizing profusely to each other.

The next day was a busy one. Four times we journeyed between car and meadow, carrying our supplies by means of a hastily made travois. But when we went to bed that night, we were comfortably set up in our new campsite about fifty yards from the creek, just within the shelter of the forest, with the meadow outside the tent.

Yukon and I had established ourselves on the southeastern edge of the Fraser Plateau, in a veritable paradise of nature. Bounded on the east by the Cariboo Mountains and on the west by the Coast Mountains, much of the plateau is still wilderness. The waterways that thread through this tableland drain into the wild and twisting Fraser River, which eventually empties into the Pacific Ocean at Vancouver. A notation in my logbook made a week after we moved into the meadow may be of interest:

What a fabulous, wonderful land! Not a sound of humanity is to be heard, not a sign of my own species have we yet glimpsed. The sounds are pure wild, so are the sights. Distant mountains appear to surround the plateau, but this is not nearly so flat as its name suggests. There are rolling heights, smallish mountains, and at least one tall one that we can see from our meadow.

So far we've traveled within a fifteen- to twenty-mile radius of our camp. We're at that in-between time, neither winter nor spring, and this makes for hard and treacherous going. Even so, we've already encountered a number of moose, one fox, a chattering pine marten, two coyotes, and a bobcat that nearly committed suicide by almost waiting too long when Yukon took after it. He'd have killed it, I'm sure.

For seven weeks we explored this vast wilderness, wandering at will, sometimes taking day trips, on other occasions sleeping out, huddling together under a lean-to shelter. Day by day, winter gave ground to spring. Then, at last, the land wept clear, cold tears, and the migrant birds began to arrive.

One morning in April I woke up to the honking of Canada geese and emerged from the tent to see three big wedges as they flew over our meadow. A few days later the loons came and cackled deliriously during an entire night, and Yukon joined them, singing his own haunting melody.

May arrived. With it came an unexpected hot spell that brought the mosquitoes and an early crop of blackflies. The creek had settled down to a purposeful flow, still augmented by floodwaters, but only moderately so. It was time to travel again, to seek and to explore new lands.

Chapter 8

FROM Riske Creek we retraced our way to Williams Lake and drove north to Prince George. There we turned west along the Yellowhead route that ends on the Pacific coast.

Today the Yellowhead route is a smoothly paved highway that passes through spectacular country, but in those days the scenery was perhaps grander because there was less development, and the road was a much humbler affair. At New Hazelton, I learned that there was a restricted road, owned by a logging company, which led north from the town of Terrace and eventually linked up with the Nass River. "It's just past the volcano," said my informant.

A volcano? *That* interested me. I couldn't learn too much about this fascinating and unexpected piece of news. The volcano was thought to be extinct, I was told, and there was a big area of lava over which the logging road traveled. Furthermore, it was doubtful that I could get permission to use the road at this time of the year and, even if I could, I would find it muddy and rutted.

Back in the car, I examined the survey map closely. Sure enough, a volcano was marked on it, and so was the lava bed through which ran the Nass River. "That's where we're going, Yukon. Even if we've got to carry the canoe all the way," I told my friend.

He wagged his tail and licked my face. I could tell that he had already had enough of automobile travel. So had I.

We spent that night in Terrace. The next morning, early, I visited the logging company's offices and received a permit to use the road at my own risk. It would be a rough trip, and so much was made of this that I almost backed out of the plan. Just then a driver walked into the office. He had come from an Indian village called Aiyansh and he said the road wasn't in bad shape to there. Then he remarked, "The oolachans are running on the Nass."

Later I learned that oolachans (more properly eulachons) are a species of seagoing smelts that enter rivers to spawn every spring. They die afterward, like salmon. The little fish, eight or nine inches long and silvery gray in color, are extremely rich in oil and were once the source of a brisk industry. Coastal Indians rendered them down for their fat, which was traded to inland natives. In 1877 the Canadian government built Grease Harbour, an oolachan oil factory on the Nass River. The factory is no longer operative, but the "grease trails" used by the native traders are still passable in places.

By now I was in a froth to get started, planning to go directly to Grease Harbour, so as not to miss the oolachan run. Then I would return to explore the volcano and lava bed at my leisure.

THE logging road wasn't as bad as the official said. With Yukon's head hanging out the car window, we drove through mud that was four or five inches deep in places. The winding route crossed small rivers and creeks, and within two hours we encountered Lava Lake, a long, thin body of water with a small lava bed at its northern end. It is ten miles from here to the Nass River and the village of Aiyansh.

The road was better now because it passed over the lava, but when we reached the Nass River we learned from a group of Indian teenagers that the going was bad farther north and that the trail to Grease Harbour was too narrow for the car. The three lads were Niskas from Aiyansh, and they were returning from the river with sacks full of oolachans. I was about to leave the car to take a look at their catch when Yukon began to growl and to show his teeth, unusual behavior on his part. I put his lead on and tied it to the steering wheel before stepping onto the road.

The Niska teenagers were shy, but friendly. One of the boys, Jimmy, who looked about fifteen, offered to show me how they fished. I accepted readily, but there was still Yukon to deal with.

Out of the car, the dog would not make friends with Jimmy, my would-be guide. The best I could do was to make him stop growling and to tolerate the lad's presence. Since Yukon had never acted this hostile before, I concluded that it was the memory of Alfred, the Indian who had sold the dog to me, that caused this reaction.

Jimmy was not the talkative sort. He smiled a good deal and replied in monosyllables when spoken to, but he didn't volunteer information. As we walked over the lava, I asked questions.

"How many people live in Aiyansh?"

"Some."

"Do you go to school?"

"No."

"Do you work?"

"Yes."

"What do you do?"

"Trap some. Fish."

It was not until the next day, after he had helped me make camp and came to chop wood in the morning, that Jimmy really started to talk. Then he wouldn't shut up.

That afternoon he demonstrated the method he used for catching oolachans. It was not complicated. In fact, the fish gave themselves up. Teeming thousands of darting, glittering fish filled the Nass from bank to bank. Racing upstream, jumping out of the water, they could be scooped up by hand. That was Jimmy's method. In five minutes we had pulled some three dozen out of the water. We then returned to the car and set up a temporary camp. Jimmy had supper of broiled oolachans with us that night. Yukon loved the greasy little fish. He ate fourteen at one sitting, raw.

When Jimmy arrived the next morning, Yukon remained merely aloof while the lad cut and stacked wood. Afterward we walked down to the Nass again, and Jimmy was soon plucking oolachans out of the water. While he amused himself, I looked speculatively at the swollen river, debating our next moves.

After concluding that the Nass was running too swiftly for comfortable upstream paddling, and since we had not yet explored the volcano or properly seen Lava Lake, I decided to drive back there and camp near the lake for a week or two. Jimmy, by now almost a camp fixture, offered to come, to help with the chores. But it was ten miles from his home in Aiyansh to the northern tip of the lake. Too far, I thought, for him to travel twice a day.

"Gotta bicycle," he said, nodding his head in a way that indicated the matter was entirely settled.

It was. For a fee of three dollars per diem, he would ride over and be the chore boy, guide, and general factotum. I didn't need him, but I rather suspected he needed us. We were an unusual event in his young life. And he certainly needed the money. He made himself very useful, and he and Yukon became reasonably good friends during the ten days that we camped near the lake.

The creek that flows into Lava Lake at its northernmost tip comes spilling down from the flanks of a mountain, the peak of which stands guard five miles west of the roadway. The mountain has no name; neither has the creek. In fact, few of the mountains that form the Nass Range have been named. However this may be, the unidentified creek passes under the gravel road by means of three corrugated iron culverts and shortly merges with the waters of Lava Lake. It is an insignificant little creek, but the tiny lagoon it has carved out of the lava cries out for attention.

This pool is filled with crystal-clear water, and dotted with forms of naturally sculptured lava on which grow small willows, ferns, wild grasses, and a variety of mosses and fungi. No Japanese gardener could compete with this pool designed by nature and lighted by shafts of sunlight slanting through trees.

Sticking out of the pellucid water, the dozen or more pieces of lava are each shaped differently: a dog's head, or it could be a wolf's; a rough-hewn heron standing on one leg, beak rather thick and foreshortened. The shapes seem actually to live as the dancing light and the slowly flowing water endow them with movement.

On our first day beside the lake I became lost for an hour in contemplation while Yukon and Jimmy, who had struck a truce by now, were hauling firewood. We had driven here from the

Nass, tying Jimmy's bicycle behind the car and giving the lad a ride in the back seat. Because I had by now formulated a long-range plan, I had also concluded a business arrangement with Jimmy. Yukon and I would, in due course, seek the source of the Nass River, traveling by canoe and leaving the car behind at the lava flats. For ten dollars down and another ten dollars when we came out, Jimmy would act as guardian of my vehicle. But first I intended to spend some more time beside Lava Lake. Then, before setting out, I would drive to Terrace to buy enough food supplies to last until the following spring, for we might winter in the mountains.

When Jimmy left for home that evening, I called Yukon and we set off to visit the volcano. Walking at a leisurely pace, we climbed the gentle slope that would lead us to the place where the crater yawns with black mouth at the blue sky.

It is not much of a volcano. It was probably not much even during its days of fire and brimstone. Yet it managed to spread its molten matter over an area of one hundred square miles, more or less, flowing downslope in a south-southwesterly direction.

Almost a century has passed since then. About fifty percent of the lava bed is now covered by vegetation, much of it still scrubby: willows, spruces, larches, and some lodgepole pines mingling with aspens and birches. In fewer than one hundred years, no time at all, in terms of evolution, the green things have come to reclaim much of the land.

LOGBOOK ENTRY: Night. Black night relieved only by the flickering of the campfire. Darkness under a volcano; no wind. Hardly any sound except for the murmuring of the restless creek. With full belly, sipping coffee, I sit and listen to the wilderness, thinking about tomorrow and the ten-mile walk back to the lava flats with Yukon, to see Jimmy and perhaps catch some more oolachans.

The next morning the sun shone brilliantly in a dark blue sky. There was coffee in the pot and bacon in the pan, three extra slices for Yukon's token breakfast. We left the campsite at eight o'clock, walking uphill along the slope of yet one more unnamed mountain. We could have driven to the Nass; but Yukon, no less than I, was tired of the bone-rattling drive we had endured getting to the lake. After a few hours of hard walking we encountered a fairly large meadow dotted with a number of good-sized boulders. It was an inviting place, and I decided to linger awhile, to smoke a pipe while resting on the grass.

Free, Yukon streaked toward a talus slope. Within seconds I saw the attraction: a big groundhog was running toward the talus, where no doubt lay its burrow.

My attention was suddenly taken by a shape that appeared on the left, about one hundred feet in the air. It was an eagle. I looked through the field glasses. To my amazement and delight, it turned out to be a golden eagle, the first that I had seen in North America. In fact, during twenty-four years of wilderness watching I have seen only six of these great birds.

Flying an erratic course through the thin timber, the eagle was evidently aiming at the groundhog, ignoring Yukon. The dog, at full stretch now, was aware that the bird was beating him to the prize. As the terrified quarry ran a straight course for the talus, the eagle, with a wingspan of more than six feet, went into a dive. Yukon accelerated, running so that his belly seemed about to touch the ground.

Down came the eagle, a blur of dark brown. Suddenly the great taloned feet shot forward. A thud as the bird hit the rodent; a scream from the groundhog. One heartbeat later the eagle lay sprawled on the grass, both claws fastened in the groundhog.

Yukon was getting closer, perhaps thirty yards away. I was afraid he would kill the eagle, or get clawed by the steely hooks. The bird righted itself and lifted the still struggling rodent up into space while beating frantically with big wings. Yukon was closing fast. The eagle rose in seeming slow motion, weighted down by the twelve or fifteen pounds of groundhog. Yukon launched himself straight up, stretching every muscle so that he almost hung in the air. I heard the snap of his jaws missing their target. The eagle had won its prize. Soon it disappeared over the top of the mountain.

Yukon, crestfallen, came back to me. As we resumed our walk, I wondered what would have happened between Yukon and the eagle if the bird hadn't pulled off its risky gambit.

EARLY ON THE MORNING of June 7 we began our journey north to the source of the Nass. The car was left parked at the lava flats, and Jimmy had come to help pack the canoe and see us off. He had a scruffy haversack slung around his neck, but he made no reference to it. I launched the canoe and stowed the stores and equipment that Jimmy carried to me. By the time we were done, the boat was loaded with almost seven hundred pounds, close to its maximum capacity. There was just room enough left for Yukon to sit forward and for me to kneel aft. Jimmy untied the mooring lines; then, in an embarrassed way, he opened his haversack and shyly offered me a brown paper parcel.

"Salmon. Smoked. For you," he muttered.

Touched by the gesture, I thanked him. In silence he pushed the canoe into the Nass and stood watching as I turned the bow upstream. Then I waved the paddle and yelled, "Good-by." Not to be outdone, Yukon raised his head and howled.

The river wasn't wild now, but the current was strong and the paddling was hard work. We reached Grease Harbour three hours later, our average speed five miles an hour. If we could keep that up, I thought we could probably reach the source of the Nass in five days, six at most, but I had no intention of trying to complete the journey in that time. There was no point to it; we had plenty of time and plenty of food.

I had meant to stop at Grease Harbour to look at the oolachan oil factory, but as we neared the village, a pack of snarling, yapping dogs rushed down to the riverbank, followed by two Niska men. When I waved, they ignored my greeting, scowling at us as we approached, so I kept on going. We made camp that afternoon on a tiny islet in the middle of the river, thirty-five miles from our starting point.

That night I did some planning. I was determined now to winter in this wilderness, either by building a small log shanty or, if luck was with us, by finding an abandoned cabin that could be made habitable. I hoped to live largely off the land, but I knew from experience that those who depend on nature's bounty for sustenance do so on a feast-or-famine basis. What I was trying to figure out that evening was the most likely region in which to winter, at the same time calculating the amount of food to leave in a cache along

70

the route, in case we needed supplies on our way out next spring.

As I sat beside a smoky fire intended to keep the mosquitoes away, my thoughts turned to living in the wilderness. There is something particularly unnerving about the prospect of a man's end coming to him when he is alone in some remote place, there to lie unburied and become food for the foraging animals. For some years now it has been easy for a man to place himself in the deep wilderness if he has the money to pay for a chartered aircraft and pilot. It is another matter altogether to enter the wilderness the hard way, furnishing your own power to propel a canoe *upriver* while being vitally aware that if anything goes wrong, it may well have fatal results.

The country into which Yukon and I penetrated that June was unknown only to us, for we went guided by survey maps that, though vague at times, could tell us in a general sense what lay ahead. But I had such confidence in Yukon that I believe I would have taken the trip even without maps. With him beside me, I always felt confident; without him, I do not believe I would have dared to cut myself off from civilization and venture alone into a country where I would not encounter another human being.

I wonder sometimes whether I led him, or he led me. I was always aware that we relied heavily on each other. He was my "auxiliary engine" when we had to portage around rapids, over sand flats, or around swamps. He was always eager to have his harness strapped and to carry forty pounds over the detour, returning briskly by my side for another load. At night he slept with me inside the tent, but he was on guard and ready to spring up if a marauding animal was close to our camp. On numerous occasions he alerted me to the presence of bears, several times when they were actually walking into camp.

In this and so many other ways Yukon was to me what his kin had been to the newcomers to this land. He was a living reminder of the great northern sled dog, the half-wild breed that made possible the harvesting of furs, carried people and supplies from Canada's Labrador to Alaska's Point Barrow. Without these dogs, Peary would not have reached the North Pole; neither would Amundsen have gotten to the South Pole. Without Yukon, I would not have reached the source of the Nass River.

THE FOOD CACHE was built just past the junction of the Nass and Bell-Irving rivers, some seventy-five miles north of Aiyansh, on the bank of a creek that is shaped like a Y. When the cache was finished, we reentered the river and continued on our way in a leisurely fashion. I had lost track of the time by now, but I *think* it was a few days later that we arrived at another creek, called Damdochax. This is the point where the Nass changes from a northeasterly course toward the northwest. For nine miles we followed this riverlike creek and soon reached Damdochax Lake.

Here was a surprise. At the junction of lake and creek were two excellent cabins. So good was their condition that I felt sure they were used as a fly-in camp by some big-game guide who brought in rich tourists to hunt and fish.

"Well, Yukon, we're going to call this home for a time. If the owner shows up and chucks us out, we'll find somewhere else."

Yukon turned around in the bow and galloped over the top of our load, almost upsetting the canoe in his eagerness to give me one of his sloppy caresses. It was hard not to yell at him, but there was no harm done, so I yielded to his blandishments. After he had slurped against my face and made the canoe stern-heavy, I paddled the last few yards to a rickety, but serviceable, dock. Yukon was ashore instantly, running to investigate the buildings.

When the canoe was secure, I followed, and we entered the larger of the two cabins. Inside were two double bunks, a table, four homemade benches, and a sturdy cast iron stove. On one wall was a cupboard containing a number of well-used pots and pans and some metal plates, as well as knives and forks. On the table was a faded piece of wrapping paper with a message: "Welcome. Use the place, but leave it as you found it." The note was signed "W.H." No date, no reference to the owner's future plans.

"I thank you, W.H., whoever you are," I muttered.

The cabin was sixteen feet wide by twenty-four feet long and made of round logs throughout. One two-foot-square window was let into the east wall, facing the lake, but the glass was covered by plywood to keep out the animals. The place was hot and stuffy, dust lay thick on everything, but it was made to order.

Two days later the cabin was spotless, the plywood was off the window, and all my food and gear were inside.

Judging by the heat and by the fact that the blueberries nearby were turning dark, I supposed the month was July. I guessed at the third, and marked that date on the calendar I had brought with me but never used until now.

By the end of the month Yukon and I had walked many miles of the wilderness around our cabin. We had met a number of black bears, grizzlies, and moose, and found a wolf rendezvous where the pack's five pups were waiting until they were strong enough to travel with the adults. Between trips, I built a smokehouse, roofing it with an elementary thatch of cattail leaves that allowed the smoke to get out slowly. Two racks were next installed for holding the fish and meat I planned to smoke for winter use.

By now I was using the smaller cabin as a storehouse for my flour, oats, and beans, as well as for the smoked fish. Once our provisions were secure from marauders, we took trips that lasted several days. We traveled light, frequently without the tent, being satisfied at the end of day to lie before a good fire, thankful for chilly nights that banished the vicious mosquitoes.

In this way we headed toward the small lake that gives birth to the Nass River. It took us five days to cover the sixty miles in an unladen canoe because of a set of fast rapids, and because of a large swamp that chokes the river with marsh grasses during the low-water season. I felt a tremendous satisfaction at seeing the source of the Nass, even though it took us twelve days to complete the round trip.

Next, we explored a good part of the Telegraph Trail, which runs parallel to the Nass for a time. When it turns away from the river, it runs through a valley on the northwestern side of a place called Muckaboo Creek. About eight miles up, we found a tumbledown log cabin, which nothing could have induced me to approach had I suspected what was going to transpire.

Yukon began to show signs of excitement some time before I was aware that the building lay ahead of us. Before he could run off, I snapped on the lead. A little later I noticed the cabin. The closer we got to it, the more intense Yukon became.

The building, I saw, was a wreck, with gaps in its walls and ragged holes where window and door had once been. I also noticed something else—the cause of Yukon's excitement—a terrible

73

stench, the sweetly sick smell of putrefaction. As we approached the gaping doorway, Yukon pulled hard. I wasn't anxious to discover the source of the awful stink, but what if some unfortunate person lay dead inside that place? I *had* to go in. With great reluctance I allowed Yukon to drag me toward the doorway, but before we reached it, a swift gray animal came hurtling out of the gloomy interior. It so startled me that I dropped the lead.

It was a coyote. Yukon closed with it in a trice, and my ears were filled with the sounds of savage battle. The hysterical yaps came from the coyote. As usual, Yukon was silent, single-minded. His jaws clamped tightly around the smaller animal's neck. The coyote's snarls became weaker. It started to thrash around violently, gasping. Yukon hung on, biting deeper. Then, heaving, he turned the coyote on its back and closed his fangs on its throat. I thought I had seen him in every kind of mood, but this was different, a chillingly intense killing passion never before displayed to me. I yelled at him, going as close as I dared and trying to find his lead. It was between his legs, and I was not about to stick my hand down there.

Suddenly it was finished; the coyote became silent, its body twitched, then went limp. Its eyes stared right into mine, accusingly, I felt.

Yukon started to drag the carcass away, but I stepped behind him and picked up the lead when it emerged from under the dead animal. Ignoring his resistance, I yelled at him, "Drop it! You bloody butcher!" He let go and wagged his tail, looking into my face like his old genial self. I was confused, as much upset by the needless killing of the coyote as I was by the change in Yukon. And now that most of the excitement was over, the awful stench of rotting flesh was obvious again.

I tied Yukon to a tree, returned to the cabin, and forced myself to enter. The smell was unendurable. I held my breath and walked a little closer to a dark mass on the floor. It was a bear that must have been dead for days. This is what the coyote had been feeding on so intently that it failed to notice our approach. I hurried outside, wondering about the cause of the bear's death.

Years later I learned that wolves will unhesitatingly kill coyotes whenever they get a chance. I also learned that wolf and dog will mate and breed, and dog and coyote will do likewise, but wolf and coyote will not do so in the wild. Evidently this is nature's way of keeping the species separate.

LOGBOOK ENTRY: The marks placed on the calendar show that tomorrow is Christmas Day. Cliché or not, time most definitely does fly! At least, it does when every day is full of interest and fascination. When I committed us to staying here after freeze-up, I wondered if I would become bored. I have six books that I read according to mood: Thoreau's *Walden*, Steinbeck's *Sweet Thursday*, Darwin's *Origin of Species*, Claude A. Villey's *Biology*, Gordon MacCreagh's *White Waters and Black*, and Plato's *Republic*. Some might think this a strange mix; for me, it's just right. And I have Yukon for affection, companionship, and talk. He listens intently as I read excerpts aloud for his benefit. He *never* argues.

Christmas menu: fried Canada goose, stuffed with rolled oats, raisins, and blueberries; boiled bullhead lily roots for potatoes; wild onions simmered in powdered milk; and bannock bread. Dessert is my own version of rice pudding: rice boiled with powdered milk and raisins and sugar. Then coffee (precious stuff now) and two tots of Scotch. Yukon shared everything but the whisky and the coffee; afterward we went out to walk the meal down.

I forgot to bring a thermometer, so I have no idea what the temperature is, but the hairs are freezing inside my nose, so it must be about twenty below zero. The snow is *deep*. Yukon has quite a time leaping through it. He still takes off for short trips on his own when I let him. Just now I won't; there are two large packs of wolves in the area. They're big, bigger than Yukon, some of them. Last week one of the packs was on our lake. Yukon got very excited and wanted to go out, but I tied him to the bunk. We've seen both packs quite a few times, but they always run from us.

We've now been six months away from civilization. I don't miss it; Yukon never did enjoy it. What a dog! In early September, when there was a little snow in the valley but quite a lot on the peaks, we climbed Blackwater Mountain, which is just behind us. Halfway up, Yukon registered great interest and pulled me off our course toward a ravine littered with rocks. We were about four thousand feet up, in about eighteen inches of snow. Because of

Yukon's interest, I unslung the rifle and put a cartridge in the breach. The clicking noise made by the gun produced a young mountain goat in the ravine, a billy. I shot it. Yukon looked at me and *wooo . . . woood,* as though he were saying, "Good shot. But you'd have gone right past it if it wasn't for me."

The high country was crying torrents the day the first Canada geese flew over Damdochax Lake and filled our valley with the age-old call of spring. On the darkling waters, slabs of ice, some of them bigger than a tennis court, screaked and groaned as they bumped each other in their anxiety to be set free. Behind our cabin, nine creeks running down the northeast face of Blackwater Mountain rioted exuberantly, producing a continuous rumble as each bursting channel hurried ice-cold water to the river. According to the markings on my calendar, it was April 14.

Yukon had been very restless of late, unusually so. I was puzzled by his mood at first, and watched him carefully. He had done a lot of howling at night during the last few weeks. Three times in two weeks he had regurgitated part of his supper at my feet. This was something he had done on only two previous occasions, an act that, if rather revolting to human sensitivities, denoted his affection and fealty. It was the wolf in him that caused it, prompted by a desire to share with me. Wolves often carry meat back to their families in their stomachs. They gorge at a kill, then return to regurgitate for the benefit of the stay-at-homes.

Mulling over these events, I realized that Yukon was always deeply affected when the wolves howled at night, which they did often during January and February. It seemed he was suffering from spring fever. He wanted to run into the wilderness and seek the affections of a female of his own kind. Some of the wolves were interested in him, too, for I had recently found enough tracks outside our own door to suggest that the wolves were drawn there by Yukon's scent. Whether they were interested in him as a meal or because they detected his wolf strain was impossible to determine. So I made sure that he stayed close beside me when we went out.

We had fared well during the winter. In early fall we had hunted enough small game to provide variation from moose meat. I managed to shoot five Canada geese from among a flock that landed on the lake. In the lowland forests, we hunted snowshoe hare and grouse, while higher up, ptarmigan became our quarry. I knew that if we were to survive the deep winter, when game tends to seek shelter, we were going to need a good reserve of meat.

For vegetables I harvested a supply of bullhead lily and cattail roots, both of which make a fine substitute for potatoes. Later, when the land was frozen and fresh vegetables were no longer available, I made a point twice a week of cutting down a small spruce. The bark was peeled and the cambium layer scraped off; the pulpy material, rich in vitamin C, I ingested raw as medicine against scurvy. And, on the premise that it wouldn't do him any harm, I regularly mixed a ration in Yukon's food too. I had brought a fair supply of raisins and dried apples with us, but these were used sparingly, either as a dessert or as emergency rations during long trips. With plenty of exercise every day, a ravenous appetite that was always satisfied, natural vitamin C, and the clean, crisp air, I kept fit, without even getting a minor cold. As for Yukon, he was superbly healthy and as hard as iron.

Before the winter was halfway spent, our partnership had become so close that we could anticipate each other's needs and actions, especially when hunting. Yukon knew that if he flushed a hare, I would immediately shoot it. He would wait for the shot and then dash to retrieve, or to complete the kill if the quarry was wounded. If my aim was bad, he attempted to rescue the situation, often succeeding where I had failed.

His hunting skills had become more and more important to us as winter wore on and the game began to thin out. Our stocks of protein dwindled alarmingly under our ravenous assaults, and it was necessary to hunt almost every day. Sometimes we would prowl for hours without discovering anything bigger than mice or squirrels. Without Yukon, I would have failed to see many of the game animals as they squatted rock still and indistinguishable, camouflaged by their surroundings. But their scent was inevitably picked up by the dog's sensitive nose.

When not hunting, we just walked, and I learned about the wilderness and its many life forms, reserving a time each evening for sitting by the light of the kerosene lantern, making copious notes. It was to take many years to correlate all these observations and to begin to acquire an understanding of the intricate checks and balances that govern nature. Indeed, I am still engaged in this task and have added considerably to the lexicon begun during those unforgettable months that Yukon and I spent in the wilderness of northern British Columbia.

When the last ice melted and the pregnant waterways became delivered, the insects arrived, an incessant torment of bugs that told me that it was time to go. The last day marked on the calendar was May 15. The next morning I packed the canoe, wrote a note for W.H., and left him a supply of beans and rolled oats. When that was done, I went outside, closed the door, and made sure the latch was firmly in place. Then I stood for some minutes looking at the white-capped mountains, the green trees, the lake lying placid as a mirror, reflecting the blue of the sky and the white of a few fluffy clouds. Near the far shore a loon was bobbing up and down. All around the cabin the birds were singing. It was hard to leave at this new and joyous time, but we had to.

WE MET the oolachans a few miles north of Grease Harbour. It just didn't seem possible that an entire year had passed since I last saw the interesting fish. When we swept past the place and the same dogs came snarling to the shore, it was as though I were experiencing déjà vu. Twenty minutes later I caught sight of a group of young Niskas at the water's edge. The Indians were scooping up oolachans. Moments later I recognized Jimmy.

The lad was up to his knees in water, a disreputable dip net in his right hand bulging with a mess of struggling, glittering fish. He was looking our way, waving. I waved back, then steered for the shore. Yukon leaped out of the canoe and delighted Jimmy by greeting him like an old friend, knocking the Indian lad down and climbing on top of him to lick his face. But when the other Niskas approached, Yukon backed away, staring at them balefully. The other teenagers retreated hurriedly. Jimmy positively preened. The big dog's special treatment of him gave the boy status. It made him a sort of unofficial *smoket*, which means "chief" in the Chinook jargon common on the coast.

"How's the car, Jimmy?" I asked.

"Car good. I keep all these bloody kids away!"

It seemed that Jimmy had taken his job very seriously. The old and battered Chevrolet was where I had left it, but instead of finding it covered in pumice dust, its scratched and rusting body was as beautifully clean and shiny as the aging paint would allow. Jimmy had also kept it in running condition. He had earned his money.

While Yukon and I looked over the vehicle, I heard Jimmy organizing his companions, speaking in his fluid and musical native tongue. I presumed he was ordering them to unload our supplies and to carry them to the car. He was.

When they had finished, I gave Jimmy his ten dollars for looking after my car. The other lads each received one dollar and all my remaining stocks of raisins and dried apples.

As we pulled away, the youngsters stood in a group, clutching bag or parcel, waving good-by, and yelling Yukon's name. The big dog sat on the front seat with great dignity. He did unbend at last, though, sticking his head out the window to look back at the young Niskas.

Retracing our route to civilization, we drove past Lava Lake and reached Terrace at suppertime. We ate in the car outside one of those instant-food places that do greasy chicken and stick-dry French fries. It was all very strange after a year's absence from the haunts of mankind, strange and *shoddy,* when compared with the clean beauty of the wilderness. I bought a newspaper and looked at the date. I was behind in my estimates of time by no fewer than nine days.

Trying to read the first news reports in more than a year, I found little taste for them, and in less than five minutes I crammed the journal into the nearest garbage container. Back in the car beside Yukon once more, I felt at a loss. What were we to do now? The dog was already restless. I took out my wallet and counted my money. The total was more than expected, almost $350, but not nearly enough to get us out of the clutches of civilization.

Suddenly I felt impelled to quit this town, to get back on the highway, and to drive where there were trees and green fields. Without debating the matter further, I backed the car out of the parking lot and turned east, leaving Terrace behind.

Seventeen days later found us in Winnipeg, and every one of

those days was crowded with doubts and frustration. From town to city we had traveled, stopping in each place just long enough to learn that none of the newspapers needed editorial staff. During all this time Yukon was disconsolate, and my heart ached for him. If it was difficult for me to accept this sudden plunge into urban life, it was doubly hard for him. Those were not good days for either of us.

When we reached Winnipeg, my cash was down to $135, and I was determined either to find work in this city or to return to the homestead and hire out as a logger. If I took up logging, we would be able to live in the backwoods, but with little opportunity to earn more than a subsistence income. Work in the city offered a chance to free-lance and earn extra money. I knew that I could stand the urban life for as long as it took me to buy our independence; but Yukon would suffer more than he had in British Columbia. There was no chance of finding such suitable quarters here.

I stopped at a service station, went into the washroom, and put on my one outfit of city clothes. At best, my new ensemble would have been described as humble; but it was better than my worn and not-so-clean bush clothes. Togged out in this way, I left Yukon in the car outside the offices of the Winnipeg *Tribune* and marched upstairs to seek audience with the managing editor.

He was friendly, but not too hopeful when he learned the reason for my visit. I don't think he was too impressed with my cover story about taking a year off to get to know Canada while writing free-lance articles. It all depended on his city editor's needs, he explained, but as we continued to talk and it turned out that we knew journalists in common, he seemed to warm up to the idea of hiring me as a reporter. In any event, I got the job.

Outside, an enormous policeman directed me to a part of town where I might hope to find inexpensive lodgings and be allowed to keep the dog. I was turned down five times, inevitably being refused the moment the landladies caught sight of Yukon. Dejected by the speedy refusals, I almost walked past the sixth Rooms for Rent sign. The building looked as though it might well collapse at any moment; maybe this landlord was more desperate to rent? Yukon and I walked down the broken cement pathway to the front door, and I thumped on the wood. My knock was an-

swered by a woman who could have hired out as a Halloween
witch: prune-wrinkled, rouged like a neon sign, and with a cigarette hanging from her tight-lipped mouth.

"You wanna room, you'll havta keep the dawg in the yard.
Ain't got no time to clean up dog dirt. An' it'll cost you an extra
three bucks a week."

I was struck speechless, but I managed to nod. The matter was
thus settled, and she even agreed to give the dog his supper if I
had to work late on assignment.

My room, at nine dollars a week, was what one would expect
for the price. It was at the back of the house and overlooked the
yard, where at least I could keep an eye on Yukon. And despite the
fact that the landlady was a dreadful woman in many ways, with
a mouth that would have silenced a longshoreman, I was grateful
to her. She was essentially kind, and her house was home to both
of us for some months.

As a reporter in Winnipeg, I found my pay was considerably
more than the meager wages I had earned at the British Columbia
sweatshop. Soon I was saving money, doing my best to curtail
social life, and making use of my spare time to free-lance. Most
weekends I was off duty, and I would take Yukon on camping and
fishing trips in Manitoba and Ontario. We both lived for these
outings, poor Yukon especially. But after a number of weeks, and
despite my determination to remain uninvolved with other people,
I found myself coming under the spell of one of the newspaper's
librarians. Joan Gray was her name.

Joan was dark-haired, vivacious, calm, and charming. (I am
biased, of course, but others would say the same about her.) She
was fairly tall at five feet seven inches, strong and practical, as are
most women who have been farm raised. And she was quite tough,
but tough in a nice way. She could tote that bale all right, ride a
spirited horse, paddle a canoe. Yet she was all female and had,
in addition, that remarkable quality that I prize almost above all
others: a great sense of humor.

By autumn I knew I had a problem. I loved Joan, the woman
who was to become my wife, but I also loved my wolf dog. I knew
I could not expect any woman to share the kind of life Yukon and
I had lived. Nor could I expect Yukon to share the kind of sub-

urban existence that loomed on my horizon. What could be done?

I was not being deliberately cunning when I invited Joan to join Yukon and me on one of our fishing trips, but I confess that I hoped she would like that sort of thing. She had never gone fishing before and was not then familiar with the wilderness. As it turned out, she loved it, but it was to be some time before she became as wholehearted about the wilds as I was.

In the meantime, Yukon was becoming more restless. When I faced the fact that I was now intent on making a lasting commitment to another person, I knew that the vagabond existence he and I had been leading had to end. For a long time I was split down the middle. I wanted to be with Joan, to work for her and for our future together, yet I wanted to be with Yukon, for whom I felt a deep loyalty. He wasn't a tame house dog who could be content with walks on his lead in the city. I didn't know what to do, and as a result, I stalled them both.

Joan spent that Christmas with her parents, while I stayed in the city, doing a shift on the newspaper and celebrating the holiday in my room with Yukon. What a contrast this was to our last joyous Christmas together in the Damdochax Lake cabin!

Chapter 9

EXCEPT for the empty barn and the snow that covered the driveway, the homestead had not changed during the thirty-three months that we had been absent from it. It was mid-January and mild when Yukon and I stepped out of the car and pushed our way through some two feet of snow to get to the house. The dog was wildly excited at being back in the Ontario woods. My own emotions were a compound of nostalgia, concern, and self-recrimination, the last generated by a sense of personal failure.

During the six-hour drive from Winnipeg, my mind had worked feverishly seeking a solution to the dilemma that faced all of us, but try as I might, I could think of nothing that would remedy our situation. Every course I considered returned me to the one inescapable truth that I was trying to avoid: I must give up Yukon— or Joan. I couldn't bring myself to accept either alternative and felt disloyal to both.

So I had returned to the homestead, searching for inspiration. Leaving Yukon outside, I busied myself lighting the fires. We had come here to seek peace and tranquillity, and we had three weeks of vacation to run the north woods together. Surely, I thought, some solution would present itself during this time.

I walked to the window and looked out at Yukon wading happily through chest-deep snow, evidently making for the forest. I moved toward the door instinctively, meaning to call him back, but a voice in my mind said, "Let him go. Let him run wherever he pleases; he's due some freedom."

There was that determined look about him that one often sees in dogs when they set out intent upon a definite errand, trotting along purposefully without stopping to sniff or wet. His line of travel would take him into an area that offered shelter to a variety of animals. Perhaps he wanted to hunt, or rediscover old haunts. It didn't matter. He was free of my landlady's desolate yard and able to do as he pleased for the first time in many months.

The sun was edging toward the eastern tree line, creating long shadows on the snow and highlighting the spruces with a pinkish glow that spilled over the snow and made a charcoal sketch of Yukon's body. As I continued to watch him, my mind returned to worrying. At the hub of the matter was Yukon's nature and ancestry. He was not as other dogs; he was *wild*. To attempt to subdue his wildness was to destroy the very qualities that made him such an extraordinary and magnificent animal.

Because I had wanted to believe it was possible, I had at first pretended to myself that he could learn to live in the city with Joan and me, perhaps somewhere on the outskirts, knowing, even as I dissimulated thus, that he could not, that he needed the wilderness if he was to survive as himself. Civilization was alien to Yukon; he didn't understand it and he couldn't accept it. He would fight it, and he would become savage and dangerous again.

Indeed, he had already become dangerous! Five days before, he had attacked a drunken man who had stumbled against the yard fence of the Winnipeg house. Luckily I was home and I was able to run out to stop him; otherwise, Yukon might have killed the man, or else the victim's screams would have brought the police, who would undoubtedly have shot the dog.

I had just come from a late assignment and, as was my habit, had spent some time with Yukon in the yard before going up to my room. He had seemed distant, failing to rise on his hind legs to lick my face. His behavior concerned me, but I chose to believe that he was merely more restless than usual.

The screaming started some fifteen minutes after I entered my room, a frenzied, terror-inspired shrieking that told me at once that Yukon was attacking somebody. I was so sure of this that I didn't waste time looking out the window; I ran out of the room and down the stairs, taking them three at a time.

Yukon had the man's forearm in his mouth and was shaking it savagely, his grim silence the more frightening in contrast with the hoarse screams coming from the man, who had already been pulled halfway over the fence.

Yelling as I ran, knowing that it wouldn't stop Yukon but hoping to give some encouragement to the man, I reached the dog and grabbed his collar, pulling him forward and twisting his head. Yukon let go, but for an instant he seemed about to attack me. I held him more firmly, speaking to him quietly.

"Okay, that's enough. Settle down now."

He recognized me. But I couldn't let him go or he would have charged the man again. I had to drag him away and secure him by his chain before returning to assist his victim.

After some moments, I managed to calm the man long enough to fasten a makeshift tourniquet around his arm, which was gushing blood badly. The police and an ambulance arrived eventually, and the man was taken to a hospital. I was left to answer a lot of difficult questions. Later I learned that the fellow had needed twenty-three stitches. Fortunately there was no lasting disability.

The next day, pleading personal reasons, I took time off for vacation; then I talked the matter over with Joan.

"I don't think you're being fair to Yukon," she told me. "He needs room to run. He's not a city dog, you know that!"

I knew that she thought I was being selfish, putting my feelings ahead of Yukon's happiness. She was right, but I could not bear to think of life without the wolf dog.

The following day Yukon and I left Winnipeg for the homestead, as I sought desperately for a solution. I wanted to have a wife *and* to keep Yukon with me; I needed to live and work in the city, *and* I wanted an untrammeled life in the wilderness. I knew it couldn't be done.

Watching Yukon now as he jumped joyfully through the deep snow, I asked myself aloud, "What the hell am I to do?"

AFTER entering the forest, Yukon stayed away for two days and three nights. On the morning of the third day he awakened me by pounding on the door. The agonizing that I had done during his absence may best be imagined. There had been wolf tracks in the snow when we arrived. Each night since then the wolves had howled from different parts of the forest, which meant that there was more than one pack in our section of wilderness. I had faith in Yukon's ability to take care of himself, yet I worried.

Now he greeted me as usual by licking and rubbing against me. When he was done, I got a meal ready for him. He sniffed at it, disdained it, but picked up a bone and took it to his favorite place beside the door, wagging his thanks. There he flopped down and chewed halfheartedly, but soon went to sleep.

I looked at him as he lay with his head resting almost on the bone. He was in top condition, obviously not hungry. His coat was somewhat matted, but otherwise he was fine. Stepping closer to him, I noticed he smelled particularly doggy. The odor is characteristic when the male of the species is seized by the mating urge. I wondered. . . . Was his arousal merely the result of frustrated desire, or had he actually met a wolf bitch out there?

I felt a tiny glimmer of hope. Could this be the answer I had been searching for? Would Yukon be able to form his own pack and live the rest of his days in wild freedom?

At first I rejected the last concept. It wouldn't be safe. He might step into a trap, or some other animal might kill him, and I would never know what had happened to him. I forced myself to be objective as I examined the possibility of his having found a wild mate. There was really nothing so very unusual about this; Yukon himself was proof that dogs and wolves interbreed freely. At the end of half an hour I knew I must give him the final choice.

I rose to put fresh wood on the fire, and Yukon woke up. He yawned noisily, then got to his feet and stretched. He came to me, and I patted his head and scratched his chest for a few moments. Afterward he walked to the door and pawed it. As I went to open the door, I almost decided to go with him, knowing that he would have stayed with me. But I let him go. It was not in me to deny him what I, too, craved so much.

BETWEEN mid-January and early March, depending on latitude and weather conditions, wolves that have not yet selected mates, or those whose partners have died, begin to pair off in preparation for the breeding season that usually occurs during the last half of March. The packs become increasingly restless during late winter, howling often and traveling great distances.

When two animals of opposite sexes meet at such times, they often pair off to form their own pack of two that will almost certainly become increased by the birth of pups sixty-three days after mating.

The night that Yukon disappeared into the forest for the second time, I put on the snowshoes and went for a tramp through a wilderness that was lighted by the fullness of a silvered moon. As I walked, I thought about Yukon's relationship with Sussie, his solicitude for her, and his concern for the pups. I remembered the sadness of it, the dreadful moment when I had to shoot her, and the death of the pups. When I reached the flat granite rock where Yukon and I had rested so often in past summers, I remembered the last occasion that we were here together, recalling once again the lake, the bushes, and all those other details of this landscape in summer that will never fade from my memory.

A single wolf howled. Its ululating voice issued from the west. Two howls replied to the solo, but these came from behind me in the area of the homestead. For a time there was quiet. The wilderness, shrouded in its white cowl under the moonlight, seemed to be waiting for more of the wild songs. In the sky, the North Star pulsed directly over my head, and the Dipper looked so close that it seemed possible to reach up and touch its pointers. The two mournful voices rose again in a prolonged song that echoed throughout the forest, a ghostly duet that, to my imagination, was destined to travel through space until it reached eternity and became preserved there for all time.

Four days after leaving for the second time, Yukon returned at dusk, but now he would not come inside. Wagging his tail and whining softly, he danced on the porch until I stepped out. Then he rose on his hind legs and licked my face. I went to get the field glasses, joined him, and scanned the forest at the edge of the clearing. His trail in the white snow was easily discernible. Yukon sat on his haunches and looked at me intently, then looked at the darkening forest. Suddenly he howled, a long-drawn, deep cry that rose high, held an instant, and slowly came down the scale. Then, his call was answered from just inside the trees. A lone voice somewhat higher in pitch, rose bell-like over the clearing.

Yukon turned to me and whined. He got up and walked toward his trail. He stopped, looked back, and whined again, apparently undecided, but it was obvious that he wanted to go. Now I knew that he had found his mate, just as I had. We were gripped by the same emotions, and though neither of us wanted to leave the other, the age-old forces at work within us could not be denied.

Yukon's life was out there in the forest, with his mate. Mine lay in the city, with Joan. This was right, as it should be. He belonged to the wild, and I could not deny him his right to live, or to die, in the wilderness that had created him. Love, I realized, is whole only if it is capable of letting go when necessary.

"Go, Yukon. Go to your lady."

He stood broadside to me, a dark outline against the white snow. His head turned my way, and when he heard my voice, his brush moved slowly upward and settled into its tightest curl. High-stepping, he left. Soon he was swallowed by the darkness.

I lingered, listening. Two voices were presently raised in the wolf song.

I NEVER saw Yukon again. But I heard him and his mate sing often during the remainder of my stay. I saw the signs he left on three occasions when he visited the house during the night, noting his familiar footprints, made distinctive by an old wound to one paw. His mate's smaller, finer tracks mingled with his right to the back door. Once, when I was walking through the wilderness, I became aware that I was being followed. I turned quickly and *thought* I saw movement some yards to my rear.

Later, on my return, I found his tracks in the snow, and those of his mate. Evidently he was still drawn to me, but she wouldn't dare a closer approach. She now exerted greater influence on him than I did.

The next morning I left the house at sunrise, determined to follow Yukon's trail, secretly hoping that he would come to me, but telling myself that I merely wanted to make sure that he was all right. At first I was bemused by many tracks within the shelter of the forest, but a definite trail emerged inside a heavy stand of cedars. Following it, I was led deeper and deeper into the forest. By early afternoon I was in country new to me. It seemed that the two were marching purposefully northward, Yukon's tracks leading his mate's.

At three o'clock I gave up following them. It was clear to me that they were moving out of the country, seeking a new range of their own in the deep wilderness away from the other packs and away from the haunts of man. The journey back to the homestead was gloomy. Try as I might, I could not reconcile myself to his going. It was depressing to realize that we would never again run the north woods together.

During the last week of my stay, Yukon's trails became buried by new snow, erased as though he and his mate had never walked across the clearing. By now the forest was silent; the pairing-off time was over.

Yukon was gone. I was happy for him the day I got into the car to drive back to Winnipeg. But I was sad also. I would always miss him, yet in my heart I knew that I had done the right thing, for he was free at last. Yukon would continue to live in my memory; just as his great spirit would continue to roam the north woods so long as these remained.

R. D. Lawrence

Born at sea of English parents, Ron Lawrence grew up in the coastal city of Vigo, in Spain, where his father was a journalist. Even when he was a boy, his love of nature revealed itself in the clay figures he modelled of the wildlife in the sea and hills that were his early playgrounds. As Lawrence relates in *The North Runner*, his adolescence was cut short by service in the Spanish Civil War and World War II, experiences that left him profoundly affected. "I anaesthetized myself against death,"
he explains now. "I developed an armour plating against emotion. Yukon ended that. He made me feel the need for a being other than myself. When we were together, I found peace with nature. Nature was and is a healing agent for me."

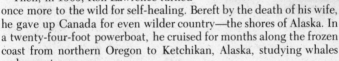

A prolific writer, driven to share his discoveries and enthusiasms, Lawrence has published ten books on the northern wilderness, *The North Runner* being the latest. In 1967 and again in 1968, he received the Frank H. Kortwright Award for excellence in writing in the field of conservation.

Then, in 1969, Ron Lawrence turned once more to the wild for self-healing. Bereft by the death of his wife, he gave up Canada for even wilder country—the shores of Alaska. In a twenty-four-foot powerboat, he cruised for months along the frozen coast from northern Oregon to Ketchikan, Alaska, studying whales and porpoises.

Today the author is back in Canada. Now married to the former Sharon Frise, a schoolteacher with red hair and a gentle charm, he spends his winters in Midland, Ontario, a small town not far from Toronto. But from spring to autumn he still roams the wilderness. To anyone interested in exploring nature on his own, he gives this advice: "First learn about your environment in your own backyard. Choose a patch of land and observe it through all the seasons. That's nature in action, humble, but like magic."

A Ship Must Die

A CONDENSATION OF THE BOOK BY

Douglas Reeman

ILLUSTRATED BY CECIL VIEWEG
PUBLISHED BY HUTCHINSON

Captain Richard Blake, VC, was a hero.
His skill was impressive, his courage
unquestioned. But there came a time, in the
Indian Ocean, when the cards seemed
stacked against him, when neither skill nor
courage were enough.

His private life was in ruins, his professional
career in serious danger. The task the navy
had set him appeared impossible: to locate
and destroy, in all that vast area of ocean,
the disguised German raider that was
decimating vital Allied convoys.

Privately, he believed there were *two*
raiders. But his superiors were hard to
convince. Was it really necessary that a ship
captained by one of his closest friends must
die before the truth could be revealed?

Once again best-selling author Douglas
Reeman has written an authentic story
of sailors at war—human, dramatic, full
of surprises.

1
Help from on High

The New Year of 1944 was only two weeks old but already it looked as if this might be one of the hottest Melbourne summers on record. The sun which blazed down across His Majesty's Australian Naval Dockyard at Williamstown was so fierce that it stripped the sky of colour, and the crowded berths and wharves twisted and danced in an ever-changing mirage.

It was Sunday, and the working parties about the dockyard were reduced to a minimum, leaving the main berth devoid of movement, the gantries motionless like dozing storks, the massive wooden concourse covered with a litter of pipes, wire, anchor cable and debris of all sorts.

Halfway along was a cruiser. From her sharp stem to the ensign which drooped from her quarterdeck staff she stood apart from the vessels around her. Despite her seven thousand tons she had the grace of a destroyer, with her funnels trunked into a single structure to add to her air of power and speed.

Where a sentry stood at the foot of her bow a lifebuoy hung with the ship's name: HMS *Andromeda*.

She, of any ship in the Royal Navy, was a veteran in the clearest terms. She had steamed thousands of miles from one theatre to another—to Norway, Dunkirk, the Atlantic and finally to the Mediterranean, from where, after two years of some of the hardest sea warfare, she had come far south, to this dockyard in Australia.

Soon now, she would be paid off, and given a full refit before being recommissioned into the Royal Australian Navy. The Pacific war was spreading, and although the United States Navy was taking the lion's share of operations, the Australians were in need of more ships to reinforce their scattered fleet.

On this sweltering Sunday, all the members of *Andromeda*'s company not required for duty were ashore. The ship was very still, with just the gentle murmur of fans and the faint throb of a generator to show any sign of life.

Right aft in his day cabin, *Andromeda*'s captain sat alone at his desk, sipping a glass of iced gin.

Captain Richard Blake, VC, was just thirty-three years old. At the outbreak of war he had commanded a destroyer. As the war increased momentum, he had advanced in promotion, "forced up under glass", as they called it, and had joined *Andromeda* as her acting commander. He had been with her ever since, and when her captain, Tom Fellowes, was killed by a bomb splinter on convoy escort to Alexandria, Blake had been put temporarily in command.

And he had stayed—fighting with E-boats, submarines, dive-bombers, heavy cruisers, shore batteries, humping stores and fuel to Africa and beleaguered Malta, eventually protecting the flank of the Allies when they took their first, tentative stab at the enemy's own territory, the invasion of Sicily. He had survived where many, many others had not.

Three months after Sicily had come the invasion of Italy. Blake looked round the quiet cabin, feeling his stomach muscles contract as he relived the experience which, in hindsight, might have been planned for him. A double column of landing craft, packed with troops, tanks and ammunition, had been heading for the beaches with *Andromeda*, two elderly destroyers and an even older anti-aircraft cruiser trying to maintain discipline. It had been a Sunday then as now, he thought, his mouth suddenly dry.

Three ships had been sighted to the northeast, closing fast. They were Italian cruisers, now in German hands, racing at full speed towards them. *Andromeda* had increased speed and had curved away to place herself between the enemy and her vulnerable charges.

What had occurred next was a part of history. At the close of the day, one enemy vessel was on the bottom, the second stopped and unable to move. The third had made off, streaming smoke, to be sunk the following day by a submarine.

Andromeda had finally managed to reach Gibraltar, down by the bows, riddled with holes from bow to stern, barely afloat. But back in 1936, when the ship's keel had first tasted salt water, they had built well. In a month the sights and horrors of battle were cleaned away, the hull patched, the blackened paintwork redone. In two months she was out of dock, and on her way to Australia. . . .

There was a tap at the door and Moon, the captain's steward, peered in. Chief Petty Officer Moon was an odd-looking man, gaunt and bony like a scarecrow, mournful of face, but like a guardsman when tending to his duties.

"Will you be goin' ashore today, sir?"

Blake shook his head. "Doubt it. Into Melbourne tomorrow. Get things started for the hand-over."

Moon nodded gloomily. "I'd like to stay with you, sir, when you gets another ship."

Blake looked at him gravely. "I don't think I could manage without you."

The chief steward seemed satisfied. "I've got your best whites ready for tomorrow, sir." He held up a freshly-ironed tunic. "Can't 'ave them Aussies thinkin' we don't know how to do things!"

Blake barely heard him. He was staring at the crimson ribbon which Moon had pinned on the white tunic. The ribbon with the tiny cross in the centre of it.

He still could not believe it. The Victoria Cross.

He could see himself in the mirror above the sideboard. He had even features, with brown hair bleached fair by many months of seagoing in the Med. A youthful face. The *boy captain*, one stupid journalist had labelled him. But it was not the sort of face he would have expected to see on the holder of a VC. He did not know if it had changed him in any way, or might in the future.

He held out his glass. "Another, please."

Moon padded to the sideboard. Captain Blake was the best he had ever served.

He watched quietly as Blake tilted the glass. Then, with the tunic and its crimson ribbon over his arm, he left the cabin.

COMMANDER VICTOR FAIRFAX of the Royal Australian Navy opened the bedroom curtains carefully and looked out at the brilliant moonlight. The house was in a quiet, tree-lined road on the outskirts of Melbourne.

Fairfax was thirty-one, a professional to his fingertips, and tomorrow he would join his new ship, the British cruiser at Williamstown. He was to be second-in-command, for the immediate future, under an English VC. It was an exciting prospect. He listened to his wife's gentle breathing in the bed behind him and felt his heart warm towards her. Leaving her would be painful. They had been married for only eight months, after a whirlwind courtship. A wedding with all the trimmings, raised swords, the admiral, the whole lot.

The war had seemed a long way off then, despite the news from Europe and the Pacific.

She stirred, and he knew she was awake. "What is it, Vic?"

He shrugged. "I was thinking, Sarah, about tomorrow. *Today*, actually."

"Come to bed. It'll be all right. We'll manage. Who knows, you may be in Williamstown for months. New captain, new crew, it'll all take time."

He sat down on the bed and she rested her hand on his cheek. "You *need* the sea, Vic, as much as I need you."

He climbed in beside her and without words they made love.

Afterwards he lay with her yellow hair across his shoulder. She said huskily, "What do you know about Blake?"

Fairfax smiled at the darkness. "A real hero by all accounts. God, his last action reads like something from a film."

"That all you know?"

"He's young for his appointment. Bit of a loner, someone told me. He's married, but it's on the rocks."

She snuggled against him. "He's not another death or glory boy, is he?" She hugged him tightly. "I don't want to lose you."

Fairfax grinned. "He'll be off soon, I expect. Back to England and the real war."

She hugged him again, and he held her until she had fallen asleep. It would be interesting to meet a real hero, he thought. He was still smiling as he, too, fell asleep.

IT WAS A TEN-MILE drive from the dockyard to the Navy Office in Melbourne and, as Blake sat in the fast-moving staff car, he tried to build up some enthusiasm for what he had to do. Nobody stayed with any ship for ever. However, with Diana gone, *Andromeda* had become his world. There was nothing else.

The car eventually jerked to a halt in a patch of dusty shadow, and Blake was shown into a cool office. Two Wrens were typing busily. Their officer, who was leafing through a folder on the opposite side of the room, stood up. "Captain Blake." She was tall, her face and hands tanned, as if she were more used to the open air than an office. "You're expected, sir. This way."

In the inner office a stoutly-built captain, old for his rank, ambled round the large desk and shook his hand.

"Sit down and take it easy." He glanced at the impassive Wren officer. "OK, Claire, you can organize some tea when you get a moment." The door closed.

The captain said, "I'm Jack Quintin. My job is to liaise intelligence between the RAN and your people. I'm sorry to drag you here first, and I know you've an appointment with the First Naval Member of the Board in thirty minutes. However . . ." he perched himself on the edge of the desk, "I thought you'd want me to soften the blow. Fact is, you will not be leaving *Andromeda* just yet. Her full refit will have to wait. You and your ship are needed at sea. It's as simple as that."

Simple? Blake stared at him. Under half the ship's usual company for crew, much of the machinery in need of overhaul, even replacement?

He said, "I understood that HMAS *Devonport* would be ready for any emergency while *Andromeda* is fitting out."

Quintin said, "It's top secret, of course. *Devonport*'s gone."

Blake exclaimed, "How?" *Devonport* was a sizeable cruiser, a powerful force to be reckoned with.

Quintin spread his hands. "She was on the long patrol, the Cape Town to Melbourne convoy route. . . . Truth is, we've lost trace of several ships in the past few months. But mostly merchantmen sailing independently. You know the sort of thing."

"You think the enemy's got a raider in these waters, is that it?"

Quintin rubbed his chin. "Could well be. Fact is, we've been in regular contact with the Admiralty in London, and someone *very high up* has decided to loan you to us so that we can find out for sure."

Blake considered the prospect. Even with her own seasoned hands to back up the new company, *Andromeda* was still unfit for immediate service. But against this he could appreciate that the next few months were very important for the Allies, even crucial. It was obvious an invasion would be launched against Occupied France while the armies continued to push up through Italy from the south. The war in the Pacific was reaching a climax. Every convoy round the Cape would be vital. If there was a raider in these vast sea areas, the German command could not have picked a finer moment. . . .

The door opened and the Wren officer said calmly, "The admiral's ready for Captain Blake, sir."

Blake looked at her. "Thanks." He nodded farewell to Quintin.

As the door closed behind him Quintin said, "Well, Claire, what did you make of him?"

She brushed a strand of hair from her forehead. "I think they expect too much. He looks like a man who has been through hell and back."

As soon as he returned on board, his mind still buzzing from his interview with the admiral in Melbourne, Blake went to his day cabin and opened his new orders.

Two cruisers, *Andromeda* and *Fremantle,* under the overall command of Commodore Stagg, RAN, were to be used to track down the raider if there was one reported, and be at first-degree readiness to carry out a search in whatever area it was known to be. Simple. A needle in a haystack would be gigantic by comparison. Blake thought of *Andromeda*'s motto. *Auxilium ab Alto.* Help from on High. They were all going to need it.

Moon appeared. "Commander Fairfax 'as arrived, sir."

"Ask him to come aft, will you?" Blake sat back in his chair.

Blake liked what he saw of Commander Fairfax. A neat, athletic man with dark hair and a pleasant smile. Crow's feet at the corners of his eyes as evidence of prolonged sea duty. They shook hands and Fairfax sat down.

98

Blake eyed him gravely. "*Andromeda* will remain in commission." He saw the man's astonishment and added, "What's your first name, by the way?"

"Victor, sir."

"Well, Victor, in about two weeks we will proceed to sea to join company with one other cruiser. In that time we will take on the necessary complement of replacements, although thank God I still have most of the key ratings and marines. But the rest will have to be led, trained; thumped if necessary into shape, all right?"

"A question, sir. Will you speak with the officers, or shall I?"

Blake smiled. "You will. You're the commander."

As commander, Fairfax would have to wear two hats. He would have to take charge of routine affairs, from manning to discipline, and at the same time present the ship to her captain as a going concern, a team, a weapon which Blake could use with confidence.

Fairfax stood up. "I'll get on to it right away."

"Join me for a glass later, Victor. I've a ton of paper to go through. You've not asked me *why* there's such a flap on?"

"I can wait, sir."

"Well, *they* think there's a raider hunting in this territory. We are going to find her. At. least, that is the general idea." As Fairfax turned towards the door Blake asked, "What do you know of a commodore named Stagg?"

Fairfax swallowed. "Very thorough, I believe, sir."

"You don't like him?"

"I didn't say that, sir."

"It doesn't matter. We will be under his command." He smiled briefly. "Carry on, Commander. There's a lot to do."

Outside the door Fairfax felt as if he were walking on thin ice. Blake was no fool, neither would he tolerate one.

ALTHOUGH *ANDROMEDA*'S new operational role remained a well-kept secret, the speed of her partial refit became something of a joke around the Williamstown dockyard. Above the cruiser the gantries swung and plunged, while hourly the piles of equipment on the berth alongside grew less and less.

Ten days after Captain Quintin's bombshell, Blake took a breather to consider the ship's state. The new hands had arrived and were soon sorted out. They had done well, and Fairfax's part had been invaluable. He had never worked so hard in his life, and he had loved it.

In the ship's company of four hundred and fifty, Blake had only two who had been with *Andromeda* from the beginning. Bob Weir, the engineer commander, who always managed to keep the shafts turning, no matter what was happening on the decks above his roaring world of machinery and noise. Weir's whole family had been wiped out in the first big air raid on Liverpool. He looked far older than his forty years and had the pallid features of a man just out of prison.

Then there was Lieutenant Palliser, the gunnery officer, who had begun in charge of B turret and had been about the only man there who was left in one piece after the last fight.

By and large they were a good company, and what Blake had seen of the newcomers he also liked. There had been the usual banter between the Aussies and the Poms, but that would pass. Apart from Fairfax, there were a couple of Australian lieutenants, some petty officers and over two hundred and fifty ratings.

As HE WAS finishing his lunch alone in his quarters, he heard the marine sentry in the outer flat moving his boots and knew a visitor was about to appear. It was Villar, the navigating officer, a tanned, tough-looking lieutenant with an Afrikaans accent you could slice with a knife. He was wearing the sword belt of officer of the deck.

"Signal from Melbourne, sir," he said. "Commodore Stagg will arrive on board this afternoon at six bells."

Blake smiled. "Tell the commander, would you, Pilot? Better pass the word to the marines, too. Farleigh will enjoy a visit. Bags of bull."

Farleigh was *Andromeda*'s debonair captain of marines.

Blake added, "But otherwise no change. We will work ship as usual."

Villar marched out and Blake glanced across at his locked desk, picturing the folder inside. Commodore Rodney Stagg, DSC, one-time prisoner of war in Sumatra. It might be an interesting meeting.

100

TIMED TO THE MINUTE, a large staff car rolled along the main berth. Blake stood beside Fairfax at the top of the brow, while nearby in a neat khaki line a marine guard waited on deck to honour the visitor.

Blake watched the commodore as he climbed slowly from the car. A big man, even at a distance, his white drill uniform unable to disguise his ample girth.

Captain Farleigh gave a quiet cough, the line of marines stiffened as if a steel rod had been passed through it, and Farleigh snapped, "Carry on, Colour-Sar'nt!"

Sergeant Macleod brought his men to the shoulder arms position as Commodore Stagg strode up towards the side. The marines presented arms, the boatswain's mates' calls shrilled in salute and Blake stepped forward to greet his new chief.

Commodore Rodney Stagg was impressive. Broad-shouldered, heavily-jowled, with dark brows which almost met above piercing eyes. He shook hands and nodded to Fairfax. Blake led the way to the after companion.

In the day cabin Stagg prowled restlessly around, his head nearly brushing the deckhead fans. "Busy ship," he said. "I guessed I wouldn't catch you slacking."

Moon appeared and took his cap from him. Stagg had thick, iron-grey hair, all bunched to the top of his head. "Would you like a drink, sir?" Moon asked.

Stagg sat down. "Why not?" He breathed deeply. "God, the smell of a ship. It's worth ten of anything."

Moon asked dolefully, "What will you take, sir?"

"Brandy an' ice." His accent was barely Australian, Blake thought, and it sounded slightly unreal, like an actor with an unrehearsed role.

Blake took his pink gin. "Here's to us, sir."

Stagg downed his drink with a nod. "This raider—" He leaned forward in the chair, his gilt buttons tugging in protest. "*Our* raider. What d'you think about her, er, Richard?"

"I've studied the reports, sir, the past sinkings and cruises of other commerce raiders, but I'm not convinced—"

"Of course you're not. This one's quite different. A wily bastard." Stagg rubbed his hands together noisily. "Pete Costello

101

commanded *Devonport,* by the way. I knew him well. Nice enough chap, but too careless, too *easy.*"

"I can see you really believe in this raider, sir."

The eyes fixed and held him like twin gunsights, searching for anything which might hint at disbelief or amusement.

Stagg nodded. "I can go one better. I know who it is."

He sat quite still, watching Blake's reaction. "Thought that would make you sit up, Richard. Both the First Naval Member and the Chief of Staff think I'm halfway round the bend. But you see, I know his habits. I've met him before." Stagg's èyes were distant. "I'll not forget. Ever. He sunk my ship. Then handed me over to the Japs. No, I'll not forgive that one."

Blake suddenly remembered about Stagg. Taken prisoner when his command was set on fire and beached near the Sunda Strait. Immediately after the fall of Singapore, that was it. Blake had imagined Stagg's ship had been sunk by the Japs, not by a German raider.

Blake said, "You're obviously very certain it's the same ship."

"I am. I can't wait to get my revenge on the murdering bastard!"

He stood up. "Must be off now. Just thought I'd meet you before we work together. Matter of fact, I was against your staying." He searched Blake's face. "But I think we'll get along."

Blake saw the commodore over the side and watched the car roll away in a cloud of dust.

Fairfax joined him by the guardrail and saluted. "Signal, sir. We're to take on ammunition tomorrow." He turned to follow Blake's gaze. "All right, sir?"

"I'm not sure." Blake walked aft again, deep in thought.

IT WAS EARLY EVENING, but Blake's shirt was like a wet rag. Something which Weir and the dockyard staff needed done had meant the ventilation fans were switched off for half an hour. In minutes the cruiser had become a sweltering oven.

"I think, Victor, we've just about earned a drink," Blake said.

Only three days since Stagg's brief visit, and the work had been all but completed. A holding job.

Fairfax, like Blake, looked damp and uncomfortable. He said,

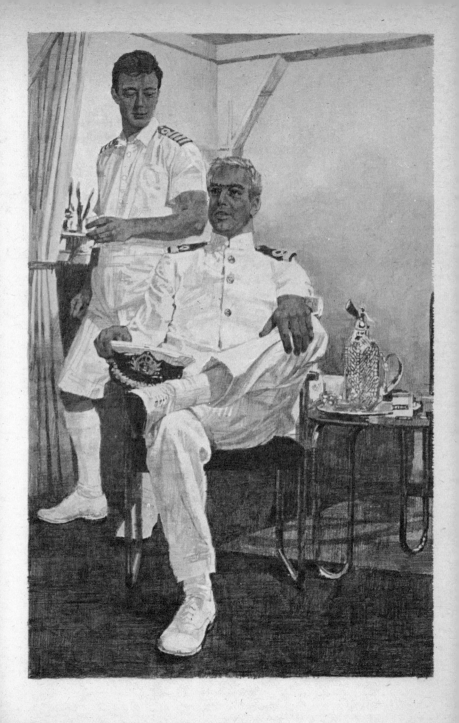

"I could certainly use a glass, sir." Blake rang Moon's bell and forced his mind away from the irritating fact that no new flying boat had been received to replace the old Walrus, which had been shot down by one of the Italian cruisers. Now *Andromeda* had only her fragile Seafox, a seaplane which had been obsolete for a year. He had mentioned it to Stagg in his last report. Stagg had sent the report back, his comment, *Make do*, scrawled across the page like a shout.

Moon padded across the cabin with a jug of ice which was already two-thirds water.

Fairfax asked quietly, "D'you really believe in this raider's identity, sir?" He took his drink gratefully. "The commodore's always been a bit wild. He had a bad time from the Japs before he escaped. Even if it's the same one, the German captain who sank his command probably had no choice but to hand him over to his little yellow allies."

Blake had thought about it a lot and had sorted through every intelligence folio which Captain Quintin's department could lay its hands on.

The German officer in question was a remarkable man. Kapitän zur See Kurt Rietz, holder of the prized *Ritterkreuz*, had already commanded two commerce raiders and had successfully sunk or captured over one hundred thousand tons of Allied ships. His daring and infuriating sorties against solitary ships or small groups of unescorted vessels had given the Admiralty headaches from the Atlantic to the Tasman Sea.

He was also an enigma, with just the bare details of his background in Quintin's files. But in all the reports, the eye-witness statements from released prisoners and survivors, there had been no mention of a single atrocity beyond the demands of combat.

Blake turned his mind back to Fairfax's comment. He obviously disliked Stagg. It would probably come out later on. Right now there was too much to do for idle speculation.

A midshipman, his face peeling painfully from sunburn, tapped at the lobby door and stepped carefully over the coaming.

"Yes, Mr. Thorne?"

"The first lieutenant's respects, sir, and there is a visitor from the Melbourne Navy Office."

"Send him in.

"It's a *her,* sir. Second Officer Grenfell."

Fairfax said, "Quintin's aide, sir. You met her, I expect?"

Blake recalled the Wren officer. Cool and in control. He caught his reflection in the mirror and pushed his hair back from his damp forehead.

She stepped into the cabin and looked at him calmly.

"Captain Quintin sent me, sir." She flipped open her shoulder bag and took out a narrow envelope. "For your intelligence pack."

"Can you tell me briefly what's in it?" Blake asked.

She looked at him directly. She had nice even features with steady grey-blue eyes. Beneath her cap her fair hair jutted forward like two pale wings. It was like seeing someone watching you from behind a mask, he thought.

She shrugged. "Nothing definite, sir. But reports are coming in about a possible incident. A ship called the *Bikanir,* carrying chemicals, two and a half days out of Cape Town, on passage for Adelaide. An American patrol picked up a garbled distress signal and part of the ship's position. Commodore Stagg is sailing in *Fremantle* this evening."

Blake ripped open the envelope and read quickly. *Andromeda* would be required to proceed to sea without further delay. He would be sent a rendezvous with *Fremantle* in due course.

Blake could feel the girl watching him. He said, "Ask the Chief if he can spare a minute, Victor. And tell Number One to recall the liberty men."

It was very quiet after Fairfax had gone, and then there was a sudden whirr. Cool air spilled into the cabin from the fan ducts.

He leaned back in his chair. "I needed that!"

She said, "I wish you luck, sir. You and your ship." She adjusted her hat and closed her shoulder bag. "I'll be off then."

Blake made to accompany her to the companion ladder but she said, "I know the way, but thanks."

Fairfax came back and watched the girl's legs until they had vanished through the hatch to the quarterdeck.

Blake smiled. "I suppose you know her?"

Fairfax sighed. "After a fashion. She keeps her distance. Hands off." He hurried on, "Not that it matters to me, of course.

I knew her brother quite well. But he's dead now. Bought it off Libya eighteen months back."

Blake saw Weir approaching the door. His overalls, fresh that day, were already black with grease.

"Be ready to move, Chief. What's still missing will have to wait." He thought of Stagg's *make do*. "There *is* a raider, so we'll have to keep our wits about us. We've two cruisers for the job, but one hell of a lot of ocean to cover."

"It wouldn't be the navy if we weren't expected to do the bloody impossible." Weir caught sight of Moon through the hatch and nodded. "Thank you, a dram would suit fine."

Blake watched him affectionately. He would never really know Weir. Not in a thousand years. But they suited each other well. More to the point, they both suited the ship. Suddenly, he thought of Diana. What was she doing at the moment? He tried to accept it, show that it no longer hurt. But he could not, and it did. . . .

2
Evidence

The SS *Argyll Clansman*, twenty days out of Sydney on passage to Cape Town, faced another bright morning. She was a fairly new refrigeration ship, her holds packed from keel to deck beams with frozen carcasses, rations for the people in Britain.

The first mate stood on the starboard bridge wing, puffing at his pipe. It was still very early, but the boatswain was moving around the hold covers with a party of seamen, getting some of the work done in time to beat the scalding heat of the day.

The mate turned as the master stepped onto the freshly scrubbed gratings, his binoculars slung around his neck.

"All quiet, Mister?"

The mate nodded. "Making a good twelve knots, sir. We'll be at anchor on time."

The master grunted. "I'll not be sorry to see Table Mountain again, believe me. No more news of the *Bikanir*, I suppose?"

The mate smiled. The Old Man would have been the first to be told. They had had an Australian sloop as escort, but after the garbled distress signal from the *Bikanir* she had dashed off.

"Smoke, sir! Port bow!" the masthead lookout called.

Master and mate bustled across to the opposite wing.

The master said, "Ship, right enough." He lowered his glasses, his face worried. "What was *Bikanir*'s position again?"

"Longitude thirty east. That was all they could pick up."

The master glanced up at the lookout, then with the mate behind him he strode into the chart room. They stared at the chart.

"We're four hundred and twenty miles nor'-nor'east of the Prince Edward Islands." The master rubbed his chin. "Can't be that raider. Couldn't possibly have got down here in half a bloody day." He looked at the mate. "Could it?"

The mate shook his head. "No chance."

The boatswain appeared at the door. "Masthead lookout reports that the ship is stopped, sir, and apparently on fire."

The two officers hurried back to the bridge.

"What d'you think, sir?"

The master peered at the distant smoke. "Think? Alter course, Mister, but tell Sparks to prepare a signal, just in case. Have the guns manned, and pass the word to all hands."

He picked up a handset and cranked the handle. "Chief? This is the captain. Get ready to shift yourself. There's a ship on fire. Might be the victim of an attack. I'll see what I can do."

The captain watched the distance falling away. On the poop, his ancient four-inch was already manned, and the one below the bridge was trained across the bulwark, its crew standing up to watch as the other vessel took shape.

A light stabbed through the smoke. The mate read slowly, "Radio's gone, fire in forrard hold. They need medical help."

The master asked, "What ship?"

The mate replied, "*Mont Everest*, she's bound for—"

"Not on your bloody life! I know that French ship well, this one's too big—" The master jumped forward. "Hard a-starboard!" he yelled. "Full ahead both engines! Tell Sparks! Send our position! *Now*, for God's sake!"

Telegraphs clanged, and as the quartermaster spun the spokes of the big wheel someone shouted, "She's hoisted her colours, sir! God, it's a Jerry!"

The smoke was thinning away even as the other ship's length began to shorten and she turned slowly towards the *Argyll Clansman*.

The master's lips moved in time with the stabbing light and the fresh hoist of flags at the other ship's yards.

Stop instantly. Do not use your radio.

Through the door he heard the urgent tap of a morse key, the sudden commotion on the deck below.

Two long orange tongues stabbed through the thinning smoke. The enemy's shells hit the ship's side like a fall of rock, and a great blast of searing heat burst through the bridge. More shells crashed alongside, and the master felt the broken screen bite into his chest. He heard the old poop gun fire just one shot before it was smashed to fragments by another violent explosion.

There was blood all over the telegraph, and he knew it was his own. Scalding steam shot up the side of the bridge as the sea burst into the boiler room, then, like his ship, the Old Man died.

FAIRFAX STEPPED into Blake's day cabin, his cap tucked beneath one arm, as he said, "Ready to proceed, sir."

Blake smiled. "Good." He looked round the cabin. He would not see it again until they anchored. The sea cabin on the bridge was his place from now on, his command post. From there he could reach the forebridge in seconds. "Has the pilot come aboard?"

"He's on the bridge now."

Blake climbed to the deck above and hurried along the port side, past X and Y turrets, the tier of boats, the catapult with its Seafox perched upon it like a delicate bird, the great trunked funnel. He felt the sun, hot already, through his shirt. He put on his sunglasses as he ran up the next ladder to the upper bridge and glanced around at the figures who filled it. Villar, the navigating officer, standing high on the compass platform with Lieutenant Trevett, RAN, who was assisting him for the moment. Boatswain's mates, messengers, Harry Buck, the chief yeoman of signals, portly as a toby jug; a marine bugler, and two signalmen.

The harbour pilot touched his cap. "Fine day, Cap'n."

Blake climbed up onto/the fore-gratings and glanced briefly at the wooden chair which was bolted there. How many days and nights had he sat there, trying to sleep, trying to stay awake? Out here, in the sunlight, it seemed like a dream. A nightmare.

Calmly he gave the necessary orders to cast off from the shore. On the forecastle, the first lieutenant, Lieutenant-Commander Scovell, characteristically hands on hips, stood right in the bows, the eyes of the ship. Near him a signalman waited to haul down the jack the moment the ship got under way.

"All gone aft, sir."

Blake crossed the bridge and leaned over the warm screen. A tug was ready to pull the stern out. There was no wind to help.

"Stand by."

"Slow ahead starboard."

A boatswain's mate called nervously, "Beg pardon, sir, but the W/T office has an urgent signal."

Blake snapped, "Read it out, man!"

Almost imperceptibly *Andromeda* nudged forward as the tug gently pulled the cruiser's elegant stern away from the piles.

Through it all the boatswain's mate's voice intruded: "Signal intercepted from SS *Argyll Clansman,* sir. 'Position latitude forty-one degrees south, longitude thirty-eight east. Am being attacked by German raider.' No further transmission, sir."

Blake watched the shadowed arrowhead of water expanding steadily between the ship's side and the berth's stout piles, the sunlight flooding down to fill it.

"Let go forrard."

His mind was like ice. *Frozen.* Somewhere a ship had been killed. That last pathetic signal hung over the bridge like an epitaph.

"Stop together. Cast off from the tug, if you please. Tell her 'Thank you', Yeoman. . . . Starboard twenty, slow ahead port."

He waited for the bows to swing out, saw the land sliding away. "Midships. Slow ahead together." He glanced impassively at the harbour pilot. "All yours."

Blake turned to the Australian lieutenant. "Trevett, isn't it?

Well, I'd like you to help the navigating officer to maintain a special chart from now on. Positions, possible sightings of the raider, distances, anything which might help us to get the *feel* of his movements."

He swung round, raised his glasses and trained them on the shore. On the last jetty he saw a parked car. In the back he recognized the shape of Captain Quintin, but beside it he saw the Wren officer, leaning against the door as she watched the cruiser turning slowly clear of the other shipping and towards the Bay.

Fairfax asked, "Shall I fall out harbour stations, sir?"

"Yes. We will exercise action stations the moment we have dropped the pilot." He saw the surprise on Fairfax's tanned features. "I want the new hands especially to get their confidence, their bearings." He gave a sad smile and touched Fairfax's arm. "We're back in the war, as of now."

BLAKE FELT A HAND on his shoulder and in seconds was awake. He turned and looked at Moon's face, pale in the small light above the bunk. A cup of tea vibrated gently in his hand.

"Dawn comin' up, sir. Very quiet. As per usual."

The door closed silently behind him. Blake put his feet on the scrap of carpet and felt *Andromeda*'s heartbeat pulsing up through each deck and flat, magazine and cabin. She was managing to make nearly twenty knots, which after her short refit was asking a lot of her.

Ten days out of Williamstown. He sipped the scalding tea and thought about it. Just three days after the *Argyll Clansman* made her frantic call for help there had been another—an old Greek freighter named *Kios*. She had lost her screw, she had been alone, helpless. Security didn't count. There was not much for her skipper to do but fill the air with his calls for aid.

Then the signal had changed. Blake had been in the W/T office with Fairfax. It was much like the last one, he thought. The *Kios*'s position, she was being attacked, then nothing. The Greek's position was nine hundred miles east of the *Argyll Clansman*'s. *Nine hundred miles in three days.* That would put the raider's speed at some fourteen knots.

He put down the cup and stood up, put on his cap, slung his glasses around his neck and stepped out of the cabin.

Vague figures loomed past him or stood respectfully aside as if to become invisible. On the bridge the morning watch had settled down. Scovell was lounging in one corner of the bridge, while his young assistant, Sub-Lieutenant Walker, a New Zealander, stood apart by the ready-use chart table.

"Morning, Number One." Blake crossed to his chair and climbed into it. The smooth wooden arms felt cold. In a matter of hours they would be like furnace bars.

Scovell moved towards him. "Nothing to report, sir."

Blake nodded and put his unlit pipe between his teeth. By *nothing to report,* the first lieutenant meant there was nothing which *he* could not handle. Lieutenant-Commander Scovell was excellent at his job. A tall, thin officer with a disdainful manner, he was due for a command, but a difficult man to work with. Intolerant over carelessness and small breaches of discipline. God help anyone unfortunate enough to serve under him, Blake thought.

"How are they all settling down together, Number One?"

"All right, sir. I've a few defaulters, but the commander will deal with them." He sounded bored.

A voice said quietly, "Radar wants permission to shut down, sir."

Scovell swung on the man, "What the *hell? Again?*" To Blake he added in a controlled tone, "May I go and see the senior operator, sir? He's reliable." He gave a rare smile. "Which is more than can be said for the equipment!"

Blake replied, "Carry on. I'll be here until we exercise action stations at six bells."

They could moan as much as they liked, but he knew that they were in no way ready to meet the enemy on a level footing yet. So he had kept it up every day since leaving harbour: action stations, fire drill, damage control, man overboard, the whole book.

He heard the sub-lieutenant moving and said, "Come here, Sub."

Walker moved up beside him. A slim, dark-haired youth of nineteen, he would be a good example to the unruly midshipmen under his care, Blake thought. He came from Wellington, the "windy city", he called it.

"Well, Sub, what do you make of all this?"

Walker shifted his feet. It was the first time he had ever been alone with the captain.

He said quietly, "I think we'll catch the raider, sir. Trouble is. . . ." He fell silent as Blake turned to look at him.

"No, go on. Tell me."

"I think we need a carrier, sir. It's too big an area for us and *Fremantle*. The German might be anywhere."

Blake nodded. "True. But to have any success a raider has to cross and re-cross our main trade routes. In the past, the raiders have cut the sea into a grid, each square a rendezvous for meeting a supply vessel or for marking down a convoy for shadowing or attack. And anyway, Sub, every carrier is pure gold at the moment. Cruisers are the best bet, with the range and the hitting power. What we need now is a bit of real luck. Then we shall see."

Walker, who had been on the ship for seven months, and had survived the battle in the Mediterranean without a scratch, said, "I'd not want to leave this ship, if she were mine."

Blake looked at him, moved by his sincerity. "I know. I was of two minds back in Williamstown. But when my chance came to stay with her I didn't hesitate." He added simply, "When you get a command, you'll know. You may serve in a dozen ships, but there's always *one* which stands out." He reached out and touched the quivering steel.

Scovell came back into the bridge and Blake faced the sea again.

As sunlight spilled over the horizon and brought colour to the ship and the sea around her, the gongs jangled like mad things and the tannoy bellowed, "Hands to exercise action!"

The bridge shook with feet stampeding up ladders and through doors. Hatches clanged shut, clips rammed home, while voice-pipes and telephones kept up their chorus.

"A and B turrets closed up, sir!"

"Damage-control parties closed up, sir!"

"Short-range weapons closed up, sir!"

From end to end, from range-finder to the depths of the deepest magazine, until Fairfax reported smartly, "Ship at action stations, sir."

Blake glanced at his watch. Better. A *little* better anyway.

"Very well. Fall out. Port watch to defence stations. But pass the word to all lookouts. The radar's playing up again, so no slacking on reports."

Blake slid from his chair. Another day.

Walker stood up sharply from a voice-pipe. "Sir! Masthead reports wreckage in the water, dead ahead!"

Blake jumped back to his chair and stabbed his thumb on the red button below the screen. Action stations shrilled through his command once again, and startled men cannoned into each other in confusion, rushing to obey the call.

Blake raised his glasses and watched the dark, bobbing fragments. "Slow ahead both engines." He looked at Fairfax. "Tell the doc to take charge down there. We shall lower two boats, one port, one starboard."

Fairfax hurried away, relieved that he did not have to watch the pathetic, grisly remains which parted across the bows and drifted slowly down either beam.

A lifeboat, its gunwale shot away almost to the waterline. At least two corpses lolling inside, covered with oil. Other bodies floating nearby in life jackets, pieces of men. A lifebelt, lettered *Kios*.

Blake said, "Check with Asdic, Number One. I'm going to stop." He did not wait for the telegraphs. "Send the boats away. Doc will know what to do. He should, by now."

Nobody spoke as the first boat, a whaler, shoved off from the side. Blake saw Surgeon Lieutenant-Commander Edgar Bruce squatting beside the boat's coxswain and guessed that his assistant, Lieutenant Renyard, would be in the other one.

Buck, the stout chief yeoman, trained his telescope on the boat's bowman who was semaphoring with his arms. The boat had stopped among some drifting woodwork.

"One survivor!"

Blake swallowed hard. A survivor. From that filthy, obscene flotsam. It did not seem possible.

He levelled his binoculars with difficulty as *Andromeda* rocked

113

more steeply in the swell. "Recall that boat, Number One. Tell the chief boatswain's mate to have his party ready to winch the survivor aboard."

The other boat reported no survivors, and headed back.

Scovell reported flatly, "Boats hoisted inboard and secured, sir."

"Very well. Resume course and speed. Fall out action stations."

The deck began to tremble again. Blake tried not to think of the men in the shattered lifeboat. One had been staring up at the cruiser, his eyes black holes. The sea birds had done that to him.

BLAKE CROSSED the *Andromeda*'s upper bridge and paused to watch the remainder of the sunset. It was very red, spilling over the horizon like blood. It was three days since they had run down on the drifting flotsam and human remains. Three days while they had waited for the sole survivor to die. He had died that morning and been buried at sea.

And of all the members of the *Kios*'s crew, the survivor had been a steward, a small, terrified Greek. Had he been an ordinary seaman he might have been able to gasp out a description of hull design or a hint of the raider's age, but as a steward he had had no understanding of such things. Big, he had said. Maybe eight thousand tons. Nothing more.

Blake climbed into his chair and placed his cap below the screen. There had been no more attacks reported . . . yet. This time tomorrow they would rendezvous with Stagg in HMAS *Fremantle*. A pencilled cross on the ocean. Two ships meeting to discuss what they should do next. For all they had achieved so far they could have stayed in harbour.

Stagg would be fed up too, he thought. *Andromeda*'s slowing down would not help. The cruiser was steaming at reduced speed and rolling uncomfortably in a quarter sea. Weir had asked permission to reduce speed. Blake never questioned his judgment. In real need the chief engineer would pull out all the stops, warning markers or not.

Lieutenant Palliser had the watch, and Blake could hear him muttering sharply to one of the lookouts. Palliser, the gunnery officer, had never suffered fools gladly, and after the last Mediterranean battle he had an even harder job controlling his temper.

A torch showed itself briefly on the gratings and Fairfax stepped up beside the chair.

"Just finished my rounds, sir. All quiet."

Blake nodded. How different we are, he thought. Fairfax had a wife in Australia, someone to wait for him. He remembered Diana, how she had looked. *I'm leaving you, Richard. You go back to your ship. I've had enough.* Beautiful, demanding, tantalizing. And yet he felt now as if he had not known her at all.

"When we make the rendezvous," he said, "the commodore will most likely begin another search. We've most of the information about previous raiders, their grid system and so forth."

Fairfax replied, bitterly, "He'll expect something dramatic."

Blake twisted round in his chair. "What is this thing you've got against the commodore?"

Fairfax sounded surprised. "He didn't tell you, sir?"

"I'm asking."

Fairfax shrugged. "It was after Singapore. Like a bloody rout, a stampede. Nobody knew where or if the Japs could be held. Anyway, I was straight from a command course. I had a fleet minesweeper and two MLs." He smiled sadly. "Not exactly an armada. My orders were to probe along the escape routes from Singapore. Thousands of blokes had tried to escape before the sell-out. Sorry, sir, I mean, the surrender. I was supposed to hide during daylight amongst the islands. Any people who had got that far, I was ordered to collect and carry to safety." He lifted his chin slightly. "We did it, too, soldiers, nurses, kids even."

Blake waited, knowing they should not be talking like this.

"Stagg drove a destroyer in those days, sir. He was all blood-and-guts even then, a man's man. Well, his ship ran into a German raider. The destroyer caught fire and the German took her company prisoner." He turned away. "Then something happened. The Jerry landed his prisoners to be picked up later by the Japs. We happened along soon after. But I was already loaded to the scuppers with refugees. Then a Jap plane flew over, bombed one of my MLs, and I had to pick up what was left of her people. I couldn't cram another soul aboard, let alone Stagg's ship's company. I tried to explain, but it was useless."

"So he was taken prisoner again?"

"I'm afraid so. The Japs killed most of Stagg's people, and tortured him and his officers. But especially him. Somehow he escaped. Went native, and was eventually picked up in a drifting prahu. But he's never forgotten. He blames me for leaving him to the Japs, and also the German, Rietz. It's an obsession with him."

Blake said, "Thank you for telling me. In your place I would have done the same." *Probably in Stagg's place too.* . . .

Palliser stepped out of the gloom. "W/T office have decoded a signal, sir. *Fremantle* is in contact with a German ship. Lieutenant Villar is in the chart room now, working out the details."

Blake slid from the chair. "Right." To Fairfax he added, "This might be an end to it."

Later, as they grouped round the vibrating chart table, Villar looked up. "She's heading our way, sir, with *Fremantle* in pursuit." He tapped his teeth with a pencil. "Weather's worsening to the nor'west of us and the glass is still falling. We might make first contact ourselves if we can increase speed."

Blake felt the familiar pain against his ribs, the excitement which always lay hidden. "I'd like to speak with the Chief. Let me have another look at your calculations, Pilot, then we'll alter course to intercept. A lot will depend on the weather. A full-blown storm would make things difficult."

The navigator's yeoman held out a telephone. "Engine room, sir."

"Chief? Captain. I think we have a German raider. Can you give me full revs when I call for them?"

"Aye, sir. Just give me another thirty minutes."

Blake handed the telephone back to the young seaman, thinking that after *Devonport*'s loss Stagg would have no use for carelessness. He said, "I'd like to see our airman. We may be able to fly off the Seafox at first light."

Villar grimaced. "Pity we don't have the old Walrus, sir. I'd not fancy ditching in our little kite, not if the sea gets any worse."

Moon's doleful face peered around the chart room door.

"Coffee an' sandwiches, sir."

Their eyes met. All those other times. The racket of gunfire, the dazzling panorama of burning ships and exploding ammu-

116

nition. Moon had always been there. Now as then, the sandwiches would seem like something special. Tea at the Ritz.

"Thank you. I'll come now." He looked at Fairfax. "Call me if you hear anything. Alter course when you're ready."

He left the chart room as the ship plunged and swayed through the outer darkness. He would have liked to stay, but he knew that his presence would be seen as a lack of trust. Later that could prove fatal.

BLAKE trained his binoculars over the screen. The sea's face had changed, giving an impression now of endless movement and power. Fairfax joined him. Dawn was close, the ship at action stations. He peered up at the scudding clouds. "Soon now," he said.

Fairfax asked, "Will we use the plane, sir?"

Blake nodded. "Otherwise we could lose him completely."

He thought of his talk with the Seafox's pilot. A temporary RNVR officer, Lieutenant Masters was the one real oddball in *Andromeda*'s wardroom. He had an outsized private income, was easy-going and well-liked by his men. Never happier than when he was risking his neck, he had flown in pre-war air races in his own plane and had raced cars at Brooklands. His young observer, Lieutenant Duncan, another reservist, was serious, over-conscientious, his exact opposite. But he and Masters got along like a house on fire.

Blake had emphasized the difficulties. In such an expanse of ocean, bearing in mind that the fragile Seafox had a range of only four hundred miles or so, it did not leave much room for error.

Masters had said cheerfully, "Piece of cake, sir. No bother."

Feeble light played across the bridge, the intent faces, the eyes of men screwed up against the spray drifting over the screens.

Blake said, "Slow ahead both engines. Port ten."

He felt the ship rising to respond to the alteration of speed and rudder, saw the sea's roughness ease away as the cruiser turned to make some sort of leeward barrier for the plane's launching.

There was a coughing roar from aft. Masters was ready, crouching at his controls while the catapult was swung outboard to meet the wind's challenge.

117

"Midships. Steady."

"Steady, sir. Course two-nine-zero."

"Very good. Yeoman, make the signal!"

The muffled Toby Jug marched to the screen and triggered an Aldis towards the seaplane. With a snarling roar it shot along the catapult, dipped, faltered, and then swung crazily round so close to the leaping water that it looked as if the sea would snatch it down, and climbed steeply away.

Blake let out his breath slowly. "Resume course, Pilot. Increase to one-one-zero revolutions." To Fairfax he said, "Tell the W/T office to keep a close check on Masters's timing. I don't want to have to start searching for *him* just now!"

As Fairfax hurried away, a metallic voice from the rear of the bridge made everyone start. The radar office.

"Ship bearing red one-oh. Range oh-nine-two."

Above them the range-finder and control tower came to life.

"A, B, X, Y turrets to follow director!"

Below the bridge the two forward turrets purred evenly to port, their slim barrels rising and depressing slightly as the crews tested their controls.

Blake bit his lip. The other ship was less than five miles away. With better visibility they would have picked it up much earlier.

He said, "Stand by, all guns."

Scovell, the first lieutenant, had put on a steel helmet. It made him look like a yeoman soldier at Agincourt.

"All guns with semi-armour-piercing *load . . . load . . . load!*"

Blake snapped, "Starboard ten! Midships. *Steady.*"

Scovell said, "We'll never be able to speak with the Seafox in this murk, sir. That R/T set has never been any good after the bouncing around it got off Tobruk."

Blake said, "Masters will fly back when he's ready." He glanced at the fat yeoman of signals. "Tell your people to keep their eyes peeled."

The Toby Jug nodded. "Will do, sir."

They were a team, thinking as one at times like these.

"Ship bears red two-five. Range oh-eight-five."

Blake strained his eyes through his glasses. He blinked and held his breath. There it was again. Flash . . . flash . . . flash, vague

118

orange distortions through the spray and feeble dawn light. Gunfire. *Fremantle* must be close by. It would be light enough to see everything in a matter of minutes.

"Hoist battle ensigns."

Someone gave a cheer as the first big flag broke from the upper yard, the white bunting with its vivid red cross very clear against the clouds.

Blake listened to the growl and crash of gunfire. Heavy weapons, they had to be *Fremantle*'s eight-inch armament.

Scovell shouted, "Signal from *Fremantle,* sir. 'Am engaging German raider.'"

"Target on same bearing, sir. Range oh-seven-five."

Blake gripped the rail below the screen as he saw the other ship, a vague, bulky shadow against the curtain of falling spray from Stagg's last salvo. The enemy.

He heard himself call, *"Open fire!"*

The rest was lost in the crash and recoil of the two forward turrets.

LIEUTENANT MASTERS turned the aircraft in an easy banking dive through a thinning bank of cloud, and suddenly there it was. The ship, steaming diagonally below, smoke pouring from her funnel.

The seaplane bucked wildly as a great salvo ploughed into the sea and exploded in a towering wall of spray and smoke. Masters saw the other ship's wake start to twist as her captain manoeuvred to avoid the next fall of shot. He searched for the warship.

Through his earphones he heard Duncan yell, "There she is! Starboard bow! That's *Fremantle*! Going like the clappers!"

Masters shouted, "I'm going round again! Hold on for tracer!"

The German ship swung into view again, smoke belching from her foredeck and blotting out her squat bridge. A big merchant-man, freighter of sorts, and fairly high in the water. Masters began to weave the seaplane from side to side as tracer drifted up from her towards the port wings with deceptive gentleness.

Duncan swore, and sent a single line of tracer spitting over the side of the cockpit with his ancient Lewis gun, which almost immediately jammed. Then he yelled, "Look at that!"

That was the arrival of *Andromeda*'s first sighting shots. Tall

119

waterspouts shooting from the sea in pairs. Palliser was red-hot all right. His first salvo was within half a cable.

Duncan shouted hoarsely, "Men, Skipper—coming up on deck!"

Masters put the Seafox into a steep dive. Through the racing prop he saw the ship reaching out on either side like a massive breakwater. But he could not drag his eyes from the mass of stampeding figures pouring up from the hatches. To his astonishment some of them were waving and cheering.

Duncan sobbed, "God, they're *our* men! It must be a prison ship!"

Masters veered away. Of course, that was it. A supply ship for the raider, her holds packed with the crews of captured prizes.

"Call up *Andromeda*! Keep sending and I'll try to reach her!"

A full broadside, eight shells, each weighing a hundred pounds, smashed across the enemy's hull in a perfect straddle as Duncan gave·up on the R/T and triggered off his urgent signal with an Aldis lamp. *Cease firing. . . . Cease firing.*

And Masters watched as that last deadly salvo blasted the German ship into a fiery ball.

3
The Enemy

Moon, his small silver tray beneath one arm, stood in silence until Blake had re-read his typed report and signed it. Through one of the cabin's polished scuttles he could see the shoreline of Port Elizabeth, South Africa, rising and falling gently as the cruiser swung to her cable.

Blake sat back. He had read his report but all he could see in his mind was the tiny seaplane rising and dipping through the wind, a lamp blinking frantically even as *Andromeda*'s broadside fell on the target like an avalanche.

With *Fremantle* steaming in a protective circle, Blake had stopped his ship and the too-familiar work of clearing up the mess had begun. The choking survivors had mostly been crewmen from the *Bikanir*, the first reported victim to fall to the raider's guns.

But a Dutch freighter called the *Evertsen,* given up as a storm loss some weeks earlier, had also been sunk. Some of her people were dragged gasping into the boats.

There had been a report of another ship in difficulties to the eastward, but too far away for the raider to have reached her. So Stagg had made a brief signal instructing *Andromeda* to take the survivors and the few German prisoners to Port Elizabeth where they would await escort and interrogation by the proper authorities.

Only one German officer, a lieutenant, had survived the bombardment, and he, needless to say, had divulged little when Blake had questioned him. His ship, the *Bremse,* had been a supply vessel trying to get back to Germany.

Any further information had gone to the bottom with the ship's confidential books and codes when the German captain had first sighted *Fremantle.*

The raider had kept all his officer prisoners with him, but the boatswain of the Dutch *Evertsen* had been able to supply some valuable information. He spoke German well and had heard his guards discussing their chances of getting home again.

The man who commanded the raider *was* Kurt Rietz, so Stagg oddly enough had been right about that. But at no time had the Dutchman heard them speak of the cruiser *Devonport,* which was strange, as she must surely have been quite a victory for them.

There was a tap at the door and Fairfax stepped into the cabin.

"The last of the wounded have been taken ashore, sir. Captain Farleigh's marines have the uninjured Germans under guard, on deck."

Blake stood up. "I'd better come down. Have the awnings and booms rigged and all boats lowered."

On the quarterdeck it was oppressively hot, the shore shimmering in the haze. The Germans, in borrowed clothing or wrapped in towels, stood like beaten animals, eyes fixed on the land, while they waited to be taken away to a prison camp.

Fairfax said quietly. "They don't look much, sir."

Blake had seen plenty of German prisoners. He said, "The intelligence people will get nothing out of them. They just carried the supplies. They'll know nothing."

Captain Farleigh stepped smartly forward. "Boat's alongside, sir." He pointed at the prisoners. "For them."

"Very well." Blake turned away. He thought of Masters's return in the Seafox. He recalled the pilot's bitterness and anger as he had clambered up to the bridge.

"What the hell are we? Bloody butchers? That was no raider. God Almighty, Stagg must be raving mad!"

His words lingered in Blake's mind. Stagg had over-reacted, had seen only what he had wanted to see. The grim fact remained, however, that *Andromeda*'s guns had made the kill.

The officer of the deck, Lieutenant Friar, the new torpedo officer, saluted and reported, "Launch approaching, sir. There's a captain aboard."

Fairfax snapped, "Man the side there!"

The approaching launch swept round in an impressive arc towards the accommodation ladder. Marines moved into position, the OOD and quartermaster stepped smartly to the head of the ladder. The boatswains' calls twittered in salute. Then, with his hand to the peak of his cap, Captain Quintin stepped onto *Andromeda*'s quarterdeck, followed by the Wren officer, Claire Grenfell.

Quintin shook hands with Blake and nodded to Fairfax.

"We flew," he said simply. Then he ran one finger round his collar. "What about a drink?"

He waited for the girl to join them. "Now what's all this? You can forget the report you've got ready for our superiors. I want the inside view." He fell in step beside Blake. "Whether it hurts or not."

ON THE EVENING of the same day that *Andromeda* anchored off Port Elizabeth, the German raider, *Salamander,* lay hove to some one hundred and eighty miles southwest of Madagascar. Of eight thousand tons, *Salamander* had been built originally for general cargo and passengers on the South America run. Also stopped, and less than a cable away, was the Swedish merchant-man, *Patricia*. Between the two vessels a German motor launch plunged towards her parent ship, with some seamen and the Swedish captain.

122

High on the raider's square, businesslike bridge her commanding officer, Kurt Rietz, studied the returning launch through his powerful Zeiss binoculars. It had been an easy capture, he thought. Relying on her neutrality, the Swedish ship had not even used her radio. And how *clean* she looked!

Rietz was well aware of his own ship's shabby appearance. But a raider had to live by her wits and her ability to survive against odds. He carried paint by the drumload—not to make his ship smart but to change her appearance and alter her identity. Like now, with the name *John A. Williams* painted in great white letters on her hull below the Stars and Stripes. He also carried wood and canvas, wires and cordage, so that a false funnel could be hoisted to be a twin with her single one.

Rietz turned on his heel and re-entered the wheelhouse. Looking down from his high perch there was little to show the raider's power. Her eight big 5.9 guns, heavier than those of the British cruisers that were hunting her, were either concealed behind steel shutters cut in her hull or beneath false deckhouses, as were her two new Arado seaplanes and their catapult. Torpedo tubes, mines and six other cannon completed her armament, and her maximum speed of eighteen knots made her hard to catch.

Storch, his first lieutenant, strode into the bridge and saluted smartly. "The prisoner is aboard, sir!"

"Bring him." Rietz was forty years old but appeared younger, slightly built with dark, glossy hair and brown eyes, a composed, thoughtful man with little to show of the hunter, the corsair.

The Swedish captain stepped into the wheelhouse and opened his mouth to protest.

Rietz held up one hand. "Please, Herr Kapitän. We are wasting time. My boarding party signalled to me what you are carrying, where from and where bound. Coal from the north of England, taking the long route for Port Said, yes?"

The Swedish captain said huskily, "I am a neutral. Sink her and I lose my livelihood."

Rietz shrugged. "Your coal would have been used by the tommies, Herr Kapitän."

A lookout called, "The rest of the prisoners are being brought across, sir!"

Rietz looked at Storch. "Make them comfortable. We will release them later. But now. . . ."

Storch said, "Torpedo, sir?"

Rietz smiled gently. "I have to tell you too often, Rudi. Waste nothing. Signal the boarding party to set charges. The coal will do the rest." He turned to the Swedish officer. "We cannot risk your keeping silent." Then, to Storch, he murmured, "No word from *Bremse*. The British cruiser must have caught her."

Storch nodded. He was just twenty-six. Badly injured in the Baltic, he was still a first-class navigator and would have died willingly for his commander.

Half an hour later the demolition charges on board the *Patricia* barely made more than an echo against the raider's bilges. When the coal shifted to crash through the protective barriers and machinery broke loose in the hull, her end came quickly.

The Swedish captain watched in silence and then was escorted below. Froth mounted from the raider's screws as she gathered way.

In the chart room Rietz switched on the deckhead lights. Opposite him, pinned to the bulkhead, was the front page of a Sydney newspaper: CAPTAIN RICHARD BLAKE, VC, ARRIVES IN AUSSIE! HERO OF THE *ANDROMEDA* A WELCOME VISITOR!

Rietz smiled grimly at Storch. So much for security.

The German secret agent who had put the newspaper in with the last pack of dispatches had written one line in pencil. *Why is he here? What is his mission?*

Aloud Rietz said, "I expect *we* knew that before he did!" He took down his bulky recognition manual and added curtly, "To work. We will assume the *Patricia*'s approximate appearance tonight. Put both watches to painting and re-marking the hull. Swedish flag, so I hope we've plenty of yellow paint."

Night closed in around the darkened ship, while far astern there was nothing left to betray that the German raider or her victim had ever existed.

CAPTAIN JACK QUINTIN dabbed his mouth with a napkin and nodded approvingly. "Damn good lunch. . . . You were saying?"

Blake waited for Moon to remove his plate. He had been speaking with hardly a break since Quintin and his Wren had stepped aboard.

She was sitting at the opposite end of the table, her hair shining in the sunlight from an open scuttle, her face in shadow. She had said very little during the interrogation, and then mostly to her boss, to clarify some point or other, which she immediately noted on a pad.

Blake said, "That's about it, sir. I spoke with the prisoners and the survivors from the *Bikanir* and the *Evertsen.* I've set up a team on board who plot the findings on a special chart and vet all the W/T signals we can pick up." He shrugged. "As for the *Bremse,* well, we may never know about her. She was probably going to another rendezvous—one she wouldn't even know until she got the signal."

The girl said suddenly, "If she'd been less heavily attacked. . . ."

Blake met her gaze calmly. "I know. I acted on the assumption that she was the raider. I was wrong."

Quintin held up his hand. "Easy now, Claire. Commodore Stagg gave the instruction."

Blake wondered if she was trying to antagonize him. "But you are right, of course. If we had captured the German supply ship intact we might have discovered something more, codes or not."

Quintin relaxed slightly. "Anyway, Stagg was probably thinking about *Devonport*'s loss."

Blake said, "That's just it. But for *Devonport,* I could accept the official view on this raider. But think about it, sir." He felt for his pipe. "According to my calculations, if *Devonport* was sunk in the manner everyone believes, the raider has destroyed her and four other ships in a matter of weeks." He drew a rectangle on the tablecloth with his pipe stem. "That means the raider has covered an area of some two and a half thousand miles east of the Cape and as far south as the forty-fifth parallel. It would seem that she was tearing about the ocean at full throttle, sinking ships which she just 'happened' to come across."

He saw that the girl was watching him intently while Quintin stared at the pipe stem. "And there's another thing," he added. "Why did the German captain take such good care of the Dutch crew and that of the *Bikanir,* yet slaughter those from the *Kios*?

And we can't even *guess* what happened to the survivors of the *Argyll Clansman*."

In the sudden stillness he was conscious of the ship around them, the gentle sluice of the current beneath the open scuttle. Then the girl said quietly, "I understand, sir. You think there are two different men, two separate raiders."

Blake nodded. "That's what I think. Two of them. Crossing and recrossing the area with arranged supply points whenever and wherever they are needed. And since the *Kios* sinking we've had to stop practically all independent movement. It's tied down dozens of warships, held up convoy sailings, made a mess of everything."

Quintin stared at him. Then, very deliberately, he lit a cigarette and stood up. "I'd like to use your radio."

Blake looked for Moon, lurking in his pantry. "Take Captain Quintin to the W/T office, will you?"

When they were alone together, the girl said suddenly, "That was something. You really came out with it, didn't you?"

He smiled bitterly. "It's only a tiny lead, but it's something. The German character has given us our one clue. There *must* be two raiders. Working an area like this, it would make the needle and haystack problem simple by comparison." He broke off, suddenly tired of the subject. "Whereabouts do you live? In Melbourne?"

She smiled. "Change of subject? Fine. No, my people live farther out. Small town. You'd call it a village, I expect."

Blake studied her. She had a nice smile, warm, but sparing, like her words.

Then she said, "When you were in the Mediterranean, did you ever come across the destroyer *Paradox*?"

"Yes."

She had pushed her chair back and turned from him. The question had been just that bit too casual.

He put his pipe on the table and walked to the open scuttle. The sea had been as blue as this one, he thought vaguely. Two lines of merchantmen plodding hopefully towards Alexandria. A week earlier there had been three lines.

He said quietly, "I remember her well. She was a wing escort that morning. We'd had a terrible battering. They came over in waves. German, Italian, the sky was full of them."

Instead of Port Elizabeth's placid shoreline he saw the lines of ships, the waterspouts of a hundred bombs falling around them.

"God, I remember the *Paradox* well enough. The last time I saw her she was drifting, ablaze from end to end."

He broke off as he turned and looked at her. She was wiping her eyes with the back of her hand, but not quickly enough to hide her tears.

He exclaimed, "I'm sorry. Your brother was lost in her. Commander Fairfax told me about him. I should have put two and two together."

She sniffed and stood up. "It's all right. I don't usually behave so stupidly." She shook her head, the hair bouncing across her cheeks in confusion.

"If there's anything I can do?"

She swallowed hard. "There is. If you come back to Williamstown, and I think you will, I'd like you to tell my mum and dad all about it, if you can bear it. Will you do that?"

He nodded. "If I can."

Quintin stepped through the door rubbing his hands. "By God, I'll bet that signal has got 'em all jumping! But they'll not like it. They've got the east and westbound convoys held up for want of additional firepower, and your little theory will go down like mustard and jam!" He looked at his watch. "Would you call away my launch, please? I'd best get ashore and get things moving."

The girl held out her hand. "Goodbye, Captain." It was all she said, but her handshake was like a truce.

Blake saw his visitors over the side and watched the fast-moving launch until it had reached the harbour. His reserves were battered, leaving him vulnerable, and that brief contact had given him a kind of strength. Or was he just making a fool of himself?

In his cabin he tossed his cap on a chair.

"Any brandy left, Moon?"

Moon gave a toothy grin. "'Course, sir." He produced a glass and bottle from the sideboard. "A celebration, perhaps, sir?"

Blake sat down. "Perhaps."

Moon hurried away. There had been a moment at lunch when he had nearly accidentally, but on purpose, spilled a dish of tinned peas over the Aussie Wren officer. Now, he was not so sure. She might be just the job.

FAIRFAX STEPPED OVER the coaming of the captain's cabin, his eyes immediately noting the half-packed grip which lay on a chair, the newly-pressed suit of white drill draped across another.

Moon, bustling about, saw him. "Captain's takin' a shower, sir. There's a flap on, sir."

A curtain jerked aside and Blake, his hair plastered down, his bare feet making a trail across the carpet, hurried to his desk.

He nodded to Fairfax. "Just had a message from Quintin, Victor. They're flying back to Australia tonight." He sorted through his papers. "I'm ordered to go with them. Bit of a rush job. We'll fly to Fremantle via Colombo with a couple of island stops to refuel."

Fairfax said, "Must be important, sir. What about us?"

"I've left written orders for you. Finish taking on fuel without delay. No shore leave. Any problems, you can make a direct signal to our people at Simonstown."

"And then?"

Blake smiled gravely. "*Then*, you will proceed to Williamstown as ordered. You shouldn't have any trouble." He tried to sound encouraging. "Good experience for you."

"Sure thing. Yes."

Fairfax was too surprised to think clearly. He was in command of *Andromeda*. Not only that, he was expected to put to sea in the morning and take her safely across the vast desert of the Indian Ocean to the port from which it had all begun.

He said, "I'll do my best, sir."

Blake slipped into his newly-pressed trousers. "You'll do better than that. You know the score. It can happen any time. It was how I got command of her. My skipper was killed and I took over. This is no different." He forced a grin. "Anyway, I'll be waiting for you on the pier, so don't scratch the paint!"

Lieutenant Palliser appeared in the doorway. "Your boat's alongside, sir. And there's a car on the quay."

128

"Thank you, Guns. I'll be up in a jiffy."

Fairfax saw Moon strapping up the captain's grip. God, he thought, Moon's going to miss him. And so shall I.

They climbed to the quarterdeck. Blake shook his hand in the dying light. "Take care of her. Good care." Then, with a nod, Blake hurried away down the ladder to the swaying launch.

The big staff car was waiting, his travelling companions already inside. Quintin, smoking as usual, said brightly, "That was fast!"

The car jerked into gear and he added, "Be a long flight. The Americans have a Catalina laid on. It was going our way and better than waiting for something larger. It will take us as far as Fremantle. The RAN will fly us to Melbourne from there, right?"

The girl, pressed in one corner, was worried. A Catalina—the big transport they'd come in had been bad enough. She hated flying.

An hour later they were embarked in the small flying boat and taxiing heavily across choppy water. Bump, bump, bump. . . . Then, with a shudder, they were off the surface, and the pilot took the Catalina in a shallow climb away from the lights on the shore.

Blake felt the girl's fingers gripping his wrist, but when he looked at her she shook her head desperately.

"Don't talk, *please.*"

Blake understood. In a few minutes she would either be sick, or get over it.

An American, presumably one of the crew, stumbled aft towards them. "OK back there? Great! There'll be coffee and some chow shortly when my buddy stirs himself!"

Blake smiled to himself. A young, unknown American, flying above the Indian Ocean, thousands of miles from home, and loving it. The fingers on his wrist relaxed. The girl had leaned away from him, her pale hair pillowed on a rolled blanket.

BLAKE PEERED at his watch. They had been flying for over ten hours. Now, the morning light through the perspex was searing, and far below the ocean was deep, deep blue, smooth as a millpond.

Quintin groaned. "Another three hours of this, goddammit! I'm as stiff as a board!"

When the young American came aft again, the daylight revealed him to be a sailor. He looked maddeningly fresh and relaxed.

"More coffee just a-comin', folks!"

Blake glanced at the girl. She was combing her hair. Without turning she said, "What wouldn't I give for a swim."

The sailor turned to reply but one of his companions shouted, "'Nother plane up thar, Billy!"

The sailor leaned out over one of the Catalina's machine-guns. "Navy plane. Must be nearer than we thought."

The pilot's voice cut through the intercom. "*God! It's a Kraut!*"

The Catalina twisted violently, and then Blake heard it, the sound too familiar ever to be forgotten. *Brrrrrrrr! Brrrrrrrrr!* The aircraft seemed to leap bodily from its course, the hull cracked and bucked, and he was almost blinded by smoky sunlight which suddenly probed through the dim interior. Holes appeared everywhere and he could smell burning.

He heard the pilot yelling, "*Mayday . . . Mayday . . . Mayday!*"

More violent cracks and bangs, and Blake shouted, "We'll ditch!" The girl stared at him, terrified. He gripped her wrist. "Keep hold of me!"

A shadow blotted out the sunlight, and Blake heard the roar of an engine and saw the brief flash of wings as the other aircraft rushed past.

It all registered in his brain in a single, despairing second. The black cross on the wing, the spitting tongues of two powerful cannon, the twin floats beneath of a German seaplane. It could have come from nothing else but a ship. *The raider.*

Air swept through the Catalina and the sound of the engines was rising to a maniacal scream as the pilot fought to level off. Then all at once the sea was there. The plane hit violently, lifted free and smashed down once more, swinging round with the port wingtip dragging under the surface like a giant scoop. Water surged through the hull and burst over the crouching occupants like waves on a rock.

Blake gasped, "*Now!* We're getting out!"

The sailor reeled through the surging water towards him. "I'll get the rafts ready! You open the hatch!"

More bangs and grinding noises. Sunlight tipped through the

hatch and then the sea was washing around them, throwing them about like sodden dolls as they fought towards the exit. Quintin and two or three other figures were struggling through the hull, one of them obviously wounded.

After being shut up in the small interior everything seemed larger and even more violent. The great surging wash sweeping over the tilted wing, cruelly beautiful in the harsh sunlight.

A dinghy-like raft bobbed into view on its lanyard and the sailor gasped, "Get in, miss!" He helped the girl over the side and then cowered down as the enemy plane came back, its guns stammering as before.

A man shrieked and fell headlong into the sea.

Quintin rolled heavily into the rubber dinghy. "The bastard caught my leg!" he groaned.

Blake, who was already in the dinghy, saw blood running down Quintin's thigh. A moment later, the sailor leaped in, then cut the dinghy free.

The Catalina seemed to veer away in seconds, and Blake saw the other Americans framed against the starboard wing, struggling with their dinghy even as the German seaplane roared at them. Sickened, he watched feathers of spray darting around the last survivors until the men had vanished and, with something like a sigh, the broken Catalina lifted its tail and began to sink.

Blake gasped, "Down! Down, all of you!"

He could feel the tiny boat falling and lifting beneath his spreadeagled body, the girl pressed against him, her face hidden in his shoulder. He waited for the impact of the bullets, but the seaplane's engine buzzed on and on. It was going away. The pilot was satisfied.

Carefully, Blake lifted his head. There was no aircraft, no Catalina. The sea was empty. With a sigh he looked at the sailor. "It's the smallest command I've ever had, but I'll do my best. What's your name?"

The youth was shaking badly. "They call me Billy."

"Well, Billy, you help Miss Grenfell—"

She interrupted, "Claire. Call me Claire." She touched the sailor's sleeve. "Give me a hand to make Captain Quintin comfortable, will you?"

Blake turned away and began to search for an emergency ration pack. He heard Quintin groan and when he looked over he saw the girl's hands bloodied to the wrists, as she tried to clean his wound before covering it with a makeshift dressing.

Afterwards she made to trail her hands in the sea alongside, but Blake took them in his own and wiped them carefully with part of his shirt. He did not say anything, and he could tell from her sudden tension that she understood.

Not far from the boat was a dorsal fin. It would remain there until the end.

BLAKE CLUNG to the dinghy's lifeline and knelt beside Quintin's crumpled figure.

"How does it feel?"

The endless swoops of the dinghy were sickening. *And this was the second day.* It was unbelievable that they had survived.

Quintin peered up at him, his eyes sunken with pain.

"Only hurts when I laugh." He opened his eyes wider. "Is our bushranger still with us?"

Blake looked over the side and found the dorsal fin without difficulty. "Yes."

His back, naked to the blazing sunlight, felt as if he was being flayed alive. But Quintin's wound needed fresh dressings, and as the girl had said, "Wrens' shirts make the best bandages." She had stripped off her shirt and handed it to Billy.

She was wearing Blake's drill tunic now.

Blake tightened his grip on the lifeline to contain his bitterness. But for his insistence about a second German raider, Quintin and the girl would have waited for the usual air transport. He had brought them to this—to two cans of fresh water, some boiled sweets, chocolate which had melted into a thick paste, and a rubber dinghy, drifting well away from land, and farther still from the direct air routes. A tiny yellow dot. Their world.

THE LITTLE DINGHY drifted on. Billy, the young American, crouched against the side, a makeshift fishing line tied to his wrist, while the girl slept and Quintin endured his suffering in silence.

Blake watched the sea and the occasional movement of the

133

shark. Through his dulled and aching mind the realization of his responsibility for their predicament seemed to force its way like a probe.

Quintin was badly injured, and the girl and the young American would never survive against such odds. It was his job and his alone to get them to safety.

Blake threw back his head, his lips cracking as he shouted hoarsely, "A hero, are you? Then bloody well act like one!"

He felt the girl jerk awake against his shoulder and knew the others were staring at him apprehensively.

He said, "Sorry." He tried to lick his lips. "How many sea birds can you think of, Billy?"

The youth blinked. "Er, I—I'm not sure, that is . . ."

The girl clutched Blake's arm. "Let me. Skua, osprey, gannet. . . ."

Quintin struggled up on one elbow. "I can do better than that. . . ."

And the shark glided closer, one eye blank and staring.

4
Convoy

Commander Victor Fairfax gripped the arms of the captain's chair and leaned forward to peer through the salt-smeared screen.

Around him the ship was going about its affairs, to outward appearance everything as usual. *Andromeda* was enjoying the freedom of speed. It was eight o'clock in the evening and the starboard watch had just closed up at defence stations.

Fairfax stared wretchedly at the horizon. It was beautiful now that the real heat had gone for the day. The horizon was shark blue, the sky above tinged with orange. It should have been one of the best evenings in his life.

He tried to think back clearly, see what he had committed himself to. *Andromeda* had been under way, standing clear of the mainland with a solitary patrol boat to see her clear, when they had received the signal about the missing Catalina. Some sort of a search had been ordered, but Fairfax knew that there were few big aircraft to spare for proper coverage. An eastbound convoy around the Cape would soon be due and a northbound one from Australia too, both needing air cover.

Andromeda was ordered back to her temporary home at Williamstown. She had no part in the aircraft search and would be needed for another patrol as soon as she reached Williamstown.

Quite suddenly Fairfax had made up his mind. He had sent for Scovell and the engineer commander.

"I intend to alter course and look for that Catalina. It may be afloat and only damaged. They'll need help. There's nobody else."

Scovell had said in his precise manner, "Local patrols will be alerted. A flying boat on the surface, even allowing for drift, should be visible."

It had sounded like a challenge. As if Scovell was stating his own position before things went wrong.

Well, things had gone wrong all right. At maximum revolutions the ship had swung round and headed northeast away from her proper course. For two days now they had kept it up, with only rare reductions of speed for minor repairs. And they had found nothing.

Weir had been like a rock. He had never complained and, when Fairfax had last spoken with him on the telephone, Weir had said curtly, "It's no' a matter of choice, sir. You did the right thing, in my view."

Fairfax removed his cap and ran his fingers through his hair. Weir's view would not be the one laid out on the court-martial table. Scovell was a hard man. He disliked him for some reason, and was watching his every move.

He thought of Sarah. How would she take his ruined career? If it had not been Blake in the Catalina, *Andromeda* would have maintained her proper course and speed. Fairfax knew it and everyone aboard would be thinking it. He turned in the chair and beckoned to Sub-Lieutenant Walker.

"Get Lieutenant Masters up here, will you, Sub?"

He returned to his thoughts. The Catalina must have sunk. He was wasting time as well as risking his own neck.

135

Villar came up, his face grim. "Signal from W/T office, sir. To *Fremantle* repeated *Andromeda*." He peered at the signal pad. "'Most immediate. Unidentified vessel reported in position latitude thirty-six degrees south longitude sixty east. Sighted by whaling supply vessel *Tarquin*. No further information.'"

Fairfax slid from his chair, his mind cringing, and led the way to the chart room where Villar's yeoman was already plotting this latest sighting on his chart.

"Where's *Fremantle*?"

Villar's brass dividers measured off the vast span of ocean. "Too far, sir. Whereas we. . . ." The dividers moved remorselessly to the pencilled line of *Andromeda*'s original course.

Fairfax gripped his hands tightly behind his back. But for having turned to search for the crashed aircraft, *Andromeda* would be within half a day's steaming of the other ship's position.

As if to rub salt in the wound Villar added, "Very close to where the Dutchman *Evertsen* was sunk."

Masters lurched through the door. "Ouch. Sorry, sir, but the old girl's rolling a bit."

Fairfax asked, "Is your plane ready to fly off?"

Masters nodded. "Yes, sir. When?"

Fairfax was staring at the little pencilled crosses on the chart, at the widening triangle between *Andromeda* and her recommended position. Even now, if Weir could coax some more knots out of his overworked screws, they might still be able to track the enemy, especially if another report came through.

Villar said softly, "Shall I lay off a course to intercept, sir?"

They were all looking at Fairfax. Masters, unusually tense, Villar, dark and watchful, and young Wright, the navigator's yeoman. What did they feel? Contempt, anger, indifference?

Scovell ducked through the door, his gaze moving curiously across the little group at the table.

Fairfax did not reply directly. To Masters he said, "I shall want you airborne as soon as it is light enough for you to make a recce." And to Scovell, "We shall reduce to twenty knots."

Masters said, "Fine."

Scovell stood his ground. "So you're not going after the raider yet, sir?"

"Is that what you would do, Number One?"

Scovell shrugged. "I'm not in command, sir."

Fairfax said quietly, "No, you are not, Number One. But I think you just answered my question anyway. Well, don't worry too much. You will be whiter than white, whatever happens!"

He swung back towards the open bridge, conscious of Scovell's look of shocked surprise and his own petty victory.

A shadow moved up from the interior companion ladder. It was Moon, his jacket pale against the grey steel. He held out a small tray and uncovered a pot of coffee. He did it with a kind of shabby flourish, as if he was trying to convey something.

"Made it from me special store, sir. Just like the cap'n 'as."

Fairfax took the cup. "Thanks. That was a nice thought."

Moon blinked through the screen, eyes watering in the breeze.

Fairfax said softly, "It's all right. We're still looking. I'm not turning back."

Moon dusted an invisible speck from his napkin. "'Course not, sir. Told 'em you wouldn't. Not your style, sir, that's what I told 'em."

USING THE YOUNG American sailor's shoulder as a support, Blake rose unsteadily to his knees and stared around. It was barely dawn, but already bright enough to reveal a clear sky, which within hours would be a furnace once more.

It had been a bad night, made worse by the American youth's obvious suffering. Blake suspected he had been wiping his face with seawater and had been tempted to swallow some to ease his thirst.

All the previous afternoon Blake had kept them at it, asking questions, awarding marks, telling jokes. Anything to keep them from falling into what they probably imagined was a harmless sleep.

He looked down at the others, feeling their despair like something physical. The girl's tongue moved painfully across her lips. Her borrowed tunic had fallen open to her waist without her caring.

Blake sat down carefully. "Get the water, Billy." His voice was hoarse, a rusty murmur.

The American cradled the container between his knees as if it were pure gold. "It's the last! There'll *be* no more after this."

Blake said wearily, "You have mine, Claire, I'm not thirsty."

She held the cup to his mouth, her hand firm. "Don't pull rank. It's forbidden here." She watched him as he sipped the water. "Anyway. You promised. We'll keep together."

He studied her. "You're quite a girl, Claire. Did you know that?"

She passed the cup to be refilled for Quintin. "You're not so bad yourself, *sir*," she said quietly.

The sun surged over the horizon, reaching out in either direction, laying bare its emptiness. Blake cradled the girl in his arms and tried to keep their combined shadow across Quintin's face.

He could no longer gauge the dinghy's motion properly and was being flung about like a drunken liberty man. He closed his eyes. Suddenly he blinked them open as Billy rolled over, struggling to rise.

Billy stared at him wildly. "Don't you *hear?*"

Blake gripped the lifeline. Billy had gone mad. He would have to do something. . . . Then he heard it. A low, humming throb, the engine of a small aircraft.

It could only be a seaplane right out here. Stagg's *Fremantle* was hundreds of miles away, so it had to be the raider's. Frantically he groped for the American's pistol. Just a few shots from the plane would destroy the dinghy. Then there would be nothing between them and the shark.

The girl put her hand on the pistol. "Use it. *Please!*"

Quintin muttered thickly, "Might miss us. Fly right past."

Blake shaded his eyes and peered. From a small vessel the raft might be invisible, but from the air. . . . His heart stood still as sunlight lanced across the aircraft's cockpit and changed its propeller into a solid silver disc.

The girl gripped his arm. "*Hold me!*"

Louder and louder, until the engine's roar seemed to stun them, smother them.

Blake put his arm round her. "It's all right, Claire. It's ours. *Look!*" He pointed at the opposite horizon, towards the tiny smudge of smoke, motionless in the sunlight. "It must be *Andromeda*. God knows how she did it, but she found us."

The Seafox swept overhead and seconds later a Very light exploded in a vivid green peardrop high in the sky.

Blake thought he saw Lieutenant Masters waving, but his eyes were too misty to be certain.

SURGEON LIEUTENANT-COMMANDER EDGAR BRUCE grunted with exasperation as he peered at Blake's blistered shoulders.

"Easy, sir. You can't expect to carry on as if nothing had happened."

Blake, naked but for a towel, sat in his day cabin, trying to accept what had so recently been an impossible dream. *Andromeda* had steamed in a slow circle around their rubber dinghy and, as a motorboat had been lowered and sent to collect the four survivors, Blake had seen his men lining the guardrails to wave and cheer.

It must have been a strange sight, he thought. Captain Quintin being carried across the quarterdeck by the sick-berth attendants, the young American sailor, almost blinded with emotion, and the girl, so beautiful in the soiled drill tunic.

He glanced at Fairfax who had stayed with him since he had been hoisted aboard. "See that the American lad is well looked after. Let Masters have a chat with him, show him the recognition cards. I think the attacking plane was an Arado 196, but Masters may be able to glean something I've missed."

He winced as the surgeon dabbed something on his back. "What did you make of Quintin, Doc?"

Bruce smiled. "He's too old for this sort of lark, sir, but as tough as they come. He'll not be up and about for quite a bit. But for the dressings he'd have lost a leg, no doubt about that." He stood back and wiped his hands. "There, sir, best I can do if you're determined not to take it easy."

Blake said, "A shave and a clean shirt will do for the present, Doc." He hesitated. "How's Second Officer Grenfell?"

"I've put her out, sir. She'll sleep like a top until tomorrow. I've got her in my cabin. I'm quite at home in the sickbay myself."

Blake knew Fairfax was watching him with sudden interest but he did not care. "She's going to be all right?"

"I've examined her thoroughly. Nothing broken. Outwardly she's as good as new." Bruce shrugged. "Later . . . well, we'll have to see."

Blake looked away. He said, "I'll be returning to the bridge, Doc. Keep me posted."

As the surgeon left, Blake turned to Fairfax. "Any further sighting reports on the unidentified ship?" He knew it was troubling the commander more than he had admitted.

Fairfax said, "No, sir. I guess the whaling supply vessel made off at full speed, just to be on the safe side. D'you think there'll be trouble about it when we get in?"

"We'll worry about *that* later."

Blake stood up and felt the deck reel under him. It had been like that since he had been hauled from the dinghy. Survivors rescued from lifeboats after weeks, even days, on the open sea could rarely walk properly at first.

Fairfax watched him, moved by his words. "Can I ask? D'you still believe there are two raiders?"

"I'm not sure. I'm certain of one thing only. We're going to finish him or them!"

As Fairfax moved to the door he called after him, "There's not much I can say. Thank you sounds too feeble for what you did, for what it might have cost you. Whoever eventually gets command of *Andromeda* will be damn lucky to have you, too." He tried to grin. "I shall bloody well tell him so!"

Fairfax walked briskly from the cabin, along the upper deck, and past a small working party who were lashing the yellow dinghy to the boat tier like a trophy. He climbed to the upper bridge, past the lookouts and signalmen and the massive bulk of Harry Buck with his old-fashioned brass telescope.

Lieutenant Palliser had the watch and threw up a real gunnery salute as Fairfax climbed into the bridge.

"New course is one-four-zero, sir." He could not contain a smile. "No further reports from W/T."

Fairfax nodded and smiled at the other watchkeepers. They seemed different. They *were* different.

He stepped up to the fore-gratings and stood beside the empty, freshly scrubbed chair.

Andromeda had decided. He was accepted.

KAPITÄN ZUR SEE KURT RIETZ steadied his glasses on the slow-moving dot in the sky. He could feel the tension around him like a steel mesh.

Under her assumed colours and Swedish markings the raider was moving at a reduced cruising speed, her wake cutting a frothing track through the glittering blue water astern.

They had sighted the aircraft two hours ago. Unhurriedly, the raider's company had gone to quarters. The aircraft was a naval flying boat, one of the old Walrus type, so there was no room for doubt. There was a British warship somewhere beneath the horizon. One of the hunters. The old enemy.

Rietz heard his first lieutenant beside him and said, "It was as well we sighted the aircraft in time to alter course, Rudi. The real *Patricia* will not be reported missing as yet, and we are *approximately* on her original course for Port Said." He gave a wry smile. "Give or take a hundred miles or so. But with these German raiders about who could blame her for taking avoiding action, eh?"

The gunnery speaker rapped out from the rear of the bridge. "Ship bearing green four-five, sir! Range fifteen miles!"

A dozen sets of binoculars swung over the screen and from the lookout stations. Rietz steadied his glasses on the first sighting of the newcomer. The merest flaw on the horizon, a hint of smoke which might have been sea mist parting before a powerful fighting ship at full speed.

He shifted his glasses to watch the flying boat. "Tell all hands not to stand with their glasses on that aircraft, Rudi." He controlled the sudden edge in his tone. "Put some men to work on the forecastle. That plane will come nearer soon."

Rietz thought of his two previous voyages. One hundred thousand tons of enemy shipping put down. A tremendous effort. But this voyage was even more important. For the first time since the army had marched into Poland in 1939, Germany was on the defensive. In Italy, in Russia, even in the Atlantic. She had to have more time. He remembered the second raider, the *Wölfchen*, and

141

the big Australian cruiser *Devonport*—he had wondered more than once what had happened to the survivors, if there were any. He thought of the other kills made by the second raider, the *Argyll Clansman* and the crippled *Kios*, and set them against the face he remembered of the man who commanded *Salamander*'s twin, Konrad Vogel, with his flashing smile and jaunty beard, the tiger of the convoy routes.

Storch called from the bridge wing. "Aircraft closing to port, sir!"

Rietz snapped, "Be ready to reply to the challenge, Rudi. But tell Fackler to make his number *slowly*. This is a Swedish ship, remember? Not a damned battle-cruiser!"

It brought a few nervous laughs, as he knew it would.

The Walrus rattled down the raider's side, and then an Aldis light stabbed from the cockpit. *What ship? Where bound? Number? Cargo?*

Rietz watched Petty Officer Fackler, the way he was cradling his lamp on his elbow. It was convincing.

The light flashed again and the signals petty officer said, "Requests we alter course two points to starboard, sir."

Rietz nodded. "Alter course, Rudi. Steer zero-two-zero. Warn the engine room to stand by for immediate increase of speed."

He removed his cap and waved it towards the aircraft. It was already heading away, and when he lifted his glasses again he saw that the oncoming ship had gained identity within minutes. It was the Australian cruiser *Fremantle*.

Rietz walked out into the sunlight to study her.

He saw the sea sweeping back from her stem in a great moustache of white foam. She was capable of thirty-two knots, according to Storch's copy of *Jane's Fighting Ships*.

A powerful light blinked across the water like a diamond.

"Heave to!" Fackler peered at his captain uncertainly.

"Stop engines." He pictured his gun crews between decks, waiting behind the steel shutters, ready to swing out the muzzles and blaze away.

He studied the Australian cruiser. She was steering diagonally towards the drifting raider, her three turrets angled round and no doubt loaded with armour-piercing shells.

142

Storch said between his teeth, "The officer you captured, sir, he may be watching you." He sounded anxious.

Rietz shook his head. "Two years. And I had a beard then."

He tried to remember the man whose broad pennant now flew above the oncoming warship. Commodore Rodney Stagg. But he could recall only his size, his uncontrollable anger.

A lookout called, "She's preparing to lower a boat, sir!"

This was the moment. Once aboard, the enemy would know. Even alongside it would be too close for deception.

Rietz said quietly, "All guns stand by. Release the shutters over the torpedo tubes."

Feet clattered through from the chart room and Schöningen, the navigating officer, hurried towards him.

"Sir! We have intercepted a signal to *Fremantle* and *Andromeda*. Unidentified ship reported."

Rietz turned swiftly as the first lieutenant exclaimed, "They are hoisting their boat again and the Walrus is preparing to come down alongside the ship!"

Rietz said softly, "Fingers crossed, everybody!"

The light began to blink again, and only the squeak of the signalmen's pencils broke the silence.

"'From HMAS *Fremantle* to *Patricia*. Proceed to Port Said as instructed. You will meet with northbound convoy and escort. You will remain with same until otherwise ordered.'"

Rietz said calmly, "Reply, 'Thank you for your help.'" He looked at Storch's confused features. "If we are near a convoy, why not do as the commodore suggests?"

A messenger called, "The *Fremantle*'s radio is transmitting, sir!"

Rietz looked at Storch again. "See? We will be expected."

He turned to watch the Walrus rising up on its crane to the cruiser's deck. The ship was already getting under way.

Storch exclaimed hoarsely, "The convoy, sir? The *whole convoy?*"

Rietz shrugged. "We need supplies. We have so many mouths to feed, so far to steam. I did not choose the killing ground, Rudi." His eyes hardened as he watched the cruiser turning end on and increasing speed towards the horizon. "*He* did."

143

"CONVOY IN SIGHT, SIR!" The petty officer stepped aside as Rietz levered himself from the plot table and walked out into the sunlight, raising his glasses.

Storch said, "Seven vessels, sir, and two escorts. Northbound. The gunnery officer tells me the destroyer is an old one from the Great War and the other is a corvette."

Rietz considered it. A small convoy in two unmatched lines steaming across blue, untroubled waters. The *Fremantle* would have signalled the escort commander. It would all be a matter of timing.

"Increase to fifteen knots, Rudi. Tell the gunnery officer I wish to engage on both beams simultaneously. The destroyer first. Torpedoes, full salvo. We will engage *her* to starboard."

He watched the two lines of ships, the sudden stab of a signal lamp from the outdated destroyer. The signalman was sending in careful, precise English, just for the Swedish master's benefit. *Patricia* was to take station at the rear of the port column to make the lines even. Just as Rietz had anticipated. A tidy arrangement for the escort commander.

"Acknowledge the signal."

It was a very slow convoy, and in the ocean's comparative calm the lean-hulled destroyer was rolling sickeningly as she sought to keep station on her charges. Two sizeable freighters, a coaster with a top-heavy deck cargo and a small tanker. The other three were masked by their consorts. The stubby corvette was the problem. She was at least two miles ahead of the convoy. With her tiny armament she presented no menace, but her radio was something else entirely. But it was a convoy, and to destroy it would create pandemonium.

Rietz watched the destroyer narrowly. She was on the starboard bow now. "Alter course, Rudi. Steer for the port line, astern of that freighter."

He walked to the rear of the bridge, picked up the red handset and waited for the engine room to answer.

"Leichner? This is the captain. Full speed in about three minutes. Everything, do you understand?"

"Yes, Captain." The line went dead.

Rietz moved to the bridge windows and peered down at the

forward welldeck where some seamen below the bulwark were dragging up heavy machineguns and ammunition. Somewhere deep in the hull a bell set up a clamour, and Rietz could picture the torpedo tubes training on the bearings being passed down from the gunnery team.

The destroyer was almost abeam now, barely half a cable away.

The speaker intoned, "Aftermost guns will now bear, sir. Ready to fire."

Rietz made himself wait, counting the seconds. "Stand by!"

A seaman strolled with elaborate nonchalance to the foot of the foremast, and Rietz knew he was carrying the German ensign inside a roll of canvas.

He glanced over at Storch and nodded. "Now."

Bells jangled throughout the ship, and Rietz felt the deck shudder as the massive steel shutters fell open along either side of the hull and the big 5.9 guns swung outboard.

Within ten seconds of the order three torpedoes leaped from their tubes and speeded towards the destroyer. The bridge began to quiver as the chief engineer obeyed the telegraphs.

"Open fire!"

The great guns crashed inboard on their springs, smoke billowing over the rusty plates in a solid bank. Machineguns hammered through the drifting fog, the tracer vivid and deadly across the destroyer and the ship immediately ahead of her.

From the guns on the port side long orange tongues stabbed towards the nearest freighter as *Salamander* turned in between the two lines of ships.

A towering column, then another, burst up the side of the destroyer, followed instantly by a violent explosion and a jet of escaping steam. The third torpedo had missed its target, but the others were more than enough. The escort was swinging round, one funnel toppling overboard like cardboard, while smoke and then searing flames burst through the fractured deck. Blasted apart by her magazines, she went into a plunge as the screws continued to drive her down.

Rietz heard his gunnery officer, Busch, rapping out bearings and targets as the individual weapons sought out the merchant-men. Two of the ships in convoy seemed to have collided and

145

were soon ablaze as the starboard battery's shells slammed into them, hurling sparks and fragments high above their mastheads.

Someone was attempting to send a distress signal, but the transmission ended as shells transformed the tanker into a blazing inferno, spilling burning fuel amongst the other vessels and screaming swimmers to add to the horror.

The *Salamander* seemed to be hemmed in by blazing ships and blinded with smoke. One ship, a medium-sized tramp steamer, apparently undamaged, had almost stopped.

Rietz shouted, "Signal her captain: 'Await our boarding party! Do not transmit! Do not scuttle!'"

A lookout pointed wildly. "Sir! The enemy!"

Rietz ran to the forepart of the bridge, and stared through the smoke towards the small grey corvette, her battle ensigns raised, her solitary gun already flashing from her forecastle as she pounded back towards the stricken convoy.

Rietz felt the hull lurch under him, heard a chorus of cries as a shell exploded somewhere between decks.

Storch said incredulously, "By God, he's attacking!"

Foolishness? Supreme courage? They often went hand in hand.

"Starboard guns, change target! Warship bearing green one-five!" Obediently the smoke-stained muzzles trained round even farther until they were locked on the tiny, defiant warship. "*Fire!*"

The corvette seemed to stop dead, as if she had hit a submerged reef. Then, as another salvo tore the sea apart in spray and flames, she started to settle down by the bow, the gun abandoned as the sea surged aft towards the bridge.

Rietz called, "Cease firing! Away all boats. Lieutenant Ruesch to that ship which is unharmed. The rest pick up survivors."

He turned away as the corvette dived. "See what you can do, Rudi. We will keep under way until we know what is happening."

He ran his gaze over the listing and burning victims of his attack. Both escorts gone, the oil tanker and the biggest freighter also sunk. The others, apart from the solitary freighter which awaited the boarding party like a guilty spectator, were either sinking or beyond aid.

"Order them to abandon and take to their boats. As soon as they are alongside we will sink the ships by gunfire."

Moving now very slowly, the raider edged past the smoking ships, her shadow covering the drifting corpses and flotsam like a cloak.

Storch hurried back to the bridge. "That shell from the corvette penetrated the medical store and killed the doctor, sir. Who will take care of the wounded from these ships?"

Rietz raised his glasses to examine the nearest lifeboats. More mouths to feed. Men to guard, and no doctor to care for the injured and dying.

He said, "Tell Lieutenant Ullmann to take charge below, then report all damage and casualties. I cannot leave a single survivor behind, Rudi. To do so might endanger this ship, our people. We must manage. We *shall* manage."

Petty Officer Fackler called, "Lieutenant Ruesch has signalled that he is in command of the prize, sir."

"Signal him to get under way and follow us. I will send him further orders for a rendezvous when he has listed the ship's cargo."

"Gunnery officer requests permission to open fire, sir."

Rietz climbed onto a grating and looked down as the first lifeboat came alongside. "Stop engines." He watched the shocked and dazed men scrambling up ladders to the entry ports. Then he crossed through the wheelhouse to the opposite wing, needing to be alone. He thought of the little corvette, knowing that was how he would like to be remembered when his time came.

The first gun crashed out, the explosion swift and echoing as it found an easy target on the nearest abandoned ship.

5
The Party

In the room in Melbourne which had been given over to the investigation into the German raider's movements and intentions, Blake glanced at Commodore Rodney Stagg. Stagg seemed to dominate the room with his presence.

They had met only briefly when Blake had been driven

straight from Williamstown within an hour of docking. Stagg had said little, and Blake had sensed his anger, his apprehension too.

An officer from intelligence was saying, "In spite of intensive interrogation of the *Bremse*'s survivors and the released prisoners after their landing at Port Elizabeth by *Andromeda*, no further information of use to our operations against the raider was discovered." He flipped over a page of his notes. "This latest attack on an escorted convoy can only add to our difficulties."

Blake recalled his own feelings when he had received the signal about the complete destruction of the northbound convoy. To date, no survivors had been picked up, and in spite of intensive patrols over the area no further evidence had been found.

The officer added dryly, "We shall have to do something—and quickly."

Commodore Stagg rose to his feet. "That's great, coming from you! Sitting nice and snug in your plush office while the men doing the job are getting their backsides shot off!"

Blake saw discomfort moving round the room. He was still not sure if Stagg was respected or feared.

Stagg rasped, "I was given the job of finding and destroying the raider. I know the man himself, how he works. He's trying to get you all in a panic. From the look of it, he's succeeding without too much sweat! But no raider can survive without supply ships. We've done for one, and I'll make damn sure we scupper the rest!"

A small rear-admiral representing the First Naval Member said mildly, "But all told, Commodore Stagg, the enemy have destroyed or captured *fifteen ships* including, for good measure, the cruiser *Devonport*, which, I might add, was larger than your own flagship, and a couple of escorts! I hardly think you can expect a fanfare of optimism for your efforts so far?"

The admiral's words hit Stagg like a sledgehammer. He said thickly, "I need time, sir. I've ordered an increase in vigilance, more patrols, and with luck some air cover over part of the shipping lanes. It's a tough job, but one I'm equal to." He sat down and stared grimly at the floor.

The rear-admiral looked at Blake. "Captain Blake. We have all seen your reports, which in view of your recent misfortune were clear and helpful. However . . ." the word hung in the air like a threat. "Captain Quintin has already informed *me* of your personal opinion about the raider. Perhaps you would enlighten the rest of my department?"

A door opened quietly, and Blake saw the girl slip into the room and sit in a vacant chair. She was wearing dark glasses. He had barely spoken to her as the ship hurried back to Williamstown, with the air filled with news about the massacred convoy.

He stood up and looked at the faces around him. All but Stagg and the girl were total strangers. Briefly he wished that Quintin were here. But any strain or excitement might have delayed his amazing recovery.

"Like everyone else," he said, "I have been keeping a close check on the raider's movements. I have not met the German referred to by Commodore Stagg, but naturally I have read all I could discover about the man." He paused. "The *man*. A professional naval officer, gentlemen. We know from his past record that this Captain Rietz is conscious of his duty to others. I will not dwell on it, but it is there. And it is totally at odds with the butcher, with the man who machineguns helpless people in the water, who leaves them to suffer and die without hope or mercy."

He added quietly, "I believe we are up against two different kinds of man. There are *two* raiders. I think they are working together, and that our present search system is inadequate. The quick changes of location, the apparent disregard for fuel economy, are firm indications that there is more than one raider at large."

Stagg got to his feet. "I don't go along with Captain Blake's ideas, gentlemen! Of course the German hurries about—I'd do the same in his shoes. And of course he changes his methods— Germans write beautiful music, but they also butcher women and children."

He paused. "Captain Blake has been in the thick of the naval war. We know that. And we have seen his record, including the decoration of the Victoria Cross."

For the first time he looked at Blake. "I'd not like to think that Captain Blake is under the impression that just one raider is too small a reward for his services. I'd hate even more to believe that the *second* invisible German is being put on record just in case we can't deliver the goods!"

The admiral snapped, "That's enough, Commodore Stagg."

Blake felt the room closing in around him. He heard himself say, "In wartime you have to put up with a lot, sir. Putting up with an insult like Commodore Stagg's doesn't happen to be one of them. I'll stick by my opinion, sir!"

The admiral rose lightly to his feet, like a cat. To the room at large he said severely, "We will destroy the raider, and any other which comes our way. I will tolerate no interservice recriminations." His eyes flitted between Stagg and Blake. "From anyone!"

The officers moved to the door, but Stagg said abruptly, "A word, Blake."

They stood a few feet apart by one of the broad windows.

Stagg said calmly, "Sorry I had to do that. But I'll not beat about the bush. I'm straight, always am. In a matter of weeks you'll be sent out of here. An Australian officer will command *Andromeda,* and things will be as our masters intended. But in the meantime the war is beginning to go our way, and neither the Yanks nor the Brits are going to take over from me. You start to throw rumours like that about and some desk admiral in Washington or Whitehall will get in a panic. We'll have flotillas and squadrons out here we'll never need, and *not one* will be under Australian control!"

Blake nodded. "And that's what you care about?"

Stagg grinned. "That, and getting the German raider. So think about it. You'll be sitting pretty, it won't be your problem any more."

He left. Alone in the big room, Blake felt anger burning him like acid. Did Stagg really see him as the glory-seeking hero? A man so full of conceit that he needed to invent an enemy?

The door opened and she stood there watching him.

"Thought you'd be coming out with the others."

He walked across to her. "It was good of you to wait."

She tossed her head, the movement drawing Blake's anger from him like balm.

"They were rough on you," she said. "But the admiral's no

150

fool. He'll be thinking about it." Then she added slowly, "Unless you've got anything planned for lunchtime, perhaps you'd like to meet my family? Like you said." She looked away.

"I'd like to very much, Claire."

She nodded and smiled. "That's settled then. I'll get a car, and be ready as soon as you've telephoned the ship."

THE CAR SWUNG OFF the main road and slowed to take a sharp bend. Blake kept a firm grip on the door, conscious of the girl beside him, the fierce way she drove, as if every minute counted.

Melbourne fell a long way behind, and the countryside into which the car was heading was empty, with sunburned scrub, timeless hills, with the sea showing itself every so often.

Blake sank down in his seat and watched the landscape pass. From time to time, he glanced at her, at her well-shaped legs as she jammed on the brakes while the car rattled round a bend. Her white uniform shirt left little to the imagination and he could see small freckles on her skin where she had bared it to the sun.

Eventually, the land lifted like a shoulder and the sea disappeared altogether. The car began to descend, and Blake saw houses in the distance, and on a hillside some sheep clustered together like an untidy patch of scrub.

"Home sweet home."

The car slowed while she pointed out the individual houses, a store, a sturdy little church and a war memorial with some parched flowers at its base.

The car rolled to a halt outside the church, and she switched off the engine.

"This is it. Not exactly Melbourne or Sydney, but the people here like it."

Blake got out and stretched his legs. He felt hot and sweaty, but in a strange way more relaxed than he had felt for ages.

He saw a tall, lean man in a flapping white jacket, striding down the path from the church, a pipe jutting from his jaw.

He said, "You'd better move the car. This looks like the vicar!"

She picked up her hat and bag from the seat and pushed the hair from her eyes.

"Yes, it's the minister, so mind your language, please."

151

Then, as Blake watched with astonishment, she ran across the road and threw her arms round the minister's neck and kissed him.

"Hello, Claire! This really is a nice surprise!" He looked past her at Blake. "And who have you brought with you?"

She turned, her eyes suddenly bright. "Dad, I want you to meet Captain Richard Blake. He's a sort of friend."

Blake took a firm handshake. "I'm glad to meet you, sir."

The girl watched them, trying to recover her aloof guard.

Her father grinned at her. "He's quite nice. For a Pom."

IT WAS A beautiful evening for a party, everyone agreed, as they stepped aboard *Andromeda*'s quarterdeck with its awnings and

colourful bunting. It could almost have been a peacetime affair.

It had been the paymaster commander who had suggested an impromptu party. And Fairfax, thinking of giving Blake a warm welcome on his return from Melbourne, had supported him.

Fairfax stood with his wife to receive the new arrivals. Sarah, her long fair hair hanging across her shoulders, in a gown which she had warned him had taken a month's housekeeping money, stared around at the bustle and excitement with disbelief.

"After reading in the papers about that raider, I thought you'd all be in a state of shock." She looked at him. "Is Stagg coming?"

He nodded.

"I think you're mad. After what he said to your captain?"

Fairfax shook hands with a major of marines. "It's not that easy," he said softly, "to leave out your own commodore."

Sarah studied the jostling throng. "Where is Captain Blake?" she asked. "I only met him once, but I liked the look of him."

"He'll be up in a minute. There were some signals for him."

"Pity he hasn't got someone nice to be with. With his wife on the loose he could do with some cheering up."

Fairfax replied, "You remember Second Officer Grenfell?"

His wife stared at him. "Claire Grenfell? Your captain'll get frostbite if he gets too close to that one!"

Fairfax shifted awkwardly. "Perhaps you've got the wrong idea. Maybe we all did. And she had a bad time after the plane was shot down." He stiffened as Blake appeared on deck and moved towards them.

"You look very lovely, Mrs. Fairfax," said Blake. He took her hand. "Too good for him."

"It's what I keep telling him." She flushed with pleasure. "But even I can't compete with *Andromeda*!"

Moon eased his way through the throng to Blake and raised his small silver tray on which stood a solitary glass.

"For you, sir. Special."

Blake downed the drink and only just held back a gasp.

Moon beamed. "Thought you'd like it, sir. Learned about it in the old *Bombay Queen*, runnin' out of Shang'ai in the thirties."

Lieutenant-Commander Scovell came aft from the gangway and said, "Your guests have arrived, sir."

While Moon retreated, satisfied, Blake walked over to the two figures stepping aboard: a tall man with a clerical collar, the girl, in uniform, beside him.

"I'm so glad to see you both again so soon," he said.

Fairfax, who saw the exchange of glances between his captain and the girl, said quietly, "Sarah, for just once in your life I think you've misjudged someone badly. I really do."

BLAKE SAT AT his desk, half-heartedly reading the various papers which the new chief writer, Brazier, was methodically laying before him. Brazier was another Australian, one of the latest draft which had come aboard as replacements.

Each time Blake left his quarters he heard new voices, different dialects, and saw the lost expressions of men exploring fresh surroundings. It took some getting used to.

He thought suddenly of the wardroom party, two days ago. A great success, everyone had said. But he had seen very little of Claire during the party because of Stagg's arrival, and his obsessive conversation about the raider.

Now the girl was in Sydney. Whether she had been ordered there or had volunteered to get away from him he did not know.

Blake recalled exactly when things had gone wrong. He had taken her to the deserted upper bridge, briefly leaving Stagg with two admirals. Under the stars, the bridge had seemed strangely ghostlike.

She had asked him about England again, what he would do after the war. They had stood side by side on the gratings, looking aft where the quarterdeck awnings glowed from the little lights hung like garlands along the guardrails and stanchions.

He had said, "The navy will be cut back to the minimum. I'll probably be politely put on the shelf, until the next blow-up."

She laid her hand on his. "Why not come out here? It may seem a bit quiet to you, but it'll be different one day."

She had not resisted as he turned her towards him. But he had immediately felt a change, passive resistance where seconds before he had sensed longing.

A messenger had arrived panting on the bridge and so saved the situation. . . .

Chief Writer Brazier said, "That's the lot, sir."

Blake smiled at him. He tried to keep his thoughts in order but the girl kept coming back. Then the door opened and Fairfax entered. He looked relaxed but tired. Blake switched his mind with an effort, thinking of the beautiful Sarah. Fairfax was lucky.

Fairfax waited for Brazier to leave, then said, "Signal from HQ, sir. Two days' readiness as of noon today. The last of the supplies will be aboard by the end of the first dog-watch. After that, it's anyone's guess, I suppose."

Blake waved him to a chair. He really wanted to be alone, but he knew the reason and despised it. More new men, changing methods, fresh routines. Only outwardly would *Andromeda* be the same ship. Soon he would not even have her. Probably his future was a nice soft job in the Admiralty, or lecturing young hopefuls on the merits of command. He sighed.

"Something wrong, sir?"

"I keep thinking about the lack of news. No more sinkings, so where the hell is or are the enemy?" He smiled ruefully. "See? Even *I'm* doubting my own ideas."

Fairfax watched him thoughtfully. "I see that they are allowing individual sailings as of this week. That may bring out the wolves."

Blake said, "Apparently Jerry was making a big thing of it on the radio. Convoys wiped out, us looking like bloody fools, all the usual stuff." He did not mention the propaganda from Berlin which had laid full stress on his own Victoria Cross. *Britain's best meets his match.* There was no need to. It was doubtless all over the ship. Without realizing it he was on his feet, pacing about the cabin. "Maybe I've been in combat so long I'm out of my depth on this sort of mission. I know in my heart the enemy is out there somewhere. Watching our every move like a tiger." He grimaced. "It must be this heat, Victor, I'm too steamed up."

Fairfax fiddled with his cap. "You ought to get away for a day, sir. There's some great country round Melbourne."

"No—but thanks." Blake looked through a scuttle. What the hell was the matter with him? He had come through when many better men had died. He had been given his country's highest decoration. *For Valour.* Yet, just because he was being moved on, because his personal affairs were in a muddle, he was acting like a lovesick midshipman.

But it was not like that. He wanted the strange, enigmatic girl with the sun-bleached hair and the rare smile. But, like Diana, he had driven her away, destroyed their brief association.

The telephone buzzed and Fairfax whipped it to his ear. Then he said, "Dock office, sir. The commodore's on his way." He stood up. "That'll make everything just perfect."

Later, as Stagg stood with his large feet well apart on the quarterdeck and regarded the activity along the jetty, littered with crates and bundles which were waiting to be checked aboard, Blake sensed the commodore's new glow of urgency and confidence.

156

When Blake led the way to his cabin, Stagg got down to it right away. "This is the toppest secret you've ever handled, believe me. But I've at last convinced the right people that we need to take the initiative."

Blake waited, conscious of the big man's latent power, watching the way he moved about the cabin.

Stagg said calmly, "The Germans monitor all our broadcasts, right? They have some good agents in the field, and probably get their hands on most of the local codes, too. There's a dockyard clerk here, the bastard—"

He broke off as his mind switched to something else. "We are letting individual ships sail on the safer routes, by the way."

"Yes, I know."

Stagg grinned. "On the ball. What I like to hear. Well, now we're going to provide some bait on the obviously dangerous routes. The admiral's given it the go-ahead. The rest is up to us."

He leaned forward. "I intend to 'create' an unescorted merchant-man, preferably neutral, and lay it on the table for our German friends. With *Fremantle* and *Andromeda* working together, and using what air coverage we can put up ourselves, I think we shall flush him out." He sat back and asked, "*Well?*"

Blake nodded. "It could work. It's worth a try anyway."

Stagg stood up. "Settled then. We shall put to sea day after tomorrow. If the raider stays quiet, we'll work into position. If not, we'll go after him as before. But this is to be treated with absolute secrecy. For the moment not even Fairfax is to be told."

"What d'you mean, sir? Not *even* Fairfax?"

Stagg grinned hugely. "'Cause he is to command the bait! Your first lieutenant can do his job. Good experience for him."

Blake followed Stagg on deck. It was like travelling in the wake of a whirlwind.

"What shall I tell him, sir?"

At the side, Stagg regarded him calmly. "Send him to Sydney. I'll lay it on for you. He can liaise with the boys there while Quintin gets his sea legs again in the hospital. Tell Fairfax he can take his wife."

At that moment, Fairfax himself appeared. He saluted. "Are you leaving, sir?"

Stagg nodded curtly. "It looks like it."

Surgeon Lieutenant-Commander Bruce was on his way aft to make his sick report to Fairfax, and watched as the commodore was duly piped over the side.

He remarked quietly, "He looks as if he means business. I shouldn't be surprised if he ends up running your navy after the war."

Fairfax grinned. "The navy, Doc? He'd like his head on a coin as the first king of Australia!"

Blake walked past them without a word. Now Stagg had gone, his plan of action had already lost some of its steam. It would all probably blow over. Schemes like this one usually ended in some Admiralty filing cabinet.

Moon was waiting for him in the cabin.

"Second Officer Grenfell just called from the Navy Office, sir. I told 'er you was with the commodore but she wouldn't wait."

Blake sat down and seized the telephone. It seemed to take an age before he got through to the intelligence department.

He heard her voice and said quickly, "It's me. I was on deck when you rang. Is something wrong?"

"It . . . it's nothing. I'm sorry. I just got back from Sydney." She sounded a hundred miles away. "I was going to explain. To apologize. I treated you so badly. I . . . I behaved like a stupid schoolgirl."

Blake said, "I want to see you. Can we meet somewhere?"

There was a pause, then she said, "I'll fix it. Give me time." The line went dead.

Blake filled his pipe slowly. The telephone buzzed again and he had it in his hand in two seconds.

She said quickly, "I can't get away yet. Could you, I mean, would you come into Melbourne?"

"I'm practically there." He tried to sound relaxed.

"I know about your orders. When you'll be leaving. Tomorrow I can get time off—I thought you might like to come to my home again."

"I'd like that a lot, Claire. It will do us both good. I'll get some civvies and—"

"No. Come as you are. For me."

Blake replaced the telephone and pressed Moon's bell.

"I'm going ashore, Moon. You've been in Melbourne lots of times, I suppose?"

"Me, sir? I should jolly well think so. Indeed, when I was in the old *Renown* we come 'ere once with royalty."

"I should have guessed. Well, there's a particular shop I want to know about. . . ."

THE TWO MEN lounged companionably by the back porch of the white-painted house beside the little church, their pipes glowing. They were waiting to go inside for lunch. It was amazing how easy it was to talk to Claire's father. Blake felt he had known him for years.

Blake said, "I was sorry about your son."

"Yeh. Dave was the apple of his mother's eye. She misses him terribly." Grenfell turned the matter aside and asked, "What about our Claire? You seem to get along just fine."

Blake stared straight in front of him. "I expect she's told you about me. That I'm married? And my marriage is finished? I'm not blaming Diana—these things are a product of our times."

"No, Claire hasn't. But the fact you told *her* makes a difference." He waved his pipe in the air. "Of course, some people misunderstand Claire, you know. She's not a big-city girl, and despite the fancy uniform and the trust she's been given by Captain Quintin, she's still unsure, vulnerable. Then there was this Kiwi she met in Sydney. He's gone now. Just as well." He added mildly, "Otherwise I'd probably have forgotten my cloth and beaten the hell out of him." He tapped out his pipe. "She loved him, or thought she did, and that's what counts, isn't it? But he only wanted one thing from her, and then he turned out to be spliced already to a nice girl back in New Zealand."

Blake listened to the hurt in the man's voice. It explained a lot. Especially the girl's aloofness when he had first arrived.

The minister cocked his head. "Time to eat, by the sound of it." He touched Blake's arm. "I'm glad we talked. You saved Claire's life—if there's anything you need from me, just ask."

They walked indoors.

Throughout the meal Claire said very little. She sat opposite

Blake, and he was very conscious of her nearness, the way she watched him.

Suddenly the telephone jangled. The call was from Melbourne and the message for Blake was brief. When he re-entered the room, he saw the way the girl had screwed up her napkin, not apparently noticing it.

He said, "I have to go back." He looked at her. "They want you, too, Claire." He felt suddenly deflated, embittered by the interruption.

She said quietly, "I'd have driven you anyway. Those HQ drivers are crook."

As she went for the car her mother took Blake to one side. "I hope you can come again, Captain Blake."

"Please. Call me Richard."

She smiled. "When you come again." She stretched up and kissed his cheek. "Take care of yourself, and God bless you."

THEY DID NOT SPEAK MUCH on the way back to the city, but as the car made the last turn towards the sea, the horizon glittering in the sunset in an unbroken line, Blake said abruptly, "Stop the car on that headland, will you?"

She obediently pulled off the road. They got out and stood by the car, looking down at a tiny beach, listening to the boom of the surf.

"What's wrong?" She sounded guarded.

"I have to say something." He reached out and took her hand from the wheel. "I want you to like me so much I'll probably make a mess of this. But even if I do, please, Claire, don't shut me out."

He pulled her hand towards him, feeling her resisting, knowing that in seconds he could smash everything.

"I went shopping in Melbourne before I met you at the Navy Office." He lifted the ring from his pocket and gently slipped it over her right-hand ring finger. Then he said, "I'm in love with you and there's nothing I can do about it, even if I wanted to. Later, if you can feel something towards me, put the ring on your left hand. Then I'll know." He waited, his heart pounding painfully. "It can be our secret."

She gripped her hands together and he thought she was trying to drag the ring from her finger.

Then she said huskily, "We'd better get going if it's urgent."

They got back into the car and, as she put her hand on the wheel, Blake suddenly saw that she had moved the ring to her left hand.

Almost defiantly she said, "They can all think what the hell they like."

She leaned over and kissed his cheek and he thought he could feel the dampness of a tear. "As far as *I'm* concerned, we're engaged!"

The rest of the journey was like a dream. Before they entered the Navy Office, she said, "You can kiss me, if you like."

He held her carefully but she kissed him with such tenderness that he could barely contain his longing for her.

Then she stood back, straightened her cap, and said shakily, "That's settled then."

6
"It Happens..."

The map room in the Navy Office was glaring bright. The overhead fans had stopped for some reason and the faces of the officers around the big table were glistening with sweat. Insects banged at the lamps.

The double doors swung inwards and Captain Quintin was wheeled into the map room by an orderly. He had discharged himself from hospital and he was pale beneath his suntan, but his face was set with determination.

"Evening, all!" He saw Blake and grinned. "Hello, Dick, sorry about this summons, but I had no choice." He glanced at the girl, sitting to one side, at a small desk. "You're here, too, Claire. Fine." To the room at large he said, "An oil tanker was sunk yesterday. She was sailing alone as the area was supposed to be clear. Fortunately, she got her Mayday off in time and most of her lads were picked up this morning."

Blake leaned over the table with its bright counters and flags. Allied ships, convoys, sinkings, hostile sightings, the panorama of war. A black cross marked with the name SS *Kawar Shell* showed where the latest sinking had been.

Then he glanced at the other officers around him. Mostly lieutenant-commanders, and he guessed they were escort commanders and from the local patrol services.

Quintin said, "I've not got the whole gen yet, but the signal I received leaves no doubt; the tanker was put down by a mine, and the minesweeper boys have discovered another 'drifter' in the same area and landed it. It was German, so it must have been dropped by a raider. Anyway, gentlemen, this is to keep you in the picture. I suggest you return to your commands and be ready to reinforce the convoy escorts." His eyes settled on Blake. "Except you, that is."

He waited for the orderly to wheel him to a table with some decanters upon it and said, "You can shove off, son. I'll call when I need a tow."

He looked at the girl. "You pour the drinks, Claire. Just like old times."

To Blake he said, "*Fremantle*'s weighed. She's on her way northeast to take a look at the area. Too late of course, but we have to go through the motions."

Blake doubted if Quintin had been out of hospital long enough to hear about Stagg's bait.

"Fact is, Dick," Quintin held his glass to the light, "that area *was* clean. Nothing but a mouse could have penetrated the patrols."

He looked at Blake and added, "There was *one* ship reported heading north, the Swedish *Patricia*. She was vetted by *Fremantle* and ordered to join a convoy. The one which was blown to hell." He waited. "Are you thinking what I'm thinking, by any chance?"

Blake looked across at the big map table. It would destroy Stagg if it came out. That he had been hoodwinked by the raider in broad daylight and had even opened the door for him to blast the convoy into scrap.

"It's possible. *Barely* possible. . . ." He added slowly, "I think it's best left alone. The raider will feel more secure, think we have taken the hook, line and sinker. And if the admiral was to blame Stagg, I feel the friction might do us real harm."

Quintin nodded. "And that means you would decline to take over the command? Stagg would act differently in your shoes. Well, it's not up to me, but still—" He groped in his pocket and dragged out a small package. "Here, Claire, unwrap it while our gallant captain wheels this old relic to the table again."

As she stooped over the chair Quintin seized her wrist. Her ring shone from her finger like a tiny star. It was fashioned in the design of a shell, with a solitary pearl set inside it.

Quintin nodded slowly. "Very nice." He pulled her down and kissed her cheek. "I know you've both got a lot of problems, so I'll say nothing more for the time being, Claire. But I'm sure it will turn out just fine for you both." As Blake wheeled him to the table he watched her, seeing the confusion on her face. But she was pleased too, excited by the old captain's acceptance.

Quintin barked, "Well, don't just stand there, girl. Open the package!"

She unfolded the wrapping and held out something shiny.

Quintin passed it to Blake. "Take a look."

It was an ordinary boatswain's call, the metal whistle that was seldom absent from any mess deck throughout the navy. Blake turned it over and saw a scratched inscription on the keel, *Tasmanian Devil.*

Quintin grabbed a pointer and tapped it on the chart. "A whale-catcher on her way to the Cape from the ice put a party ashore *here.*" The pointer touched some tiny scattered islands, specks on the Indian Ocean, some three and a half thousand miles away to the west-southwest. "They were looking for some fresh water for their tanks. There are plenty of islands scattered around there, most of them unpopulated. Anyway, one of the whalers found this bosun's call jammed in a rock." He looked up, his face grim. "*Tasmanian Devil* was HMAS *Devonport*'s nickname."

Blake stared at the map. Tiny islets, south of the forty-fifth parallel and off all the sea routes. It was just possible.

Quintin said, "I've got top approval. You'll sail today. Round up your people or leave without them if necessary. I want you to search those islands, and that one in particular. It may be nothing.

But that bosun's call didn't get there on its own." He sat back. "Off with you now and get some sleep."

Blake looked at the wall clock. It was nearly midnight. Claire followed him into the corridor. "I'll be thinking of you," she said.

A night worker from the code room paused and looked. A naval officer with a Wren in his arms! Just like the movies. All right for some, he thought.

BLAKE RAN THE last few steps of the ladder to the upper bridge. After the sticky humidity of his sea cabin it was a relief to be on the bridge again.

This was the morning of the seventh day out of Williamstown after Quintin's dramatic announcement about the whaler's discovery. And now, here were the islets, sprawled untidily across the starboard bow, colourless in the strange grey light.

For a week they had pushed through a vast, empty ocean, with depths falling away nearly three thousand fathoms to a dark unknown world. The sea had risen, and for the past three days they had battered through ranks of angry rollers while the ship had been washed with heavy rain and incoming waves until there was barely a dry set of clothing to be had. Then, with startling suddenness, the seabed had showed itself in tiny groups of scattered islands, boundaries of the Mid-Oceanic Ridge.

Blake touched his cap to Lieutenant Friar, the Australian torpedo officer, who was in charge of the watch.

"All quiet?" He had to shout above the rumbling din of water.

"Aye, sir. Revolutions for twelve knots, course two-five-two."

Blake left it to Friar, who had already proved himself a good officer, and returned his gaze to the islands.

He had had a lot of time to think during the restless, uncomfortable week. He missed Fairfax, and Scovell was withdrawn into his haughty shell even more than usual. Blake had been left much to himself. It was good for him, he thought.

He felt the deck sidle more comfortably into an oncoming sea. He raised his glasses and levelled them on the nearest islet. Like a basking sea monster, ugly with spray-soaked bushes and brown grass. A few hillocks but no trees.

Scovell appeared on the bridge.

Blake said to him, "We'll do it as planned, one island at a time. Take the best motorboat and handpick your landing party. See that they're armed. Just in case."

Scovell, who had once served down here in a survey ship, shrugged. "There's nothing there, sir. I think we're clutching at straws. Wasting time."

"Perhaps."

Blake felt suddenly irritated by Scovell's attitude. He said, "Be ready to hoist out the boat in about an hour." He met Scovell's flat stare. "Carry on."

As the first lieutenant left the bridge, Villar, the navigating officer, called, "Nearest islet has a landing place, sir. Protected from the breakers for the last fifty yards or so."

"Good. Pass the word to Number One, will you? Then close the shore for another half mile. We will stand off but retain contact with the landing party." He turned to "Toby Jug" Buck. "Make certain there's a good signalman with the boat, Yeoman."

Buck nodded. "Already done, sir."

The seaplane's crane swung out above the boat tier, and small oilskinned figures scrambled amongst the tangle of blocks and wires.

"Slow ahead together." A pause. "Steer two-seven-one."

Blake watched the motorboat swinging outboard while the cruiser's side made a lee against the heavy swell.

"Stop engines. Lower away."

He saw Scovell standing by the motorboat's canopy, a webbing belt and revolver round his waist. His men were huddled together, some gripping Lanchester sub-machineguns, the rest clinging to the gunwales as the boat's keel dug into the water, the screw frothed into action, and the boat bumped and lurched like a speedboat at the seaside.

LIEUTENANT-COMMANDER SCOVELL was tired, dirty and his stomach felt raw with hunger. It was past noon. He looked around the litter of fallen rocks, dead bushes and weed with distaste. The fourth island so far. His men, equally tired and irritable, were wandering about, their first interest having gone two hours back.

Andromeda's boatswain's mate, Chief Petty Officer Flint, looked across at Sub-Lieutenant Walker and asked, "Can't we shove off, sir? I'm missing me tot badly an' so are the lads."

The young New Zealander peered at his watch. "What about it, sir?"

Their combined fatigue gave Scovell strength. "Take half the men up to the ridge, Sub. I want a line right across the island. We're not leaving here until we're satisfied . . . *I'm* satisfied!"

Under his breath Walker murmured, "That's never, then."

And so it went on, made no easier by the sight of their floating home standing off the shore.

Leading Seaman Jack Musgrave, the bearded leader of *Andromeda*'s forecastle party, plodded away from Flint's group with his own smaller squad. He was prepared to amble along, wait for the snotty-nosed first lieutenant to give up and then get back to the ship. A tot of neaters, and another from his secret bottle, and then head down in his mess for the seven days back to Aussie.

He saw the ordinary seaman called Digby sitting dejectedly on a stone. Poor little Digby. He eyed him sadly. Poor little sod. He was frightened of his own shadow. He passed his water bottle to the pinch-faced seaman. "'Ere, 'ave a wet, Diggers."

The youth peered at him timidly. "Water, is it?"

"Well, it bloody would be with old high an' mighty Scovell runnin' things, wouldn't it?"

He glanced round. They were out of sight of the others. Musgrave sank down and stretched his legs on the wet sand.

"What the '*ell* did you do before the war, Diggers?"

Digby searched his face, expecting sarcasm or an insult.

"I—I worked for a museum. I was hoping to get a degree." He waved his hands vaguely. "Old buildings, Roman fortifications, and that kind of thing."

Musgrave, whose home had originally been in an East London slum, studied him with amazement. "What, *you?*"

The other two seamen in the party grinned and moved nearer.

"Well, yes." He stood up, ignoring the grins, and pointed at the barren island. "I—I could tell you about the layers, the styles and substances of this place. How it has been changed, the pattern influenced over the years. Here! I'll show you!"

Seizing a spade, he walked towards a fallen bank of sand and small stones. Suddenly he reeled back against Musgrave.

Musgrave stared at the object sticking out of the sandbank. Then he snapped, "*You*, Adams! Take 'old of Diggers!"

With surprising tenderness one of the seamen took Digby by the arm and turned him away from the hole. "Easy lad, *easy* now."

Then Musgrave took a spade, his stomach muscles in hard knots as he began to dig the wet sand from around what Digby had seen. Two clenched skeletal hands, bound together with cord, and below them the naked spine of a rotting corpse.

Musgrave said quietly, "Fetch that Scovell. Tell 'im to get up 'ere fast." He turned his face from the stench. "There's more than the one buried 'ere, if you ask me."

BLAKE STOOD APART from the rest of his men.

It was unreal, a scene from some macabre painting. The shallow trench, one side of which had already collapsed under the heavy overnight rainfall, the double line of canvas bundles. Thirty-three bodies. All through the previous afternoon Surgeon Lieutenant-Commander Bruce had worked on an improvised examination of the corpses.

Thirty-three bodies. Every identity disc or scrap of clothing had been torn from them, and it was impossible to tell exactly who they had once been. Except for their probable common bond as sailors. They had all suffered war wounds before being dragged or carried ashore to this miserable scrap of land in the middle of an ocean, stripped naked, their hands pinioned behind them, then shot, one by one, in the back of the skull, to fall into a hastily dug grave. But why? Surely the Germans had a doctor, or *some* means of getting their wounded captives to safety?

At least one of the murdered men must have been from the Australian cruiser *Devonport*. Which, Blake wondered, was the man who had managed to drive a boatswain's call into the rocks so that one day it might be discovered and he and his companions might be avenged?

Captain Farleigh saluted smartly. "Burial party ready, sir."

Blake nodded and walked slowly through his men as they gripped their spades. The chaplain stood very upright by the grave. ". . . They that go down to the sea in ships, and occupy their business in great waters—"

Most of the original landing party were present, even young Digby. But for him the secret might have remained.

Farleigh snapped, "Royal Marines, *Ready! Present! . . . Fire!*"

The volley crashed out and sent a cloud of screaming sea birds wheeling from their hiding places.

Blake saluted and turned his back as Flint's burial party moved in. He'd not forget. Not till he'd put the murdering raider captain down.

BLAKE AWOKE gasping as the telephone buzzed above his bunk.

"Captain speaking! What is it?"

"Officer of the watch, sir." It was Palliser. "Radar reports a ship, almost dead ahead. Range about eight miles."

"I'll come up."

Blake rolled off the bunk. The islands lay two days astern, and after making a brief signal of their findings there, he had turned his ship back towards Australia, the worsening weather doing much to keep his men too busy to brood on what they had discovered.

He peered at the bulkhead clock. Four o'clock in the afternoon. It would be early dark in the foul visibility. What was a ship doing out here, miles from anywhere? He hurried to the bridge.

Palliser said, "Radar say that they are getting a poor reading, sir. The conditions are bad and—"

"Who have you got on radar?"

"Gibbons, sir. He's good."

Blake crossed to the telephones and lifted one.

"Gibbons? This is the captain. What do you make of it?"

"The range is about the same, sir, but I'm almost certain she has altered course. We're getting a lot of interference." He sounded apologetic. "But I'm pretty sure she was steering southeast. Now we're on the same track."

"Good work, Gibbons." He put down the handset. "Sound off action stations, if you please. Tell the engine room to increase revolutions for twenty knots."

169

The other vessel was not equipped with radar, otherwise they would have detected it by now. She must have been keeping a damn good lookout to spot *Andromeda*'s upper works in this visibility. That was unusual for a run-of-the-mill merchantman, even in these waters.

Seconds later the alarm bells jangled throughout the ship and men surged towards their stations. Palliser left to go to his director control tower, and Blake moved to the plotting table. "Muster your plotting team, Pilot. I want every move put on paper!"

"Ship at action stations, sir."

"Very well. Alter course. Steer zero-eight-zero. Tell radar to keep watching for any change of course by the other ship."

"Aye, aye, sir."

The bridge groaned and rocked as the mounting revolutions reached up through the glistening steel.

Blake heard the gunnery speaker click on and then Palliser's voice from the director.

"Ship bears green oh-five. Range one-five-five."

Blake moved restlessly about the bridge, his shoes slipping on the wooden gratings. He thrust his hands into his pockets. Was he over-reacting?

He said, "Yeoman, write this down and pass it to the W/T office. *Am investigating strange ship in position. . . .*" He broke off, strode back to the chart, told Villar, "Give the yeoman a position about *here.*" He pointed to the north of their position. "A nice easy one, about a hundred miles away. If that other ship is an enemy, he'll think we're in company and that it's our consort farther north who has made the contact. We'll see what he does about it."

They ducked out into the wind and Villar handed the position of the mythical sighting to the Toby Jug before asking, "What then, sir?"

"He'll get the hell out of it, thankful that we were stupid enough to go after the wrong ship. But if he's on the level, he'll not only fail to comprehend our signal, but will remain thankfully on his lawful occasions."

Beam on to the big rollers, *Andromeda* heaved and swayed to a sickening angle. The minutes ticked past.

"Radar . . . bridge!"

Blake had the telephone to his ear in a second. *"Captain here!"*

"The ship *is* altering course, sir. Turning to starboard."

To confirm this, Palliser's voice came through the speaker again. "Ship now bears one-three-oh. Range one-six-oh."

Villar exclaimed, "The bastard's heading away, sir. He swallowed it, the whole bloody bit!"

Blake stared at him, his mind like ice. "Bring her round, Pilot. Course to overhaul and intercept. Twenty-five knots."

Like an avenging beast, *Andromeda* swung steeply to starboard, her guardrails buried in spray as she pointed her stem towards her invisible quarry.

WHILE *ANDROMEDA* pounded after the unknown ship, low cloud and a heavy downpour reduced visibility to less than a mile. Only the radar's invisible eye and the gunnery control's blurred glimpses of the other ship told them they were not charging after a phantom.

"Range now down to three miles, sir."

Blake wiped his mouth with the back of his hand. It was hard to think with the rain sweeping across the bridge like pellets, the ship lifting and surging forward in great sickening swoops.

"Warn Guns. Be ready to open fire instantly." Blake thrust an empty pipe into his mouth and bit on the stem. There was no sense in prolonging the wait.

"Fire star-shell. Yeoman, use your big light and signal her to heave to. You know the drill."

The biggest searchlight clattered into life. *Stop instantly. This is a British warship. Do not attempt to scuttle.*

A four-inch gun crashed out, and seconds later the low cloud exploded into life from the star-shell.

It was all there. The other ship, almost end on, her high stern glistening in spray and the glare from the drifting flare.

Villar said, "God, he's switched on his navigation lights. Pretending to be a neutral, the crafty bastard!"

More lights appeared through the rain, and Blake saw Spanish colours painted on the vessel's side, the urgent flash of a morse lamp from her bridge.

171

The Toby Jug growled, "Says she's the *Jacinto Verdaguer,* sir." His pronunciation was clumsy. "She's not stopping, sir."

Blake picked up a handset but kept his eyes on the fading shape of the other ship as the flare began to die.

"Guns? One round. Close as you like."

The violent crash and recoil of B turret's right gun made the bridge jump as if kicked.

Blake saw a leaping column of water, which had it been any nearer would have exploded inside her hull.

"She's stopping, sir." A seaman strapped in his Oerlikon gun gave an ironic cheer.

Walker shouted, "From W/T, sir! That ship's transmitting! Says she's being fired on by British warship. It's an SOS, sir!"

Scovell appeared on the bridge, his boots skidding in the slopping water. "Shall I send off a boarding party, sir?"

Blake levelled his glasses again. One of the other ship's boats was beginning to jerk down the falls towards the waves alongside as the ship began to drift downwind.

He said, "Signal her again! *Do not scuttle! Do not abandon! Stand by to receive my boarding party!*"

The swift change of events, the other ship's sudden call for help, seemed totally at odds with her previous movements.

Scovell said, "We'll have to get closer if we're to send a boat across, sir."

Blake glanced at him. "If we don't put some hands aboard, every scrap of evidence will go over the side, you can bank on that!"

Walker yelled, "That was an explosion, sir!"

A dull, metallic thud rolled against *Andromeda*'s hull, and smoke belched through the other ship's forward deck, to be driven instantly downwind.

Scovell rasped, "Bloody hell! Look, they've fired a scuttling charge!"

Blake looked across at the ship. "Make to her once more. Do not abandon."

The lamp clattered and the yeoman said, "No acknowledgement, sir, *and* they're lowering another boat."

The ship had begun to list.

172

"Slow ahead together. Pilot, alter course to make a lee for those boats." Blake could not disguise his bitterness.

Another bang echoed across the water, a scuttling charge or some internal explosion, it was impossible to tell.

"She's settling down."

The navigator's yeoman peered through the rain. "I've checked her on the list, sir. The name's genuine anyway. Spanish ship under charter to a company in South America. Buenos Aires, to be exact."

Scovell said softly, "Well, there's a thing."

The tannoy bellowed, "Stand by to take on survivors. Scrambling nets, lower away!"

Villar said savagely, "Survivors, my ass!"

Blake looked at Scovell. He said, "Number One, I want every man from that ship put under guard."

Scovell's eyes were in shadow. "You still believe it was an enemy—" He broke off as the ship heeled over and plunged beneath the surface in a welter of boiling foam and steam. "A supply vessel of sorts?"

Without waiting for an answer he left the bridge, calling for some armed marines to receive the boats.

Blake said, "Fall out action stations. Lay off a new course for base, Pilot."

Villar looked across the ticking gyro-compass. "Well, *I* think she was a bandit, sir."

The speaker intoned, "Fall out action stations. Port watch to defence stations. Hands to supper."

Blake walked aft to the ladder, going over the fast-moving chain of events. Villar shared his views. Why had the ship displayed no lights nor an indication of her neutrality? How had an ordinary merchantman under charter managed to detect *Andromeda*'s approach and her sudden alteration of course?

But suppose he was wrong. In his sea cabin, the sides of which were running with condensation despite the fans, Blake threw his oilskin on the deck and lay on the bunk.

It was no longer a matter of luck. You had to be right, and to go on believing you were right, no matter what. The Spanish merchantman had been a supply ship for the raider. No other explanation fitted. But the evidence now lay on the seabed. Her captain had obeyed his masters very well. No evidence.

Blake rolled onto his side, but the sleep he so badly needed stayed away.

7
Secrets

Engineer-Commander Weir stood on the opposite side of Blake's littered desk and said firmly, "I understand all that you're doing and trying to do. Lord, we've been in each other's pockets long enough for me to know that. But the engines are my responsibility, and I'll not be able to answer for them if we go on like we have of late."

Blake stared past him, his eyes sore from lack of sleep and long hours on the bridge. Through an open scuttle he could see a tall gantry, drifting smoke from some dockyard machinery. Williamstown again. They had docked in the early morning, to be met by an armed escort for the crew of the merchantman, some intelligence officers and then the usual horde of officials and workers.

His orders were brief. Take on fuel and stores. Local leave only to be allowed, but no loose talk. One hint about what had happened, and as a cheerful Australian naval officer had said, leave would become something as unknown as a good cup of coffee.

He thought of the *Jacinto Verdaguer*'s captain when he had had him brought to the bridge. Angry to the point of hysteria, but behind all the bluster Blake had detected a defiance, too, a sort of wild triumph. As if by sacrificing his ship the man had done his best to crucify Blake.

Fremantle was due in this afternoon, her patrol having passed without incident. Stagg would send him packing when he heard what had happened. Once he might not have cared. But now it mattered. Because of the girl, and for a lot of other reasons, too.

The telephone buzzed. It was Friar, the torpedo officer, who was OOD.

"Sorry to bother you, sir, but there's a commander come aboard to see you, a Commander Wilfred Livesay, sir."

Blake stared at the bulkhead, a face emerging like one at a séance. Wilfred Livesay, a slightly-built youth, with dark plastered-down hair. They had been in the same training cruiser as cadets, and had met up again several times since.

"Show him down, please."

Weir grunted, "I'm away, then."

Blake stood up and looked at himself in the bulkhead mirror. There were deep lines at the corners of his mouth. His hair was untidy and thick with salt. He looked like an unmade bed, he thought wearily. What was Livesay doing in Australia? he wondered.

The door opened and Livesay, perfectly turned-out, stepped over the coaming. They shook hands, and sat down.

Livesay looked round the cabin. "Quite a ship." He sat back, hesitated, wrestling with something. "Fact is, er, Dick, I've just arrived. I'm attached to the Navy Office on behalf of our High Commission. Sort of staff job." He stood up. "Look, the fact is, I've been sent. It's all a bit beyond me. But I was summoned by their lordships before I was flown out."

Blake tensed. *Flown out.* It had to be important.

Livesay turned to peer through a scuttle. "I think they chose me because we've known each other for a long time." He swung round, his eyes troubled. "You know the navy, Dick. It's a family. People talk. News gets round. Everybody in the UK is too keyed up about the coming invasion to bother much about what's going on here, but in the Service, *they* know."

"Know what, for God's sake? If you mean that I'm trying to help catch a raider, all I can say is—"

Livesay wriggled in his chair. "Oh, *that!* No, Dick, it's about, well, you know, your personal life."

"I see." He felt for his pipe but had left it in the sea cabin. "Diana's been on to you, has she?"

"Well, yes and no. You remember Vice-Admiral Tasker? Well, he's at the Admiralty, and I was on his staff before I was sent out here. It's because of our friendship that they sent me—they know you wouldn't discuss your private affairs with just anyone."

Blake stood up. "I think I should ask you to leave, Wilfred, old friend or not."

Livesay flinched. "Don't do that." He took a deep breath. "Your wife wants to come back to you. The fellow she's been going with, well, he's pretty senior and a friend of sorts of Admiral Tasker."

So that was it. Maybe the man she had "been going with", as Livesay had so delicately put it, was also married and wanted to clear his yard-arm.

Blake looked at Livesay, suddenly sorry for him. "So this is a sort of warning. Either be a good boy, a hero for the people to cheer, or I'm in the cart, eh? Everybody surfaces looking nice and clean, and discipline will prevail! Well, thanks, Wilfred. You did your best."

In a small voice Livesay said, "I've a letter here. It tells you to report to our office in Sydney while the ship has three days to overhaul. *Andromeda*'s duties will be partially covered by an armed merchant cruiser which is coming from Bombay." He tried to smile. "We're doing all we can."

"What's the purpose of my visit?" Blake glanced at the sideboard and suddenly needed a long drink.

"Well, our people in Sydney will want to go over the matter of the Spanish ship, of course. There's one hell of a hullabaloo coming from their consul and also the Argentinian authorities. But then, I imagine you anticipated that?"

He stood up slowly and then blurted out, "The fact is, Dick, your wife is there, too. She flew in the same plane." He recoiled as Blake turned to face him. "I had absolutely nothing to do with it, I swear!"

He placed the sealed envelope on the desk and made for the door.

Blake picked up the telephone. But there was no shore line yet, because of another priority, they said. It was more likely that someone had been told to keep *Andromeda* and her captain as isolated as possible. As he was replacing the receiver, Scovell entered.

"Well, Number One?"

"There will be some defaulters shortly, sir. Three of our ABs threw a dockyard worker off the pier, sir. He apparently shouted something they disapproved of."

Blake frowned. He could well imagine what it had been. That the cruiser had sunk a helpless neutral.

He pressed Moon's bell and when the steward appeared he said, "Pack a bag, Moon. For a couple of days. I shall be in Sydney." He looked at Scovell. "So *you* deal with the defaulters, Number One. In fact, you take charge of everything until I return." He looked slowly around the cabin. If they let me return.

Scovell excused himself and left. The telephone buzzed. The switchboard said, "Shore line's been connected, sir."

Blake nodded. "Thank you, but I don't need it now."

He put down the telephone and stared at it. What could he tell her anyway? Don't worry, I'm going to see my wife. But we can still be friends, can't we?

He felt the anger surging around his head like a fever.

But I love you, Claire, I want you so much.

Moon called, "I'm runnin' a bath now, sir." He hovered by the door, his gloomy face troubled more than usual. "The lads is all be'ind you, sir. Never did like the bloody Spaniards anyway." He shuffled off, shaking his head angrily.

To Moon, as always, the ship and her captain came first.

BLAKE WAITED for the hotel porter to lay his travelling bag by the bed and close the door behind him before he strode to the window and opened it. The sound of traffic rose to greet him.

Sydney. Much as he had imagined it. The great bridge, the pale buildings, and beyond the harbour the open promise of the Tasman Sea, dull like pewter beneath low cloud.

He had been bustled straight from the airport to Garden Island, where he had found himself confronted by an imposing table full of senior officers and some men in plain clothes. A British rear-admiral had been in overall charge, and had laid it on well and truly, as if to prove to his Australian colleagues that there was going to be no favouritism.

"You say the *Jacinto Verdaguer* altered course after your original contact. But you admit that conditions were bad and even your most experienced radar operator was unsure. You have stated that the ship was not sunk by the one shell fired by your main armament. But there is no proof. Nor is there any proof that she was a supply ship for the enemy, or that she carried advanced radar detection equipment. The Spanish master has admitted he was steaming without lights. But that was his own risk. The only *fact* you have laid before us is the discovery of thirty-three murdered men."

Blake had said, "Spain has helped the Germans often enough, sir. They are bound to make a strong protest. The Spanish captain was well briefed. He knew he could not escape my ship, but was determined to make the most of his own loss by screaming to the world that we were attacking him."

"Be that as it may, Captain Blake, I have ordered the release of the *Jacinto Verdaguer*'s company, and no doubt His Majesty's government will eventually be faced with a heavy bill as the result of this, er, escapade."

There had been more. A whole lot more. The rear-admiral had skirted around what would happen next, but Blake had no doubt he would be replaced as soon as possible and sent home.

The bedside telephone jangled loudly, making him start.

"Hello? That you, Blake?" The voice was so loud he had to move the telephone away from his ear.

He relaxed. It was Stagg, angry, out for a quick kill.

"What can I do for you, sir?"

"God, you're a hard man to find. . . ." There was a gurgling sound and Blake guessed Stagg was drinking.

"I've heard *all* about it! Every white-livered, pansy-minded load of crap which you had to face up to. Man, if I'd been there I'd have told them a thing or two!" He was shouting. "I've just been with the First Member to put in my pipeful. I told him, and I told him straight. If you want to interfere with one of my captains *you will do it through me!*"

· Blake swallowed. "Thank you, sir."

Stagg laughed. "Thank me when we've caught those Krauts." In a more controlled tone he added, "I saw that old fool Jack Quintin, too. I suppose he means well." He was finding it hard to say something. "He . . . told me about the *Patricia*. I've had a

178

sneaking suspicion in my own mind since I let the ship join that convoy without a closer inspection. To think that it was very likely that cunning bastard Rietz. I'll bet he was laughing all over his bloody face. I keep thinking of the convoy. Wiped out because of me. . . . Anyway, I just wanted to thank you. For saying what you did to Jack Quintin. There's many an eager-beaver who'd have used it to knock me down, I can tell you." He guffawed. "I was wrong about you. In fact, I've been wrong about quite a few things." He chuckled. "But don't rely on that. I'll still be a pig if need be!" The line went dead.

Blake walked to the window. It must have cost Stagg a lot to admit he had made a mistake. All at once Blake needed to get out of the room, to walk about, to see people. People with normal lives.

In the hotel lobby he was about to hand in his key when he heard Fairfax's voice.

"Hello, sir! I'd heard you were in Sydney and found out where you were staying. Sarah's in the lounge. And your wife." He dropped his voice. "I had no part in it. I wanted to tell you that before you see her. *I've told her nothing.*"

Blake replied, "Maybe I won't see her."

"I think you should, sir." Fairfax was pleading. "For your sake, and for Claire Grenfell's."

Blake took time to think about it as Fairfax walked with him to a wide lounge. A waiter with a loaded tray stepped to one side and there she was. Diana.

She was watching him, smiling in the way he remembered so clearly.

"Why, there you are, Richard. At last."

IT WAS LATE AFTERNOON. The thin, dark line of a tiny islet, almost covered at times by the long, booming ocean rollers, acting as a breakwater for the three ships—the two raiders and a heavy freighter named the SS *Waipawa* loaded with mining machinery, the sole survivor from Rietz's attack on the convoy.

He stood on the *Salamander*'s flying bridge, hatless, his face damp from the salt air and the low, humid breeze. There was a storm about. He watched a motorboat moving clear of the other raider's shadow. *Wölfchen*'s captain was coming aboard, as Rietz had requested, for their first meeting in months.

He heard the boat coming alongside, then saw the navigating officer watching him from the wheelhouse.

"Yes, Schöningen, what is it?"

The lieutenant had a weighted signal file in his hand. "Our bulletin, sir." He looked sick. "From Berlin." He handed it to Rietz without another word.

As Rietz was reading the decoded information Storch ran up a bridge ladder. He opened his mouth to speak, saw Schöningen's expression and shut it again.

Rietz said eventually, "It seems our most gallant and courageous comrade has solved the problem of wounded men in his charge." He thrust the file at his subordinate. "*Read this*, Rudi. Read about thirty-three men who died in the name of Germany!"

For a long moment there was silence on the flying bridge. Lieutenant Busch, the gunnery officer, appeared and saluted with a flourish. "*Wölfchen*'s captain is here, sir."

Rietz took the file back. "You will tell no one about this. That bulletin would have been decoded aboard Vogel's ship while he was on his way here." He did not explain what he meant. "I will be in my stateroom. Show the good captain there also."

Fregattenkapitän Konrad Vogel was junior to Rietz but walked with the springy step of a conqueror. There was something theatrical about him . . . his cap set at a rakish angle, the jutting beard beloved by the photographers.

Rietz waited for his visitor to sit down.

"I have taken the unusual step of arranging this rendezvous so that we can prepare for the immediate future. With *Bremse* gone and our Spanish supply ship also on the bottom, things are bad, although not critical. *Yet*."

Vogel regarded his superior blandly. "My command is in better shape than your own. As we fitted out originally in Japan we had to steam shorter distances. My fuel and machinery are thus able to serve me longer. I notice from the scars that you were hit by that convoy's escorts. Nothing serious, I trust?"

Rietz made himself speak slowly. "I have some wounded, and my surgeon was killed. I am filled to capacity with prisoners and neutral seamen." He ticked off the points on his fingers. "Food and ammunition are in good supply. Fuel and machine spares are not. I have only three mines left. The end is near. Time to discontinue the attacks and return to base."

Vogel stared at him in amazement. "But that is fine for you to say! You with nine merchantmen sunk, one captured and two warships destroyed."

Rietz stood up and walked across to one of the scuttles. "You destroyed a heavy cruiser, as well as two merchantmen. That is surely enough? Between us we have made our mark. To prolong it further is to invite our own destruction."

"The prize which you have at anchor. Could you not use her?"

"With such a cargo? Mining machinery?" He drew himself up to his full height. *Now.* "When you return to your command, Vogel, you will discover a bulletin waiting for you. It is mostly information obtained from enemy newspapers and radio broadcasts. About those men you murdered and buried like beasts. You, Vogel, a hero of the Reich, the long arm of Germany's might who can still stoop to such filthy degradation, *you make me sick!*"

Vogel, too, was on his feet. "I acted as I thought fit. I did my duty to my men as I saw it!" His voice grew louder. "There can be no half measures in war. I am proud of what—"

Rietz said harshly, "*Proud?* You have no pride, Vogel, only conceit. By your vicious, contemptible action you have defiled the name of Germany! Now get back to your ship. All your prisoners are to be ferried across to *Salamander* immediately. I want every boat in the water right away. And I am taking your surgeon from you also."

Vogel exclaimed thickly, "I shall not forget. After the war things will be different. Then we shall see who was right, *sir.*"

As he made to leave, Rietz called, "Write me a full report, Vogel. The names of those dead men, and the officer you ordered to execute them. I will hand that report to the grand admiral if we ever get home again." He watched Vogel's defiance begin to wilt. "Now get out of my sight!"

After Vogel had gone, he sat at the table, his head in his hands. He had to make plans, to think and prepare. How dare that bloody swine talk of *pride* to him. . . .

181

FAIRFAX got to his feet and said, "We'd better go now if we're to meet the others on time." He stared hard at his wife. After several drinks, Sarah seemed to have no intention of leaving Blake alone with his wife. "Come *on*, my dear."

Blake forced a smile. He felt like death. "You two go and enjoy yourselves. It may be some time before it's possible again."

Only when they had left did he say, "Well, whatever you've come to do, Diana, let's have it out in the open."

She sat back in the deep chair, one leg crossed over the other, an amused smile on her lips. She was elegantly dressed. Her dark hair had been washed and set that day. She was beautiful. Even desirable.

His mouth going dry, Blake said, "You shouldn't have come. It won't work, Diana. It's over, finished. You'll have to sort it out with your lover, whoever he is. As I said, I've had enough. A divorce is the only thing left."

"Don't be bitter, Richard." She leaned back, entirely relaxed. "I've come to make up, darling, to forget the past and try again." She reached out for his hand, pulling it beneath her breast while she said softly, "You know you want me. I can make you forget. Bring us closer than we've ever been." She looked at the door. "We'll go to your room."

Blake withdrew his hand. "You think I'm joking? In a minute I'm going to walk through that door. Things are quite bad enough at the moment without you making them worse."

He expected anger, scathing words. But she simply stood up and smoothed her skirt. "Divorce then. But we'll do it my way." She added quietly, "And when your poor little Wren gets her name dragged through the courts, and her father's, a *reverend* gentleman, I believe, *don't come crawling to me!*"

Blake clenched his fists. It was a nightmare. "It's nothing like that, and you know it!"

"Perhaps I do, but try to ask yourself who will be believed?" She took a pace away from him. "I'm still here. Waiting."

People in the lounge were staring curiously. The dark, beautiful girl and the young captain with a crimson ribbon on his jacket.

"I'll tell you this, *dear* Richard. If you won't do as I ask, I'll not give you a divorce without a fight. When I've done with your little madam she'll loathe the ground you walk on!"

"You bitch!"

She picked up her handbag. "I am staying down the road from here, at a somewhat better hotel. If you change your mind, find me. If not, don't say I didn't warn you."

She was mocking him, enjoying his torment. And she meant every single word of it. His need for Claire would destroy them both.

After she had gone, Blake walked from the lounge. All the way to his room her words kept coming back. After losing their son in the *Paradox*, Claire's parents were in no position to withstand another hurt. In a small town like theirs the minister was important.

Once in his room, Blake sat down on the bed. There was no point in delaying. Claire would be at her quarters now. He reached for the telephone and then gave a start as it began to ring. A bored voice said, "You're through, sir."

It was Quintin. "Glad I found you." He broke off in a fit of coughing. Then he continued, "Can't talk much over the phone, but things are moving at this end. You can forget about courts of inquiry, being sent home and all that stuff. You are going to be needed right here, and soon, if my information is correct. But enough of that. Walls have ears."

Blake found he was holding the telephone with such force that it was a wonder it did not split in half.

Quintin said, "There's something else, Dick. I . . . I'm very fond of Claire, but then you know that. Well, she's been through a lot, and when I saw what was happening between you two I thought I should add my weight. And now, with people asking questions, snooping about like spies, being in charge of intelligence here has given *me* an advantage. I heard about your wife's arrival in Sydney, and what I could not guess about it I dragged out of that spineless halfwit Livesay."

Blake heard him take a deep breath and then say, "Now hold on to your hat and don't hang up on me. Your wife has tried to get you both together again, is that right?"

"Yes, but I don't see . . ."

"You will, Dick, you *will*." Quintin lowered his voice. "The man she's been living with in London, and he outranks both of us pretty considerably, by the way, wants her to get a divorce from you, then marry him, all very neat and dignified so far. He's an ambitious man and wants no scandal. It would not look too smart to take the wife of a VC, now would it? So the plan was for her to divorce you, after laying the blame firmly at Claire's doorstep, with all that involves. You know the idea, man away from home, service love affair, mud-slinging all round."

Blake sat very still, his heart pounding at his ribs.

Quintin spoke slowly. "Well, she failed to allow for one small thing. She got herself pregnant. Whether it was by our senior officer or somebody else doesn't matter much. The man she wants to marry would run like a scalded cat if he thought there was a scandal in the offing!"

Blake felt light-headed. "So Diana needed me just for one night."

Quintin sounded suddenly cheerful. "Right! Think about it. How you would have looked. Giving your wife a child even though you were having an affair with Claire. She would come out whiter than white, and you and Claire would be right in it up to your necks!"

Blake asked, "How did you get all this out of Livesay?"

Quintin chuckled. "I threatened to tell the admiral he was no good out here and to have him sent back to the UK with a duff report. Rank has its privileges."

"Thanks for telling me. I don't know what to say. A few minutes ago I felt like jumping off the harbour bridge. I'm still a bit stunned by all of it."

"I've got to go." Quintin added brightly, "I feel a whole lot better myself!" He slammed down the telephone.

Blake sat for a long time. Out there somewhere was Diana, still expecting him to find her. People didn't change. . . .

The telephone rang again and Blake picked it up. Jack Quintin again perhaps, or Stagg with some crazy new scheme for catching his German raider.

She sounded very close. "I hoped I'd catch you."

"Claire! I was just going to ring you. To try to explain—"

184

"Please, you don't have to explain anything. I love you, Richard. I know about your wife. . . ."

"Yes, but you don't know what's happened."

"Please. I do know. She came here to see me. It was horrible to start with. I'm no good at that sort of thing. And then I thought of you. Us. In that terrible raft. With the shark always there. It was then I began to fight her, Richard. When she threatened me and my family I told her to go to hell." She tried to laugh. "Not like me at all."

"Claire, I do love you."

"I know. I think I knew from the beginning. Anyway, Captain Quintin's told me the rest now. He's been pretty wonderful."

Blake said, "I must see you. I'm so sorry to get you mixed up with this. But I'll make it up to you."

She was half laughing, partly crying, as she said, "What's it like in Sydney?"

Blake looked at the window. It had begun to pour, the rain like steel needles across the rooftops.

"It's suddenly very beautiful!"

"Here, too!" There was a metallic click and she said huskily, "Sorry. That was your ring. It hit the phone. It's still there, I've not taken it off since that evening."

He said, "Can you come, Claire? Here, to Sydney? I'm not certain how long I've got before . . ." No, he had to shut that from his mind. Nothing mattered now. "I want to see you so much."

She could not control the tears any more. "Tomorrow. Captain Quintin will fix it. I love you."

Blake lay back on the bed, staring at his own thoughts. He was still lying there when darkness closed over the city.

IN WILLIAMSTOWN, a small, inoffensive man paused to watch some tipsy sailors lurching towards the heavily-guarded dockyard gates. He was a clerk in the dockyard, on his way home at exactly his usual time, pausing only at this one shop to buy some cigarettes and an evening paper. Then he would take his dog for a walk, and sit down for the evening meal with his wife and mother-in-law. All as usual.

The man behind the shop counter nodded to him and passed

over a pack of cigarettes. The little clerk gave him in return a small envelope. Then he went on his way.

The shopkeeper bolted the door and went into his back room, opening the envelope without haste and whistling quietly to himself.

In an hour the contents of the envelope would be flashed across the ocean, a thousand miles or more. To the German raiders.

COMMODORE RODNEY STAGG took a heavy lighter from his desk and lit his cigar with great concentration.

Across the desk, his face lined with fatigue, Captain Quintin watched him warily. Two days back from Sydney, he had been in his Melbourne office for most of the night, and Stagg's booming cheerfulness was getting on his nerves. Through the windows he could just discern the early-morning sounds of the city coming to life for another day.

"What time's Fairfax getting here?" the commodore asked, glancing at the wall clock.

His massive shadow loomed over Quintin's map of the Indian Ocean and at the latest markers placed there.

"No more sinkings reported. It makes sense. The raider's running out of fuel and supplies. I'll bet my pension that Blake was right about the Spaniard. That's two supply ships down and another prevented from reaching the area."

Quintin smiled wryly. It was a change for Stagg to admit anything at all.

Stagg added, "You've checked everything yourself?"

Quintin sighed, hating the smell of the cigar. "Yes. I had a signal from Aden. Fairfax's fleet oiler, the *Empire Prince*, is ready to sail. She's loaded with fuel, too. Any extra subterfuge like filling her with ballast instead of oil would only involve more people and cause a bigger security problem."

Stagg nodded. "Good thinking."

"The Second Naval Member was not slow to point out what would happen if we make a mistake," Quintin said. "The raider will get his hands on enough fuel to last him for months, and we'll have egg on our faces."

"*Worse,* if I know him!" Stagg moved away from the map. "A

186

small, handpicked crew of volunteers, with Fairfax in command. Huh. Well, we shall see. What about the latest on the German agent?"

Quintin grinned. "He'll be taking his dog for a walk about now, before he goes to work."

"The bastard. I'd like to choke him to death with my own hands!"

"Any other way would have been a risk," Quintin said. "Laying a false trail would have been smelled a mile off. This way the Germans will know that it is real and that the bait really is worth the taking."

A Wren looked through the door. "Commander Fairfax, sir."

Fairfax entered, carrying a briefcase and looking surprisingly fresh after the flight up from Sydney.

Quintin described how far the mission had so far progressed. "It was the dockyard office which gave my people the idea. There is no other place where so much information comes in about stores and equipment needed by incoming ships. The *Empire Prince* will make a signal when she's on her way to Williamstown. To say that she has suffered damage and needs immediate dockyard facilities on arrival. That way she will be able to point out the necessity of off-loading her fuel without delay. I imagine that our little spy will be only too eager to pass on that information to the raider when it comes. He's already sent one message to his contact." Quintin kept his face blank. "I've also had it spread around that I am preparing a decoy which will be sailing in a couple of days from Perth. This decoy to be shadowed by *Fremantle* and *Andromeda*."

Stagg had been watching Fairfax. "Well?"

"If I was the German captain, I'd think it about perfect, sir. The two cruisers away in another direction with their Perth decoy, while the real prize comes unexpectedly from Aden. The *Empire Prince*, equipped for oiling at sea. It should work."

Stagg said shortly, "Should? It bloody must!"

Fairfax said evenly, "We've had our differences, sir. But I still maintain I was right. I couldn't have saved your men without losing every passenger under my command."

Stagg rolled the cigar in his thick fingers. "Maybe. But if you'd been made to watch your boys lined up and slaughtered, and then had the little bastards going over you with their knives and bamboo needles, I guess you'd be a bit sour on the subject!"

It was as near to an agreement that they would ever reach, Fairfax thought.

Stagg said, "I've given orders for both my ships to be ready to sail for Perth tomorrow afternoon. It won't do any harm for people to see us doing what we say we are going to do. Where we go once we're out of sight of land is nobody's business." He made for the door. "I'll be in touch."

As the door closed Quintin said to Fairfax, "You'll have a very small crew for the *Empire Prince*. Just enough to keep her moving. The cruisers will keep their distance and the first hint you'll probably get will be a Jerry aircraft coming to take a look at you. If they order you to shut down your radio, do it. You'll be riding on real juice, and I don't want you blown up. Your lovely wife wouldn't like it."

"About Captain Blake, sir." Fairfax watched him for a reaction. "I met his wife in Sydney. If there's anything I can do. . . ."

Quintin grinned. If Fairfax could worry about Blake and his bloody-minded wife when he was about to begin a mission which, to put it at its best, was extremely hazardous, he was a good hand.

"It's being taken care of. The best I can do. And thanks for the offer."

The door from the operations room opened and a tired-looking lieutenant said, "Transport's here for Commander Fairfax, sir."

Fairfax walked round the desk to prevent Quintin from struggling to his feet.

"So long, sir." He hesitated. "If anything happens, goes wrong, maybe you could see Sarah for me?"

"Will do." Quintin shook his hand. "Do the same for me if I fall out of this bloody chair, eh?" He forced a grin. "Have a good flight out to Aden."

At last Quintin was alone. He went over the plan for the hundredth time. If there was a flaw Rietz would see it. If circumstances changed in the next few days, a lot of men would die for nothing.

8
Last Chance

Blake had never seen Claire in a dress before and, as he waited at the airport to meet the plane from Melbourne, he was almost sick with disappointment, watching the hurrying passengers.

Then he spotted her. In a simple yellow dress, looking at him across the busy concourse, her eyes shining with pleasure.

They dropped off her case at the hotel, and then she told him of a small restaurant on the city's outskirts, one she had discovered during her time in Sydney.

They parked the hire car and dashed across to the restaurant in the biggest, noisiest downpour Blake had ever encountered.

But it did not matter. Nothing did. Inside the restaurant, he put his arm round her. Then she turned, her breath warm on his mouth as she said, "I'm suddenly not hungry, are you?"

They sat quite still, the implication as strong as if it were being shouted aloud.

"No." He put his hand on her neck, feeling his longing, not wanting to spoil things. "I love you, Claire."

She kissed him, gently at first and then, as he came closer, she pressed against him. "I think we should go," she said.

The drive back to the hotel was quick. They gave the keys of the car to the doorman and together they went straight to Blake's room.

It was like a delicious madness. Blake knew he should have taken a separate room for her, should have made certain his wife had already left Sydney, should have done so many things. But for these few, precious moments he could think of nothing but the girl.

She said breathlessly, "I feel wicked! How long do we have?"

Blake felt her tense as he loosened the strap across her tanned shoulder. "Only tonight, my darling."

She gently pushed him away. "Let me," she said quickly. She stepped out of the dress and threw it onto a chair. She said, "You do the rest. I'm shaking so much, I. . . ."

189

He kissed her shoulders, and saw the pale skin where her swimsuit had covered her from the sun. Then he held her away, taking in every detail of her nakedness. It was the purest thing in the world.

She lay back on the bed and watched him as he undressed. Then, as he came towards her, she held out her arms to him and said, "No matter what happens, my darling, this is for ever."

BLAKE LAY VERY STILL, conscious of the girl's breath against his chest, the beat of her heart. Dawn was opening up across the city.

He felt completely spent and yet elated. They had made love at first with tenderness and then with an almost desperate abandon. He moved his fingers down her spine, planting each memory of her in his mind. She stirred drowsily. "Is it time?"

"Soon."

She ran her fingers over his chest, her breath suddenly unsteady as she sensed his returning desire. He knew that the instant they were parted he would think of all the right words. Now, instead, he pushed her gently onto her back and kissed her. . . .

They were still lying together when the telephone rang.

It was Quintin. "Time to make tracks, Dick. Transport's laid on. All you have to do is *be here*." He hesitated and then said, "Tell Claire that her desk is waiting for her."

Blake raised himself on one elbow and looked down at her. "Did you hear that, Claire?"

"Yes. I'll be there."

He kissed her again and then slipped off the bed and dressed with feverish haste. He would not even stop to shave. Any second now and she would give way to tears.

As if reading his thoughts she said softly, "I'm all right. Really."

He tried to smile. "I know. Like me."

He opened the curtains and stared across the water. A fine day, the rain clouds gone in the night and neither of them had noticed. He turned and bent over her. He felt her touch the ribbon on his jacket as she said, "Promise you'll take care?"

"It's a promise." He kissed her lightly. "I'm off."

LIEUTENANT-COMMANDER SCOVELL'S eyes followed Blake around the *Andromeda*'s day cabin like needles.

"I must say, sir, I've been wondering what all the flap was about. So we're going after the enemy in earnest and the decoy ship is just a double bluff?"

Blake, back from Sydney, had been aboard for two hours, each minute of which had been crammed with making and answering signals, dealing with the dockyard manager and his men, as well as trying to keep Scovell's questions at arm's length until the ship was at sea. Now it was time.

He said, "In earnest, Number One. I shall speak with the ship's company later on. I don't want them to think it's just another useless patrol. I'll leave it to you to spell it out to the wardroom."

Scovell gave a thin smile. "Bad flight, was it, sir?"

"Average. Why?"

Scovell gathered up his files. "I noticed you'd not had time to shave, sir."

"I'll attend to it right away."

Scovell glided to the door. When he had gone Blake walked into the adjoining bathroom. In front of the mirror he paused. His face looked younger, more relaxed than he could remember. . . .

"SIGNAL FROM *BOUNCER*, sir. 'Are you ready?'" *Bouncer* was the tug at the stern.

Blake turned to Sub-Lieutenant Walker. "Very well."

He walked over the scrubbed gratings. He had to put all else behind him. This steel tower, the bridge, was his domain. To it, and so to his brain, went every telephone line and voice-pipe. Others did the work, his was the responsibility.

As he peered over the screen, a handful of dockyard workers came from huts and sheds to watch, and Blake found himself wondering if the spy was looking, too, from his office somewhere at the end of the yard. What sort of a man would do it? Blake could understand a man who spied for his country. But to pass information to an enemy who was intent on killing your own people was beyond him.

"Ring down, 'stand by'."

He looked forward where Scovell, hands on hips as usual, was watching the forecastle party fighting with coils of mooring wire.

The telegraphs jangled. *Andromeda* would go out stern first. He stepped across to the port gratings. "Let go aft. Tell *Bouncer* to take the strain."

He saw the Toby Jug waddle to the special flags he kept for the rare occasions they needed tugs.

"All clear aft, sir." Walker sounded keyed-up.

From his compass platform, Lieutenant Villar took a couple of test fixes, his gaze lingering on the ancient tower in the dockyard, the device which in the old days had signalled the exact time to every ship in harbour so that their chronometers would be reasonably accurate.

Wright, his young yeoman, looked up at him. "I've got the charts you asked for, sir."

Villar gave his wolfish grin. "Well done, Shiner. I'll make a navigator of you yet."

The stern was already moving slightly from the jetty, the dripping rope fenders being hauled inboard and rushed farther forward as the well-bruised piles edged dangerously near to the paintwork.

"Slow ahead port."

Blake waved his arm to Scovell and saw his men slack off the spring which, as the ship nudged forward, lifted until it was bar taut. Slowly but surely, using the pull of the tug and the springing action of the wire, the cruiser angled away from the jetty.

"Stop port. Let go forrard."

"All clear forrard, sir."

Blake turned and looked at the anchorage. A few ships in the distance, nothing dangerously close. The land was swinging past as the cruiser continued to drift with her way and current.

Villar said, "Ready, sir."

Blake ran his eye over a harbour launch, but it was staying well clear.

"Wheel amidships. Slow ahead together. Tell the tugs, 'thank you'."

The *Bouncer* turned away, her seamen hauling in the towline while her skipper gave a shrill toot on his siren.

Blake climbed into his chair. "In fifteen minutes you can tell the hands to fall out from harbour stations—"

He broke off as a man yelled, "Hell, sir, look at *that!*"

A Walrus flying boat was hurtling past a slow-moving freighter, in danger of colliding with two corvettes which were about to leave the harbour. It hit the water, bounced off again with its pusher engine spluttering madly, then settled within feet of the freighter's side.

Scovell appeared on the bridge, his usual calm gone as he shouted, "What is that bloody madman doing?"

The Toby Jug lowered his telescope. "I think it's Commodore Stagg, sir." He coughed politely. "I gather 'e wants to come aboard."

"Away seaboat's crew!" Blake's voice brought the astonished bridge party to movement again. "Lively with it!"

He turned to Walker. "Tell the Chief, Sub. Dead slow. We don't want to hit anything."

There was chaos enough. The two corvettes were trying to recover their proper station, while from the freighter's high bridge there came a stream of obscenity magnified by a loud hailer for all the harbour to hear.

Blake had no need to use his glasses to recognize Stagg's towering shape. Why was he here? Perhaps the mission had been aborted. Blake did not have long to wait for the answer.

Beaming to all and sundry, Stagg arrived on the bridge, shook hands, and boomed, "Fast as you like, Captain Blake. I'm sailing with you." He added, "The fact is, *Fremantle* had a bit of bother. We had just cleared the bay when we met with an incoming destroyer. An American, naturally."

"*Met* with, sir?"

Stagg eyed him coldly. "She ran into us. Right down the bloody side of the fo'c'sle. I've sent for tugs. The destroyer got the worst of it, and I'll see her skipper in bloody irons when we get to the court martial!"

Stagg looked at his oily hands. "All right if I use your quarters aft? Good. I wasn't going to be left behind, not now, by God. I'd have crippled that Walrus pilot if he'd missed you." He grinned. "I had a feeling it would turn out this way. Just you and me

193

against the bloody world." He went off, tossing casual salutes to all as if it was one great joke.

Blake slid off his chair and laid his cap below the screen. Had it only been this morning? Another place, where the world had been the four walls of a small hotel room?

He looked at his watch. She would be at her desk now, neat and cool in her uniform. The thought helped to steady him, and he said to Scovell, "I'm going round the ship, Number One. We shall exercise action stations at dusk. Just to blow away the cobwebs."

When darkness fell the land was well astern, and *Andromeda* had the ocean to herself.

AFTER MAKING HER RENDEZVOUS west of Perth with the phoney decoy ship, *Andromeda* turned towards the Indian Ocean once again. The five days it had taken to complete the passage to Perth had been almost leisurely. Despite regular drills with main and secondary armament, damage-control exercises and fire fighting, the ship's company seemed relaxed by their solitary cruise. But, as Moon had gloomily predicted, it was the calm before the storm.

Even the weather was strange. Long hours of bright sunlight, but lacking warmth. The sky was harsh and difficult for the lookouts to scan without using coloured glasses. Sometimes, when he went onto the upper bridge, Blake thought it was like sharing it with a crowd of blind men.

The secret signals arranged by Quintin came at regular intervals. Fairfax's *Empire Prince* had cleared Aden and was heading on a southeasterly course, maintaining complete radio silence.

Blake had gone over the plan with Stagg in the chart room. It was unnerving to compare the vastness of the ocean with their own puny resources, which had been halved as a result of *Fremantle*'s collision. Their job was to work into position about two hundred and fifty miles from the *Empire Prince*. When she sighted the German it would then take them about eight hours at full revs to run down on her. The raider would be caught still pumping out her fuel.

Eight days out of Williamstown the sea changed. It altered its colour and the horizon seemed blurred. When *Andromeda* shipped water over her forecastle the spray looked like yellow lace.

Blake stretched his legs around the bridge, a mug of coffee in his hand. Up, down, roll. He felt the ship sliding into a trough, sensed the urgent race of her screws as the stern lifted towards the surface.

Stagg loomed up the ladder, his shirt soaked with spray, a doused cigar jutting from his jaw.

"Morning." He nodded to the watch and then moved to Blake's side. "Looks bad. What d'you think? Will it affect our rendezvous?" he asked.

"It could." Blake glanced abeam at the glass-sided rollers, their crests as yet unbroken. "Probably a cyclone, sir, but I believe we'll cross the edge of it. Once we're on station it won't be so difficult. If we get a hint of the enemy, we can close with him and use our speed to good advantage."

Stagg rubbed his chin. "Fairfax might get cold feet."

So the old antagonism was still there, like a canker.

"I think it's unlikely, sir."

"We'll see." He squinted his eyes as the spindrift floated over the bridge and splashed against the fire-control tower. "Bloody weather!"

Blake turned away. He wanted Stagg to go aft again to his cabin, to leave him with his thoughts. The fact that the commodore was obviously getting rattled did not help at all. There was a raider out there somewhere. Somewhere.

RIETZ OPENED his eyes and looked at Storch for several seconds without recognition. He had been trying to sleep in the hutchlike cabin at the rear of *Salamander's* charthouse.

"Sorry to rouse you, Captain." Storch waited as Rietz threw his legs over the side of the bunk. "We have received a signal."

"About the decoy, Rudi?"

Storch shook his head. "No, sir. She sailed just as our agents reported. This is another. A naval oiler, the *Empire Prince* outward bound from Aden with a full cargo. She is in trouble and requires attention when she berths at Williamstown. Our man there has done well."

Rietz got to his feet. Where better, he thought, to have a special spy? The brief but powerful transmissions were virtually undetectable amid the mass of radio traffic which came and went from Williamstown and Melbourne.

His ears picked out the noisy clatter of loose gear, the hull's groan as she swayed in a steep swell. The glass was steady enough, but there was a big storm coming.

"Is our captured freighter still anchored?"

"Yes, Captain. But Lieutenant Ruesch requests permission to weigh and stand offshore. The *Waipawa*'s anchor is dragging. If the swell gets worse he'll have to steam away from the island."

Rietz felt the deck pitching heavily. Even *Salamander*'s eight thousand tons was no substitute for fuel reserves. He stared at himself in the cabin mirror, hating how he felt, the smell of unwashed clothing. He had been forced to order the rationing of all essential stores, from fresh water to soap.

"Very well, Rudi. Signal the group to get under way. Then we will steer north while we examine the enemy's intentions and the exact position of this oiler—" he smiled "—from heaven."

In the brightly lit chart and plotting room, Rietz went over the chart and his navigator's calculations, item by item.

There was talk of another troop convoy en route to the Pacific. To be able to scatter that would offer a suitable moment to retire from the area. But to do it they had to have fuel, and be certain that the cruiser force was nowhere within possible contact. While Stagg, he knew, would give anything to run him to ground.

He was still unsure. Suppose the decoy ship had been a deliberate hoax, to give the raiders the impression they were safe to move at will? It would be just like Stagg to think of that. The cruisers might even now be making another sweep, in the hopes that he and Vogel would go for the troopships.

Petty Officer Fackler lurched through the door from the bridge. "Captain! Another signal." He was grinning. "The Australian cruiser *Fremantle* has been seen in Williamstown with her bows stove in!"

Storch exclaimed, "You are certain, man?"

Fackler nodded excitedly. "She hit a Yankee destroyer!"

Rietz turned back to the chart. This made everything different.

Decoy or not. With *Fremantle* out of the game, and even with the weather worsening, the odds had shifted.

"Tell Schöningen I want him to lay off a course to intercept this *Empire Prince*. Advise *Wölfchen* of what I intend and prepare the Arado for take-off."

He rubbed his chin thoughtfully, "Then find out all you can about the oiler and plan accordingly. We may have to go alongside in a heavy swell, so I want every hammock, fender, spare cordage and canvas on deck ready to be slung between the two hulls."

With the *Waipawa* trailing astern, the two raiders steered away from their tiny islet.. Rietz left the charthouse and walked onto the flying bridge. If they could fill the oil bunkers, even half fill them, there was a good chance for their survival. They had done what they had set out to do, and his men deserved far better than the misery of a prisoner-of-war cage with the additional smear of Vogel's cruelty on their heads.

All the same, he would take no chances. A wild animal was caught usually because of hunger and a deadly moment of carelessness. The trap did the rest.

9
"Am Engaging!"

Blake put down a half-eaten sandwich as Villar stepped into the sea cabin.

The motion was less violent, but Blake knew the signs, and the most recent signals confirmed a storm of unknown intensity approaching from the southwest. With luck they might pass through the fringe, but they might still never find the oiler.

Villar grinned at him. "Provided the *Empire Prince* is on station, sir, we should be close enough tomorrow morning."

Blake stretched his arms. Another day, and now another night. The ships blundering towards each other like helpless drunks. One signal between them would be enough, but if Rietz was anywhere near it would be all that was needed to smash everything.

The weather was the one enemy they had not allowed for. Fairfax was to make another signal when he was in contact with the enemy. An ordinary follow-up to his original one about damage. The rest was mostly up to Weir and his engines. But they had to be certain where Fairfax was. An auxiliary oiler was not the most manoeuvrable of vessels. She could have drifted in the swell, been forced miles off course.

Villar said quietly, "You could send Masters at first light, sir. He's done it before."

"I'll think about it, Pilot." Against the risk of Masters being spotted by the German's Arados he had to set the strong possibility of their missing Fairfax altogether.

Andromeda's bows lifted and then smashed through a steep roller like a giant plough, the impact making the bridge shiver, the guns rattle on their mountings.

Down on the forward messdeck there was a chorus of shouts and curses from the off-watch hands as a few unguarded plates and mugs scattered in fragments amongst a growing pile of sea-boots and oilskins.

The tannoy came on. "Aircraft handling party and catapult crew will be required at oh-six-thirty tomorrow. Cooks and sweepers clear up messdecks and flats for rounds."

The seamen began to tidy up their mess, where they lived, slept, slung their hammocks and endured. Leading Seaman Musgrave looked round his domain with approval. "Fair enough, lads."

Someone asked, "Who's doin' rounds tonight, Hookey?"

Musgrave frowned. "Lieutenant Blair, 'our Micky'."

He was the Australian quarters officer of B turret. He was quite popular with the lower deck, but they still thought him a bit odd.

Musgrave explained, "You know, the one 'o comes in an' says, 'Owarewealldoin' then?'"

A marine's bugle shattered the calm and a petty officer bellowed, "Attention for rounds!"

Lieutenant Michael Blair came through the watertight door, swaying unsteadily as the ship took another plunge.

He gave a cheerful smile and asked politely, "How are we all doing then?"

COMMANDER VICTOR FAIRFAX pressed his face against the bridge windows and stared towards the oiler's blunt bows. The rollers had eased away into a long running sea, with great streaks of foam writhing across the ship's path. It should still be daylight, but it was barely possible to make out the forecastle from the oiler's high bridge.

The *Empire Prince* was so well loaded she seemed indifferent to the angry water around her. A rich prize for any raider.

He walked to the rear of the bridge which, compared to a man-of-war's, was spacious. He glanced at the faces of the men on watch. It was strange to be serving with men he did not know. Few of them knew each other, and he guessed it was the usual arrangement for a special mission, or an "early suicide" as Lieutenant Williams, his temporary second-in-command, had described it. Williams was a real expert. An RNR officer, he had served most of his peacetime life in oil tankers. He was a laconic, nuggety Welshman from Cardiff.

He entered the bridge now, banging his sodden cap against his thigh, his eyes nevertheless taking in the compass, the ship's head and the general alertness of the watchkeepers.

He nodded to Fairfax. "I suggest you get your head down, sir. You'll be busy in the morning, I shouldn't wonder."

Fairfax replied, "I feel OK."

"Mebbee." Williams jammed the battered cap on his head and took out his pipe and pouch. "But you know I'm right, all the same." He glanced at the interwoven gold lace on his sleeve. "I understand ships, sir, but I'm not much of a man of action. I'm a survivor, if you like."

Fairfax watched him as the blue tobacco smoke went jerkily upwards into the fans.

"Why did you volunteer for *this*, then?"

Williams grinned. "Perhaps I misunderstood the offer, sir."

"Well, I'm glad you're here." He peered aft towards the squat funnel and the remaining superstructure. "I'm more used to being able to shoot back!"

Williams smiled. Fairfax seemed all right. Not one of those hell-for-leather madmen who were usually the first to crack wide open when they were most needed.

He said, "What d'you reckon our chances, sir?"

Fairfax walked to the chart table. "*Andromeda* will be about here." He tapped the pencilled lines. "Pity about *Fremantle*. We could do with a bit more muscle."

Williams shrugged as if it was no concern of his at all. "Well, we have our orders. No heroics, no matter what. Surely a cruiser can cope with a bloody armed merchantman, sir?"

Fairfax looked at him grimly. What was the point of reminding him that if this was the raider that had sunk *Devonport,* it must be more than just an ordinary armed merchantman? "I expect *Andromeda* will cope," he said.

He lay down on the campbed by the chart space, and turned on his side listening to the muted beat of engines, the occasional flurry of blown spray across the windows.

Tomorrow. Nothing might happen at all. He thought of Sarah, could almost feel her pressed against him.

Fairfax had had quite a few girls before he had settled down with Sarah. Even after their marriage he had played around once or twice when his ship had been away from her home port. It had been a part of his life, something everyone treated as normal.

He closed his eyes tightly. *Not any more.* They both knew that now. He slipped suddenly into a deep sleep.

Hours later, Lieutenant Williams was just thinking of sending for his relief when the starboard door slammed back and an oilskinned figure lurched into the wheelhouse, streaming with rain and spray. It was a lookout from the bridge wing.

Williams regarded him coldly. "Well?"

He gulped and wiped his reddened face. "I—I'm not sure, sir, but—"

Fairfax woke and hurried across the bridge and asked, "What's happened?"

The seaman said, "I thought I heard an aircraft, sir."

Fairfax said sharply, *"All lights out!"*

The wheelhouse was suddenly pitch-black, except for the luminous glow of the gyro-compass which reflected in the helmsman's eyes so that they shone like two white marbles.

"Open the door."

Fairfax groped out onto the slippery plating, his ears useless against the roar and hiss of the sea, the sluice of water along the oiler's fat flank.

Williams said dryly, "Aircraft, you say? We're nowhere near any air cover and out of range of everything but the bloody birds!"

Fairfax gripped his arm. "Listen! *Now!*"

There it was. A faint, indistinct drone, lost almost at once in the ocean's noises.

Williams stared at him in the darkness. "By God, the Hun's found us. He'll have seen our lights before we doused them."

They strained their ears for a few more moments but there was nothing. In silence they re-entered the wheelhouse.

Fairfax said slowly, "I think a drink all round is indicated, and one for the lookout."

LIEUTENANT JEREMY MASTERS groped his way cautiously across the upper bridge, each hand seeking a firm hold before letting go with the other. It was dawn, but when he peered over the screen all he could see was the foam boiling along the side or rising over the guardrails, and beyond, the sea, as black as a boot.

He made out Blake's familiar shape in the bridge chair, shining faintly as the rain and spray bounced across his oilskin. Masters measured the distance, took a deep breath and hurled himself towards the forward gratings.

Blake half turned and said, "Look at it. You can't fly in this."

Masters sensed his anxiety, his frustration, as the ship plunged over the dark water. "I could have a go, sir."

"No."

What was the point in discussing it? The Seafox's range of four hundred odd miles left no room for error. Masters and his observer could fly on and on into oblivion and discover nothing.

A small figure hovered by the chair, trying to guard a steaming jug from the salt and rain.

"Cocoa, sir?" It was Digby, the one who had discovered the grisly remains on the islet.

Blake nodded. He felt stretched out, like piano wire. Damn the weather. He sipped the cocoa. It was scalding, in spite of the long haul from the galley. He asked, "All right, Digby?"

The youth stared at him, astonished that anyone remembered his name, especially the captain, and at a time like this.

"Y-yes, I mean, aye, aye, sir."

Masters was saying, "You're certain it'll be today, sir?"

Blake turned angrily. "I'm not bloody sure of anything!"

He was about to apologize, ashamed of his anger, when Villar clawed his way across the bridge. "Signal, sir! *Empire Prince* has sent her arranged message. She must have made contact with the German. My team is plotting the position now, but as far as I can gather she's about two hundred and seventy-five miles south-southwest of us."

Blake thrust past Masters to the chart table. "Alter course to intercept, Pilot. Increase revolutions. Warn the engine room."

Fairfax could not possibly have sighted the raider. His situation would be like *Andromeda*'s. Desperate the German might be, but he would not risk seizing an oiler in pitch-darkness. He must have launched an aircraft. An Arado was bigger and far more powerful than Masters's Seafox. The German pilots would be the best available, professionals well-used to tracking surface vessels under all conditions. So they were there. More to the point, the lure of fuel had pushed caution aside.

Blake stood up, waiting for his eyes to get accustomed to the darkness again. What would he do in Rietz's place, with the only chance of survival a tempting cargo of fuel with the means to bunker at sea? Rietz was probably shadowing the oiler, keeping well back until he was ready. The pity was that they didn't know where he was, or even from what direction he'd come.

Scovell peered round. "Rain's getting heavier."

Blake turned away. A storm and a battle did not go hand-in-hand. He listened to the screws' mounting beat, felt the ship's violent motion as she hurled herself into the weather as if she hated what they were all doing to her.

He said, "Call the hands half an hour earlier, Number One. I want them fed and ready to go to action stations as soon as we've got some daylight." He added, "Tell Paymaster Commander Gross to get his department on top line. Sandwiches and tea to all the gun positions. Chocolate, too, if he can spare it. Then make sure the commodore's been roused."

Blake heard Scovell's boots clattering down a ladder. Probably thinks it's unnecessary. A waste of time. Sentiment, when all they needed was a firm hand. Behind him Digby crept round the bridge, gathering up empty mugs.

The ship's company was wide awake now. Soon cooks and stewards piled small mountains of sandwiches on trays, while stokers of the damage-control party went round the ship looking at life rafts and Carley floats, timber for shoring up bulkheads, all the odds and ends of survival.

Both the boiler rooms and the engine room were fully manned, with overalled figures scrambling through the steamy haze. Weir watched from his catwalk, his face set in a grim mask, while the din roared and rattled around them.

On the thick watertight doors the clips were greased and ready to be slammed shut. Safety for some, death by fire or drowning for others. On the long messdeck in *Andromeda*'s forecastle, Leading Seaman Musgrave ran his eye quickly over the bare neatness. The messdeck, like the others below his feet or aft, was prepared for battle.

He rapped the nearest empty table with his torch. "All done 'ere, sir." He looked at the officer who had been sent to check the messdecks with him.

Midshipman Steven Thorne nodded stiffly. He was frightened. He wanted to discover the kind of strength the seaman seemed to take for granted. He asked huskily, "You were aboard when you fought the three Italian cruisers, Musgrave?"

"'S'right." Musgrave felt both sorry for and irritated by Thorne's misery. He added, "Any reason for askin'?" He dropped the sir. It was his way of finding out how far he could go.

"I—I just wondered what it was like."

He sounded so wretched that even Musgrave felt a twinge of pity. He looked along the broad messdeck, remembering the savage gashes in the side, the sea streaming past as *Andromeda* pressed on with her attack. A lot of good blokes had bought it that day.

He said, "It was rough. But this one will be a piece of cake. I think the skipper's 'ad just about a gutful of the Jerry. I wouldn't give much for '*is* chances!"

Above the door to the messdeck was a red-painted gong.

Musgrave said quietly, "Listen. In a moment or two that bloody thing is goin' to sound off like the clappers."

Thorne said, "I know. Action stations."

Musgrave swung the door shut behind them. "More to it than that. We're goin' to *fight* today. I feels it. When that 'appens there's blokes up top 'o'll be lookin' to you, God 'elp them. 'Cause you're an officer. The fact that you 'ave never been in a scrap like this one'll be never comes into it. So when the shit starts to fly, *sir*, just remember not to let 'em down."

Thorne nodded, his fists clenched to his sides. "Yes, I see. Thank you." He straightened his cap. "Let's get on with it then, shall we?"

Musgrave grinned. He thought, I'll bet nobody's spoken to him like that since he was caught pinching apples.

It was at that precise moment the alarm began its clamour.

"Action stations! Action stations!"

Musgrave ran for the nearest ladder. Just before he scrambled through the hatch to the deck above, he paused and looked back. It struck him then that he was never going to see that messdeck again.

SCOVELL SALUTED. "Ship at action stations, sir."

Blake peered at the sky. Dawn had broken and the cloud was breaking up, with patches of steely blue showing occasionally. "What do you think, Pilot?"

"Another two hours' sailing, sir. It's my guess the Germans will have stopped the *Empire Prince* by now and are taking on fuel."

Blake peered at his watch. Two hours. It was too long. He looked at the sky again, hating it, dreading what might happen to Fairfax and his men.

He glanced round as a rain squall hit the ship with drenching intensity.

A seaman thrust a telephone towards Blake and shouted, "Engine room, sir!"

Blake jammed it to his ear. "Captain!"

Weir called, "I can give you another two knots now, sir."

The rain roared through the bridge, battering Blake's cap and oilskin like a flail. Yet through it all he heard Weir's quiet confidence, the prop he needed more than Weir would ever know.

"Everyone seems good and busy, Captain."

Commodore Stagg walked to the bridge chair, oblivious to the downpour. "Got bored aft." He shot Blake a questioning glance as he joined him by the screen. "Something bothering you?"

"It's still going to take two hours. Longer than planned."

Stagg growled, "Rietz will need a whole lot longer to get his fuel across in this swell, you can be sure." He rubbed his wet hands. "He's lost his safety margin. *Andromeda* will have him by the guts long before that. He'll know he can't outpace us."

They both turned as the gunnery speaker barked, "Ship bearing green two-oh, range one-four-oh."

Stagg glared at Blake accusingly. "You said two hours!" Then, surprisingly, he grinned. "So Rietz got suspicious after all. So much the better. Go get him."

Again the speaker's metallic tones: "Two ships, repeat *two* ships, at green two-oh, range one-four-oh."

Blake lowered his glasses, the misty picture fixed in his mind. The rain passing on and over, the sea riding in long, undulating rollers to meet them, and then, just off the starboard bow, two blurred, oncoming shapes.

He shouted, "I was right! There *are* two of them!"

Stagg stared back at him, his jaw hanging open.

"Ships altering course. Now steering zero-four-zero. Rate two hundred, closing."

Blake looked at Villar. "Tell W/T to make the signal. 'In contact with two German raiders. Am engaging.'" He watched him move to a voice-pipe. "Fast as you like, Pilot."

Scovell asked, "Shall I stay here or go aft to damage control, sir?"

"Carry on aft, Number One. Tell Masters to be ready to fly off immediately and to make sure his plane is fully armed. He'll understand." Blake then looked at the Toby Jug. "Very well, Yeo. Hoist battle ensigns."

"All guns with semi-armour-piercing, *load, load, load!* Follow director!"

Blake wiped his binoculars with his handkerchief. A faint

shadow moved over the bridge, and when he glanced up he saw one of the big ensigns running up to the yard, the white like snow against the dull clouds, the red cross like fresh blood.

"Open fire on leading ship!"

Both forward turrets fired together. Blake saw the vivid red flashes, the pale waterspouts which shot skyward to mark the fall.

"Up two hundred. *Shoot!*"

Blake looked at Villar as his face lit up in the flames. "Alter course two points to port. That'll give the guns a chance."

He felt the deck tilt to the pressure of rudders and screws as Villar said tersely, "Course one-nine-zero, sir."

"*Shoot!*"

Blake saw the glow of flames, like tongues, changing shape and spreading as he watched. The leading ship was hit, probably badly. There was a lot of smoke about, billowing low across the sea. Beyond it, at a range reduced to about six miles, the flames were adding to the confusion.

X and Y turrets opened fire at an extreme angle, the shells ripping past the cruiser like express trains.

"*Captain, sir!*" Sub-Lieutenant Walker waited for Blake to look at him. "Masthead reports that the first ship is the *Waipawa*, sir, captured in that convoy!"

Blake snatched up a handset below the screen. Rietz had fooled them after all. He had sent the merchantman ahead for this sole purpose, to draw their fire while he worked into an attacking position where he would be unhampered by the extreme range.

"Guns! Shift target! The leading ship is—"

The bridge seemed to rise under his feet. He heard no explosion but was momentarily rendered speechless by concussion, by the terrible lurch which threw men about like dolls.

Then he heard Palliser's faint voice and realized the handset had been blasted from his fingers and was swinging on its flex.

"Captain! Direct hit!" There was someone screaming in the background. "Can't cope here. . . ." His voice was getting fainter. "All dead up here. . . ."

Blake peered aft at the director control tower. There were several holes punched through the plates, which were pouring out smoke. There were eight men inside there. Or had been.

"Shift to local control." He strode back to the compass. "Hard a-port."

"Thirty of port wheel on, sir."

Stagg was yelling, "What are you doing?"

Blake stared past him, his eyes stinging with smoke. "He's got his sights on us now, and he's outranging us. We must close the distance."

"Midships. *Steady.*"

Loose equipment clattered across the bridge. Someone was calling for a stretcher-bearer.

Walker called, "First Lieutenant Scovell, sir!"

Blake took the telephone. "Yes?"

"That shell passed through the starboard flagdeck," Scovell told him. "It exploded on the port side. Couple of boats are gone and an AA gun has been flung overboard."

"Casualties?"

Blake winced as the hull bucked violently and he saw two great columns of water rise over the bridge before roaring down on the forecastle in a solid mass.

"The DCT is knocked out, sir. Guns is dead. About ten men in all. The doc's got some splinter cases aft."

The phone went dead.

Blake said, "Alter course again. Hard a-starboard!"

As the helm went over once more, the four turrets were already swinging across, their muzzles crashing back as they fired again. Without the control tower and main range-finder, each turret had to fend for itself.

"Midships. Steady!" Blake raised his glasses. If only the sky would clear. It was like fighting shadows.

Crash. A shell exploded right alongside, shaking the hull from stem to stern. Blake ran to the side, and saw the flag deck directly below him. It was hanging down towards the water like buckled cardboard, its signalmen and Oerlikon crew flung into the sea and already far astern.

"*Shoot!*"

That was the Australian, Lieutenant Blair, in B turret, his voice unemotional over the speaker, as if at target practice.

"Over. Down one hundred. *On! Shoot!*"

"Target's altered course, sir. Steering due north."

Stagg shouted hoarsely, "Probably going to launch his tin fish at us! Some hopes in this sea!"

"Pass the word aft to Masters. Stand by to fly off the instant I reduce speed." Blake lowered the glasses. "The German is turning to get his seaplanes airborne." He saw Stagg's disbelief. "He's nothing to lose, has he?"

"All ready aft, sir!"

Blake wanted to tell Masters and his observer. But tell them what? That he was sorry they had to take a terrible risk? But the Arado seaplane carried bombs. Perhaps the raider could be stopped. Not big bombs, but enough.

"Stop engines!"

Andromeda seemed to lean forward as the way went off her shafts. A few moments later two shells exploded directly ahead. Where she would have been but for Masters.

Blake's heart sank as the little Seafox shot along the catapult and tilted drunkenly to the driving wind and rain.

Then he said, "Full ahead together!"

The freighter, which had been deliberately used to draw *Andromeda*'s opening salvoes, was already moving closer, her hull down by the bows and one anchor cable dangling in the sea. There were several fires raging, and tiny figures were racing about with hoses. Someone had run up a white flag. But the *Waipawa* with her German prize crew would have to fend for herself. It was a race. Who would get to her first? The storm or the victor of the fight?

"Aircraft bearing green four-five! Angle of sight three-zero!"

Blake saw the aircraft coming straight for the starboard bow. There were two of them.

"Barrage! *Commence . . . commence . . . commence!*"

Tracer lifted from the sponsons to join the small, vicious shellbursts from the anti-aircraft guns. The noise, blanketed every so often by the main armament, was shattering.

The first seaplane flew directly for the ship, turned at the last minute, its cannon ripping across the bridge structure like a steel whip.

A bomb hit *Andromeda*'s forecastle and skidded over the side

208

without exploding. Another burst in the water, fragments clashing against the armour plate, while others cut through some signal halyards high above the bridge. Blake had to duck as the second aircraft roared overhead, guns hammering, a bomb already on its way down.

"A hit!" Someone was cheering like a maniac. "We got him!"

Blake lifted his head in time to see smoke and sparks spreading away from the other ship. The deck shook under his feet and metal shrieked past him, punching through steel and slapping hideously into solid flesh. Three men were down.

"Stretcher-bearers to the bridge!"

The second aircraft was swinging away, trying to gain height as the tracers followed it with merciless concentration. Fire rippled along its wing and belly like droplets of molten liquid, then it exploded and threw fragments as far as the ship.

The first attacker was standing well away, waiting for a chance to cut through the smoke and perhaps rake the open bridge.

In the Seafox, Lieutenant Masters peered at the terrible panorama below him.

The listing freighter had stopped altogether and was in a bad way, her hull sliding into each successive trough and finding it more difficult to rise up again.

The raider was badly hit, too, with fire and smoke trailing astern as she continued to shoot from her hidden mountings. Great patches of white froth drifted nearby where shells had exploded, while from *Andromeda,* with her wounds made small by distance, came the regular flash of gunfire.

Provided *Andromeda* could avoid a fatal hit in a magazine or shell room, it would soon be over, Masters thought.

His earphones crackled and he heard the observer say calmly, "Sorry to disturb you, Skipper, but there's a ruddy great bird coming just underneath us!"

The Seafox was a midget by comparison, and with only a single Lewis gun. But the two Germans in the Arado's crew were not even aware of Masters's presence as they overtook the Seafox about two hundred feet below its floats.

Masters said quietly, "If they spot us, Jim, we're done for. What about it?"

Duncan was still grinning. "Ready when you are!" He cocked the outdated Lewis and swung it over the side. To the gun he shouted, "Just don't jam on me, that's all I ask!"

Masters dragged the stick over and saw the Arado right beneath him. A last-second warning made both Germans look up together. They were still staring, unable to believe what they saw, as tracer smashed through the cockpit and turned it into a torch.

Masters watched the blazing plane reel away in a tight spiral, a greasy plume of smoke marking its fall, until with a silent explosion it hit the side of a long, crested roller and vanished.

It was nearly over. As the thought touched his mind he saw a great mushroom of fire burst through the raider's welldeck, tiny feathers of spray darting from the sea around her as wreckage was scattered in confusion.

Then even as he watched Masters saw the sky clearing far beyond her, and the sea changing again into those great, smooth rollers.

He stopped breathing, the glasses pressed against his eyes until they watered with pain.

Far away on the brightening horizon was a single ship. She was bows-on, and even at such a distance Masters could see the rising moustache at her stem which left no room for doubt.

He spoke into his microphone with deliberate care.

"Jim, old son, we were celebrating too soon." He put the Seafox into a banking turn. "We have company!"

10
Just a Man

Like two wallowing juggernauts the *Salamander* and the *Empire Prince* had headed into sea and wind while the work of pumping the oil got under way.

On the port wing of his bridge Rietz watched carefully. It was all going remarkably well, in spite of the rain and the deep swell. The oiler's crew had not put up any real resistance, and after the *Salamander* had followed up her signal to heave-to with a shot across the other ship's bows, there had been no trouble. Rietz had sent sixty of his own men to help with the complicated derricks and guys which were used for swaying the hoses over the strip of surging water.

Rietz had been surprised to learn that the oiler's master was a naval commander, but the *Empire Prince* was a fleet auxiliary, an important vessel by any standards. He had been the only casualty, clubbed down by one of the boarding party as he had been trying to reach the radio room.

Rietz glanced outboard at the smoothing sea. They might miss the full brunt of the storm. He no longer cared much. With full bunkers he would be free again, able to move as he chose.

He thought briefly of Vogel in the *Wölfchen*, miles away to the northeast, making certain *Salamander* could replenish her empty bunkers without interruption.

Then he heard a door slam back inside the wheelhouse. It was Schöningen, the navigating officer.

He exclaimed, "Captain, we have just received a signal from *Wölfchen*! She is engaging a British cruiser. The prize ship is badly hit, but Captain Vogel has reported severe damage to the enemy."

Rietz looked away. He snapped, "Call up Lieutenant Storch. We will discontinue oiling at once. See that all our prisoners and neutral seamen are sent across to the *Empire Prince* without delay."

He was still on the bridge wing watching the prisoners emerge on deck, when Storch came hurrying up the ladder.

"Is it true, Captain?"

"It is, Rudi. Vogel is taking on a British cruiser."

Storch stared from him to the growing lines of figures being herded on deck.

"What are you going to do, Captain?" His face looked stricken. "Are you going to help him?" When Rietz did not answer, Storch said, "Leave him, Captain. He has betrayed the name of Germany. *Leave him.*"

Rietz smiled gravely. "You know it is not possible. It is a matter of convenience as well as honour, my young friend. That ship will be the cruiser *Andromeda*. There is none other in these waters. I think I knew it would be like this." He became suddenly brisk. "Now get those people passed across to the oiler and cast off the hoses." With a sudden impulse he added, "Bring the oiler's captain to me. Quickly!"

By the time Fairfax arrived, his head bandaged, most of the prisoners had already been transferred. Fairfax glanced around the bridge. The prisoners were being sent over for a reason. So that the *Empire Prince* could be sent to the bottom with the last of the evidence. But before the terrible act of murder it was to be his turn. The guard beside him was fidgeting impatiently with his submachinegun.

Faixfax felt very calm, almost empty of emotion. All he could see in his mind was Sarah.

Rietz stepped forward and nodded curtly. "You are Commander Fairfax of the Royal Australian Navy, yes?" He gestured towards the swaying oiler. "In a moment you will be free to go. I regret your radio must be destroyed, but it is a small price to pay."

Fairfax stared at him. He had never seen a real enemy before. Not close to, as a human being. Perhaps that was almost as unnerving as the German's words.

Rietz said, "You will know soon enough, there are two raiders. I suspect some of your people have always thought as much. It is no longer important. What is important is that you should know my ship was in no way responsible for the murder of helpless seamen. In war we have to do many cruel things, but not that."

Fairfax said slowly, "I am not sure what you are talking about, Captain."

Storch thrust forward angrily. "Because of our prisoners we have wasted valuable time when we could be many miles away and you left to drown! And because my captain is not the man you British think he is, we are going to fight *your* ship!"

Rietz turned on his heel. "Take him back to his ship."

A seaman seized Fairfax's arm, but he shook him off.

"Captain Rietz." Fairfax waited until the man had turned towards him. "Thank you for giving your prisoners a chance to live."

He saluted and then followed the armed seaman down the bridge ladder.

Rietz watched the last boat being run up to its davits.

"Ring down for full speed. We will steer northeast."

As *Salamander*'s screws began to beat the sea into a powerful froth beneath her stern, Rietz turned away. "It will feel cleaner, Rudi, to fight under our true colours for once," he said.

COMMODORE STAGG sat on the bridge chair, a cigar glowing from his great jaw as he watched the busy figures around him. The dead and wounded had been taken away, most of the smoke had cleared, and *Andromeda* had reduced to half speed because she had taken on a slight list to starboard. But the underwater damage was reported to be in hand, and Weir had managed to keep all the pumps going.

Sub-Lieutenant Walker lifted his glasses to look at the blazing raider. All her main armament had fallen silent, but *Andromeda*'s guns were still moving slowly on their mountings, watching for any sign of defiance.

Blake put down the telephone. "W/T office report on the storm, sir. It may give us a miss. Once I'm sure of the raider we'll signal her to abandon and take to the boats. But her list is much worse." He wiped his face as if to clean away the sights and smells of battle. "Close thing though."

"Seafox in sight, sir. Fine on the port bow."

"Warn the handling party."

So Masters had survived. Perhaps it was even he who had brought down the second Arado.

A dull explosion deep inside the German ship flung more glowing sparks high in the air. Was Rietz dead? Blake wondered.

"Seafox is signallin', sir." It was flying so close to the surface that the morse light was reflected across each long roller.

"'German raider approaching from the southwest.'" The Toby Jug spelled out each word impassively.

Stagg said hoarsely, "Can't be! Bloody fool's wrong!"

Blake turned to look at the blazing ship with its clutter of splintered woodwork and rigging. Then he looked along his own ship, at the scars and blackened holes. So he had been proved right after all. But it was cruel, unbelievably so.

He heard himself say, "Pass the word to all positions, Pilot, then warn the Chief."

Stagg swallowed hard then threw his cigar over the side and lurched to his feet. "Give me the microphone. I'd better speak to the ship's company." He saw Blake's face and said quietly, "No, it's for you to do. The ship *knows* you."

Blake took it in his hand and pressed the button as he had a thousand times.

"This is the captain speaking. We thought we had finished work for the day, but now we shall be engaging another German raider. After that, most of us will be going home." He gripped the microphone until his hand ached. "I just want you to know how proud I am of you—"

He thrust the instrument into Walker's hand, unable to continue.

Stagg muttered, "Well done. Not easy."

Blake watched the little Seafox. "Tell Lieutenant Masters to continue spotting, will you?"

Moon appeared. "I'll fetch some sandwiches, sir," he said mildly.

Blake gripped the steward's shoulder and shook him gently. "You do that, Moon. I shall look forward to them."

"From Seafox, sir. 'Enemy closing!'"

Stagg looked at Blake and spread his big hands. "Ready?"

Blake nodded. "All right, lads?" He studied each face in turn. "Ring down for maximum revolutions. Stand by to engage!"

STAGG was on his feet, restless and grim-faced, as the *Andromeda*'s bow wave peeled away on either side in steep banks of white foam.

"What d'you reckon he'll do?"

Blake raised his glasses and stared at the horizon where the storm clouds were massing.

"He'll make a diagonal attack, sir. These converted merchant-men usually have their armament in halves, one full battery on either beam. Torpedoes, too, but he'll not reduce speed to use those."

He felt the deck lift slowly and then surge forward and down again. The raider probably had the latest range-finder, whereas *Andromeda*, damaged now, was almost blind. He knew the only chance was to get as close as possible and beat down the enemy's fire-power.

Walker said in a hushed voice, "Engine room, sir."

Blake strode to the telephone. "Chief? Captain here."

Weir said, "I'll need to reduce speed, sir. Starboard outer is giving me trouble. Must have taken a bad knock from a bomb or shell splinter. If we cut the revs on the port screws for a time it will give me a better chance."

Weir knew what he was doing. *Andromeda* would need all her manoeuvrability. She could not manage on helm alone, and with unequal thrust on her screws it would take longer to alter course, to avoid those first deadly salvoes.

"How long, Chief?"

Weir did not answer directly. He said, "We're losing fuel, too."

"I know. Do your best."

Weir gave a short laugh. "Aye, sir. I've no wish to swim home."

Villar snapped, "Enemy's opened fire, sir!"

There was a thin, abbreviated whistle, and a column of water shot from the sea barely half a cable from the port beam.

The two forward turrets began to whirr round, their guns lifting to their maximum sixty degrees elevation.

"*Open fire!*"

The gong gave its tinny warning below the bridge, and A turret, followed closely by B turret, belched fire towards the horizon.

Over the speaker Blake heard Lieutenant Blair call, "Range one-double-oh. Inclination one-one-oh right!"

Blake blinked rapidly to clear his vision, then as some of the mist parted he saw the enemy for the first time. A solid dark shape, guns flashing from her hull.

Whoosh . . . crash! The raider's shells exploded close alongside like twin thunder-claps. Two more heavy shells arrived seconds later, bracketing the cruiser in shining waterspouts and filling the air with the shriek and crash of white-hot metal.

Blair's voice came through the din. "*Shoot!*"

The four guns recoiled together, and Blake saw the shellbursts to the right of the target.

Walker yelled, "X turret is jammed, sir! Seven marines wounded!"

A boatswain's mate stood back from his voice-pipe. "Two pumps have carried away, sir! Damage control need more men aft!"

Blake snatched up a handset. A frightened voice called, "D-damage control, sir!"

"Get me the first lieutenant, *quickly!*"

The voice broke off in a sob. "He's dead, sir!"

Blake asked, "Who is that?"

"Thorne, sir."

A face swam through the smoke. A replacement midshipman. Straight from the training school. A boy.

"Well, listen, Mr. Thorne. Send a petty officer and some stokers aft to help your party there. Can you do that?"

There was a pause, and in his mind Blake could see the

splinter holes, the blood and upended switchboard and damage-control panel. Scovell, who had wanted his own command so much, lying dead with his men.

Thorne said in a whisper, "Yes, sir. I'll do it now."

Blake ducked his head as a great explosion smashed against the bridge, buckling steel plate and hurling broken glass and fittings amongst the crouching figures.

Two men were down, kicking out their lifeblood, and Commodore Stagg was gripping his shoulder and staring at the stain spreading down his side.

Blake yelled, "Starboard twenty! Midships! *Steady!*"

The raider continued to draw nearer, apparently unmarked as her short-range weapons opened up. A solitary star seemed to detach itself from the shellbursts above her and fall slowly towards the sea. Just before it touched the water it exploded, to leave a dirty smudge against the sky.

Blake watched the wind drive it away. Masters had got too close and had paid with his life.

Several of *Andromeda*'s company who were working on the exposed upper decks saw the Seafox fall like a comet. One of them was Ordinary Seaman Digby who, with a handful of assorted ratings, was rushing to hack some blazing canvas from a searchlight mounting and throw it overboard.

He paused, sobbing for breath.

A petty officer bellowed, "Over here, lads! Lively now, there's two blokes trapped under this lot!"

Then a shell burst somewhere below, and the world seemed to erupt in smoke and flying metal.

The seamen were hurled down, scattered like butchered meat, and the petty officer, who had been calling to some men pinned beneath the collapsed flagdeck, dropped to his knees. He had no head.

A voice rasped through the smoke, "'Ere, lend a 'and, someone!"

It was Leading Seaman Musgrave. He was badly cut about the face and there was more blood shining beneath his lifejacket.

The sight of Musgrave gave Digby strength, and wheezing like an old man he seized his arm and began to drag him beneath the shelter of the trunked funnel.

"'O's that then?" Musgrave was moving his head from side to side, and Digby realized he was blind.

"It's me, Jack, Diggers!" He could barely stop himself from weeping for man's frailty.

"Diggers?" Musgrave grimaced as the pain grew worse. "Good lad. 'Ow bad is it?"

Men were shouting, and smoke billowed through a gaping hole by the boat tier as if the whole ship was ablaze.

Digby said, "I'll get help. You'll be all right."

Musgrave gripped his wrist. "No, Diggers. You stay along of me. Just for a bit, eh? Feel dicky. Real rough."

Digby sat down beside him. "I'm here."

Musgrave tried to touch his eyes. "You'd make a good officer, Diggers. Don't you forget it. . . ."

His head lolled and he was dead.

Digby stood up slowly. He did not even duck as a splinter slammed through the funnel and ricocheted over his head.

He might be going mad, but he was no longer afraid. It was as if all the strength of that coarse, violent seaman had somehow drained into him.

SUB-LIEUTENANT WALKER, his hat gone, and some flecks of blood on his forehead was tying a crude dressing round Blake's arm.

"Might help, sir!"

Blake looked past him, seeing the smoke pouring from the ship's wounds. He had not even felt the blow on his arm.

Stagg was roaring like a bull. "The bastard's turning away! He's going to fire a full broadside at us!"

Blake levelled his glasses. There was the raider, angled away across the starboard bow, smoking from several hits now, but moving as firmly as before. He guessed the German was preparing a final straddle before he closed in to use his torpedoes.

It would not take much longer. *Andromeda* was barely answering the helm as, with her pumps unable to cope against the racing screws, she was listing more and more to starboard.

Blake looked down at the angry sea and knew there would be few left who would be able to tell of their fight and their sacrifice.

Forward of the bridge, and sitting on his little steel seat at the rear of B turret, his eyes glued to the sights, Lieutenant Blair studied the blurred target with something like despair.

He knew that forward of his turret the other two guns were silent, their crews killed by a direct hit. Down aft, X turret was still jammed solid, and Y was unable to train on the enemy.

Blair heard the hissing sounds of the shells being guided into the smoking breeches, the hoarse bark of orders and then the slamming click of the locking mechanism.

"Both guns loaded, sir!"

Blair adjusted his sights with elaborate care. The enemy was moving on a different angle now, but what was more interesting was that she was heeling over steeply whenever her stern lifted above the crested rollers.

Sweat ran down the side of his nose as he watched the magnified picture of the raider's bridge, a tiny pale sliver as it rolled once again towards him.

"Sights moving! Sights *set!*" He held his breath. "*Shoot!*"

Blake saw a single explosion directly on top of the enemy's bridge. It was a brief orange flash, and then as the armour-piercing shell plunged down through the decks, aided by the raider's steep turn, it exploded against one of the magazines.

Two more vivid flashes cut through the drifting spray, and then as some of *Andromeda*'s men jumped up from behind their gun-shields the sky seemed to dim to one tremendous explosion.

Stagg pointed beyond the German ship. "What's *that,* for God's sake?"

Blake stared, mesmerized, at a pale line behind the raider. The line was a bank of rollers, built up into a single, massive force over hundreds of miles of ocean with nothing in its path but the stricken raider.

Blake shouted, "The fringe of the storm!" He tore his eyes from the oncoming mass and . shouted down a voice-pipe, "Slow ahead together! Wheel amidships!"

He swung round, trying to switch his mind from the fact that he had now destroyed both the German ships and dealt with the safety of his own.

"Pilot, have it piped round the ship!"

220

He noticed Villar's body below the compass platform, a small red stain just below his heart.

Lieutenant Trevett said, "I've taken the con, sir." He glanced at the dead South African. "Reckon I had a good teacher."

Blake nodded, and turned back to the second German raider.

The unending bank of water seemed to roll against her side without any sort of urgency. Then, as the pressure mounted against her bilge keel, thrusting her over and down, the ship began to turn turtle. One final explosion blasted her hull wide open, and as the sea surged over her shattered plates, the side of the wave was lit up from within. Then she was gone.

Perhaps the fringe of the storm had really spent its fury. It reached *Andromeda*'s stem and lifted her effortlessly towards the smoky sunlight. Then, before anyone could accept that it was over, it had passed quietly astern.

Sub-Lieutenant Walker had a telephone in his hand and said huskily, "It's the Chief, sir."

Blake took it but kept his eyes on his ship.

Weir sounded tired. "Thought you should know. I can give you more revs now." He gave what might have been a chuckle. "The old girl was playing me up, nothing worse."

"Thank you, Chief."

Blake handed the telephone to Walker and rejoined Stagg by the broken screen.

"Fall out action stations. Post extra lookouts in case there are any survivors in the water."

Stagg was staring at the sea where the enemy had been just moments earlier. "I thought it would mean something." He sighed and allowed the Toby Jug to fold a shell-dressing over his torn shoulder. "But Germans are nothing special after all. Just men." He looked at Blake. "Like the rest of us."

He pulled a silver flask from his hip pocket and took a long swallow. Then he wiped it on his sleeve and passed it to Blake.

Blake drank silently. He needed this moment. For Claire. What he would say to her when he saw her again.

Stagg eyed him thoughtfully. "After this I'll be needing an assistant in Melbourne. How would it suit you?" He grinned suddenly. "I can see it would!" He watched Moon as he crept onto the bridge with a vacuum flask and some sandwiches. "Of course, the new commanding officer will take over from you soon, so that's no real problem."

"You already know who it will be, sir?"

Stagg picked up a sandwich. It looked like a postage stamp in his great fist.

"Fairfax, of course. If he's still in one piece, that is." He grunted. "Better make a signal. Tell the people in Melbourne that we did it."

The Toby Jug had his pencil poised.

Blake said quietly, "Make this signal to the Navy Office, repeated Admiralty. 'Two German raiders destroyed. With help from on high, HMS *Andromeda* is returning to harbour.'"

Quintin would see that and show it to Claire. She would know that he was safe.

They picked up the survivors from the German raiders. Then, slowly, *Andromeda* turned and headed towards the eastern horizon.

Douglas Reeman

Like most really successful authors, Douglas Reeman works regular—and long—hours. His mornings are spent dealing mostly with research and his extensive correspondence—he receives mail regularly from his readers all over the world, and does his best to answer every letter personally. And in the afternoons, from two till dinner-time, he works on his writing. Furthermore, he's not a man to take long holidays—he's never really happy, he says, when he doesn't have a book in hand.

It's hardly astonishing, therefore, that *A Ship Must Die* is his thirty-third novel. He has now published twenty-one stories of modern naval warfare and twelve historical sea

adventures, written under the pseudonym of Alexander Kent. His books are all about the sea because it's a subject he knows better than any other. He served in the Royal Navy throughout the last war, mostly aboard motor torpedo boats. And he clearly led a charmed life, since he survived the sinking of no less than three ships beneath him.

After the war he joined the Metropolitan Police, and worked in London's East End, attached to the CID. After meeting his future wife, Winifred, he found work with more regular hours, as a social worker in Battersea. It was Winifred who first started him on his career as an author when she suggested that he write down one of the many stories he had told her and submit it to *The Navy* magazine. It was accepted instantly, and only a very short time after this tentative beginning he was able to leave the social services and settle down as a full-time professional writer.

Nowadays Douglas Reeman is a world-wide bestseller. And as far as the British Navy is concerned, they consider him their number one recruiting officer. The Royal Australian Navy, too, treated him as an honoured guest when he was in Melbourne recently, researching for *A Ship Must Die*.

He remains, for all this, an unassuming man, friendly and hospitable, and—with his inexhaustible stock of fascinating anecdotes—excellent company.

ERROR OF JUDGMENT

A CONDENSATION OF THE BOOK BY
Henry Denker

ILLUSTRATED BY BARBARA FOX
PUBLISHED BY MACDONALD AND JANE'S

For lovely Cynthia Horton the painful
wrench from the excitement of her wedding
plans to the loneliness and uncertainty of a
hospital bed had taken three short days.

And it was within only minutes that a
surgeon's decision would radically change
her whole future—as a wife and as a
mother.

Undeniably the surgeon was a superb
technician. But the doctor assisting him at
Cynthia's operation was appalled by his
lack of concern for her total welfare.

As Cynthia and her fiancé face a married
life that is potentially devastated, the young
idealistic doctor dares risk his career to
expose what he considers a crucial error
of judgment.

CHAPTER ONE

TALL, black-haired, a scowl turning his handsome face craggy, Dr. Craig Pierson glanced at the wall clock as he raced down the hospital corridor. Already ten minutes past seven. He had not completed his morning rounds of patients, and he was due to assist in the operating room at eight. One interruption after another, this latest most irritating of all. He caught sight of the distressed young intern waiting outside the patient's room.

As he reached him, Pierson demanded angrily, "What is it, Blinn? Can't you take a simple presurgical history?"

Willis Blinn blushed, embarrassed. That blush reminded Pierson that only two years ago he too had been an insecure intern. He must learn to control his impatience with younger, less experienced men. But, then, he had days when he was impatient with older colleagues as well.

Constantly he had to remind himself that medicine was a craft practiced by mere human beings. With the best of intentions, they were bound to make mistakes. As a second-year resident in obstetrics-gynecology, he had already made his share.

Blinn, a willing young man who worked harder than any other intern on staff, was not yet up to the demands of the job. Still, it was Pierson's duty to cope with such inadequacies. Next year, when he became a senior resident and, he hoped, chief resident, he could devote more of his time to surgery. The residents under him could worry about interns.

Painfully aware of Pierson's impatience, Blinn attempted to explain. "The patient is highly emotional. I couldn't get her to answer any questions."

Pierson said sharply, "Look, Blinn, maybe you should choose another specialty. Gynecology is fraught with patients who have emotional problems."

Blinn did not respond. Dismissed, he turned and started down the corridor. Pierson again felt a rush of guilt. He decided to take the patient's history himself rather than add to Blinn's embarrassment by having another intern do it.

He looked up at the room number—442. Through the half-open door he could see that the bed was still neat, its corners tightly squared. There seemed to be no patient. He pushed the door open a bit wider. She was there, a young woman, hardly more than a teenager, to judge from the size and contour of her body, staring out the window. She did not appear to hear him. Craig picked up her chart.

PATIENT: Horton, Cynthia. BIRTH DATE: May 12, 1956. AGE: 22. ADMITTING PHYSICIAN: Dr. H. Prince.

Another of old Goldfingers' admissions, Craig observed. Old Goldfingers! That title had been bestowed on Dr. Harvey Prince both by residents who stood in awe of his brilliant surgical technique and by staff surgeons who envied his six-figure income.

Craig read the remaining entries on the history form.

ENTRANCE COMPLAINT: Ovarian mass.

PROCEDURE: Exploratory laparotomy.

Gently he began, "Miss Horton? It is miss, isn't it?"

Slowly she turned to him. He was struck by her beauty. Finely cut features in a pale face were accented by deep violet eyes and lustrous black hair. She appeared even younger than twenty-two.

"I shouldn't be here!" she said in a strained voice. "I should be getting the final fitting on my wedding gown this afternoon. Instead, I'm going to die. I know it. It's a curse!" The word unleashed a flood of tears. She buried her face in her hands.

228

"Miss Horton," Craig coaxed, "no need to be so upset. What you're going to have is really a simple procedure, an incision into your abdomen. Most patients are home in four days. As to the possible findings, statistically three out of four of these masses are benign. And even if Dr. Prince finds something, it probably can be completely removed. He's the best g-y-n surgeon around."

Cynthia Horton looked up at him. He introduced himself. "I'm Dr. Pierson."

She did not acknowledge the introduction but responded, "It's an accident that I'm here at all. Mother said it was a good idea, before Pete and I got married, for me to have a physical. So I went to Dr. . . ."

She could not control her tears again, and turned away. Craig tried to help her.

"So you went to your family doctor. He did a routine examination and discovered something. Did he do a Pap smear?" She nodded. "And it came back negative?" Again she nodded.

"That's a good sign," he encouraged. "I have to ask you some questions. Will you answer them? Please?"

"I'll try," she said, but refused to face him.

Craig followed the hospital's form for gynecological history. Then he asked questions concerning her present condition.

"Noticed any weight loss in the last month?"

"No."

"Any pressure on the bladder?"

She hesitated. "Yes. Is that important?"

"Probably not," Craig said, hoping to calm her. "Did you notice any other effect of this mass on your bodily functions?"

"I didn't even know there was a mass!" Cynthia now turned and stared hard at Craig. "Mother kept saying, before a girl gets married she should have a complete physical. To make sure there are no impairments. 'Impairments to what?' I asked. And she said, 'Impairments to having children.'"

Craig changed the subject, hoping to put her at ease. "What kind of work do you do?"

"I work in an ad agency. Secretary."

"Parents still living and well?"

229

"Yes."

"Any family history of cancer?"

She faltered. "I . . . I don't know."

"You mean if there had been, your mother and father would have kept it from you?" he asked.

"I mean what I said, *I don't know*. I don't know! I don't know!" She was weeping again. "Now leave me alone."

Craig waited. He knew it would do no good to pressure her. Eventually she recovered sufficiently to say, "*I* don't know because *they* don't know. I'm adopted! I don't know my family history."

"I understand," Craig Pierson said sympathetically.

"*Do* you?" she demanded vehemently, "I wonder! I wonder if you know how it feels to go through your life with half of it missing! All those questions, simple questions, like the one you just asked me, and I have to say, I don't know!

"Don't you think I've read that cancer can run in families? It was the first thing I thought of when Dr. Corbin discovered that mass. I wanted to find my mother and ask questions like 'What drugs did you take when you were pregnant with me? Did you ever have cancer?' But where do you go? Whom do you ask?"

She was now very tense. "I thought marrying Pete would wipe out my past. Our children would know who they were, their family history. Then this happened. I thought, I've never seen my mother, but she's put a curse on me. From the day I was born. Now I won't even live to get married."

"Miss Horton, your fear is quite unrealistic," Craig assured her. "You'll have surgery. You'll recover. You'll be married. Probably even without postponing the date."

"And if you *find* something?"

"The odds are greatly against its being anything serious," he said truthfully.

"If there's a way to destroy me, she'll find it," the girl said grimly. "Someday I'll search for her. Find out why she gave me up. Why she won't let go of me, even now. I'll find her. Adoptees do it all the time."

"I know," Craig said. "I did it."

"Did what?" Cynthia asked.

"Searched. Found her."

"You mean you're adopted too?"

"Members of the same club," he said, smiling. He held out his hand to her. She stared at him before she shook it.

She did not relinquish his hand as she asked, "What was it like? When you found her?"

"I was apprehensive," he admitted. "After all, maybe she had a family of her own. I would be an unwelcome intrusion, a shock. Then I saw her. She turned out to be small, frail. I don't resemble her. We had nothing in common. We couldn't even make conversation. She seemed relieved that I had grown up well. But that was all. She had no impulse to embrace me or kiss me. And I had no feeling for her. We were strangers. At that moment I knew who my mother and father really were.

"I told my parents. They weren't surprised. They had expected I'd do it one day. But they were relieved that it was over."

"That's all there was?" Cynthia Horton asked.

He smiled. "That's all. Except afterward I felt a bit foolish."

"Why?"

"I forgot to ask her about *my* family medical history."

Cynthia Horton now relaxed sufficiently to smile with him. "You didn't make all this up, did you?"

"No," he said. "I *am* adopted, I *did* find her."

The pretty, dark-haired girl was pensive for a moment. "I want children," she said. "Children who will grow up free of all the fears and doubts I've always had."

"I see no reason why you can't have them."

In the normal course of a new admission, Craig Pierson would have done a thorough examination. However, since this girl was now beginning to relax, he chose not to risk upsetting her. He terminated the interview. "Miss Horton, there's no more capable surgeon for this procedure than Dr. Prince. If you were my own sister, Prince is the man I'd have do it."

After Craig left, he glanced into every room on the corridor until he found Blinn, taking a blood sample from a young pregnant woman. Once Blinn had sealed the test tube and handed it to the technician, Craig beckoned him to the door.

"It wasn't your fault," Craig said. Blinn was surprised. "She's extremely apprehensive," Craig went on. "Highly emotional. And for good reason. Sorry I blew my top."

PIERSON completed his rounds. Then he scrubbed and assisted at four surgical procedures. One, a hysterectomy, he performed himself with the woman's surgeon standing by to observe. The surgeon complimented him on his technique and proficiency.

His long day done, Pierson changed from his OR greens into his gray tweed jacket. Since Kate was away at a seminar, he could go back to his small bachelor apartment and try to catch up on a high stack of medical journals. Every month obstetrics and gynecology produced a prodigious number of new findings. What specialty in medicine, Craig used to joke, had a better right to be so productive?

He was crossing the hospital lobby when he felt a sudden need to see the Horton girl again. Though he had reassured her, to himself Craig had to admit the seriousness of her condition. Women in their early twenties did not often present gynecological malignancies. Yet in her case, one ovary was suspect. And ovarian malignancies, though third in frequency among gynecological cancers, were more fatal than all other kinds combined.

He reached her room, heard voices—low, soft. The door was slightly ajar. Craig knocked nevertheless. "May I come in?"

"Dr. Prince?" a young man asked as he opened the door.

"I'm the resident. Pierson, Craig Pierson. I saw the patient this morning. I wanted to check on her before I left."

"Of course," the young man said. He was no more than twenty-six, tall and rangy, with a tanned, weathered complexion.

Cynthia Horton was sitting up high in her bed. She said, "Dr. Pierson, this is Pete Tompkins. My fiancé."

"How do you do," Craig said, shaking hands with him.

"We were expecting Dr. Prince," Pete explained. "He said he might drop by this evening."

"Good," Craig replied, though he knew it was not like Prince to visit the hospital in the evening unless an emergency developed. However, Craig was relieved to observe the improvement in

233

Cynthia Horton's attitude. She smiled easily, and when she did, he appreciated even more how unusually beautiful she was. He thought, With her beauty and Pete's physique, they're going to have magnificent children.

Conversation was light, casual. When Craig excused himself, Pete volunteered to walk him to the elevator. Smiling, Pete kissed Cynthia, saying, "Be right back, honey."

Once outside the door, Pete Tompkins turned grim. "Doctor, tell me the truth. Is it bad? I swear I won't tell her."

"We won't know a thing until Prince does the exploratory."

"I called a friend of mine," Pete said as they walked down the corridor. "He's a doctor. When I said 'exploratory laparotomy,' he was stunned."

"Mr. Tompkins, the term itself is nothing to be frightened of. It simply means performing an exploratory by opening up the abdominal cavity."

"But if you find—" Pete started to say.

Craig interrupted. "We don't speculate. That's why we go in. As for what we might find, there's been no bleeding, no pain, no obstruction. If anything's there, we've caught it very early. And cases like that we can cure. Possibly the luckiest thing that ever happened to her is that she went for a checkup."

At that moment the elevator arrived. As the door opened, a middle-aged couple emerged. The woman threw her arms around Tompkins, saying, "Oh, Pete, Pete . . ." and she began to weep. He embraced her, then introduced the couple to Craig.

"Mr. and Mrs. Horton, Cynthia's folks. This is Dr. Pierson, Dr. Prince's assistant."

"Just a resident," Craig explained. He shook hands with Mr. Horton, a harried-looking man with dark hair running to gray. Tompkins and Mrs. Horton started toward Cynthia's room. Horton lingered, then put his hand on Craig's arm to detain him.

"Doctor . . ." he blurted out. "Doctor, you can tell me the truth."

"Mr. Horton, we haven't lied to Cynthia. Or to Pete. There's something there. We have to find out what. When it comes to finding out, Prince is the best man there is. That's the truth, the whole truth, and nothing but the truth."

"Thank you," Horton said, his eyes filmed over with tears. "She's our only child. If anything happened to her . . ."

"The odds are in her favor, Mr. Horton."

"Thanks, thanks very much," the relieved man said, and started down the hall.

Craig Pierson could appreciate Horton's feelings. His own folks felt the same way about him. Which reminded him, he had not telephoned them in almost three weeks. He would call when he got home this evening.

Craig did not often ponder his relationship with his parents. He had always loved them. His father, a stolid, hardworking man, had been brought up on a rugged stony farm in northern New York. He had drifted into landscaping, and once he achieved a comfortable financial status, his wife, Anna, began urging that since they had no children, they consider adopting.

At the outset, it was for Anna that Bill Pierson did it. But when they were handed an infant boy for their own, Bill Pierson discovered emotions within himself that he had not known existed. At the end of the first month he was already making plans for the boy's future. He set up a savings account for him, determined that, unlike himself, his son would not be denied an education.

From an early age, Craig Pierson knew that he was adopted. There were nights when he lay awake wondering where he had come from, why he had been given up. But in the end he felt glad that he had been given to such loving people as Anna and Bill Pierson.

Through high school, though coaches urged Craig to go out for sports, he declined in favor of helping in his father's landscaping business. His dad tried to suggest there was no need to feel any obligation. But Bill was not an easy man with words. Nor could he disguise his pride when customers praised Craig's work.

Always, Bill Pierson was happy to reply, "Well, he won't be at it long. That boy is going to be a doctor, not a gardener like his dad." And on the day Bill and Anna drove their son to college, they felt they had achieved the goal of a lifetime.

During summer vacations, Craig returned home and insisted on working in the business. His father demurred. A man who studied hard all year should rest during his time off. But Craig insisted on dragging hose, tilling soil, pushing a lawn mower.

After Craig entered medical school, Bill Pierson forbade him to work at landscaping. It was not fit work for a doctor. So Craig took a job in a playground for disadvantaged children and began contemplating pediatrics as his specialty. But the year his mother had a cancer scare he began to delve into gynecological oncology, and he decided in favor of that field. Fortunately his mother's case was well handled by his professor of ob-gyn, and she recovered completely. When it was over, his dad said to him, "Anything we ever did for you, son, you repaid a million times over."

Tonight, as soon as he arrived home, Craig called his parents long-distance. His father answered, and his mother got on the extension. They talked of many things, catching up on events since he had called last. They asked how his work was going.

"It's been busy. Every day is like trying to save a stand of saplings in a hurricane. Never lets up."

"Can't do any harm," his father said, proud that his son's services were so much in demand. "The more you do now, the better you'll be when you go out on your own."

Craig made a mental note that one day soon he must tell his father that he was considering not going into private practice but staying on at the hospital, on staff and to do research. So for him there would be no huge house, no well-cared-for acreage that his father had always assumed was the just due of any doctor.

Suddenly Craig found himself telling them about Cynthia Horton, her condition, and her fears about being adopted.

He ended by saying, "I guess that's really why I called. If people love each other, maybe they don't have to say it. But I want you to know how I feel."

"It never hurts to say it, son," his mother replied. He could envision the tears in her eyes.

His father said, "Take good care of that girl."

"Talking of girls," his mother said. Craig knew what was coming. "Is there a girl yet?"

"A girl?" Craig asked. "Or *the* girl?"

"You know what I mean, son," she answered. "After all, even

for a doctor, life shouldn't be all work. There's a time for marriage. And a family."

Craig would have been delighted to share with them that there was a girl. *The* girl. But how could he explain that the world of men and women had changed in thirty years? That it had become much more free and hence more complicated. Without understanding that, they would never understand about Kate.

IT WAS just past midnight. Cynthia Horton was still awake. The night nurse had given her the sedative prescribed on her chart. But Cynthia's anxiety had defeated the mild dose.

She stared up at the pale green ceiling, breathing guardedly, fearing that to draw a single deep breath might disturb and spread the *thing* that was growing in her. She had moments when she could convince herself it was nothing. But always those moments were overwhelmed by such panic that she considered leaping out of bed and fleeing. As if she could leave the *thing* behind her.

When her mother first suggested she see Dr. Corbin for a checkup, she and Pete had joked about it. Who ever heard of going to a doctor for approval to get married? It was comic. Still, Cynthia respected her mother's wishes and went to see him.

While Corbin examined her, he asked questions about her mother and dad. Were they going to Europe this spring? Was her dad, an attorney with a large law firm, overworking as usual?

Suddenly, during the pelvic examination, his questions changed from casual to strictly medical. He had obviously detected something that startled him. He pressed again, probed again.

Ovarian mass, his fingers told him. If he recalled correctly, in a patient this young such a mass would most likely be a benign cystic teratoma, a harmless dermoid cyst.

He took a Pap smear, then completed his examination. Once she was gone, he carefully studied two texts on gynecological diseases. They confirmed his recollection. They also raised another alarming possibility—that even though the patient had no pain or bleeding, the mass could be an ovarian malignancy.

He rushed the Pap smear through. He felt some relief when the report came back negative. He called Cynthia at her office and told her that though her Pap smear was negative, he thought she should get another opinion about a possible ovarian mass. Cynthia was inclined to laugh it off, but when Corbin became quite stern, she agreed to keep the appointment he had arranged for her the next day with Dr. Harvey Prince.

She called her mother, caught her at the country club making arrangements for the wedding reception.

"Mom, Dr. Corbin wants me to see a gynecologist tomorrow."

"You know Dr. Corbin—conservative to the end. Nothing to worry about, I'm sure."

"Mother, I'd like you to go with me."

"Of course, darling."

THEY had waited over an hour when Cynthia was finally shown into one of Dr. Prince's examining rooms. A nurse told her to disrobe and gave her a white gown. The fresh muslin sheet felt cold and coarse to Cynthia's skin.

Minutes later, minutes that seemed much longer, she heard a man's voice—crisp and businesslike—ask, "This one?"

"Dr. Corbin's patient."

"Oh, yes. Check her history. Did he do a Pap smear?"

"Yes. Negative," the nurse replied.

Dr. Harvey Prince entered the room, wearing a white lab coat. A tall, dignified man with an impressive white mustache, he exuded an air of authority that transmitted itself to Cynthia at once. If there were something wrong, she had confidence he would fix it.

He asked the same questions Corbin had asked—pain, pressure, bleeding. With each answer he smiled and nodded. She felt determined to please him and thus earn a favorable verdict, so that her wedding could proceed on schedule.

He began the examination and when he was done, he dictated a note into his machine: "Ovarian mass. Seven to eight centimeters. Mobile. Tensely cystic. Suggesting ovarian neoplasm."

The words, most of which were foreign to Cynthia, alarmed her. "What did you find, Doctor?"

"Get dressed and go into my consulting room. That's your mother in the waiting room, isn't it? We'll have her in too."

238

Again they waited a very long time for Prince to join them in the lavishly furnished consulting room. Her mother camouflaged her now growing fear by talking so incessantly that Cynthia realized how grave she suspected the situation actually was.

Meanwhile Cynthia stared at the volumes on the bookshelves. *New Concepts in Gynecological Oncology. The Classification of Malignant Tumors. Carcinomas of the Uterine Cervix, Endometrium and Ovary.*

Though the word oncology was new to her, she knew well what tumors and carcinoma meant. Suddenly she interrupted her mother's ceaseless chatter about wedding plans with a tense and tearful "Mother, please!"

Her mother embraced her, saying, "It's going to be all right."

Prince finally entered the consulting room. "Well, now," he began, once he had settled himself in his leather desk chair. "I'll be as frank with you as I am going to be with Dr. Corbin."

He lifted his phone, pressed one of many buttons, and said, "Carla, get me Dr. Corbin."

While they waited for the call to go through, Prince asked inconsequential questions and seemed only the slightest bit concerned when he discovered that she was planning to be married in four weeks. His phone buzzed.

"Corbin? Harvey Prince. . . . About the Horton girl. She's sitting right here. I want her to hear everything I say.

"You were right. On bimanual, she presents an ovarian mass. I'd say seven to eight centimeters. I think we should go in and take a look right away so she can proceed with her wedding plans. I envy the lucky man." He smiled at Cynthia. "So if it's okay with you, I'll send her into the hospital tomorrow."

Prince hung up. He smiled reassuringly. "That's all there is to it. Miss Reigle at the front desk will make arrangements with the hospital. All you have to do is show up first thing in the morning. We'll run some tests. I'll probably operate the next day, if I don't have any emergencies. But don't worry about a thing.

"Now, very simply, the procedure will be done under a general anesthetic. The incision will be in the abdomen. Horizontal. Trust me to leave a very small scar. So there'll be nothing to spoil the honeymoon." He laughed. "Once in there, we'll find that pesky little thing and remove it. At that point it goes to the pathologist, who does a frozen section. Once the report comes back negative, we close you up and that's it. A few days later you go home, good as new.

"Of course," Prince added, "if the report comes back positive, we look around carefully and stage the disease—that is, map out the extent of it. Then we do the operation to remove it."

"Exactly what *do* you do?" Mrs. Horton asked.

"What the surgeon does depends on what he finds. You have to trust me," Prince said soberly.

"Of course," Cynthia replied numbly.

"HAVE it done and get it over with, darling!" Pete had said when Cynthia told him. "Make sure. Then we can go on with our plans."

He had embraced her, and for the moment she felt safe in his powerful arms. But later that night, alone in her own bed, the fears she had felt as a child returned. She had not been good enough for her natural mother to keep her. Now that she was diseased, she would not be good enough to marry.

She began to sob. In a while her father came in. He sat on her bed, gathered her up in his arms.

"Cynthie, Cynthie baby, it's going to be all right. We'll get through this. I was talking to one of my partners this afternoon. His niece went through the same thing. They operated and found it was nothing. Nothing at all. She's married now and has two terrific kids. Believe me, it'll be all right."

"I've always been a trouble to you and Mother."

"Trouble? I've always felt privileged to be your father. I want you to know that. It's been a privilege, Cynthie, darling."

She pressed against his shoulder, her tears wetting his pajama top. Tenderly he set her down on her pillow. At the door he said, "Darling, first thing in the morning I'll talk to Dr. Prince myself."

It had been almost dawn when she had finally fallen asleep, her hand on her belly trying to contain whatever was threatening her life.

240

TONIGHT, IN HER hospital room, Cynthia Horton lay with her hand on her belly, wondering what they would discover in there. Finding it impossible to believe that all this had happened so suddenly.

From the excitement and intoxication of making wedding plans to this. In only three days.

CHAPTER TWO

IT HAD been a usual harried morning for Dr. Craig Pierson. He had made his rounds on the ob-gyn floor and had been called to the emergency room to treat a young woman who had tried to abort herself. She was now resting comfortably, but Craig was concerned about her emotional recovery.

Every patient on his service had to be viewed psychiatrically as well as physically. In any gynecological situation a woman's sense of self was at stake. The patient in 403, thirty-six years of age, was scheduled for a hysterectomy to remove *leiomyomata uteri*, commonly called fibroids, which though benign were uncomfortable. All she thought of was, What will it do to me as a woman?

Always it came to the same thing in Craig's specialty: Doctor, save my life, but keep me a woman. Don't remove or damage that part of me uniquely mine and the purpose for which I was born.

The problem was always compounded when the possibility of a malignancy presented itself. Craig was reminded of Cynthia Horton. Though she was not in need of medical attention this morning, he decided to drop by and reassure her. Her door was opening and the chief resident, Dr. Burt Carlyle, was emerging.

Carlyle was a light-skinned black man, lean and of slightly taller than average height. He carried himself with a dignity that was almost aggressive. He was an excellent surgeon.

As soon as Carlyle saw Craig, he explained, "Prince asked me to have a look. Seems her father called him this morning. Kept him on the phone for fifteen minutes. You know how old Goldfingers is with families. Nice. But only up to a point. Time is money, he always says."

"Who should know better?" Craig joked. "How is she?"

"Tense. Maybe you should increase her Valium."

"I'll have a look," Craig said, starting into the room.

Cynthia Horton was lying on her side, facing away from him. She heard the door open and, without turning, said, "I don't want any more doctors! I want to be left alone!"

"Good morning, Cynthia."

She turned. "Oh, it's you. You can come in."

Craig stood over her bed. "There was a doctor in here," she said. "He said Dr. Prince sent him. Was that true?"

"Of course. He's chief resident and an excellent doctor. Wouldn't be surprised if Goldfingers tapped him for his private practice at the end of the year."

"Goldfingers?" she asked.

Craig laughed. "Dr. Prince. He's such a fantastic surgeon that we younger men call him Goldfingers."

She seemed encouraged by that.

"Well, how are you?" he asked warmly. "Have a good night?"

"Not bad," she evaded.

"You did something for me yesterday," Craig said. "Made me call home."

"I did?"

"The talk we had reminded me how terrific my people are. I sensed that you feel the same way about your folks."

"Yes."

"I feel that their whole lives are centered on me. You ever feel that way?"

"Yes."

His efforts at bringing her out had not succeeded. With each monosyllable she withdrew more. He considered having one of the psychiatric residents come to see her. Kate might help. Being a woman, she did especially well with patients on the gyn service.

He took Cynthia's pulse and found it racing. Carlyle was right, he should increase her Valium. He must check first with her anesthetist to make sure it would not conflict with what he'd use during the operation.

While Craig was on his way to make his call, he thought back to the first time he had scrubbed with Harvey Prince. It had been fascinating. The surgeon had made a neat horizontal incision, then worked deftly through layers of fat and muscle. He took a sample biopsy and sent it to the pathologist's lab. During the ten minutes they waited for the results of the frozen section, he had spoken to Craig as if he were a concerned father.

"Let me tell you, Pearsall—"

"Pierson," Craig had corrected him.

"Pierson. Of course. Let me give you the best medical advice you'll ever get. Start investing when you're young. You residents make fortunes these days. All I got when I started out was fifty dollars a month. Not fifteen thousand a year like you fellows. Whatever you save after taxes, put it into the market. Buy blue chips. And energy stocks. Don't get nervous when the market goes down. In fact, that's the time to buy more.

"Keep piling up equity. Then when you're fifty, you can decide if you want to continue to practice or retire. Myself, I don't ever want to retire. But I do want to have that choice."

At that moment the pathologist had called. The frozen section had come up positive. Endometrial carcinoma, cancer of the lining of the uterus. Prince returned to the table, and proceeded to perform a hysterectomy, first making sure the carcinoma was confined to the immediate area.

While he worked he continued to talk. "Another thing. When it comes time to go into practice . . . you *are* going into private practice, aren't you?"

"I haven't decided yet."

"That's where the money is. If you do go into practice, don't put all your available cash into office equipment. Get a bank loan. Interest is deductible from income taxes. Meantime your own money is working for you in the market. Or in tax-exempts. These days practicing medicine is only half what a doctor does. The other half is trying to outwit the government!"

From that day on, Craig knew precisely why, from the beginning of Prince's affiliation with State University Hospital eleven years ago, all the doctors had called him Goldfingers.

Burt Carlyle, who had scrubbed along with Craig that day,

must have read his thoughts. Once Prince left, Burt advised Craig, "Don't let it throw you. Just watch his fingers while he's talking finance and you'll learn a lot about surgery."

"Is he always like that?"

"When you've got his technique, you can talk about anything and still be better than most surgeons."

When Craig scrubbed with Prince a second time, he heard him utter a bit of advice that he would always remember. Prince had just received an equivocal report from the pathology lab. He paused for only an instant before he said, "When in doubt, take it out!" Prince had then proceeded to do surgery which Craig considered far too radical for the situation. Later, when he raised the question with Carlyle, Burt had said, "Study Prince's record. His cancer patients have a remarkable five-year survival rate."

This morning Dr. Harvey Prince came striding down the corridor attired in what had become his trademark when he visited the ob-gyn floor: a light gray flannel suit with a budding red rose in the lapel. He always pretended a warmth and affability which he believed won him the admiration of the entire staff.

At the residents' station, he was especially warm in greeting Craig Pierson, and asked, "Have we got a signed consent from the Horton girl?"

"I'll check and see."

"Do that. Right away. Her father's a lawyer. A nervous lawyer. They sue for malpractice at the drop of a hat." He started away, turning back to call out, "I have to delay her another day or two. Emergencies referred last evening. But get that consent signed."

CRAIG Pierson opened the door of room 442. "Cynthia?"

"Yes," he heard her answer from the bathroom.

He found her staring into the mirror over the washbasin, examining her face very carefully. Finally she turned to him.

"I look the same. Surely if there were something really wrong, it would show. All I can see is red. I've done a lot of crying."

"That's why it's best to have the surgery. Get the suspense over with," he encouraged.

She came out into the small sunlit room wearing a blue silk

244

robe. Despite her eyes, which did betray considerable weeping, she really was quite beautiful—and so young. Craig himself was only thirty. But twenty-two seemed a long time ago.

She dropped into the armchair, more self-contained than when last he had seen her.

"Cynthia, there's a standard procedure in all hospitals. Before a patient can be operated on, she has to sign a consent form."

"Yes, I know. Daddy told me."

"I assume Dr. Prince explained the procedure to you. Its purpose. The questions that might come up in the course of the operation. The pathologist's report."

"Yes, yes, he did."

He handed her the blue sheet. She read:

I authorize Dr. Harvey Prince or such associates as may be selected by the doctor, to perform upon myself the following operation/procedures: Exploratory laparotomy, surgery performed through the abdomen for the purpose of doing a biopsy on the right ovary.

In the event developments indicate further operations/procedures may be necessary, I authorize the physicians to use their own judgment and do whatever they deem advisable during the operation/procedure for the patient's best interests, except the following:

After the printed words, the word NONE had been typed in. Cynthia looked up. "That word none . . . Does that mean if they do find"—she faltered—"something, they might do drastic things to me?"

"More extensive surgery might be advisable," Craig said.

"Like what?" she challenged.

"It might be necessary to do a bilateral salpingo-oophorectomy," he said.

She tried to laugh. "You can talk clearer than that, Doctor."

"It would mean excising both tubes and ovaries. We might possibly remove the uterus."

"Then I'd never be able to have children, would I?"

"We're dealing in *ifs. If* there is a malignancy, *if* Dr. Prince

245

decides that's the proper course to take. But remember, it could be benign, nothing at all."

Her violet eyes sharpened angrily. "We're making quite a fuss over 'nothing at all,' aren't we?"

"Only in the interest of making sure."

Cynthia studied the form again, but her hands trembled and she turned away to hide her tears. "I can't. I won't sign it."

Craig decided to have Kate talk to her.

KATHERINE Lindstrom was a disarmingly small blond woman of twenty-nine who appeared to be years younger. Just over five feet tall, she was often taken for a college student. Actually she had been graduated from a midwestern university cum laude, had been accepted by its medical school, and had broken off her relationship with a law student to concentrate on her career.

Her mother, who had lived all her life on a farm, understood that. Her father, who considered himself a practical man, would never understand. Why his daughter would ask more out of life than the good prospects of a suitable husband, he did not know.

Kate had done well in medical school and had been graduated with high grades. She had selected psychiatry as her specialty and, a year ago, had become the second female resident in the history of this hospital's psychiatry department.

She met Craig Pierson during a grand rounds session devoted to postpartum depression, an area in which the departments of ob-gyn and psychiatry had a mutual interest. He was struck by her from the moment she walked into the auditorium. She was uncommonly attractive. She also turned out to be forthright in her opinions and had contributed greatly to the session.

After that meeting he had called her for a date. Within a few weeks he was in love with her. He wanted to formalize their relationship, but she was a determined person. She would make no permanent commitment until she had settled her professional future. She would have to choose soon between private practice and academic medicine.

Without spoken agreements, Craig and Kate remained faithful to each other. But they remained aloof from each other's professional duties. Except at those times when Craig felt an especially distraught patient needed psychiatric assistance.

Cynthia Horton was such a case. Craig had asked Kate to examine Cynthia's chart in detail, which she did, studying the findings of Corbin, Craig, and especially those of Harvey Prince.

She had her own private reservations about Harvey Prince. He had once made a pass at her after she had observed at one of his surgical procedures. This despite the fact that Rita Hallen, his chief scrub nurse, was within earshot. Everyone in the hospital knew that Rita was Prince's mistress and had been for years. He carried on flagrantly with her, even though he was married.

Kate respected Prince only for his surgical work. In that, she had to grant, as did everyone, that he was superb.

When she was thoroughly familiar with Cynthia Horton's chart, Kate went to see her. She found Cynthia lying on her side, facing away from the door, motionless. "Miss Horton?" Kate asked softly. "I'm Dr. Lindstrom."

Cynthia turned to stare. Kate realized how remarkably beautiful Cynthia was. Her inner torment added pathos to her beauty.

"I don't want to be examined by any more doctors! I am not a specimen! I don't want to be used as a practice dummy!"

"I'm not here to examine you."

Cynthia Horton glanced at her, openly distrustful.

"I understand you have refused to sign the consent form for your operation."

"It's not *my* operation. It's *his* operation. I'll bet he does a lot of unnecessary operations! I've read about doctors like him," Cynthia said venomously.

"I've examined your chart. There's no doubt surgery is indicated. But I'm more interested in your reaction than in the surgery itself. I think I know what you're going through."

"Oh, do you?" Cynthia demanded, trying to sound combative but on the verge of tears.

"The fact that I'm a doctor doesn't mean I'm any less a woman. I've had two occasions when I thought I felt something in one breast, and had that pang— Maybe this is it. That flood of fear— Maybe they're going to take away my womanhood. I do know the feeling. In the lives ahead of us we want to fulfill ourselves as women—to be wives and mothers."

"I was supposed to be married in four weeks," Cynthia explained softly.

"Why do you put it in the past tense?" Kate asked, slipping into a chair. "There may be no need to change your plans."

"There will be, if they find the *thing*."

"Find what?" Kate pinned her down. "Say it."

The girl hesitatingly said "Cancer."

"Instead of tormenting yourself with doubts, let the doctors find out. It may be benign."

"They all say that. But somehow I know . . . it won't turn out right. Won't!" she insisted.

Kate betrayed no hint of the concern she felt. She knew, as every psychiatrist knows, that the psychological state of a cancer patient is highly important. Patients with a positive attitude could develop a factor which, for want of a better name, had been dubbed "host resistance." If that positive attitude was lacking, the patient might develop "host acquiescence," making herself a submissive victim to the disease. This girl, Kate thought, has already resigned herself to the worst of all prognoses.

"I understand you couldn't give Dr. Pierson a complete medical history."

"Oh, you know I'm adopted?"

"Yes. And I understand your fear. But you're an intelligent woman. Surely you realize that what you're reacting to now is not the possibility of the disease. It's the fact that you feel deprived. Cast out. Never good enough. Else why did your natural mother give you away? You fear that somehow, in that operating room, the same thing will happen. They won't care. They'll let some terrible thing happen to you again."

Cynthia did not dispute her.

"Who'll let it happen? Your mother and father, who love you? Your fiancé? Dr. Prince? Dr. Carlyle? Dr. Pierson? Men who devote their lives to saving people? Are they going to single you out and say, No, this one we'll reject? Does that make sense?"

Cynthia shook her head.

248

"Unless you sign this consent, none of them can help you."

Kate drew the blue form from the pocket of her lab coat.

"That line," Cynthia said. "The one that says: 'None.' "

"It means you give the surgeon permission to exercise his professional judgment after he gets the pathologist's report."

"He could do anything . . . remove anything. . . ."

"He would take whatever steps are necessary to protect your health and your life. That's all we're interested in, Cynthia."

Cynthia Horton stared down at the form. Without a word, she held out her hand for the pen.

As she finished signing, the door opened tentatively. Barbara Horton entered. Cynthia looked up at her, tears forming in her eyes. "I signed it, Mama. I signed it."

"Good," her mother said, trying to smile.

Kate went out to the nurses' station. After she had signed "Dr. K. Lindstrom" in the space provided under "Signature of physician securing this consent," she placed the form in Cynthia Horton's chart.

She called Craig. He was greatly relieved. They both assumed that Kate had completed her work on the case.

They were wrong.

RITA Hallen had sharp, neat features which were accented by the severe surgical cap she was required to wear in the operating room, where she presided as chief scrub nurse. When she was not in hospital garb, her face, while not soft, was attractive. She was dark-haired and tall. Though she had turned forty, tense young interns and nurses, whom she dominated during surgical procedures, joked that she must be closer to sixty. As Blinn once said, "It would take that long to make a woman that tough."

A tyrant in the OR, Rita Hallen had proved most inept in her private life. She had met Dr. Harvey Prince when he had joined the hospital staff eleven years before. She had been twenty-nine at the time, and he forty-four.

Prince, then as now, had been handsome, and brilliant with a scalpel. It had been considered a triumph for State University Hospital when Prince signed on as an attending surgeon. He had had an excellent reputation in the East, where he had been affiliated with a prestigious hospital. His reason for leaving was hardly unique. He had grown weary of the hassle of life in a large old city. He preferred a newer community where he and his family could live graciously in a pleasant suburb only ten minutes away from the hospital.

When Harvey Prince met Rita Hallen, she had finally just about recovered from a long and tragic relationship with her fiancé, a young resident who had died of a self-administered narcotic overdose. She had been granted a six-month leave of absence after his death, and by the time she came back to work she had cut off all personal attachments, both in the hospital and outside. Some termed her a recluse. She would have lived out her life as one if it hadn't been for Harvey Prince.

They'd been working together in the OR for some time before they had their first meeting outside the hospital. It had taken the form of an after-hours drink. Prince had just completed a long, difficult procedure on a woman with a widely spread ovarian cancer. The operation had consumed more than three and a half hours.

He had left the OR perspiring furiously. He took a shower and dressed in his gray flannel, red rose in place. He was just emerging from the locker room when Rita Hallen passed by. She stopped to compliment the surgeon. "If that patient has any chance at all, you gave it to her," Rita had said.

"Tough case," Prince admitted. "But I never could have done it without you. You're the best scrub nurse I've ever had." Prince sighed wearily. "I'm still keyed up. Would you join me for a drink?" Rita hesitated. "Please?" he insisted. "I need someone to talk to."

She nodded finally, breaking the vow she had made never again to become socially involved with any doctor.

In a small cocktail lounge not far from the hospital, they drank and talked. Mainly Prince talked. About his past, the way his wife had worked to help him through medical school. The real reason he had left the East—professional jealousy, hospital politics. All he wanted was to practice his specialty as best he could. "I'm not a politician," he had said. "If God has given me any talent at all, it's in my hands."

"You were fantastic this afternoon," Rita said. "I don't know any surgeon who could have done as well."

He took her hand. His touch excited her.

"I work with such confidence only because you're there. Rita, I've felt something for a long time. I think there was an element of fate involved in my coming here. In meeting you. We understand each other. We need each other."

Rita had remained tense and breathless throughout this declaration. She was strongly attracted to him, but she knew that once she let down her reserve, she would have no defenses at all against this overwhelming man.

She should have withdrawn her hand. Instead, she had closed her hand over his.

He took her back to her apartment. He made love to her. For the first time in several years she felt like a woman again.

At first, nothing was said about his wife, Margaret. For Rita it was enough that she had him to herself for part of every week. But it wasn't long before she realized that their relationship held little promise for the future, so she began a persistent campaign, demanding that Prince divorce his wife and marry her. Always he had an excuse for putting it off. The scandal would cause irreparable damage to his career. But one day soon. Soon . . .

Because she needed him, Rita had permitted their affair to continue, enduring the deprivations and gossip. A frustrating existence, but, even so, her life was fuller than it had been before.

When Harvey Prince could manage the time, he would see her.

The night before he planned to do the Horton girl was one of these times. He had called Margaret in the afternoon, telling her he would be home late. His pretext was that he had a complicated case early the next morning and he wanted to devote the evening to examining X-ray films and scans.

For Harvey Prince and Rita Hallen the evening began with a few drinks, then dinner in a small French restaurant. He did most of the talking, as usual. She drank little, ate little. He suspected that this might develop into one of her morose evenings. So he talked of an invitation he had received to address a convention of ob-gyn men in Las Vegas three months from then. If he could arrange it, he would like Rita to come with him.

Rita persisted in moody silence for most of the night. Later, in her apartment, he talked about the day when he could finally leave Margaret. Rita suspected he might never do it. She knew what she ought to do. She also knew that she never would.

Harvey Prince doused himself with the bottle of after-shave which he kept at Rita's. "Have you seen the schedule for tomorrow, darling?" he said.

"I know you have that exenteration first thing. Then there's the hysterectomy."

He smiled, a bit proud as he said, "The mayor's wife. He called me himself yesterday. Wanted to know what effect the operation would have on her. I said, 'At thirty-eight, she's had all the kids she wants. So she's not going to miss whatever I take out.'"

He was chuckling until he noticed Rita was neither smiling nor amused. She was thinking, I'm forty. Whatever they take out of me, I won't miss either.

To smooth over the awkward moment, he continued quickly, "Oh, yes, if there's time, there's that young girl with an ovarian mass. Shouldn't take long. Routine exploratory."

Rita was silent. He knew that the unfortunate comparison with the mayor's wife still lingered. He embraced her as he whispered, "Darling, believe me, it's not possible right now. Unless we left here. But after all, I'm fifty-five. I can't start up someplace new at my age. I'm so well established here. It would be a crime to give it all up."

"*She* could leave here," Rita said flatly. Rita never referred to Margaret Prince by name.

"I wish I could make her. But there are the girls."

That was always his last refuge. His daughters. One in high school. The other just graduated from Smith. That he was truly fond of them Rita had no doubt. But that he used them as an excuse for inaction she did not doubt either.

He left her apartment, and Rita Hallen went into her bedroom. She sat before her dressing-table mirror. Forty years old. And hopelessly involved with a man who probably wouldn't marry her. There were times—this night was one of them—when she thought the best thing she could do was go back to the small town in West Virginia where she had been born.

She got in bed and fell asleep thinking of tomorrow's schedule.

THAT same night, Craig Pierson lay awake thinking about Cynthia. She troubled him greatly. He had an instinctive feeling that her mass was malignant. But he had been wrong before. As all ob-gyn men were. There were times they breezed through a procedure sure the growth was benign, only to receive the unhappy news from the pathologist that it was malignant. At other times the surgeon would lift a mass from a patient, consign it to the specimen tray, and begin to explain to residents and interns the procedure he would follow, since the mass seemed malignant. Then the phone would ring with the pathologist's findings: benign.

But most times there were no happy surprises. The doctor had a sense as to what he would find.

Tonight Craig wished he did not have a nagging fear about Cynthia Horton.

IN A comfortable Tudor-style house in a suburb of the city, Barbara Horton slipped quietly out of bed. She was at the bedroom door when her husband called softly, "Barb?"

"Sorry, darling. I didn't mean to wake you."

He rose, went to her, kissed her. She clung to him, trying to reassure him. "The odds are in her favor. Corbin told me so again today. We have to have faith. Just . . . faith." She started to weep.

"Barb, please?" He placed his hands on her shoulders. "Tomorrow when we visit her she is not going to see red eyes, or pity, or fear. We're going to send her up there with every hope, every chance, every bit of courage we can muster."

They were both silent for a time.

"I wonder," Barbara began. "Would it have made any difference if we'd known more about her mother?"

"No."

"How do you know?"

"The attorney for the adoption agency is a friend of one of my partners. I asked. He searched the records for her medical history. No mention of any malignant disease. Of course, she was only twenty, the last record they have of her."

"What if we tried to find her?"

After an uncomfortable silence, Arthur Horton admitted, "I've tried. She died a few years after we adopted Cynthia."

"Oh, no," Barbara Horton whispered. "Did they say from what?"

"Suspicious circumstances. Suicide possibly."

"I hope not."

"Why did you say that?" he asked.

"I don't know. I just hope it wasn't, that's all."

BURTON Carlyle, chief resident on ob-gyn, had just finished reading a recent paper on cancer of the endometrium—the lining of the uterus. He turned out the light in the small living room of his modest apartment and went into the bedroom to join his wife, who was already asleep. In the dim glow from the night-light he admired her delicate profile, her nicely carved lips.

Until she married him, LuAnne had been one of the most outstanding black models in the fashion world. And she was proud, as he was proud of her. He would have no other kind of woman for his wife. That was his grandmother's doing.

When he was a boy, while his mother was out working in other women's homes, his grandmother would drum it into him. "Be proud. And be smart. Even if you go without food, get learning. Because if you got learning, you can have pride. And if you got both, there's no limit to what you can do."

254

Through his life he would live with the ambition his grandmother had instilled in him. He made no apologies for his race and wanted no special treatment. He believed that the best affirmative action for any black man is his own affirmative action. Burt could say proudly, I stood fifth in my class at college, third at medical school. So judge me, not my skin. I am as good a physician as any man on staff, and I want people to know it!

Especially he wanted Dr. Harvey Prince to know it. For it was common knowledge around the hospital that one of Prince's two associates was leaving at the end of the year, and Prince would be looking for a replacement. Carlyle wanted to be part of that lucrative practice. It would set him up for life, financially, but most of all in acceptability.

Carlyle's last thought before falling asleep was to hope Prince would let him do one of those cases tomorrow. Probably the hysterectomy. Carlyle had done so many of those they no longer constituted a challenge. Or maybe he would be stuck with the simple exploratory on that young Horton girl.

ON THE night before her surgery, Cynthia Horton, though sedated by one hundred milligrams of Nembutal, was still far from sleep.

She pressed her side, seeking to isolate the enemy lurking there. What did it look like? How did it feel? She thought of a hundred questions she would ask if only the doctors were here. But she would have to endure the night alone.

She trembled. The next twelve hours could spell the end of everything. Marriage. Pete. Mother. Dad. Life. She had only one thought. If it was bad, she hoped she would never wake up.

She turned on her side, wet her pillow with tears. Why me . . . ?

CHAPTER THREE

IT WAS seven o'clock when Dr. Harvey Prince began to scrub for his first procedure of the morning. Alongside him Burt Carlyle scrubbed. Two washbasins away was Craig Pierson. This was one of those early mornings when Prince envied them. They were young, energetic. He was reaching the age at which, despite his success, every procedure became a chore.

A nurse stood by with sterile gown, powder, and gloves. Prince dressed and looked about. Carlyle and Pierson were ready.

"Let's take one last look at those X rays and scans on that first case," Prince said wearily.

The films had been mounted in view boxes on the OR wall. Prince, Carlyle, and Pierson studied them carefully. Cervical malignancy was strongly suggested, as was involvement of bladder and rectum. Such widespread malignancy demanded a total pelvic exenteration.

An exenteration, far more radical than a hysterectomy, could take as long as seven or eight hours. After his late night with Rita, Prince was a tired fifty-five-year-old surgeon this morning. He took one last look at the films—and then it suddenly occurred to him: Why not? He turned to Carlyle. "Are you up to it?"

Taken aback at such an opportunity, Burt Carlyle hesitated before replying with great assurance, "I've been up to it since my second year of residency."

"Good!" Prince announced. "Pierson and I will assist. Unless you get into trouble. Then I'll take over."

"Of course," Burt answered. This was the sign he had been hoping for. That Prince would demonstrate sufficient confidence in him to permit him to do one of the most intricate of gynecological operations. He would have great news to tell LuAnne tonight.

Exenteration was an involved surgical procedure in use only since 1948. In the intervening years great improvements had been made not only in the technical aspects of the surgery itself, but in anesthesia, antibiotics, and blood banking. A woman who once would have been doomed to death in months, today had a better than fifty percent chance of long-term survival.

Burt Carlyle began this surgical procedure at seven nineteen in the morning. He worked nimbly, swiftly enough to prove that he had the skill and confidence required. Rita Hallen, anticipating his needs, passed instruments to him in the proper order.

While Craig assisted, he admired the way Burt worked. He hoped that if he succeeded Burt as chief resident, he would be

256

handed a few cases like this one. That was one of the prerogatives of being chief resident: to get the challenging cases that tested your ability to the utmost.

Burt Carlyle's fingers were in the abdominal cavity, palpating liver, kidneys, bowel. He was sampling specimens to send to the path lab for immediate frozen section. In the lymph-node area, he removed suspicious nodes for additional frozen sections.

At ten past ten one of the nurses fed Carlyle sugar-enriched orange juice to supply energy. There was still a long way to go. The patient had been transfused to compensate for loss of blood. Another transfusion might be necessary and was ready.

Each report from pathology dictated Carlyle's next step. The node dissections had proved, fortunately, to be uninvolved. Carlyle turned his attention to the pelvic area. The patient was transfused again and was responding well, despite having been almost seven hours on the table.

It was after three o'clock in the afternoon when Carlyle started to close. "Very good, Carlyle! Excellent!" Prince declared.

To himself, Prince observed dryly, Good man. Too bad he's black. Otherwise I'd love to have him in my office.

Burt Carlyle stepped away from the table, ripped off his gloves. His face was soaked with perspiration. His hands and arms ached. In the back of his neck was a knot of tension.

Craig Pierson turned from the table and whispered to Carlyle, "Terrific! Old Goldfingers himself couldn't have done it better."

After a short break for a hurried sandwich, the team scrubbed again. Prince performed the hysterectomy, since the patient was the mayor's wife. When it was over, he debated doing the Horton case. It should prove a relatively simple procedure.

In addition to feeling unduly tired, Harvey Prince had to consider the dinner party he had had Margaret arrange for this evening. It included Walter Deering, the hospital administrator, and several members of the board of trustees. Since he would have to be at his best for the party, he was strongly tempted to put off the Horton case. But when he recalled how crowded his OR schedule was the next day—what he called a ten-thousand-dollar day—he decided to get the case over with.

With great concern he said, "The Horton girl's emotionally prepared for the operation. Let's not add to her worries by postponing." And the weary Prince decided to let Craig Pierson perform the exploratory.

CYNTHIA Horton was asleep when she was wheeled into the OR. The anesthetist started an intravenous infusion to provide needed fluids and to keep the vein open in the event she needed a transfusion. Then he placed a mask over her face and began to administer halothane.

Meanwhile the circulating nurse dipped a long forceps, with gauze pads affixed, into a solution of soapy Provadine iodine. Then she painted Cynthia Horton's body from mid-thighs to breasts, turning her skin brown.

At four fifty-two Craig Pierson stepped up to the table. He draped the patient's body with sterile green sheets so that only her abdomen was exposed. A square foot of brown-tinted flesh was the focus of attention of the surgical team—Craig Pierson, Prince, and Carlyle. On the other side of the table, Rita Hallen selected a scalpel and passed it across the patient's body.

Craig paused for an instant before making the first incision. In previous cases the patient had always been an impersonal object. It was part of a surgeon's discipline never to permit emotions to affect judgment. Only what he saw with his own eyes should determine his actions during surgery.

Craig wished now that he had not taken that history on Cynthia Horton, or learned that they shared the kinship of adoption. She was no longer merely the subject of a surgical procedure. She had become a kindred spirit.

Perhaps he should have refused to do this procedure. But he did not wish to appear unwilling in Prince's presence. Prince was a power in the hospital, with great influence on appointments. And Craig was determined to become chief resident.

Putting all those thoughts aside, Craig Pierson lowered the scalpel and made a fine-line transverse incision in the lower abdomen of Cynthia Horton. A vertical incision would have permitted easier access, but Prince always insisted on transverse incisions, so he could boast to his patients, "You'll be able to wear a bikini and no scar will show."

Once her abdomen was open, the field was kept clear of blood by suctioning and clamping. Rita slapped an aspirating syringe into Craig's right hand. He drew up fluid from the peritoneal area and handed the syringe to one of the assisting nurses to submit to the pathologist for cytologic examination. Evidences of malignancy might be found there.

Now began the careful examination by his gloved hands of the structures in the peritoneal cavity. He could feel no mass. He felt along the surface of the liver, seeking subtle intrusions that would warn of a dangerous finding. He carried out the same careful procedure on her diaphragm. Prince's eyes asked the question; Craig's eyes answered. No lesions. No indication of malignancy.

He then searched the large and small bowels. No hint of spreading disease. He examined the omentum. No sign of disease, but the approved procedure called for him to remove this portion of the peritoneum. He severed it from the transverse colon. There was no evidence of disease between stomach and colon.

Carefully he now began to examine the lower abdominal lymph nodes, since a malignant ovarian tumor could have spread to them. None were involved.

He came now to the right ovary, where there was the palpable mass. He did not like the feel of it, hard and irregular. But it was, until identified specifically, only an intruding mass.

He looked across at Prince, who studied the offending object, then said, "Proceed!" But his eyes had rendered the verdict. Malignant.

Craig was less dogmatic in his assumptions. Or was it that he wanted to give this girl the benefit of every doubt? He must stop thinking about the girl and concentrate on that mass.

He knew what he had to do now. Unilateral right salpingo-oophorectomy was the technical term, the removal of that right ovary and the fallopian tube. The remaining ovary, if sound, would preserve her fertility. But as he carefully excised the affected ovary and tube, Craig knew that, depending on the pathologist's findings, his work might not be over..

He lifted the ovary in a surgical clamp, consigned it to the specimen container. An orderly rushed it to the pathology lab.

Craig was aware that Dr. Sam Becker was on duty there. Becker was a good man. Some surgeons accused him of being too cautious about frozen sections, always wanting to hold off on diagnoses until more definitive findings could be established in four or five days. Craig respected Becker's conservatism.

Since it would be at least fifteen minutes before Becker called with the verdict, Harvey Prince went to the phone. One of the nurses, not required to remain sterile, lifted the receiver for him. He placed three calls. One to his office. One to inform his wife that he would be late. One to his broker.

When he rejoined Craig and Burt, he said, "Market's up again. Nine points. Remember, boys—stocks, bonds, and tax-exempts. It's the only way out of this rat race."

Craig nodded, to avoid any further discussion; he was thinking of what Becker might be discovering in the lab.

Finally the phone rang. A nurse held the receiver for Prince. It was Becker in the pathology lab.

"Sam?" Prince greeted. "Well?"

"It's not easy to tell from a frozen section, Harvey. Not in this case. I sampled one block of tissue for every two centimeters of diameter of that mass. Five sections altogether."

"Very adequate. What's the verdict?" Prince persisted.

"I'd rather look at the permanent sections and give you a definitive report in four or five days," Becker said.

"Sam! I've got a patient open, on the table. I have to know!"

"Then I would say, of the three possibilities—benign, malignant, or borderline—this one is borderline. Borderline mucinous carcinoma of low malignant potential."

"Right." Prince accepted the pathologist's verdict. "What do you think we ought to do?"

"The peritoneal fluid is not suspicious. I'll have the cytology report on that in a couple of days."

"Sam!" Prince responded impatiently. "I'm asking you what you think we should do now."

Becker was usually a soft-spoken, mild-mannered man. Some

ascribed it to the nature of his specialty, having to pronounce life and death conclusions through the course of any given day. Still, Becker could be firm when a situation called for it.

"Harvey, not having seen the patient, or all the clinical information, I am not qualified to give an answer!" Becker declared.

"You say it is carcinoma. . . ." Prince tried to pin him down.

"*A borderline mucinous carcinoma of low malignant potential*," Becker repeated very carefully. "And I still want that five days."

Prince turned from the phone, allowing the nurse to hang up.

"What does Sam think?" Craig asked.

"Borderline mucinous carcinoma of low malignant potential."

"Low malignant potential. Should we bivalve, and wedge the other ovary for a biopsy? Just to be on the safe side," Craig suggested.

"To *really* be on the safe side," Prince said decisively, "we'll do a complete cleanout."

"Bilateral oophorectomy? On a girl of only twenty-two?" Craig protested. He glanced at Carlyle, whose eyes supported Craig's challenge.

Prince glared at Craig Pierson. He was not used to having his decisions disputed, especially before an entire surgical team. He said gruffly, "I've always done bilaterals in cases like this "

"But the latest findings clearly militate against a bilateral—" Craig started to say.

Prince interrupted angrily, "Are you questioning my judgment?" Then, in his most sarcastic tone, Prince delivered a scathing lecture.

"Dr. Pierson, I realize you young residents know everything there is to know about medicine and surgery. But let an old hand at this business tell you a thing or two about ovarian carcinoma. This patient has a malignancy in one ovary, and in a large percentage of such cases there is bilateral involvement, now or later. Therefore, if you want this girl to have a chance of living out her normal life span, you do a *bilateral* oophorectomy. When in doubt, take it out. Now proceed, *Doctor!*"

Craig Pierson did not move. "This girl's about to get married! She's going to want children!"

"Then let her adopt them," Prince said simply. "Now, Doctor?"

"Sorry," Craig said.

"Do I understand you refuse to follow *my* orders in relation to *my* patient?" Prince demanded.

Slowly, and well aware of the possible drastic consequences, Craig said, "I can't carry out a procedure I disagree with. I think it advisable to close her up and wait for the definitive path report. Then, only if forced to, go in and take that other ovary."

With exquisite indulgence, Prince asked, "Is that your considered professional judgment, *Doctor?*"

"Yes," Craig said, softly but very firmly.

"Then get out of my operating room!" Prince exploded.

"The schedule calls for me to assist here today," Craig said. "So I'll remain."

Prince glared at him, then assumed the position at the left side of the table. He held out his rubber-gloved hand. Rita Hallen hesitated. Burt Carlyle glanced across at Prince. For an instant Craig thought his colleague would support him. But Carlyle said nothing. Rita passed a scalpel to Prince.

The surgeon reached into Cynthia Horton's abdominal cavity and proceeded to remove her one remaining ovary neatly and with excellent technique. He completed the procedure by removing the tube as well as her now useless uterus. He turned to Carlyle and ordered curtly, "Close!"

Prince turned and strode out of the OR. Craig Pierson stared down at the specimen container waiting to be delivered to the pathology lab. No need for haste now. The lab would have five days to perform the definitive examination of both ovaries. Then they would know for certain. One thing Craig Pierson knew for certain now. In a matter of minutes Cynthia Horton had been rendered sterile, infertile, for the remainder of her life.

ATTIRED as usual in a custom-made gray flannel suit, budding red rose in his lapel, Dr. Harvey Prince came down the corridor to room 442. He knocked gently. Arthur Horton opened the door. Beyond him, Prince spied Barbara Horton sitting numbly in a large leather armchair.

Prince smiled brightly. "Cheer up, Mother! It's over with. She's going to be fine!"

Barbara Horton began to weep in relief. Her husband asked, "What did you find?"

Prince took on an air of compassion. "It was there, all right."

"Malignant?"

"Yes." Prince reassured them: "But we got it all. That girl owes her life to your Dr. Corbin. Catching it in time is the key."

"When can we see her?" Horton asked.

"She'll be in recovery for at least eight hours. But she's good as new," Prince said. "Better, in fact!"

"Thank you, Doctor. Thank you very much," Horton said.

Barbara Horton came up out of her chair and kissed Prince on the cheek. "I can't say what's in my heart, so that will have to do."

"I am deeply touched and flattered," Prince said in a great display of humility. As a seemingly minor footnote he added, "Oh, we'll have to put her on a regimen of estrogen. But that will only be a minor inconvenience."

"I've read that estrogen can cause uterine cancer!" Mrs. Horton said, alarmed.

"In Cynthia's case, nothing to worry about," Prince said, smiling. He did not explain that since he had removed all her reproductive organs, Cynthia was no longer susceptible to uterine cancer.

Neither of the Hortons thought to pursue the topic, they were so thankful to be told their daughter was safe.

IN THE dressing room up on the surgical floor, Craig Pierson removed the top of his pajamalike OR suit and hurled it against the wall. "That bastard!" he exploded.

"Cool it," Burt Carlyle said. "Prince is the attending on the case. His was the final judgment."

"When you are faced with any doubt, you just don't remove both ovaries, a procedure with irreversible consequences!" Craig shouted.

"Hold it down, Craig!" Carlyle cautioned.

"Hold it down? He left her sterile! Unable, ever, to have children! She's only twenty-two!"

"That isn't the worst thing that can happen to a woman," Carlyle pointed out.

"It is, if it didn't have to happen! He's so damn busy doing hysterectomies at two thousand dollars per, so busy entertaining trustees, that he hasn't got time to keep up on the literature. He could have at least listened to me."

"Not so. He's Harvey Prince and you're a second-year resident who challenged him in front of the whole team. He wasn't going to let you get away with it," Carlyle said. "Suppose the Horton girl has to adopt her children instead of having them. Is that so bad? You're adopted. Would you trade your folks for other parents?"

"Of course not."

"So she can have children. She just won't give birth to them."

"And the other aftereffects?" Craig asked.

"Estrogen will take care of those."

"Provided there are no complications," Craig said.

CRAIG Pierson made his early evening rounds. Then he stopped at the nurses' station to read Cynthia Horton's chart.

He studied the last entry. Prince had made a note immediately after he came down from the OR: "Path report, malignant. Performed bilateral salpingo-oophorectomy as clearly indicated. No involvement of nodes, liver, diaphragm, omentum, or other organs.

264

Patient survived procedure well. Hormonal treatment to begin on discharge. Dosage to be indicated later." Harvey Prince had signed it with a bold flourish.

Craig stared at the entry. He reached into his jacket pocket for a big black pen with a large point for broad-stroke writing. He considered carefully, then proceeded to set down in large letters: "Path report was borderline mucinous carcinoma of low malignant potential. Advised waiting definitive path report in five days. And going in again only if report warranted it. Definitely opposed bilateral procedure on the basis of preliminary path report." He underlined the last sentence. Then signed his name as boldly as Prince had signed his.

He went up to recovery to check on Cynthia Horton. Her vital signs were good. She seemed to be sleeping peacefully. Her IV, which contained a combination of fluids—sustenance and antibiotics—was functioning well.

She opened her eyes for a fleeting moment, glimpsed him standing over her. "You're fine," he said. "You're okay."

She smiled, closed her eyes, and reached for his hand. He wondered, Had Prince told the Hortons the condition she had been left in? Soon, someone would have to tell the girl herself. This was not the time, nor was he the person authorized to tell her.

Once she drifted off, he slipped out of the room.

THAT night, in Kate's apartment, Craig told her details of his dispute with Prince. And what Prince had done.

"What did Burt say?" Kate asked.

"Not much. It was just between Prince and me." Then Craig confessed, "I saw Prince's entry on her chart. So I put mine on. I want them all to know."

"Of course," Kate said. But she knew Prince was not a man to condone such an affront. "Craig," she went on gently, "medicine is carried on by human beings. You can't demand perfection of them. Most of all, it is too much to demand perfection of yourself."

"That's why I'm at the hospital," he replied. "To perfect my science. To learn how to do things so that the patient is put at the least risk while being given the best chance of recovery."

"Very noble. But even that can be carried to extremes, darling."

"What does that mean, Doctor?" he asked a bit sarcastically. "Do you detect some neurosis at work? We have here a strange young doctor. He has delusions. He thinks that we should give as much thought to our patients as we do to our stockbrokers. We should put him under restraint, before he wrecks the system!"

Now it was Kate's turn to be offended. "There's nothing wrong in striving for perfection. What is wrong is your reaction when you or some other doctor fails to achieve it."

"What do you want me to do? Call Prince now, apologize? After all, I almost deprived him of his quota of errors in judgment for the week. Kate, do you know how that girl is going to feel when she finds out? It's a hell of a way to enter into marriage. Which reminds me—"

"Don't," Kate warned. "I haven't made up my mind yet."

"Okay." Craig embraced her. She was soft, warm. One would never suspect that she could be so tough with him when the occasion demanded.

"Doctor, I love you," he said. "Do you ever have affairs with your patients?"

"Only in exceptional cases," she said, and she kissed him.

CHAPTER FOUR

AT SIX fifteen in the morning Craig was making his early rounds. He had examined all charts to see if changes had occurred in any patients during the night and noted that Cynthia Horton had been brought down from recovery. He decided to see her last, before reporting to the OR.

He eased the door open softly. In a weak voice Cynthia called out, "Dr. Prince?" She turned and faced him. "Oh. Come in, Dr. Pierson."

He took her pulse to see how she was reacting, emotionally as well as physically. He was rewarded with a steady, if weak, beat. He examined the area of the surgery. No distension. No sign of complications.

"Was Dr. Prince by last night?" he asked.

"I don't know. I was asleep, except that moment when you came by," she said. "What . . . did they find? Was it . . . ?"

"Only borderline. And it's all been removed."

"All?" she asked, searching his eyes. "It's very important to know exactly what he found," she said with solemn intensity. "I want to be honest with Pete."

"There was borderline cancer. . . ."

"I knew it," she said. "I knew it."

"Of *low* malignant potential. Which means that it was not invasive. We found no involvement of surrounding tissue. None! Cynthia, you can live a long and healthy life. I'm sure Dr. Prince will explain it all to you."

As he was leaving, Cynthia asked, "You're sure they got it all?"

"They got it all," he said, responding to her specific question, careful not to breach his ethical obligation to her surgeon.

He slunk down the corridor, feeling like a charlatan. His beeper sounded, and he made his way to the phone to pick up his call.

"Pierson?" a deep voice asked. It was Professor Clinton Ordway, chief of the ob-gyn department. "I wonder if you could drop by my office."

"I'm on my way up to the OR, sir," Craig explained. "I'm scheduled to assist."

"That can wait," Ordway said.

CLINTON Ordway was tall, white-haired, imposing. He had been an excellent gynecologist, but for the past decade, since becoming chief of the department, he had devoted himself to administrative duties. He had become skilled at recruiting new men, advancing research, dealing with trustees. Ordway's was the best-funded department in the hospital. In a time of stringent budgets, that was no small achievement.

The chief greeted Craig a bit less amiably than usual and gestured him to a chair. Ordway remained standing.

"Pierson, last evening I happened to be at dinner in Harvey Prince's home. He took me aside and said he did not intend to countenance insubordination from a second-year resident. Now, if you will, tell me exactly what happened."

Craig Pierson recounted the events in the OR. When he had finished, Ordway remained thoughtful for a moment.

"You deemed your judgment superior to his? Harvey Prince has done more of these procedures than you are likely to do in the next ten years."

"If I may, sir," Craig said, realizing his conduct had already been judged and condemned. "Dr. Prince is the most skillful surgeon I've ever scrubbed with. But he may be a little too busy. I've read about cases like this, and only the diseased ovary is excised, unless the final path report clearly indicates a bilateral. That way there's a chance of preserving the woman's childbearing ability. That's all I was suggesting. Wait for the final report. Then go back in if necessary."

"And be accused of doing two operations instead of one?" Ordway asked. "You can't pick up a newspaper without seeing the medical profession under attack for unnecessary surgery!"

"Dr. Ordway," Craig responded, "Prince's decision was made in minutes. But that girl will live with the consequences the rest of her life. I had to voice my opinion before the damage was done."

"So now it's 'damage'?" Ordway seized on Craig's word. "Pierson, before you go making irresponsible charges, I think it would be wise for you to look at Dr. Prince's record. I must accept his judgment over that of a resident."

Craig Pierson confined himself to a respectful "Yes, sir."

"Now, I'll try to find some way of patching up things with Prince. And it wouldn't do any harm if you apologized to him. After all, I wouldn't want Prince's feelings about you to become a factor when I designate my chief resident for next year."

It was phrased as a promise, but Craig recognized it for what it was, a subtle threat.

At that moment one of the phones on Ordway's desk rang.

"Nelly, I told you, no calls. . . . Oh, put him on." Ordway held his hand over the mouthpiece. "Prince. Maybe I can pave the way for your apology." He greeted him heartily. "Good morning, Harve. Great party last—"

But it was evident from the abashed look on Ordway's face that Prince was assaulting him with a tirade.

"Yes, Harvey. Yes, I understand," he finally said grimly. "I'll deal with it. Don't worry." He hung up.

"Pierson, last night did you make a note on the Horton girl's chart that disagreed with Prince's note?"

"Yes, sir," Craig admitted.

Ordway made no effort to disguise his fury. "Patients' charts are not a battleground on which conflicts between doctors are fought. Disagreeing with Prince in the OR was foolish enough. But making that note . . ." His anger exceeded his ability to express it. "I'll see what I can do to repair the damage. But Pierson, you must apologize to Prince!"

IF THERE was one post on which Craig had set his heart, it was chief resident in his third year. But was it possible, Craig had to ask himself, that by marking the chart, he had put not only the chief residency but the remainder of his residency in jeopardy? He began to regret his bold note on the Horton chart. He stopped at the floor desk to see how bad it looked in the cold light of day. He glanced at the page. His note was no longer there.

Prince's orders and his postop report were all there. Only Craig's entry was missing. He realized that Prince had removed the original page and written a new one.

He called Ordway at once. Ordway was not surprised. "Yes, I know. Prince decided to give you another chance. Decent of him. Any other man might have been vindictive."

Craig hung up, disturbed that a chart could be altered. Yet he had to admit feeling relieved as well. His residency did not seem so shaky now. It had been a close brush.

SOON after talking with Craig, Dr. Ordway closeted himself in his office and called Sam Becker. "Sam? Do you remember the biopsy you did on a patient named Horton late yesterday?"

"Yes. Frozen section. We'll have the paraffin block and the final report in four days," Becker informed him.

"What did that frozen section show?"

"Borderline mucinous carcinoma, low malignant potential."

"You reported that to Dr. Prince?"

"Of course."

"Tell me, Sam, do you recall what he said, if anything?"

"He asked what I would recommend. It happens all the time. On the close ones, the surgeon wants a lead. And I have to tell them, all I know is what that bit of tissue tells me. And a frozen section isn't always definitive."

"Of course," Ordway said. "Sam, the second ovary—did you examine that too?"

"Frozen section."

"And?"

"Absolutely clean, tumor-free."

"IT WAS necessary," Dr. Harvey Prince explained gravely. Barbara Horton sat in the big leather chair; her husband was balanced on the arm. Cynthia, white-faced, sat up in bed, her violet eyes staring. Peter Tompkins stood by her side.

"Necessary?" Barbara Horton asked numbly.

"I take no chances with ovarian cancer. If one of those masses spreads, even a little, it can be deadly."

He turned to Cynthia. "My dear, I want you to know that it didn't spread at all. It was removed. Totally. To be absolutely certain that you could live a long healthy life, it was necessary to do what I just described. Now, you'll spend a week here, another two weeks recuperating at home, and then you'll be free to pursue all your plans, including marrying this fine young man."

Prince smiled benignly, as if he had bestowed a gift upon the patient. Cynthia continued to stare. "Explain it to me. How will it affect me?"

"Aside from not having children of your own, it won't affect you at all. You can get married and live a perfectly normal life. When you decide you'd like a family, you simply adopt. In fact, that way you can be sure of having healthy babies, without the dangers and difficulties of pregnancy."

Prince continued, "Of course, we'll have to assist nature a bit. Any aftereffects can be counteracted by hormonal supplements, estrogens. Used within limits, of course. I'll get you started on a regimen in a few days."

270

"I see," Cynthia said. But it was evident that she was beyond seeing or understanding, and far from accepting.

Prince departed. Cynthia's mother bent over, kissed her daughter on the cheek. "Thank God, everything's going to be all right."

Decisively Cynthia said, "Mother, Dad, I'd like to talk to Pete. Alone."

"Of course, darling," Mrs. Horton acquiesced. She and her husband left the room.

The moment the door whisked shut, Pete embraced Cynthia, kissed her. She allowed him only her cheek. She was intent on having her say.

"Pete, darling," she began, "you're free to end it here and now. I will understand. You agreed to marry a whole, healthy girl. You're entitled to children of your own."

"I want *you*. The way you are," he insisted, embracing her again. "You have no idea what I've gone through the last few days. I thought, She'll never make it. I'm not lucky enough to have her. What have I ever done to deserve a girl like her?"

Cynthia wept softly, pressing her wet face against his cheek.

"You won't ever have regrets?"

"Never! I swear, never!"

"I'm not the same as I was, not the same," she said emptily.

"I want you the way you are." He kissed her again, trying to stop her tears. "We're two very lucky people. It could have been worse. A lot worse. I'll settle for this, now and for all time!"

271

When he could not stanch her tears, he went out to find her mother. "Talk to her," he implored. "She'll believe you. The wedding is still on. Everything is the same! Make her believe that!"

In Cynthia's room, Barbara Horton wiped her daughter's eyes, brushed her lustrous black hair as she talked. "Pete wants the wedding, if anything, more now than before."

"What if he wants children of our own?"

"You think your father loves me less because I didn't bear you? I doubt that. A girl as fine as you? No child of our own could have pleased us more."

Barbara Horton held her daughter in a warm embrace. "Now take a nap. You need your rest."

She kissed Cynthia again and slipped out of the room.

CRAIG came to the end of another tough, tiring day. He looked forward to dinner with Kate.

He was about to ring her when his beeper paged him. He picked up the phone at the nurses' station. "Pierson," he reported in.

"Cynthia Horton calling," the operator said.

He took the call. "Cynthia? Something wrong?"

"I just want to talk to you. Could you come see me?"

"Be right there," he assured her, for he detected from her voice that her problem was less physical than emotional.

When he entered her room, she stared at him, her violet eyes quite fixed and penetrating. "Close the door? Just on the chance that he's passing by."

"He?"

"Dr. Prince."

"Oh," he said, wondering if she had heard of his disagreement with Prince. "If there's something you want to discuss, you should do it with Dr. Prince. I'm just a resident."

"There are things I don't think Dr. Prince is telling me."

"Such as?" Craig asked cautiously.

"If he had to do to me what he did, it can't be as trivial as he makes it sound, or the occasion for so much smiling."

"The surgery is over, the patient is doing well. Every time we discover malignancy this early and remove it completely, we feel

272

lucky. That's a reason to smile." He hated himself for trying to explain away Prince's unctuous bedside manner.

"There's something Prince keeps passing over very lightly, and I don't understand it."

"Ask him. Most patients are afraid if they ask the doctor too many questions, he'll resent them. So they just go on worrying silently. No need. Medicine isn't practiced that way these days."

"Okay, then," she challenged. "*You* tell me. He talked about hormones, estrogens. I thought estrogens were for older women. Women in menopause."

"True," Craig said, realizing that Prince had not fully explained her situation to her.

"I'm only twenty-two. Why would I need estrogens?"

Craig hesitated. "The ovaries not only have to do with the reproductive processes. They also manufacture the female hormones. When they are removed, the doctor can make up for that by prescribing supplements. Estrogen."

She was pensive for a moment, then said softly, "If only Prince didn't smile so much."

"I just told you the truth, and I'm not smiling," Craig said; then he broke into a small grin.

She tried to smile back. Instead her eyes filled with tears. "I thought he was holding back something terrible."

To avoid responding to her declaration, he said instead, "I think you should be up on your feet. At least for a little walk around this room. Let's try it."

She pushed back the coverlet. He was relieved to see she was wearing the white elastic stockings the hospital rules prescribed to minimize circulatory complications. She let her legs down carefully over the side of the bed. There was a moment of dizziness. Craig reached out to help her. She began to walk slowly across the room and back.

"I'll write orders on your chart. But even if the nurses fail to remind you, I want you up and walking at least half a dozen times a day. It's good for you."

He did not explain any further. The chances were excellent that he would never have to explain his real concern to her at all.

When she had walked sufficiently, he gestured her back to bed. Once she was settled, he said, "If you have any questions, don't hesitate to have me called. Understand?"

She nodded, smiling for the first time.

At the door, he felt compelled to stop and caution, "If you feel any pain, especially in your legs, or notice any swelling, tell the nurse to get hold of me at once."

"All right," she said.

On his way past the nurses' station he paused to look at her chart. Her temperature had.been checked just before dinner. Normal. He must check it again in the morning.

Though the possibility of what he feared was small, he would not rest easy until she was past any possible danger.

CRAIG had fully intended to leave the hospital at once. But his sense of foreboding made him go to the path lab on the fifth floor. He caught Becker at the door, ready to leave.

"Sam, got a minute? It's important," Craig insisted.

An experienced pathologist who had seen hundreds of residents come and go, Sam Becker had his favorites, those few who, he could sense, would become the most dedicated doctors of the future. Craig Pierson, alert, willing to learn, with exacting standards of performance, was one of Sam's favorites.

"Okay, Craig, what is it?" Sam tossed his hat toward a chair.

"The Horton girl," Craig identified. "A case of Prince's. Bilateral salpingo-oophorectomy."

"Oh, that one," Sam said. "On frozen section it was borderline. It was confirmed later."

"That was the right ovary. What about the left one?"

"The left one." Sam Becker considered. "Yes. I'll look it up." Sam pretended to search his records, all the while saying to himself, Damn it, for his sake I wish he hadn't asked me.

"Well?" Craig prodded when Sam found the record.

"The left ovary was clean. No sign of tumor."

"The arrogant bastard!" Craig reacted exactly as Sam had anticipated. "Sam, you're going to present this at the path conference tomorrow, aren't you?"

274

"Another ovarian carcinoma, another bilateral." Sam tried to pass it off.

"This is not just another!" Craig said angrily. "This is a young girl who might live fifty years with the mistake of a doctor who should have known better!"

"Let's get out of here. I don't want us to be seen discussing this."

Soon they were walking along the quiet, dark street that led away from the hospital.

"What I say now, kid, I do not want repeated," said Becker. "If it is, I will deny it. Understand?"

"Understand," Craig agreed.

"You're agitated about the Horton case. I am agitated about hundreds of Prince's cases. He does a better, quicker hysterectomy than any other surgeon in the city. He should, he does so many. Needless ones. Sometimes I think he calls his accountant and asks, 'How much do I need to make my quota for the year?'"

"Don't you ever say anything?" Craig demanded.

"A pathologist is not a policeman, he is a researcher, called upon to deliver an opinion. He does not decide on therapy. Afterward, any discussion as to whether what was done was right or wrong is up to other surgeons. To the chief of the department."

"Ordway . . ." Craig considered.

"Ordway's job is to keep the ob-gyn department running. And he does. It's a good department, better than most I know of."

"It's his job to be a policeman," Craig reminded him.

"But not *yours*," Sam Becker said. "Craig, this is not your battle. Don't fight it. All that can happen is that you'll endanger your career, possibly destroy it, and nothing will change."

"Something has to change!" Craig insisted.

"My boy, you're up against a medical windmill. And you are Don Quixote. The big difference is this: Don Quixote was an old man, at the end of his life. You're at the beginning of your career. Don't ruin it. Because we need doctors like you. Doctors who care. For *your* sake, I would prefer not to discuss this case at the path conference."

They had reached Becker's apartment house, only a few blocks from the hospital. "Discuss it, Sam!" Craig urged.

"I would rather not."

"If you won't introduce the case, I'll ask for it!" Craig insisted.

Becker finally relented. "I'll bring those slides to the conference. But think about what I said. Think about the patients you'll be abandoning to men like Prince if you get yourself kicked out."

CRAIG was an hour late arriving at Kate's apartment. But there were no recriminations. She deduced from the weary set of his posture that he needed her.

She mixed him a drink. "A psychiatrist can tell by the way the patient enters the office whether he has big troubles or little ones. And tonight my patient has very big trouble. Talk!"

He related his conversation with Sam Becker.

"Sam's a good man," she said. "If you got into a jam, he'd stand by you."

"I know that. So is that why he's urging me not to press this? Because it will put him on the spot?"

"Craig, darling, instead of trying to find selfish motives, grant Sam the courtesy of believing him. You get a reputation for being a troublemaker, you'll never become chief resident."

"So you agree with Sam."

"If I thought you could keep quiet about this and live with yourself, I'd say Sam is right. But you'd eat yourself up. So, do what you have to do. I'll be with you all the way." She kissed him full on the mouth.

DINNER and the white wine were long gone. But Kate still sensed his tension. "What are you thinking about?" she asked.

"Possibilities. Cynthia's possibilities."

"Prince'll put her on estrogen. She'll get married."

"What's bugging me is, what happens if they *can't* put her on estrogen? Because of some complication?"

"If she can't have estrogen—" Kate stopped abruptly.

"Exactly," Craig said. "She'd have a premature menopause. And everything that goes with it. Flushes. Aging effects on her skin. Possible pain and bleeding on intercourse. What kind of marriage would those two have under such conditions? Prince hasn't just removed her ovaries, he's exposed her to terrible possibilities."

"The chances of her developing postop complications are small," Kate consoled.

"No postop patient is immune from a thrombosis. That's why we put elastic stockings on them and have them walk. If we're lucky, she'll get through it all right. But for some days she'll be at risk."

Kate was silent for a time, meditative.

"What, Katie?"

"When I interned at Parkside, we had a girl with premature menopause. No psychiatrist could treat her. Not even the chief."

"What happened?".

"She signed herself out against advice. Two weeks later she committed suicide."

CHAPTER FIVE

INTERNS, residents, and staff physicians were gathering for the weekly ob-gyn pathology conference. Professor Ordway was a martinet about the presence of all staff ob-gyn surgeons at such meetings. Attending physicians, whose practice took them outside the hospital, made an effort to show up when convenient. For there was always the inherent threat that if they became too lax, their hospital privileges might be canceled.

The only man who seemed exempt from the conferences was Harvey Prince. Between Prince's office practice and his demanding surgery, it was unreasonable to expect his attendance on any regular basis. Besides, Ordway was unable to insist, since Prince was an intimate of several members of the board of trustees. Therefore it was no surprise to Craig Pierson that Prince was not in attendance today.

Ordway gave a signal to open the conference. The room was darkened. Dr. Sam Becker sat beside the slide projector.

His first set of slides involved a case of carcinoma of the cervix. The patient was twenty-eight. Her history followed the classic characteristics of such cancers, including early sexual activity and a history of venereal disease. On the basis of the high incidence of cervical carcinoma in prostitutes and the very low incidence in nuns, it was presumed that there was some causal relationship in promiscuous sexual activity, that a cancer virus might be passed on in the same way as venereal disease.

Becker completed his presentation of the case. The patient's gynecologist outlined the course he had followed. Since she was beyond surgical repair, she was to receive radiation therapy. Her prognosis was guarded. Regretfully he concluded, "This is a classic case of neglect. If she had exercised concern for her health and gone for regular checkups, this would have been picked up early. She'd have had an excellent chance for recovery."

Becker presented three more cases, projecting his slides, calling attention to affected tissue. The surgeons involved described patient, symptoms, diagnosis, and treatment.

"It's getting late," Ordway reminded the meeting.

Sam Becker said, "There's only one more case." He presented the slides of Cynthia Horton's biopsies. In his usual thorough manner he pointed out the sections he had sampled.

Ordway announced, "Since the surgeon in charge of the case is not present, we should postpone discussion." He rose abruptly from his chair, his signal that the conference was over.

Despite that part of him which warned against it, Craig Pierson blurted out, "I assisted at that operation! In fact I removed the ovarian tumor. I would like to report on the case now."

Ordway glared at Craig. Becker's eyes pleaded with him. Burt Carlyle's barely noticeable shake of the head tried to dissuade him. Craig would not relent. Finally Ordway yielded. "All right, Pierson, if it won't take too long."

"The slides, please!"

The room dark again, Becker projected the slides of the diseased ovary as before, pointing out the affected areas.

"Dr. Becker, do you have the slides on the other ovary removed from the same patient?"

Becker inserted those slides and was forced to point out the absence of any finding of tumor cells.

"Dr. Becker," Craig persisted, "wouldn't it have been possible to arrive at the same conclusion—that the left was clean—if the

278

surgeon had not removed that ovary but had presented you with a wedged sample?"

Becker decided, for Craig's sake, to sidestep the issue. "That," he said, "is a decision to be made by a surgeon, not a pathologist."

Ordway seized the moment to dismiss the entire episode lightly. "Pierson has just given us a perfect illustration of the practice of medicine with the aid of that infallible diagnostic tool known as the hindsight scan."

There was laughter. Craig expected that Burt Carlyle might point out that it was not hindsight. But Burt remained silent.

Ordway ended the meeting. "I understand the patient has an excellent chance for long-term survival. Now I think we'd best get back to our jobs."

CRAIG Pierson and Burt Carlyle left the conference room together. "Craig, what were you trying to accomplish?" Burt said angrily as they strode down the corridor. "You lost that battle the moment Prince decided to do a bilateral."

"He was wrong. Wrong!" Craig stopped and confronted Carlyle. "You didn't agree with Prince. I could see it in your eyes!"

"I don't agree with lots of things I see in surgery," Carlyle said. "But I don't make a public issue of them. All I say to myself is, Learn from mistakes. Who does a greater number of cases than Prince? So from whom can you learn most? Even from his mistakes? Prince!"

Aware that passersby were staring, Burt lowered his voice. "Craig, follow Ordway's advice. Apologize to Prince. Before he kicks you off his scrub team. You'll never get a chance to assist on as many interesting cases with any other man."

"And who apologizes to the girl in 442?" Craig said bitterly.

Burt lost his patience. "Don't be a fool! One thing I learned in my internship was never to allow any one case, any one mistake, to loom that large. Go to Prince. Apologize. For your own sake."

At that moment Craig's beeper sounded insistently. When he reached a phone, he was startled to hear his mother's voice. Quite upset, but apologetic about interrupting him at the hospital.

"What's wrong, Mom?"

"It's Dad. Yesterday he was cutting branches off a tall pine and he . . . he fell. They took him to the hospital."

"It was that bad?"

"We don't know. They haven't finished all the tests."

"Which hospital?" Craig asked.

"Good Samaritan." She added, "Sorry to bother you, son. I know how busy you are. But I'm frightened." She began to weep.

"Mom, take it easy. It might be nothing. I'll call the hospital and find out."

He called Good Samaritan and reached the doctor treating his father. "Dr. Halloran? Dr. Pierson, State University Hospital. I understand you admitted my father yesterday. William Pierson."

"Oh, he did mention he had a son who was a doctor. Yes, we admitted him for observation."

"And?"

"So far we find a concussion. And a comminuted fracture of the right elbow. We're doing more testing, possibly even a brain scan, to make sure it's nothing more."

"Maybe I ought to be there."

"It wouldn't hurt. His right arm is going to be virtually immobile. He won't believe me, so perhaps it would be a good idea for you to come."

"I'll work it out," Craig promised.

He called Kate, then tracked down Ordway, who was quick to grant him three days off. Burt Carlyle would cover for him.

Ordway was relieved to have Craig away from the hospital for a few days. By the time he returned, the whole affair should have blown over. Prince was too valuable to the department to antagonize, and Pierson was too good a resident to lose. Ordway looked upon the family emergency as a fortuitous event.

THE next morning Craig flew home. He took a taxi from the airport directly to Good Samaritan, without calling his mother. Halloran would be completely frank with him alone.

Halloran turned out to be a second-year resident. His first remark was a question. "Pierson, what's a man with a history of coronary disease doing climbing trees and sawing limbs?"

"Coronary disease?" Craig asked, startled.

"Take a look at his cardiogram. I had one taken. Just on a hunch." Halloran spread out the EKG tape. "There, and there, and there. Clear evidence of a coronary episode. Didn't you know?"

"Of course not."

"A man seventy-one, with a history like this, and then that fall." Halloran shook his head sadly. "He's got to quit."

"He wouldn't know how," Craig said. "Where is he?"

"Sixth floor. Semiprivate."

It was a small bare room, with hardly enough space to pass between the two beds. His father was fixed in a ninety-degree posterior splint, elevated, and in ice packs. His gray hair was disheveled and he had a stubbly two-day growth of beard.

When he saw Craig in the doorway, his eyes filmed over with gratitude and pride. "Craig . . . what are you doing here?"

"What happened, Dad?"

"Oh, this." He glanced disparagingly at his splint. "Nothing. They made such a fuss, like I got hurt real bad. It was a mistake to tell them my son was a doctor."

"Dad," Craig interrupted, "why didn't you tell me you had a heart attack before?"

"Who said—" the old man started to protest.

"I saw it. On the EKG."

"Oh, that. That's over with. . . . I mean—"

"When? How? Did you tell Mom?"

"Nothing happened. I had a little indigestion. So I stayed home from work for a few days. But that's no heart attack."

"Dad," Craig said, calling him to account, "I've told you a thousand times, if you feel bad, no matter what you think, let me know. I'm the doctor, not you."

"Okay, next time I'll call," his father grudgingly consented.

"We're going to make sure there is no next time." Craig was taking command. "No more work. Sell the business. Give it away. But no more, Dad. It's time to stop."

"What'll I do?" the old man lamented.

"Don't worry. I'll take care of Mom and you."

"All my life I've been on my own. Now to be a burden to my

son . . . That's some way for a man to end his days." The tears in his eyes spilled over.

Craig embraced him. "You're not a burden, Dad. . . . Dad, don't cry. It's all right."

"To tell the truth, the business isn't worth anything. I can't sell it. I tried. There are not many customers anymore. . . ."

"Dad, why didn't you tell me? There are things more important than pride!" Craig exploded.

"Like what?" his father asked, brushing the tears from his eyes. "To my generation, without pride a man is nothing."

"Of course, Dad," Craig said softly. "I understand. Now rest— take it easy. And give this a chance to heal."

"Are you leaving today?" his father asked hesitantly.

"No, I've arranged for a few days off."

"Good . . . good. I'll feel better knowing you're here. I think of your mother alone in that house. I worry about her."

"She'll be okay, Dad. I'll talk to her. Maybe it's time you both moved south. A warmer climate, a nice condominium," he suggested, wondering where he could get the money for such a luxury.

IT HAD been almost a year since Craig had last come back to the two-story frame house where he had lived most of his life. The tasteful and abundant shrubbery set it off from the other modest homes on the block. He walked up onto the porch, where the boards still creaked in the same places. Before he could open the door, his mother was there. She flung her arms around him.

"He's okay, Mom. I stopped at the hospital and he's doing fine."

"What did they say?" she asked anxiously as they went inside.

"He'll be all right. But I told him he won't be able to work anymore. He broke his elbow, so he can't use his right arm the way he used to."

A worried look creased her thin face. "Will he do it? Retire?"

"He has to," Craig insisted.

"You know . . . business hasn't been so good lately."

"He told me."

"It must have been painful for him. He had such dreams. In years gone by he would promise me that when you were through

282

medical school and he didn't have all those bills to pay, the business could run by itself. We could live comfortably, take vacations. But in the last five or six years things have got worse. It's been a struggle."

She did not say it, but it was clear it had been a great hardship for them to see him through school. Impulsively he put his arms around his mother and held her close. "Mom, did you know he had had a heart attack?"

"No." She leaned back from Craig and looked up into his eyes fearfully. "Is that why he fell?"

"Before that. Months ago."

"He never told me. Once . . . he complained of a bad upset stomach. He was in bed for a few days. . . ."

"That was the time."

"Heart attack . . ." she whispered breathlessly. "He can't go back to work. No matter what he says! But what will—"

"You'll sell the house. And move down south. It'll be better there."

"And the . . . the money?"

"I'll take care of the money," Craig assured her. "The main thing is, you have to convince him that going south is best."

The phone rang, and as it did, she remembered. "Oh, a girl called. Her name was Kate something."

He answered the phone.

"Craig?"

"Yes, Kate?"

"How is he?"

Craig reported what he had found.

"Then it's not all so serious. Good!" Kate sounded relieved. "When are you coming back?"

The question alerted Craig. Kate was too self-sufficient to become concerned about his return after only a day.

"In two days. Why? What is it?"

She hesitated. "Prince. He heard about the path conference. He considers it an attack on his reputation. The air around here is not good. Not good at all. So, as soon as things at home permit, come back, Craig."

HARVEY PRINCE had had a long, profitable day in the operating room. He had been silent, not his usual loquacious self. He did not joke with the residents or flirt with the student nurses.

He had arranged a meeting with Clinton Ordway in the office of Walter Deering, hospital administrator. The meeting was set for five o'clock, to accommodate Prince's crowded schedule. At four forty-five, almost finished with the fourth hysterectomy he had done this day, Prince turned to Burt Carlyle and said curtly, "Close!" He walked briskly out of the OR.

He showered, dressed in one of his gray flannel suits, affixed the budding rose in his lapel. He rode down in the elevator, rehearsing how he would begin the meeting. By the time he opened Deering's door, Harvey Prince was prepared.

His first words were preceded by a sigh of weariness. "It's been a rugged day, gentlemen. A man should not have to go through such a day and then be troubled by meetings such as this."

Used to Prince's theatrics, Deering and Ordway said nothing.

"However," Prince continued, launching into the attack, "this is an urgent matter. Mind you, I don't raise this question on my own behalf. After all, what difference does it make to my career if some pompous young resident attacks me?

"It's this hospital I'm concerned about! If we get a reputation for permitting insubordinate residents to attack other doctors, we run grave risks. Good men will go to other hospitals.

"But more important is this: if you permit residents to carry on open criticism, and that gets back to patients, you are opening the door to a tidal wave of malpractice suits. Things are bad enough, with greedy lawyers seeking to pounce on dissatisfied patients. Hand them such a weapon as another doctor's opinion that something was done that harmed a patient—what a field day for them!"

Both Ordway and Deering nodded in grim agreement.

"Well, the best way to end this is simply to end it," Prince suggested. "Being a surgeon, I approach every problem the same way. When in doubt, take it out!"

"Exactly what are you suggesting, Harve?" Deering asked.

"Get him to resign! And if he won't, fire him!"

Ordway sought to temporize: "Perhaps there's some other way. Why not refuse to have him scrub with you? I could have Carlyle arrange the schedule to accomplish that."

"I do not want Pierson to have any contact at all with my patients!" Prince declared.

"Even that could be arranged," Ordway agreed quickly. "Harvey, aren't you condemning Pierson on the basis of a single case? He's never been insubordinate before."

"If it happened once, it can happen again. We can't let him get away with it," Prince insisted.

When neither Ordway nor Deering picked up the cue, Prince continued, "As I was saying to Gus Wankel on Sunday when we were climbing up to the ninth tee, I said, 'Gus, as a trustee, you ought to look into things at the hospital. Not just go to board meetings. Get to know the place firsthand.'"

Prince had made clear that his social relationship with several trustees gave great weight to any suggestion he made. Both Ordway's job as chief and Deering's as administrator depended on the favor of the trustees.

"Harve, I give you my word, we'll discuss it and take some steps," Deering promised.

THERE was a note in Craig Pierson's box when he returned to the city. It was a message from Clinton Ordway: "See me!"

He had no trouble reaching Ordway, who broke out of a meeting to see him. The chief ushered him into a small side room.

"Pierson, this has become most serious!" Ordway began. "When you disagreed with Prince in the OR, I gave you my best advice:

apologize. You chose to ignore that. To make matters worse, before the entire staff in the path conference you questioned Prince's judgment. Now it comes down to this: he wants your resignation."

Craig stared hard at Ordway.

"I think Deering and I were able to satisfy him with less. You are not to be assigned to scrub with him again. And he does not want you to have contact with any of his patients at any time!"

Craig realized, as did Ordway, that this decision excluded him from a great number of patients on the ob-gyn service.

"The way I have arranged things," Ordway said, "I'll have Carlyle assign you more heavily to the wards and gyn emergency for the rest of the year. You can still scrub with some of the other men," he added.

Ordway was trying to let him down as easily as he could, and Craig appreciated the chief's concern. But at the same time, Ordway was making it clear that Craig would not become chief resident. It was even questionable whether he should stay on to become a senior resident.

"Pierson, because I respect you, I want to give you some advice. Let us say, for the sake of argument, that you were right and Prince was wrong. Let us say that not only were you right but you could prove it. Think of the harm you might be doing that girl by making a cause of this thing. Put yourself in her position. Deprived of ever bearing children through an avoidable error in judgment. That would be far worse for her than if this condition were *un*avoidable. Think about it."

Craig did not respond at once.

"And think of other doctors," Ordway suggested. "What surgeon wants a resident looking over his shoulder second-guessing his every move? Who wants a man around today who tomorrow might testify against him in a malpractice suit? You may be destroying your career before it gets started."

Ordway paused to allow his warning to sink in. "I think, with Prince, deep down, it's a matter of vanity. So massage his ego a little. It may not be too late to apologize. Of course he'll gloat, spread it around the hospital. But try it. After all, you can still learn a lot of surgery from him."

286

CRAIG CALLED Kate and asked her to meet him for coffee in the hospital cafeteria. She was late. It gave him time to consider what Ordway had said. The most significant point was the irrefutable fact that it would do Cynthia Horton no good to create an issue now.

By the time Kate arrived, his mind was made up.

He kissed her. In times of stress he knew how much he needed her. "Kate, the trip home gave me a chance to think. My dad won't be able to work any longer, and . . ."

"Tell me."

"It's . . . it's Prince. It's what happens to me if I can't stay on to complete my residency. The least I can do is relieve my dad of financial worries. I have no right to jeopardize everything they worked for, sacrificed for."

"So you've decided to apologize to Prince?" she guessed.

"The alternative would be to leave here. But where does a man go to finish his residency? Hospitals ask questions. Ordway's right. What hospital is going to want a resident who'll be looking over shoulders, watching for mistakes?"

Kate just stared at him. "How are you going to tell Prince?"

"The simplest way. Just say, 'I've thought it over; you've had far more experience than I, your judgment must have been better. My way might have necessitated a second operation. A second risk.'" He kept improvising, gave up. "I'll find some way."

"Craig, however you decide to say it, first make sure it's something you want to say."

He looked at her, then admitted, "It won't be easy."

"Whatever you do, do it for Craig Pierson. Because you're a man with a troublesome conscience. That's what I love about you."

CRAIG called the OR and found that Prince had a heavy schedule. An exenteration and three hysterectomies. Craig felt a sudden surge of envy, because Burt would probably do the exenteration. Unless he could patch things up with Prince, he would never realize that opportunity.

While waiting for Prince to come down from the OR, he examined patients' charts to learn what changes had taken place in his three-day absence. He was on his way to check on a postop patient when his beeper sounded.

The operator had a message. "The patient in 442 would like to see you."

He hung up, determined to ignore the message until he had straightened things out with Prince. But Craig did go back and consult Cynthia Horton's chart. Her signs were stable. There seemed no reason to antagonize Prince by seeing her.

The phone rang at the nurses' station. The nurse said, "For you, Doctor."

"Dr. Pierson?" He recognized Cynthia's voice. "Could you come see me? Just for a minute?"

"I'm rather busy," he improvised. "If there's something you want to ask, perhaps I could tell you over the phone."

"Remember the last day you were in to see me? You made me get out of bed and walk. And you examined me, especially my thighs. Well, now there's something about my right thigh that *is* different."

"How is it different?"

"It burns. Feels very warm."

"Warm?" He considered, cautious, trying to avoid the speculations that word invited. "Okay. Don't worry, I'll . . . I'll call you back." He hung up, turned to Veronica Ryan, chief floor nurse. "Ronnie, go into 442 and get me a temp."

Ryan stared at him, aware of Prince's orders forbidding Craig to see any of his patients.

"Ronnie! Do it! It's important!" Craig ordered.

He waited anxiously until Ryan returned. "Well?"

"A hundred point nine. Shall we put her back on antibiotics?"

"This may be more than an infection—a lot more. Call up to the OR. Find out how long Prince and Burt will be."

When she hung up, she informed him, "They're closing up one hysterectomy and have two more to go."

That would mean three hours at least. Time that could have long-lasting, even fatal consequences. He decided, To hell with Prince's prohibition.

He went into 442. He threw back the coverlet on Cynthia Hor-

288

ton's bed, drew down her elastic stockings, and pressed her legs. He detected a swelling on her right thigh, at the place where she complained of the burning sensation. He flexed her right foot upward. She reacted in pain. That, and the slight swelling, reinforced his suspicion of a thrombosis. There was only one way to make absolutely sure.

He went out to see Ryan. "Get Miss Horton onto a gurney and up to X ray. I'll call ahead and arrange for a venogram."

The look on Veronica Ryan's face demanded an explanation.

"Someone has to do something stat. I'll take the consequences."

By THE time Cynthia Horton was wheeled into the X-ray room, Dr. Romano, the radiologist, was ready. He filled a large hypodermic with dye and injected it. The X-ray technician took the films Craig ordered. Cynthia Horton lay on the table, submitting rigidly to the painless procedure.

Craig had an orderly return Cynthia to Ryan's care. Then he joined Dr. Romano in the viewing room. They moved slowly along the line of films. Romano took a red marking crayon out of his pocket and drew a circle around a dark shadow on one plate.

"There it is," Romano said. "No question."

"Thrombus. I'd better start her on an anticoagulant immediately," Craig said gravely.

"Absolutely. Unless you want to risk a pulmonary embolus."

Within ten minutes Craig Pierson had given Cynthia Horton her first injection of heparin. On her chart he wrote out dosage instructions, and ordered that she was not to be released from the hospital for ten days. That done, he proceeded with his other duties. But he was constantly nagged by the possible complications of what he had discovered. All he could do was wait and hope the patient would respond.

It WAS late afternoon when Barbara Horton came to visit her daughter. She had brought a small overnight case in preparation for Cynthia's release. She inquired at the desk what time she might call for her daughter. The nurse on duty, who had replaced Veronica Ryan during her dinner break, reached for the chart, found

Craig's new orders. "Mrs. Horton, your daughter is not due to be released for ten days."

"I was told yesterday that she could go home tomorrow."

"I'm sorry, all I know is what Dr. Pierson wrote on her chart."

"Well, we'll see about that!" Mrs. Horton said sharply.

Not wishing to alarm her daughter, she called her husband from the pay phone in the visitors' room. Indignant, she told him what she had discovered. He called his senior partner, Bruce Miller, who was chairman of the hospital's board. Miller called Walter Deering, who called Dr. Ordway.

Ordway himself came down to examine the Horton chart. He picked up the phone and reached Craig in emergency. "Pierson!" Ordway demanded. "May I see you at once?"

"DAMN it, Craig," Ordway exploded, "you were specifically forbidden to have anything to do with Prince's patients! Now this!" Ordway slapped his hand violently against the chart. "And the way I find out is through a call from a trustee!"

"Dr. Prince is up in the OR. I didn't think it wise to disturb him. It was quite clear what had to be done."

"You had no authority to do it!"

"As a resident on the service, I felt I did have authority. There was no matter of judgment involved. Not when a patient is running the risk of a pulmonary embolus."

Ordway could not dispute that, so he only grumbled, "You should have called some other resident, some staff physician."

"The patient asked for me," was all Craig could say.

"I wouldn't mention that to Prince. It will only enrage him more," Ordway cautioned. "Well, I'll do what I can to protect you. Pierson, I'm trying to make a doctor out of you despite yourself."

BY THE time Dr. Harvey Prince finished his last procedure, it was past six o'clock. He was getting out of his scrub suit when the message from Walter Deering reached him. Would he come down to the ob-gyn floor as soon as possible?

When he reached the floor, both Deering and Ordway were waiting. Deering explained board chairman Miller's interest in

290

the Horton girl and the sudden reversal of orders for her discharge.

"Who gave new orders?" Prince exploded indignantly.

As gingerly as he could, Ordway explained it was Pierson.

"I expressly forbade him to go near her!" Prince said fiercely. "I want to see him!"

"Not now," Ordway said. "The girl's parents and fiancé are in her room. They're very upset."

"I don't blame them," Prince said belligerently. "I'll talk to them at once."

Quietly Ordway warned, "I'd look at her chart first."

At the nurses' desk, Prince found Burt Carlyle examining the chart. Impatiently he ripped it out of Carlyle's hands and stared at it. But he handed it back much more slowly. "Thrombosis . . . You never detected any sign when you examined her this morning?" Prince asked.

"Nothing. But a hidden thrombus is not uncommon. In fact, that's the most dangerous kind."

"Thank you for the instruction, Doctor," Prince said acidly.

He started down the corridor. In his brisk walk to room 442, Dr. Harvey Prince prepared himself to confront the Hortons and the girl's fiancé. By the time he opened the door, he was putting forth his best and most encouraging manner.

"Well, I'm glad you're all here. It seems we have a bit of a problem. Nothing to get excited about, I assure you."

"Cynthia was scheduled to go home," Arthur Horton complained. "Suddenly they want to keep her another ten days."

"Now, just relax. And you too, my dear." He smiled at Cynthia.

"Now, then," he began, "we have here a slight complication that is not unusual after a surgical procedure. What we are dealing with is a thrombosis, a clot that has formed in the pelvic femoral vein in the thigh. The treatment is simple. We give the patient heparin several times a day and the clot gradually resolves. To be absolutely safe, we do that for ten days. So while we don't like to delay discharging our lovely patient, I'm sure we all understand why it has to be done this way."

Mrs. Horton, relieved, smiled at Cynthia, who made a weak attempt to smile back. If Horton was still concerned, and if the young fiancé was not particularly happy, Prince discounted that.

"So get a good night's sleep, my dear. We'll keep close watch on you." He smiled at Cynthia, then eased his way to the door, where he asked, "Am I going to be invited to the wedding?"

Without waiting for an answer, he left.

SHORTLY after Dr. Prince's visit, Horton had Craig Pierson paged, and arranged to meet him in the hospital coffee shop.

"Dr. Pierson, my daughter tells me that when you discovered her condition you became acutely concerned. You rushed her up to X ray. You administered some drug."

"Heparin," Craig explained. "It's mandatory in this condition."

"So I understand," Horton said. "But Dr. Prince was in to see us. He tried to make light of the whole thing. Too light. Now, I know you fellows have your professional ethics, so I won't invite you to comment on Dr. Prince's conduct. But we had a malpractice case in the office a few years back." Horton hastened to assure him, "Don't worry, I'm not thinking of suing anybody. I'm only interested in protecting my daughter. In the case we had, the blood clot developed into something else."

"An embolism?" Craig asked.

"Yes. It shot to the patient's lung and proved instantly fatal. In plain terms, is that a possibility in Cynthia's case?"

"In any patient with a thrombosis, that's always a possibility. That's why we put them on heparin," Craig said.

"Then Prince's attempt to pass this off as a slight complication was really dishonest. . . ." Horton shook his head. "Doctor, Cynthia has complete confidence in you. You're honest with her, and with me. I want you to take over her case."

"I can't do that. She's Dr. Prince's patient. He's forbidden me to see her," Craig admitted simply. "But I give you my word, if anything's wrong, I'll do something about it."

"Thank you," Horton said, greatly relieved.

IT WAS past midnight. Kate was serving coffee and trying to console Craig. "Horton didn't ask, so you didn't have to tell him."

"That's a cop-out," Craig said, angry not with her but with

292

himself. "The man wanted the truth. I gave him half-truths, empty assurances."

"Craig, darling," Kate said, "psychiatrists face that situation frequently. Often I don't force a patient to face the whole truth. I let him grow into a gradual recognition of it. If I succeed, it all comes out. When he can handle it. It's the same with Horton. What if you had told him the whole truth tonight?"

"I could have destroyed him," Craig admitted. "Still, I should have said, 'Mr. Horton, instead of worrying about what will happen if she has a fatal pulmonary embolus, worry about what might happen to her if she *doesn't!*'" Craig said bitterly.

Grimly Kate agreed. "After a thrombosis, she can't have estrogen without risking another thrombosis."

"Say it! Loud and clear. With both ovaries removed and no estrogen, what will she become?"

"A menopausal woman at the age of twenty-two," she admitted.

"Well, Kate, I may not be able to help her any longer. But I am going to try to help those who come after her!"

CLINTON Ordway sat back in his large desk chair and stared at Craig Pierson, pondering the startling request the resident had just made. To deny it would be an evasion; more simply put, a cover-up. To grant it would put young Pierson at considerable risk. Either course was distasteful to Ordway.

"I want you to think of what this can mean to your future."

"I've thought about it," Craig said.

"Overnight? Frankly, I'd think about it a good deal longer. Prince is a man with enormous clout."

"The more I think about it, the stronger my feeling becomes."

Ordway nodded sadly. "If you insist, I'll see that the case is presented at the next session of grand rounds."

As Craig reached the door, Ordway called out, "By the way, how's your father?"

"Recuperating. But he'll have minimum mobility in his right arm. He won't be able to work any longer, that's certain."

"Will that be a financial burden on you?" Ordway asked.

"Yes," Craig admitted.

Ordway shook his head sympathetically. "Too bad. Especially at a time like this."

Craig left without responding. Ordway made a note adding one more case to grand rounds, day after tomorrow.

THERE was a large turnout in the auditorium for ob-gyn grand rounds. Word had gotten around. Staff men had gathered to see an attending surgeon attacked. The attendings had come to watch an impertinent young resident get his ears pinned back.

Absent from the meeting was Dr. Harvey Prince. He had chosen not to dignify Craig Pierson's attack. His interests would be represented by his colleagues.

Doctors were still streaming into the auditorium when Burt Carlyle announced the first case. It was one in which a surgeon, during an operation which threatened to go sour, had improvised a new surgical technique. The doctor described the case, exhibited slides, detailed his new technique, then answered questions. Thus the prime purpose of grand rounds was fulfilled, sharing new information for the enlightenment of colleagues and students.

The second case involved the use of colposcopy as a means of localizing an abnormal area on the cervical surface. A diagnostic procedure used successfully in Europe, it had only recently come into use in this country. The presentation at grand rounds was done by a gynecologist who was interested in having this sophisticated method adopted at State University Hospital.

Though interesting, these cases proved only a prologue to the one most of them had come to hear. Burt Carlyle now announced, "Next is a case involving a bilateral salpingo-oophorectomy, which will be presented by Dr. Pierson."

Craig made a simple presentation of the history, from first checkup through surgery, and then raised the question as to the proper surgical procedure.

Spofford West, a short, portly, dignified man in his sixties, came down the aisle to deliver his opinion.

"Those of us who have been around for more than a few years know that in as many as fifty percent of the cases where you have one ovarian tumor, you're likely to have bilateral involvement.

Therefore, conservative surgery is not advisable. That second ovary would have had to be removed sooner or later. Or haven't you learned that yet?"

Craig felt a rush of blood to his cheeks, from both anger and embarrassment. "Recent reports indicate that appropriate treatment for this type of tumor would have been *unilateral* salpingo-oophorectomy. Then *after* the woman's childbearing years were over, for *preventive* purposes the second ovary could be removed, because of the potential for bilateral development."

West smiled indulgently. "You young fellows would subject patients to any newfangled theory that comes along."

"Not any more than you old fellows would keep inflicting the same old crimes on your patients," Craig shot back.

The moment the word "crimes" had passed his lips Craig realized he had blundered. The silence that followed his outburst confirmed his fear. Carlyle tried to diminish the effect of the moment. "It's twenty past one. With your permission I'll close—"

West interrupted and renewed his attack on Craig. "Young man, in my entire career I have never heard any doctor classify an accepted surgical practice as a crime! What was done in this case was the most effective preventive measure to take. Only inexperience makes you disagree!"

Still Craig persisted. "As far as preventive measures are concerned, if we did a hysterectomy on every thirteen-year-old girl, we'd wipe out uterine cancer in one generation. But at what price? I've always been taught that the basic principle in medicine is to cure the patient with a minimum of functional impairment."

West glared at Pierson, then turned abruptly and left the hall.

Grand rounds was over. There was considerable hostile whispering among the older men, who drifted out of the auditorium in small groups. The younger men lingered, but said nothing. It would have been politically unwise.

Among the older men, only Sam Becker made his way down the aisle to Craig's side.

Sam was annoyed. "So you made your point. Idiot! They set you up. Who was here? West, the chairman of the county board of the American College of Surgeons. And Maxwell. The man in this district appointed by the American College of Obstetricians and Gynecologists to interview applicants for admission. Do you think they will forget the word 'crimes' today? What do you think will happen when you come up for admission to those organizations? And what do you think will happen to any future appointment you might seek if you're not a fellow of the ACS or ACOG? What you did today you won't be able to undo in a lifetime."

"Sam, what would you have wanted me to do?"

"I guess," Sam Becker said sadly, "be a coward like the rest of us. I'm sorry, kid," and he patted Craig on the shoulder.

Craig started out of the auditorium. He saw Burt Carlyle standing at the head of the aisle.

"Craig, I tried to shut you up," Burt said. "But once you used the word 'crimes' . . ."

He nodded. "Okay. That was ill advised."

"Is ill advised a euphemism for fatal?" Carlyle asked bitterly.

AFTER the meeting, Dr. Spofford West called Harvey Prince.

"Spoff? How did it go?"

"Better than I hoped," West gloated. "He not only attacked you, he attacked every attending there."

"Good," Prince agreed. "Let's get rid of him once and for all!"

CHAPTER SIX

CRAIG Pierson stopped at the nurses' station to peruse the charts of those patients to whom he still had access. Instead of considering it a luxury to have so much time to himself, he felt lonely and excluded. He missed the excitement of being pressured every hour, from early rounds, to surgery, back to rounds, to emergency. It was a grind which every resident griped about—but enjoyed.

A nurse approached him. "Doctor, the patient in 442 would like to see you." She relayed the information in a formal manner. Evidently gossip about grand rounds had gotten around quickly.

"What seems to be the trouble with the patient?" Craig asked, adopting the nurse's antiseptic attitude.

"She claims to be having a fever."

"Did you take her temperature?" Craig asked.

"Ninety-eight six," the nurse informed him crisply. "She insists on seeing you. What shall I tell her?"

"I'll drop by."

Cynthia Horton was sitting up in bed. Her black hair had been tied back in a red ribbon, yet wisps of it adhered to her damp cheeks. She was pale and thin. He recalled that on her chart a nurse had noted that she did not eat well, sometimes sending her trays back untouched.

Before he could say a word, Cynthia said petulantly, "They took my temperature and they lied to me."

He recognized a frequent syndrome among patients whose course of recovery had gone differently than predicted. They began to suspect that everyone was in a conspiracy against them.

"Cynthia, they did not lie to you. Why don't you see for yourself?" He got a thermometer and shook it down. "Under the tongue, please."

The three-minute wait seemed an eternity. When the time was up, Craig reached for the thermometer, glanced at it, handed it back. Cynthia looked at the tiny glass instrument.

"Couldn't be more normal," he said.

"Then why do I get these terrible sweats?" she asked.

"Do you get them often?"

"More by night than by day," she said. "But sometimes every three or four hours. It feels like I'm burning up."

"Have you told Dr. Prince about this?"

"He hasn't been by in two days now."

Craig debated how much he should reveal to this girl who was not his patient. Finally he said, "It's not a fever or an infection. And the thrombosis is resolving."

Everything he was saying was true. Yet it was evasion. But even if he told the girl the blunt truth, it would not change the course of her condition.

No treatment was possible. It was Prince's responsibility to tell her that.

Even while Craig spoke to her, he could see a flush rise up her throat. Her cheeks, pale before, now became a deep red. Perspiration glistened on her forehead and her face. "That's it," she whispered. "That's the way it happens. Open the window!"

He lifted the window high, letting fresh air flood the room. Cynthia threw back the light coverlet to drink in all the cool air she could, to soothe her flushed and burning body.

How does one explain to a twenty-two-year-old girl that she is in the midst of a menopausal flush? In some cases, symptoms can be tempered if the physician prepares his patient. Obviously Prince had not done that. So the girl was struggling to combat symptoms that were not only distressing but mystifying.

Craig decided there was only one way to handle the situation. If Prince would not, he would. The patient's health and safety superseded any fine points of medical ethics.

"Cynthia," he began, "there are some consequences of the kind of surgery . . ."

With no word, no warning, the girl began to weep. She made no sound, but tears streamed down her face.

"Cynthia?" Craig asked gently. "Why are you crying?"

She shook her head. "I don't know," she admitted. "I lie awake at night and cry. . . . I ask myself why, but I don't know. And I'm afraid. The last few days, all the time, I'm afraid."

"Afraid Pete will leave you?" Craig suggested.

"No. He's been terrific. I'm not afraid of any special thing. I just cry," she said pitifully. "Tell me, *has* anything changed? Did the lab find something they haven't told me about?"

"No."

"Something's changed. I feel it; I know it," the girl said plaintively, beginning to weep again.

How, Craig asked himself, how do you tell this girl that she is suffering all the depressive symptoms of premature menopause, with even more symptoms to come? The facts must be revealed by someone. That she sent for him in her difficulty imposed that obligation on him.

"Cynthia, these are quite usual symptoms for certain conditions. The depression, the nervousness, the feeling of unexplained fear, the hot spells. Once a woman's ovaries are removed, those are natural consequences."

"But what do you do about it?"

"Usually we prescribe an estrogen supplement," Craig said. "Because of what happened to your vein, you can't have estrogen. Without it, you're going to be subject to these symptoms. But they are not dangerous," he tried to reassure her.

"Not dangerous," she evaluated. "Will it ever go away? Being afraid. Crying that I can't control. Can't understand."

"Yes, eventually it will go away."

She seemed to accept his answer. "If you say so, Dr. Pierson, I believe you," she agreed finally. She wiped her eyes with the palms of her hands. She could even manage a flicker of a smile.

His hand was on the doorknob when she asked, "Those hot spells . . . are they the same as you hear older women talk about?"

He turned slowly before he said, "Yes, Cynthia."

"You mean that I . . . I'm having . . . menopause. Is that what you're trying to tell me?"

"You are having what we term premature menopause," Craig said as gently as he could.

Her tears began again. This time she buried her face in her pillow, ashamed to face him. He knew he could not comfort her now.

He left, went to a phone, and dialed Kate's extension.

"Kate, when you have a chance . . . see the Horton girl."

"What happened?" Kate asked.

"I had to tell her," Craig said. "Everything, except the possible marital complications."

"I'll look in on her," Kate agreed.

KATE Lindstrom changed from her white hospital suit into the dress she had worn that morning. She preferred to approach Cynthia Horton as one young woman to another, sensing that by now the patient had become disenchanted with physicians.

Kate pushed the door open quietly. She had expected to find Cynthia in tears. Instead, she lay perfectly still, straight and stiff, like a marble sculpture atop a medieval stone crypt. Her eyes were closed. Her face a mask.

"Cynthia . . ." Kate spoke softly. "I thought if we talked, it might help."

The girl remained rigid and silent. Kate detected that this might be the first stage of a severe depression. She had spent many nights reading up on the psychological aspects of cancer patients. To some, worse than the fear of dying was surviving in mutilated condition. Especially so if the mutilated parts concerned their sexuality. A young woman on the brink of marriage could look upon her condition as devastating.

Aware of the tendency of most patients to blame themselves for their disease, Kate hoped to coax Cynthia into talking. "I know how you feel. But it's not true."

The girl did not open her eyes, but half turned in the direction of Kate's voice.

"Most patients' first reaction is to blame themselves. They feel they must have done something wrong to have earned this disease. It's true that in some cases we can attribute cause and effect, as in smoking and lung cancer. But in most cases we don't know the cause. Though we do know it's nothing as mystical as punishment for sins. Nothing you did brought it on."

Kate paused, to give Cynthia a chance to react. Silence seemed to have a compelling effect. Cynthia turned away and began to speak. Her voice had a flat, distant sound that made Kate uneasy. She had seen many depressives; she knew the signs well.

"What I can't understand," Cynthia said vaguely, "is why *this* patient? Why *me*?"

"It was something that happened. You can't blame yourself. The main thing is, you're free of the disease now. You must look forward to the rest of your life. A few months from now . . ."

Kate became silent. She could see the flush rise up from Cynthia's chest. The girl broke into a profuse sweat, rolled her head back and forth on the pillow, wiping away the sweat with her palms. A natural phenomenon over which neither patient nor psychiatrist had any control. Kate could only wait for it to pass.

The flush subsided. "How long will those go on?" Cynthia asked. "All my life?"

"In some cases a few months, in other cases a few years." Kate was encouraged that the girl had made some connection with her future life.

301

"My thoughts make no sense. Yet I can't shake them," Cynthia said. "They wake me at night. I am dreaming of Pete and suddenly he disappears, but she is there. That other mother. Hating me, accusing me. The strange thing is, she has no face. Only eyes."

The girl turned away. "If I am going mad, tell me. So it won't come as a surprise. I've had many surprises in the past few weeks."

"I think you're going through reactions we expect from patients who've been told they had cancer."

There was little more that Kate could say, and if there had been, she would have withheld it to encourage Cynthia to talk. Open expression of the girl's fears would have a therapeutic effect.

"Those dreams in which Pete disappears . . . Does that mean he's going to leave me? Not that I would blame him," she added.

"Since it's your dream, not Pete's, it's not his intentions but your fears. Has anything happened?"

"He comes every evening. He talks on, making plans. I lie here and listen, praying that I won't have one of those flushes. I don't want him to see me this way."

"What could happen if he did?"

"I don't know. He might become frightened and leave me."

"Like your other mother?"

"I guess," Cynthia conceded. Then she confessed softly, "It's terrible of me. My mother is worried sick, trying to do anything she can to make me better, but all I can think about is the other one, who deserted me. What a way to repay my parents for the love they gave me!"

"I'm sure they understand," Kate said. "There's no need to invent guilt for yourself."

"I don't know," Cynthia said hopelessly. "Sometimes I wish . . ."

"Wish what?" Kate asked gently.

"That thing in my leg . . . I understand that can break off and send bits to the lungs or heart and that would be the end of it. Sometimes I wish it would!"

"Do you feel that way now?" Kate asked.

"No. Not now. Would you come see me again in a day or two? Please? I can talk to you."

"I'll drop by. And anytime you want to talk, call me."

Kate went back to her office and made a note for herself about Cynthia. She had a premonition that at some time in the future she might be called upon to report her findings.

CRAIG Pierson had just emerged from the OR, where he had assisted one of the full-time surgeons in a complicated hysterectomy. The surgeon had permitted Craig to do part of the procedure. It had been a tough afternoon but worthwhile.

He washed up, made his final rounds, and went to see Cynthia.

She was alone. Her parents had been in but had left for a quick dinner. Pete was not there. A meeting out of town, he had called to say. Craig was relieved that Cynthia seemed less depressed than she had been earlier in the day.

"She's very nice," Cynthia said.

"Dr. Lindstrom?"

"Honest blue eyes. Friendly. Open. I like her," Cynthia said. "I wish I could believe her completely."

"Don't you?"

"Right after she left, the fears started again. I get this feeling they'll never end."

"They will. Though while it's going on, you do get this feeling that it'll never end."

Her parents came back, so Craig felt safe leaving her. As he was closing the door, Mr. Horton said to him, "Doctor, do you have a minute? And a private office?"

"Of course. Come along."

Craig closed the door of the residents' office to ensure privacy. Horton did not make any preambles, but asked directly, "Doctor, what would happen to Cynthia if Pete were to decide . . . well, if he changed his mind about marrying her?"

"He's not the only eligible young man in the world," Craig said.

"He might be, for her," Horton said gravely. "After all, at least they were in love before this happened. But starting fresh, with another man, I don't think she can . . . She's sensitive, timid . . . and this has only made things worse."

"Aren't we worrying about something that may never arise?" Craig asked. "Did anything happen?"

"I called Pete to ask him out to dinner this evening."

"Cynthia said he had to go out of town on business."

"That's what he told her," Horton said. "The truth is, he is not out of town. He simply avoided coming."

"I see."

"That's why my question, What will happen if he decides to bow out now?" Horton said grimly.

"She's going through a time of depression. She needs someone to comfort her, see her through. I had hoped he would."

"So had I," Horton said. Suddenly he asked, "Doctor, what is osteoporosis?"

Craig stared. "Osteoporosis," he explained, "is a loss of density in the bones. The mineral content of the matrix is lost and the bones become 'soft.' Why do you ask?"

"What causes that?" Horton asked.

"A number of things can," Craig answered guardedly.

"Such as removing a woman's ovaries?" Horton pressed.

"Yes. Where did you find out about osteoporosis?"

"I've been doing some reading. I don't understand a lot of it, but I get enough," the man said sadly. "Doctor, I must know the whole truth. What is the total extent of the damage that has been done to my daughter?"

Craig's immediate inclination was to refuse to answer. These were medical issues, to be settled among doctors. But Horton's direct question made him decide it was time to speak out.

"Mr. Horton, you must not tell Cynthia what I am about to tell you. She is in quite fragile emotional condition. I don't know how much more she can absorb."

Horton nodded, accepting Craig's warning with gravity.

"The consequences of your daughter's present condition will be far-reaching. It is possible that she might not be able to function as a wife in the normal way."

"What do you mean?"

"It is most natural for young husbands and wives to have regular, frequent sexual relations. In her condition, without estrogen, she might experience pain and bleeding. If that happened, it might jeopardize the chances of a happy marriage."

"If she doesn't have her marriage to look forward to . . ." Horton did not dare pursue this speculation. He went on, "You mean, in all of medical science, there's nothing . . ."

"Some conditions are irreversible and untreatable."

Horton took a handkerchief out of his breast pocket, wiped his eyes. "I wonder if Pete knows and for that reason didn't want to come to the hospital tonight," he considered. "We'll have to find a way of preparing her for that possibility. Otherwise, I don't know what will happen to her. . . . I just don't know."

FOR the next three days, though Cynthia called for him several times, Craig avoided going to her room. Ordway had again asked him to stay away, and Craig did not want to endanger his career further. But the most persuasive reason was that there was nothing he could do for the patient. The best that could happen to her now was gradual acceptance of her condition.

It was just past three in the morning when Craig's phone rang with the persistent urgency that only early morning calls inflict.

"Sorry to bother you at this hour," the operator apologized. "One moment, I'll put the floor nurse on."

The nurse took over. "Dr. Pierson? Cynthia Horton is threatening to jump from her fourth-floor window. And nobody can talk her out of it!"

"My God!" Craig exploded. "Keep talking to her. I'll be there as soon as I can!"

He called Kate, and within fifteen minutes they were both at the hospital. They raced down the hushed corridor to 442, where they could hear subdued but fearful whispers.

Craig opened the door cautiously. Inside the room, the night resident and the chief floor nurse were talking softly but continuously, trying to maintain tenuous contact with the girl who was perched in the open window.

Craig motioned them away and moved toward Cynthia. Once so beautiful, she now presented a caricature of herself. Her torment had distorted her features even as it had distorted her mind.

"Cynthia," he began softly. "It's me. Dr. Pierson. All I ask is the chance to talk to you."

She would not face him. She stared into the black night, breathing in short, convulsive gasps.

"You can talk to me, Cynthia—you know that. Because we share something none of the others do. Isn't that true?"

With those words he had hoped to make her face him so that he could make eye contact with her. He failed. He glanced at Kate, who urged him on with a nod.

"Cynthia," he tried again, "no matter how you feel about yourself, you have to think of others. Your mother and dad. Who love you so much. How do you think they'll feel? Asking themselves every day, Where did we fail her? That's a terrible guilt to put on two people who love you so much."

He edged slightly closer to her. She edged farther out the window. He drew back, not wishing to exert pressure. Now he became aware that, below them, police cars were beginning to roll into the courtyard. She seemed oblivious of them.

"Cynthia, you and I know what it means to be left, deserted. Yet that's what you want to do now, to your mother, your father. Desert them. They've given you so much. Is this all you have to leave them?"

Slowly she turned to stare at him.

"Everybody . . ." she said in a strained voice, "everybody who touches me . . . whom I touch . . . everybody is doomed. This is the way to free them all. Mommy. Daddy. Pete."

"Free them?" Craig asked. "How free will they be if you do this? Wishing they could bring you back. To tell you how much they love you. You'll be destroying their lives too."

He was becoming more apprehensive of the sounds and movements below the window. He hoped they would not precipitate some rash move on her part. "Cynthia . . . I'll help you."

She glanced back, her look betraying doubt.

"I will," he promised.

Suddenly from below a powerful burst of searchlight lit up the window and the entire room. Cynthia started, losing her balance. Craig lunged forward and was barely able to grasp her. She was out of the window, hanging precariously from his uncertain grip. For a moment she struggled. Then she went limp. Straining des-

perately, Craig increased his hold until he had both arms around her frail body. Carefully, slowly, he lifted her back through the window.

He placed her limp body on the bed, covered her, and without looking at the nurse he ordered a sedative. A trickle of sweat made its way down his chest. His face dripped with perspiration.

He slumped into a chair. Kate wiped his face dry. The nurse returned, administered the sedative, and left.

"We have to begin intensive treatment with her," Kate said. "In fact, we should move her to psychiatric."

"Wonder what triggered it?" Craig pondered, exhausted.

"She's had a lot of time to brood. And a lot to brood about."

Craig went to Cynthia's side, found her pulse. The sedative had slowed it, but it was not yet normal. As he turned from the bed, he spotted a crumpled ball of paper under the night table. Curious, he reached for it, flattened it out. It was a note which began, "Darling Cynthia." At the bottom of the page it was signed "Pete." In view of the events of the past hour, he felt authorized to read it.

I know how you must feel about my not having come to see you every night this week. It's not that I love you less. But I need time to think.

We've always been honest with each other. Honesty now is more important than ever. So I want to be open with you.

It didn't matter to me too much about not having my own children. We can always adopt. If we're lucky, we'll get a girl just like you. And maybe a boy or two as well. I don't want you to worry about that.

It's the other part. Our love has always meant more to me than sex. Yet we can't deny that sex is part of love. And now, with what the doctors say, and what my own doctor told me, I have to ask myself, Can I cope with a marriage that offers less? It's not that I love you less, it's that I doubt myself. And I have to find out.

I'll always love you. But I need time. All my love.

Craig stared at the letter, then passed it to Kate. After she read it, she shook her head sadly.

"Didn't he know what he was doing?" she asked.

"I guess he assumed she'd been told."

There were whispers at the door. The night floor nurse was being backed into the room by Barbara and Arthur Horton.

"She's fine! The emergency is over," the nurse tried to assure them. "We only called because we thought we might need you."

"We came as fast as we could," Horton explained. "We insist on seeing her."

Craig intervened. "Come in," he said. "Just be quiet. Please?"

Both parents stood at the foot of the bed and stared at Cynthia until they were reassured that she was asleep and safe. "What happened?" Arthur Horton asked.

Craig handed him the letter. Horton scanned it hastily, passed it to his wife.

Barbara Horton broke into tears. "We were going to tell her. In a way that wouldn't hurt her more than necessary. But this . . . She must have become hysterical."

"Worse," Craig said in simple honesty. "She threatened to jump from the window."

"No!" Barbara Horton blurted out. "She couldn't. . . ."

Horton sank into a chair, staring toward the bed. His wife moved to his side but could only whisper, "Arthur . . . oh, Arthur, what are we going to do?"

To ease their suffering, Craig suggested, "There's nothing you can do here. Why don't you go back home?"

"We'll stay till morning," Arthur Horton said. "When she wakes, the first thing I want her to see is us."

Craig nodded. He and Kate left the two anxious parents with their daughter. They took the elevator to the main floor, where one person was waiting to go up. Peter Tompkins. A glance affirmed that he had dressed hastily and rushed to the hospital. The Hortons must have called him earlier.

"How is she?" he demanded, breathless.

"She's all right now," Craig assured him.

"What happened?"

"Your note," Kate said frankly. "That was not the way she should have found out."

"You mean she didn't know? I assumed—" He broke off, sank

309

down onto the wooden bench near the elevators. "I was only trying to be honest. We've always . . ." He couldn't finish.

"Sometimes it's kinder not to be too honest, too soon," Kate pointed out.

Craig felt compelled to intervene. "Exactly what did you mean in your note about what your doctor 'told' you?"

"About what happens to a young woman in Cynthia's condition. How it makes sex impossible," the young man explained.

"Did he say 'happens' or 'might happen'?" Craig demanded.

"I don't exactly remember," Pete admitted.

"Did he use the word 'impossible'? Or don't you 'exactly remember' that either?" Craig asked furiously. "That's the trouble when a little knowledge gets into the hands of laymen!"

"I'm sorry if I misunderstood, very sorry," Tompkins said. "Can I go up and see her? Can I try to explain?"

"She's sleeping," Craig said.

"What can I do?" the distraught young man asked.

"I'd do a great deal of thinking before I did anything more, if I were you," Kate said sharply.

Craig and Kate stepped outside the hospital. Far to the east the sky was beginning to brighten. They stood in the cool morning air, breathing deeply.

Craig said simply, "Okay. Today I will do it. I'll see to it that Goldfingers doesn't make any more 'mistakes.'"

CHAPTER SEVEN

THE morbidity and mortality review always convened in the large conference room of the hospital. At M&M conferences, those actions of surgeons which had led to serious complications or death were discussed by their colleagues.

Clinton Ordway waited impatiently as the ob-gyn men straggled in one by one. Once everyone was assembled around a table, Ordway called the meeting to order.

The first case involved an exenteration during which the patient, having been on the table for five and a half hours, had required several blood transfusions. The patient accepted the first two with-

out adverse reaction. But after the third transfusion the patient reacted violently. Though the procedure was carried through to a
successful conclusion, the patient suffered renal failure and died
within thirty-six hours.

The obvious cause: an infusion of incompatible blood.

His face red with anger, the surgeon complained, "I'm outraged
about this case. When I send down to the bank for type A blood,
I should get type A blood!

"As soon as I left the OR, I went down to the bank myself. And
what did I discover? The orderly had brought type B up to the
floor! That's all. A little slipup. A little fatal slipup! Once that B
blood was infused into my patient, shock, renal failure were unavoidable. Because of one lousy mistake by one orderly whose
mind was probably on whether he should go out on strike or not!
You can't trust any hospital employees these days!"

"Then why *do* you?" Burt Carlyle called out.

"Why do I *what?*" The surgeon glared at Carlyle.

"You said you couldn't trust hospital personnel these days. Yet
an orderly brings a pint of blood into the OR, and neither you nor
the anesthetist checks before transfusing it. There were two professionals who could have prevented this death, yet neither of
them did!"

"It's not my job," the surgeon retorted.

"We never expected we'd need a third transfusion, so the blood
was late getting up there," the anesthetist declared. "With the
patient's pressure falling rapidly, there wasn't much time."

"Not even time enough to look at the label on the bottle and
check it against the patient's type?" Carlyle shot back.

Ordway intervened swiftly. "Gentlemen, the next case."

Several more cases were heard. Craig Pierson noted, as he
always did in these conferences, that in each instance the doctor
involved presented his explanation of how the death had occurred,
without any fault on his part. And usually at least one physician
present would defend him. At M&M conferences, a man's colleagues were more apt to justify than to judge his errors of judgment.

Two more cases were heard. Two more doctors were exonerated.

Ordway glanced down at his agenda and announced, "That brings today's conference to a close." He flipped his folder shut.

"There *is* another case," Craig said. "The Horton case."

"Horton?" Ordway echoed, as if the name were unfamiliar.

"I don't wish to use names, but I'm forced to. Cynthia Horton. A patient of Dr. Prince's."

"Oh. That case was removed from the agenda."

"Why?" Craig demanded. "After all, this is a morbidity and mortality conference. I would say that in her case morbidity is certainly a marked result."

"Because of the pressure of time, we've confined ourselves to mortality cases today. Besides, the patient's been moved out of our department to psychiatric. This meeting is closed."

Craig leaped up. Burt Carlyle, in a low, forceful whisper, said, "Don't! Did you hear me, Craig? Don't say another word!"

Craig glared at his colleague. His eyes accused: You're joining them. You're protecting Prince. After what he did.

Burt's eyes remained firm and unapologetic. It was Craig who finally relented. The other physicians and surgeons began to depart. Only Burt Carlyle and Craig Pierson were left.

"Come to the house tonight," Burt suggested. "I want to talk to you."

"What would we have to talk about, Burt?" Craig asked.

"A lot!" Carlyle said angrily. "Seven o'clock. Bring Kate. Okay?" Craig finally nodded.

THROUGHOUT dinner, conversation was stilted, to avoid open conflict. But after dinner, Burt decided to confront the issue head-on. "Okay, Craig! Let's have it! Everything you didn't say to me this afternoon. Get it off your chest."

"Just tell me one thing," Craig demanded. "Did you and Ordway conspire to bury this case?"

"Yes, we did! But do you know *why?*"

"Because of Prince. You didn't want to jeopardize a possibility of joining his office."

"Of course," Burt said. "That's the goal I've had from the first time I assisted him. I worship that man's technique. All I have to

312

do is learn from him. When my turn comes, I won't do unnecessary hysterectomies, but I'll do the necessary ones magnificently."

He paused, then admitted, "And make a fortune in the process. My wife, my kids are going to have the best of everything!"

He stood up and began to pace. "Craig, I know you won't believe this. But there was another reason. Ordway's reason. He's actually protecting you."

"Fat chance," Craig scoffed.

"Craig!" Kate insisted that he give Burt a hearing.

"Ordway's subject to pressures too. Trustees. Budgets. After all, it's men like Prince who keep the service going. His admissions are often made on Fridays for surgery the following Monday. Why? Prince'll say it gives the staff a chance to do a proper workup on the patient. But you know the labs are virtually shut down over the weekend. So the patient lolls around, at a hundred and seventy-five dollars a day or more. And the hospital picks up an extra few hundred dollars. Is it any wonder that Prince has more beds reserved for him than any other attending in ob-gyn? He's a gold mine not only to himself but to the hospital."

Craig's fury mounted. "And that's the man you're defending?"

"*You* are the man I'm defending! Because Goldfingers has muscle, Craig. Muscle enough to have you kicked out. That's why Ordway bypassed the Horton case. That's how he induced me to cooperate. But now . . . now I have to ask myself, Was it really you I was concerned about? Or myself? Craig, don't make me answer that question. Because I don't know."

Craig did not reply.

"Craig, if you feel I let you down, I'm sorry. I did what I thought was right. Especially after Ordway told me that now Prince insists you be fired!"

It was past two in the morning. Kate and Craig sat over coffee in her dinette, still pondering what Burt Carlyle had said.

"Fired." Craig was considering all the consequences of that word. "If it weren't for my dad, I'd say let 'em fire me!"

"But there *is* your dad," Kate pointed out. "What are you going to do?"

313

"I don't know," he confessed. "I don't know."

They had been silent for a time when Craig asked, "How is Cynthia getting along?"

"She'll be a long-drawn-out case. A girl of twenty-two is not going to become adjusted to what happened, not for a long time."

"It never should have happened. He won't get away with it," Craig threatened.

"It seems he already has," Kate said grimly.

"CRAIG! No!" Ordway exploded. "I will not put that case back on the M&M agenda."

The chief hesitated, considering whether to reveal what he had in mind. Finally he said, "Craig, the pressures have been building up. I've been thinking that I ought to rotate you."

"Rotate?"

"Exchange you with one of the second-year residents at City Hospital. A three-month rotation. It wouldn't do you any harm to learn how ob-gyn departments in other hospitals function. I've been in contact with Leverit over at City. He's amenable."

"Why? Do they have a troublemaker over there they want to get rid of?"

"I'm not trying to get rid of you! I'm trying to keep you out of Prince's way until he cools down."

"Old Goldfingers," Craig remarked bitterly.

"Craig, you're not just antagonizing Prince, it's the entire profession. We're under attack constantly. The government, malpractice suits, the media. Because of that, we physicians have become what you might call a highly sensitized body. You know from immunology what happens when a sensitized body is invaded. The immune system mobilizes the body's resources against the invader. In this case, *you* are the invader, the enemy."

"Dr. Ordway, if we don't clean up our own mess, then the government, or the media, or the lawyers will. We have to stop covering up for incompetents and frauds. We have to adhere to our own ethics."

Ordway nodded. "One thing about being young, Craig, all difficult questions seem so simple. A few surgeons are less than ethi-

314

cal; therefore, drum them out. Simple. But at the same time you slander every hospital they're associated with, you disgrace every physician in that specialty, you attack the profession."

Ordway paused before confessing, "Craig, I know how you feel. I've watched frauds with polished bedside manners succeed. I've seen fine doctors fail financially because they were better doctors than they were businessmen or politicians. Early in the game, I decided I couldn't be the keeper of any conscience but my own. If I could come through a day and feel that I had done well by my patients, that would be enough. So I shut my eyes to what other men did.

"Then, I made it my ambition to become chief of the service. And what have I done to myself? Become a politician. Our budgets come from the state, so we need clout in the capitol. That means behind-the-scenes maneuvering. That dinner at Prince's home a few weeks ago. He invited the mayor and three state senators. After dinner, we spent a very constructive hour in Harvey's den. I think our budget for next year will be increased.

"The point is this. The man has power. Okay, then. I don't have to be diplomatic. Prince wants you fired. I want you rotated. Take your choice."

Craig remained silent.

"You don't have to decide right this minute. Think about it. Then come back tomorrow and tell me you agree to be rotated."

Craig nodded soberly. He started for the door, stopped suddenly. "I don't have to think about it. I want to be fired."

Ordway's face flushed in both anger and frustration. "I won't accept that answer! What if I refuse?"

"I'll tell Prince you refused," Craig shot back.

"You're deliberately trying to wreck your career!"

"No, I just want to be fired," Craig said firmly.

Ordway exploded. "All right, Pierson. You are fired!" He pressed down the key of his intercom and ordered, "Nelly, come in! And bring your book!"

Unaccustomed to such brusque orders, Nelly Burnham nervously entered and sat down. Ordway swung his chair around so that he faced Craig while he dictated.

"Craig Pierson, M.D., Department of Obstetrics and Gynecology, State University Hospital. Dear Dr. Pierson: In consequence of recent events, the details of which I need not cite in this letter but which reflect an uncooperative and obstructive attitude on your part, and which disrupt the harmonious working of this department, it is my duty to inform you that your employment is hereby terminated.

"You have two weeks in which to wind up your affairs. I hope you will find yourself a place in some institution which may prove more suitable to your ambitions and personality."

He glared at Craig. "There! Does that satisfy you?"

"Yes," Craig said. "That's fine."

He left. Ordway turned to Nelly Burnham. "That'll be all."

Once she had left the room, Ordway picked up his phone and dialed a number he knew well. "Dr. Prince, please."

KATE Lindstrom glanced at the letter, then looked up at Craig.

"Before you say anything, Kate, hear me out. It was either this or run away and hide. Rotation or resignation, it was running and hiding. I know that I have my folks to think about. But I can't run out on what I believe. It won't be easy, but it beats slinking away to some small town no one ever heard of. Either *I'm* right about the way medicine should be practiced or *Prince* is. And if he is, then I don't belong in medicine. Here. Or anywhere."

"And how do you find out who's right?" Kate asked.

"By staying right here and demanding a hearing."

"Hearing? Before a group of doctors who will look on you as a radical upstart who wants to rock their very comfortable, remunerative boat?"

"Someone has to recognize the truth!" Craig persisted. "Kate, I know what this can do to my career, to our lives. But this isn't your war. If it hadn't been for me, you wouldn't be involved now. You can still back out."

"Craig, don't you think I've been doing my own thinking? Ever since the night I watched you try to talk Cynthia back from that window, I realized that in a way you were contemplating the same thing. Copping out. You were considering going to some place

316

where you'd rot for lack of teaching and research. That would have been professional suicide. You had to do this."

"Kate, there's still time to decide," Craig said. "Do you want a hero? Or a husband?"

"Just a husband who won't spend the rest of his life feeling that he failed."

WITHIN the day, Craig Pierson typed out a response to Ordway's letter of dismissal. It ended with a simple paragraph:

I am, therefore, demanding an official hearing to determine whether my conduct justifies the action taken by this hospital in discharging me.

The letter was hand delivered, and soon after, Craig was summoned to Ordway's office. He discovered Walter Deering, the hospital administrator, already there.

Ordway began straightaway. "Deering and I have discussed your letter. We feel we have sufficient grounds for your discharge. Therefore, we are rejecting your request for a hearing."

"Dr. Ordway, you've taken a step that seriously affects my career," Craig said. "I'm entitled to have that reviewed by other physicians after a complete presentation of the facts."

"We know the facts," Deering interposed. "Pierson, you got yourself into this mess despite good advice. Don't compound it by asking for official condemnation of your obstructive conduct and thus deprive yourself of all chance of another post."

"I think what Walter has in mind," Ordway interceded, "is that we might work out a letter of recommendation to ease the way for you at some other institution."

"You fire me, then give me a letter of recommendation? No, I'd rather have the hearing, if you don't mind."

"But we *do* mind," Deering said angrily.

"Then you don't leave me any alternative." Craig smiled. "I'll have to go into court and sue."

"On what grounds?" Deering demanded.

"My reputation has been damaged."

"Let me warn you now, this hospital has one of the best law

firms in the city on retainer. If it's a case of matching legal talent, or dollars, you don't stand a chance!"

Craig said nothing.

"We'll get back to you," Deering said sharply.

After Craig Pierson left the office, the administrator asked, "You think he meant it? That he'll sue?"

"I never suspected he'd go *this* far, but he did," Ordway pointed out. "Maybe we should consult our counsel."

"I already have," Deering admitted. "They were quite sensitive to the possibility of a lawsuit. They don't think we'll lose. But if we do, the way juries are these days, it could be for a sizable sum. And then the Hortons might sue for malpractice. I'm afraid we'll have to let Pierson have his hearing."

"How do we go about it?" Ordway asked. "This department's never had such a hearing before."

"It can be done either before our own medical board, or we can assemble three experts from the state specialty board."

"Our own medical board . . ." Ordway was thinking, the hospital medical board, composed of older men, zealous in protecting the hospital and themselves from scandal, would turn such a hearing into a court-martial. Exasperating as young Pierson could be, Ordway felt he was entitled to a fair hearing.

So he asked Deering, "To give every appearance of being unprejudiced, wouldn't it look better if the decision was made by outside experts?"

"Good point, Clint."

"I'll compose a list of men who might serve."

Once in his own office, Walter Deering picked up the phone.

"Harve? There's going to be a hearing."

"The medical board?"

"No. Ordway suggested an independent board of experts. Would seem more impartial. He's making up a list."

"Good idea. Show it to me the moment you get it."

CLINTON Ordway studied the names of the members of the board of governors of this district of the American College of Obstetricians and Gynecologists. He knew all twelve men, by reputation or personally. Chief candidate for his panel had to be Joseph Simmons, chairman of the board of governors. A well-established surgeon, past middle age, Simmons would surely condemn any upstart resident who had the audacity to disagree with an attending surgeon. Still, Simmons was chairman. One could not bypass him without creating suspicion. Ordway hoped that the surgeon's backlog of cases would prevent him from serving. That would give Ordway a free hand in inviting other men.

He chose to call the surgeon at a time when he was likely to be very busy. At such a moment, he was bound to refuse.

Ordway placed the call, identified himself to the operator, and succeeded in overcoming her protests about not disturbing Dr. Simmons in surgery.

When the OR phone rang insistently, Simmons demanded, "Somebody answer that thing!"

A nurse lifted the phone. "It's for you, Doctor. A Dr. Ordway."

"Ordway? Okay." He turned to one of the residents and ordered, "Close her up, Junior." He strode to the phone, bent so that the nurse could hold it to his ear, and barked, "Yes, Ordway?"

Encouraged by the impatience in Simmons' voice, Ordway began a long, involved, deliberately obfuscating explanation of the nature of his call. He was halfway through when Simmons interrupted. "I'll be glad to chair that hearing!"

Taken aback by such eager acceptance, Ordway warned, "It might take as long as a week."

"That's okay!" Simmons agreed vigorously. "Be glad to do it."

"Good," Ordway said, with little enthusiasm. "I'll round up two other men from the board."

"I'll save you the trouble!" Simmons said. "I'll select them."

Ordway had no alternative but to agree. "Of course. You understand the nature of the hearing sufficiently to explain it to them?"

"Harvey Prince briefed me. I get the whole picture," Simmons confided vengefully.

CLINTON Ordway had called Kate Lindstrom to suggest a meeting. Over coffee, which neither of them touched, Ordway explained the situation, summing it up by saying, "Simmons has picked Kearney and Fein for the panel. With those three, it won't be a hearing, it'll be a lynching."

"I know," Kate admitted.

"Then do something! Talk him out of it!"

"I can't," Kate said simply.

"Then warn him. Harvey Prince himself couldn't have picked three men who would favor him more."

"I'll do what I can," Kate said, and resolved to discuss the situation with Craig at the end of the day.

She left Ordway and went up to the psychiatric wing. She knocked on Cynthia's door. "It's Dr. Lindstrom. May I come in?"

"Oh, please."

Cynthia Horton was sitting in a big leather armchair, dressed in a plaid skirt and a cherry-red cashmere sweater. The bright cashmere set off her shining black hair. It was most encouraging to Kate, until she fixed on Cynthia's eyes. The tension was still there. And signs of much crying.

"I love that color on you," Kate said.

"Do you? It was Pete's favorite color."

Kate noticed that she spoke of her fiancé in the past tense. Cynthia realized it too.

"I keep waiting . . . for him to come back. The last time he was here I had a flush. I tried to conceal it, but I couldn't. Do you think it scared him?"

"Possibly," Kate said. "But he'll get over it. Give him time."

"I don't want him to just get over it. And I don't want him to come back out of pity. I only want him back if he wants me," she said staunchly. But despite her protest, Kate knew that Cynthia needed to have him back on any basis.

Kate spent the rest of the afternoon dealing with psychiatric outpatients. From moment to moment, she found herself barely listening to their difficulties as her mind kept dwelling on what she would say to Craig.

The day was over finally. She called Craig and he met her in the psychiatric residents' office.

"This is a conflict between doctors," Craig exploded. "What makes you think I need legal counsel?"

"Ordway says it's a stacked panel," Kate protested.

"I never expected anything else," Craig said. "I'll convince them or I'll lose. I can't be worse off than I am now!"

His outburst warned Kate that more was involved in his reaction than deciding whether to have counsel represent him. "Craig? Darling?" she coaxed gently.

Her tone defused his anger. He admitted, "Dad's doctor called. Another complication. Hypostatic pneumonia. They've got him on antibiotics and moved him to ICU."

"How does it look?"

"They won't know for forty-eight hours. I ought to be there."

"Then go."

"Now, with that hearing coming up?"

"You go! I'll attend to everything here," Kate said.

HARVEY Prince was savoring the excellent brandy of which he kept a plentiful supply at Rita Hallen's apartment. They had had dinner in a small out-of-the-way restaurant and returned to her place. This night Rita appeared even more on edge than she had been recently. She refused to take any brandy, but stared at his glass as he emptied it sip by sip.

"Darling, what's wrong?" he asked, prepared to listen to another demand for marriage. He was unprepared for her answer.

"That was a stupid thing you did," she accused.

"What?"

"That hearing!"

"I didn't ask for it. Pierson did."

"You could have stopped it."

"It's the best way to get rid of him. And make sure he's shut up forever. He hasn't got a chance."

Harvey Prince laughed, raised his brandy glass, and downed the last of the pungent liquor in one final swallow.

"What about the side effects?"

"What side effects?" he asked, irritated now.

"Who was in the OR when you made the decision to do a bilateral? Who heard the conversation between you and Pierson? Who is likely to be called to testify?"

321

"Carlyle, you . . ." He had started to enumerate when the cause of her concern suddenly became clear to him. "You mean, what happens if you're called to testify? Just tell the truth. The lab report. The disagreement. My decision," Prince said. "I wouldn't ask you to do anything else."

"What if Pierson asks about *us?*"

Prince hesitated a moment. "Men like Simmons, Kearney, and Fein are not going to be influenced by gossip. They'll only want to hear the medical facts."

"*They* won't be influenced," Rita agreed. "But the word will get around. After all, this hearing will attract a lot of attention. Then what happens?"

"It'll be forgotten the day after the hearing is over," Prince said glibly. Her appearing as a witness did not disturb him. But he remembered another potential witness who did. Burt Carlyle. He added, "I'd better have a talk with Carlyle."

"Don't forget they're friends, Pierson and Carlyle."

"I know. But Carlyle's a bright young man. He knows that friendship won't buy you a cup of coffee in these times."

"Don't do anything without talking it over with your lawyer first," she advised.

"Lawyer? Don't worry, baby, when it comes to handling himself on his feet, your Harvey is as good as they come."

CHAPTER EIGHT

DR. CRAIG Pierson raced up the steps of Good Samaritan Hospital. He hurried to ICU and slowed only when he approached the glass wall that sealed off that unit from the rest of the noisy floor. He entered quietly and whispered to a young bearded resident, "Mr. Pierson? I'm his son and a physician."

"Room 9," the resident said.

He found the cubicle where his father lay. "Dad?" Craig asked softly. Bill Pierson's eyes opened, closed, then opened again.

"They shouldn't have bothered you, son," he said weakly.

Craig glanced at the monitor behind the bed, watching the blips dance across the screen. They were as slow and tired as his father's

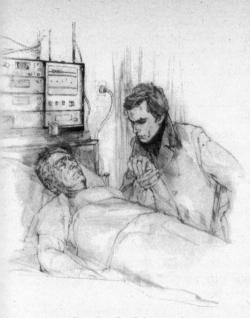

heart must be. He slipped into the chair alongside the bed, took his father's thin hand.

"What are they doing to me?"

"Just precautionary, Dad," Craig assured him. "So just rest, relax, let the antibiotics work on that pneumonia."

Content to lie there, his hand held in the affectionate grasp of his son, Bill Pierson felt at peace and secure. In a while, without opening his eyes, he said, "Remarkable what they do these days. My father was forty-two when he died from a heart attack. Here I am seventy-one, and still going. Because of young men like you. Makes me proud, son. Have you seen your mother?"

"I came here straight from the airport."

"Call her. Tell her you're here." The old man chuckled. "She'll go right into the kitchen and start cooking. And you better be ready to eat. Call her!" he insisted.

Craig went to the pay phone just outside ICU.

"Craig? Where are you?"

"At the hospital with Dad."

"What happened?" she demanded, her voice rising in concern.

"Nothing. Just thought I'd come take a look," Craig said. "I'll check with the doctors, then come out to the house."

"I'd better come in. They only let me see him twice a day."

"I'll be here, waiting. I love you, Mom."

He had just hung up when there was a flurry of activity outside the phone booth. Several doctors and nurses raced toward ICU. He followed them. Beyond the glass wall he could see them converge on his father's cubicle.

323

He raced to the door to hear the resident say, "Okay!" A technician activated two paddles that had been placed on his father's chest and back. The body heaved. There was no other response. Again the resident gave the command. The line on the monitor remained flat, the sound an ominous monotone. The third jolt of electricity accomplished nothing.

Craig rushed in and pushed aside the equipment. He began to apply tremendous manual resuscitation. He worked until sweat dropped off his face onto his father's bare chest. In a while, exhausted, and acknowledging death, he slumped on his father's body and wept. The resident cleared the room, permitting Craig to be alone with his father's lifeless body.

For a whole day and night Craig tried to reach Kate. She was not at the hospital, not at home. He was puzzled and distressed.

He called Ordway to explain why he would not be back for a few days. Ordway was sympathetic.

The funeral was a small affair. Friends came, including some Craig had not seen since high school days. Neighbors had prepared for their return from the cemetery with food, hot coffee, and sufficient people to keep the house from seeming large and empty. Later, when the mourners were gone, the phone rang.

"Craig?" It was Kate.

"Darling, where've you been? I've been looking all over for you."

"I know. Shall I come? Would it help?"

"I'd love you to meet Mother."

"Good. I'll come," she said.

He went to the small airport to meet her. It was close to midnight when the two-engined plane touched down. In minutes Kate was in his arms. He knew now how much she meant to him.

When Kate and his mother met, they embraced each other as though they were old friends. Then his mother held Kate off and stared into her face. "I always knew when Craig chose a girl she would be lovely and fine. I used to say, 'Dad, when Craig . . .'"

She turned away, wiping her eyes.

Over coffee, his mother asked Kate about herself, her family, her early life. Soon they were exchanging anecdotes and memories.

It was very late when his mother finally went up to bed. Kate and Craig remained in the parlor.

"You haven't told me where you were for two days," Craig said.

"Chasing rainbows," she said ironically.

"What does that mean?"

"I was able to get a look at Prince's file in personnel. It kept bugging me. Why, eleven years ago, would Prince leave an excellent hospital and a large practice? At a time when he should be reaching the peak of his career, why make such a change?"

"What did you find out?"

"I searched his entire file. Everything clean. His letters of recommendation are so laudatory they're almost embarrassing. So I decided to go back to his old hospital and do some checking."

"And?"

"Those letters of recommendation are genuine."

"That shouldn't be any surprise. He's a terrific surgeon."

"Still"—Kate hated to abandon her suspicion—"I was so sure. A man like Prince to up and leave a profitable situation? Why?"

Her psychiatrically oriented mind demanded a sensible motive.

WHEN Kate Lindstrom returned to her office, she found three messages that Peter Tompkins had called. She made him her first order of business.

The agitated young man pleaded that Kate see him at once. She agreed.

"You've got to help me!" were his first words when he confronted Kate in one of the consultation rooms.

"Exactly what kind of help do you want?"

"It was bad enough before. . . ." Tompkins started to pace to avoid looking at her as he confessed. "It was the way things kept growing worse. At first the operation was to be minor. Suddenly they'd destroyed any chance of our having kids of our own. I could live with that. But then her thrombosis. And everything that flowed from that. Including—"

"What it might possibly do to the sexual part of your lives?"

"Yes. Then, once she tried to commit suicide, I had to ask myself, What am I getting into? What if that happens again?"

325

"Are you sure that's really what troubles you?" Kate asked. "Or is it your own guilt at having precipitated her attempt?"

"I had no way of knowing she hadn't been told!"

"Of course not. Still, you feel guilty."

"It's more than that," Tompkins confessed. "I love her, Dr. Lindstrom. I really love her. It's the future I don't know about. Myself. I'm going to need help to find out if I can make our marriage work. I want your help."

"That may not be possible," Kate warned. "Mr. Tompkins, sit down." Once he had, she went on, "Listen to me very carefully. Cynthia is my patient. For her to have continued trust in me, I have to be completely honest with her. Before I could treat you, I would have to get her permission."

"I'm sure she'd say yes," he responded quickly.

"She loves you. Of course she'd agree. The question is this: Would my asking her for permission raise such hopes in her that if your treatment didn't work out, she would become so depressed that there might be—damaging consequences? She's groping her way to a recovery. I don't want to do anything to upset that. So I don't want to ask her just now."

"Then when?" he asked impatiently.

"That will depend on you," Kate said. "You're frightened, and have every right to be. You're confronting a very difficult challenge. Because of Cynthia's condition, sexual relations might be difficult. But the marriage can succeed if there's understanding, patience, consideration. So I want you to think about it. Then if you come back and say you're willing to work at it, hard and earnestly, I'll ask Cynthia for permission to treat you. But I don't want to raise any false hopes in her. Do you understand?"

Tompkins sat still and silent. Finally he nodded gravely.

"Call me if you decide you can do it," Kate said. "Until that time, we'll go on the basis that we have never had this conversation."

HARVEY Prince was completing his sixth case in the OR. It was Friday, and the hearing would begin on Monday.

He permitted Carlyle to close, then said, "Burt, you in a rush?"

"No. Why?"

326

"Oh, just thought if you had a little time, we might have a drink." Prince smiled. "There's something I want to talk to you about."

"Let me check on the floor. If there are no problems, I'm free."

"I'll be in the cocktail lounge across the street."

Within half an hour, Burt Carlyle found Harvey Prince nursing a Scotch on the rocks. Once Burt had been served, Prince began.

"Burt, you and I should've had this talk months ago, but things have been so hectic I haven't had a chance. Practice is growing faster than I can handle. And out of regard for those women who come seeking help, I'd have to be pretty coldhearted to turn them away. As I said, things are hectic. So I've been meaning to talk to you."

Prince took another sip of the smooth, icy liquor.

"Burt, I've been watching you for a long time now. I wouldn't hesitate to entrust any patient of mine to you. I've thought about it carefully and come to a decision. I would like you to come into my office as soon as you finish your residency."

Burt Carlyle hoped that his eagerness was not too transparent. Cool, he cautioned himself, play it cool.

Prince went on, "My boy, I guarantee you seventy-five thousand dollars a year to start. After that, write your own ticket. I don't expect to practice forever. The time will come when you and the other two men in my office will take over. And I'd say within five years you'll be making a hundred and fifty thousand a year, maybe more!"

Prince chuckled. "Take the weekend to consider it. Seventy-five thousand a year to start. Let me know by Monday."

Harvey Prince was signing the tab when he pretended to suddenly recall, "Oh, Monday. I'll be busy with that damn hearing. But I'll want your answer as soon as that's over."

Harvey Prince had no doubt at all that Carlyle got the message. Prince's offer was clearly dependent on what developed during the hearing.

THE hearing in the matter of the termination of Dr. Craig Pierson was held in the boardroom of State University Hospital. It was a luxurious room with oak-paneled walls, and a polished mahogany table fifty-four feet in length and wide enough for the three presiding surgeons to sit abreast at one end.

Simmons, a tall man with a florid face, sat in the middle, since he was the presiding officer. On his left sat Dr. James Kearney of Misericordia Hospital, stolid and grim, as usual. On Simmons' right sat Dr. Myron Fein of Mount Zion, a small man who seemed pleasant and affable. But those who had worked with Fein in the OR knew him to be a man of violent rages when the slightest detail went wrong.

Clinton Ordway and Walter Deering were present to protect the hospital's interests in the event institutional practices came into question. It had been suggested that the hospital be represented by an attorney. But since none of the parties had chosen legal counsel, the board of trustees had voted against it.

The stenotypist set up her machine and was ready. Simmons, Kearney, and Fein were ready. Sitting on one side of the table, Craig Pierson was ready. The place opposite him was empty. The chair designated for Harvey Prince. Simmons was growing impatient when the door was flung open. Prince entered in great haste.

"Sorry, gentlemen! Emergency. Ectopic pregnancy. But she's in good hands, and now I'm all yours." He took his seat and said in a condescending manner, "Good morning, Pierson. I understand you've had a loss in your family. Terribly sorry."

"Thank you," Craig said, wishing his opponent were less pleasant and ingratiating.

"Now, then," Simmons said as he opened the hearing. "We are here because Dr. . . . ." He had to consult his notes. "Dr. Craig Pierson has been dismissed during the second year of his residency. The causes are insubordination, personality conflict with attending surgeon, unethical interference in the surgeon's case. Dr. Pierson requested a hearing."

Simmons cleared his throat slightly. "Now, we'd like to accomplish this hearing in the swiftest and fairest way possible. Dr. Pierson, anything you wish to say at the outset?"

Craig replied, "Since I've been dismissed, I consider myself accused of wrongdoing. Therefore I would like to hear testimony as to the specific charges before I say anything."

328

Simmons turned his attention to Harvey Prince. "Doctor?"

"I would like a witness to be sworn. I have several witnesses."

"The first one, then," Simmons said briskly.

With a smug smile, Prince said, "My first witness is Dr. Craig Pierson."

Taken by surprise, Craig flushed in anger, glared at Prince. Simmons lowered his glasses and instructed the stenotypist, "Administer the usual legal oath!"

Once she had, Prince leaned forward on the table, staring across at Craig. "Dr. Pierson, in view of the fact that this entire series of events began with a surgical procedure, would you explain to the panel what happened in the OR that day?"

"A patient, twenty-two years of age, was presented for an exploratory laparotomy. I scrubbed with Dr. Prince. I performed the oophorectomy on the right side. It was sent up to the path lab for a frozen section. The report came back: borderline mucinous carcinoma of low malignant potential. Whereupon Dr. Prince ordered me to remove the left ovary as well."

"And what did *you* do?" Prince interposed quickly.

"I refused."

In a voice edged with disapproval, Fein asked, "Young man, you mean that the surgeon in charge of the case decided on a procedure and you refused to carry it out?"

"There was a good reason—"

"You'll have your turn, Doctor!" Simmons interjected. He turned to Prince, "What happened after that?"

"I completed the procedure myself."

Craig insisted, "I would like to explain my actions in the OR."

"Dr. Pierson," Simmons said, "no one intends to deprive you of your chance to defend yourself. But you asked that Dr. Prince submit his case first. So we will proceed. Dr. Prince?"

"My second witness is Dr. Clinton Ordway."

Ordway took the oath from the stenotypist.

Prince asked, "Dr. Ordway, Dr. Pierson was dismissed. Wasn't he first offered the chance to *resign?*"

"Yes," Ordway admitted.

"In fact, isn't it true that you and I tried a number of times to

329

keep him out of harm's way? That we agreed to have him removed from my scrub team in order to avoid further friction?"

"Yes," Ordway had to agree.

"Isn't it also true that Pierson *asked* to be dismissed?"

"Yes."

"So he could demand this hearing," Prince concluded, driving the point home.

"I wouldn't know."

Prince turned to Craig. "Surely Dr. Pierson can tell us?"

Craig announced firmly, "Yes. That was my reason."

"So you see"—Prince turned to the panel—"we're all here, at great inconvenience, to satisfy the capricious whim of this arrogant young man. Whose real purpose escapes me. Unless he's here to carry out a personal vendetta against *me!*"

"This is a purely professional matter," Craig said.

Prince ignored Craig and turned back to Ordway. "Tell this panel, Doctor, didn't this young man criticize my decision during the pathology conference?"

Ordway hesitated. "Dr. Pierson did make some critical remarks during the path conference."

"Did he also insist on having this case discussed at grand rounds? Again critical of my decision?"

"Yes."

"And did he also attempt to have it discussed at the morbidity and mortality conference?"

"It was not discussed," Ordway pointed out.

"The important fact is, this young man tried to have it discussed!" Prince turned to the panel. "Gentlemen, there's a pattern here of personal vengeance. For reasons that will become quite apparent later, this man has embarked on a campaign of vilification against me."

"That's not true!" Craig shot back.

"And the result is this hearing. Gentlemen, I must apologize to you for this whole regrettable episode."

Fein agreed compassionately. "I know how you feel, Dr. Prince, when a man with your record has to justify himself."

"You'll appreciate that even more," Prince said, "when you've

330

examined the record." He reached under the table for his attaché case and produced a thick document. He slapped it down on the conference table with dramatic impact.

"This," he announced, "is a Xerox copy of Cynthia Horton's chart. It contains all the facts in her case. Signs and symptoms. Diagnosis. Surgical procedure. Postoperative plan. You gentlemen are free to consult it." He pushed the chart toward Simmons.

"Before you gentlemen examine it, I want to warn you. One entry has been removed!" Craig charged.

"Of course it has," Prince conceded readily, to Craig's surprise.

"Under what circumstances?" Kearney asked, leaning forward.

"After surgery, I wrote up what I had done. Also my notes for the postop plan. Thereafter, Dr. Pierson wrote on the same page his complete disagreement with my decision."

Prince smiled. "At the time, I dismissed it as an impulsive, immature act. And so, to protect him from charges of insubordination, I removed that page and rewrote my entry. In view of what's happened since, I regret having done that."

Craig slowly sank back in his chair, realizing that Prince was as shrewd a tactician as he was a surgeon.

"But, gentlemen, the chart before you is incomplete in other important aspects. I must ask you to be indulgent so I can give you a more complete view than is in the written record.

"Dr. Simmons, would you turn to the first page and see who took the history of Cynthia Horton on her admission to the hospital?"

Simmons leafed through the chart. "It's signed by Dr. Pierson."

Myron Fein observed, "That's the job of interns." He turned to Craig. "I hope you have a logical answer."

"An intern had gone in to take her history. But he didn't succeed. The patient was extremely tense," Craig explained. "You might say she was in shock. Emotional shock. She has a personal history which colored her outlook."

"And that is?" Kearney persisted.

"When I asked about the incidence of carcinoma among her close female relatives, she confessed she had no knowledge of her natural family. She is adopted. She trusted me because, you see, I too am adopted. She felt able to talk to me rather freely."

"What did she say?" Simmons asked.

"She has felt—from her earliest years—that she has been the victim of fate. That destiny would prevent her from enjoying the life that other young women have."

Prince intervened. "Dr. Pierson, would you say she was obsessed with dying at a young age?"

"I wouldn't say obsessed."

"Deeply concerned, then?"

"Yes," Craig was forced to concede.

Having established that point, Prince addressed the panel. "Now, gentlemen, I wish you would consult her chart and see under what conditions she signed the consent form."

Simmons found the form. "Who is Dr. K. Lindstrom?"

Prince said, "A psychiatric resident on staff here."

"A psychiatric resident?" Fein asked, startled.

"Is he available for questioning?" Simmons asked.

"She," Prince corrected, then added, "I think she must be asked to appear."

"We'll recess. See that she's here within fifteen minutes!"

DURING the recess, Craig Pierson sat immobile, making every effort not to surrender to panic. To face three men who had the absolute power to determine his professional destiny was a terrifying experience. Three men, obviously set against him. He had begun to regret having demanded a hearing.

And Kate? What could Prince ask her?

Craig was pondering the possibilities when Kate arrived, an eager look on her lovely face. She sank into the chair beside Craig, took his hand, and whispered, "I'm glad you sent for me."

"I didn't send for you," he whispered back.

Before Kate could respond, Simmons was calling the hearing to order. "Dr. Prince, you wished this witness to appear?"

"Indeed." He smiled across the table at Kate. "Dr. Lindstrom, a question has come up about an entry in Cynthia Horton's chart. I thought you could enlighten the panel."

"I'll do my best," Kate said, and was administered the oath.

"Now, then," Prince continued. "A consent form for surgery is usually secured by the surgeon or a resident. But in this case, the consent form was secured by you. Would you explain why?"

Kate glanced at Craig, then stared across the table at Prince.

"Of course," she began. "The patient was unusually apprehensive. She had refused to sign the consent form. Dr. Pierson sent for me, thinking I might reassure her and persuade her to sign. Which I did. That's all."

"That's all?" Prince repeated. "Surely there must be more. What did she say to you?"

"I found the patient to be tense," Kate responded. "Quite suspicious of all doctors. In fact, she accused Dr. Prince of doing many unnecessary operations."

"I resent that!" Prince interrupted angrily.

"I was asked to relate what happened during my conversation with the patient," Kate explained sweetly.

Fein leaned forward, staring at Kate. "Doctor, how did this patient's anxiety manifest itself?"

"She talked of things in the past tense. Her impending marriage, for example. She seemed to have given up hope."

"I see," Kearney said, attaching significance to Kate's answer.

Prince resumed his questioning. "Tell me, Dr. Lindstrom, at the time you saw her, would you say that her overriding concern was survival?"

"Isn't that everyone's fear in time of crisis or danger?"

"I agree with that," Prince said quickly, "because I had come to the same conclusion about that girl."

Prince turned to address the panel. "I needn't tell you, gentlemen, that the night before any operation a surgeon thinks about the total patient. Not merely the body which is presented for surgery. But a total human being. A wife, a lover, a mother. A doctor must ask himself, How can I best benefit that total patient?"

Craig was sorely tempted to remark that whatever Prince had thought the night before, it was more likely what to tell his broker the next morning.

Prince continued, "That night before I operated on the Horton girl I promised myself, whatever it was humanly possible to do to assure her a long life, I would do. Because of her desperate fear of dying so young, all that mattered to me was to come down from the OR and say to her, My dear, don't worry, you're going to be fine. For the very reasons Dr. Lindstrom has so clearly set forth. Thank you, Dr. Lindstrom."

But Craig intervened. "I believe I have a right to question witnesses." Simmons nodded.

"Dr. Lindstrom, during your talk with the patient, was it only her concern about survival that troubled her?"

"She was afraid the operation would destroy her chances of getting married. And because of her adoption, she looked forward to having children of her own."

"Her ability to bear children was important to her?"

"Very much so," Kate said.

"If you were a surgeon faced with such a patient, would it be an important concern to you to preserve her childbearing ability, if at all possible?"

Prince interrupted. "Dr. Lindstrom is not a surgeon. Therefore she should not be allowed to answer that question."

Simmons agreed. "Only surgeons are qualified to express opinions involving surgery. Any more questions, Dr. Pierson?"

Craig looked at Kate. "No more questions," he said grimly.

"Dr. Prince?"

"Yes. One more question. Dr. Lindstrom, could the patient have borne her own children if she were dead?"

"Of course not."

"So that saving her life was the first and most important thing. Am I right?"

Kate Lindstrom reacted in a flush of fury. "I admit the patient was fearful about dying. But there was more, much more. And that was, as much as living, she wanted to be mother to her own children. Now, one surgeon who was there tells me that both her life and her fertility could have been preserved. Because I know him to be a man of integrity, I believe him!"

Kate was tense to the point of tears. The three panel members were all made suddenly self-conscious by her outburst. Kearney observed dryly, "I think we've heard enough from this witness."

Simmons resumed charge of the hearing. "Dr. Prince, is there any more material in the patient's chart that we should cover?"

"There certainly is. Because therein lies the real reason I asked that Dr. Pierson be dismissed!"

"Please explain," Simmons urged.

"Once the frozen section revealed a carcinoma, I felt I had no choice but to do a bilateral. I say, When in doubt, take it out. My plan was, save the girl's life. Make sure she is free of disease. Then put her on estrogens to avoid the aftereffects."

Both Fein and Kearney nodded, affirming Prince's plan.

"Of course, I did not expect a girl of twenty-two to have a thrombosis. But once that happened, naturally I was prevented from prescribing estrogen, not without inviting another and possibly fatal thrombosis.

"Now, you will find in that chart the events that led to the patient being transferred to psychiatric. One evening she made an attempt on her own life! When that crisis occurred, the nurse sent for Dr. Pierson."

Prince paused for a moment and smiled cynically. "Now, one might say, Pierson did prevent her from jumping, and thus he emerges the hero. However, consider this: I suggest Pierson told the girl of her condition. Cruelly. Bluntly. Without any preparation. Pierson precipitated her panic, caused her to make this attempt on her life!"

Craig moved to leap from his chair, but Kate restrained him. Sensing that he had scored strongly, Prince was determined to press his victory.

"Gentlemen, Pierson had been ordered not to have any contact with the girl. Yet somehow he got this information to her, with an unfortunate result. If that isn't insubordination, carried to a dangerous degree, then I don't know what the term means."

Kearney looked grimly at Craig. "Dr. Pierson, did you have contact with the patient after being ordered not to?"

Craig was forced to admit, "She kept asking for me. I tried to avoid her. But since my staying away only made her more anxious, I felt I had to see her."

"And did you tell her the prognosis of her condition in view of her thrombosis?" Kearney pursued.

"I did not," Craig said. "She discovered it from a note sent to her by her fiancé."

"And where did *he* acquire that knowledge?" Kearney persisted.

"He told me that he discussed her case with his own physician."

Suddenly Kearney accused: "You've had conversations about the patient with him?"

"Yes. But nothing improper or unethical," Craig insisted.

Kearney nodded skeptically. "You do agree that her full knowledge of her condition caused her to make an attempt on her life?"

"I have to assume so," Craig conceded.

At that point, Simmons announced, "We are obviously not going to finish today. We will resume at ten tomorrow morning."

CHAPTER NINE

"PLOWED him under!" Harvey Prince exulted to Rita Hallen that evening. He refilled his glass, slowly rotating the brandy as he inhaled its fragrance. "I'll destroy him. . . ."

"Harvey, what'll they do to him?"

"Vote to affirm his firing. Make sure he never gets on the staff of any decent hospital again!"

"He's a bright young man," Rita suggested cautiously. "I've observed him in the OR. Excellent technique."

"Too bad he never learned the technique of minding his own business. Every medical school ought to teach those young squirts to listen, learn, and keep their mouths shut. We can't have doctors criticizing doctors!"

He suddenly remembered, "Damn it, meant to call Carlyle. What time is it?"

"Just past ten."

"Not too late," Prince decided. He dialed the number. "Burt? Dr. Prince. What's your schedule tomorrow? I see, uh-huh." When Carlyle had concluded, Prince said, "The reason I wanted to know is that we're going to call you to testify tomorrow morning."

Prince listened to Carlyle's response, his face betraying a growing intolerance. "Burt, like it or not, you are involved. If my reputation is on the line, and you're coming into my office, then your

336

reputation can be affected too. In the interest of truth, I thought you'd want to say what happened that day."

Prince's voice became more impatient and dictatorial.

"I know it isn't easy for you. But you only have to say what happened! I don't see that you have any choice. Unless, of course, I've misjudged you. I'd hate to think I've been wrong about you, Burt." His meaning was quite clear.

Prince listened, nodded, and said, "Good. See you tomorrow."

"WHAT did Prince want?" LuAnne asked.

"He wants me to testify at Craig's hearing."

"Will you?"

Burt closed off any discussion. "It's late. You should get your rest. And I have to be in the OR at seven."

He turned off the light and slipped into bed. He slid his arm about her and drew her close. She said nothing. But he could sense her tension. He had to discuss it with her.

"He as much as said that if I didn't testify, he would have to reconsider his offer," Burt said. "I want that spot in his office, Lu. Two and a half years of doing everything right, and now . . ."

"Tell me what you'll say to them. I want to be sure in my own mind that you're being honest."

"Do you think I'd lie?" he asked indignantly.

" 'Two and a half years,' " she quoted. "A man dreaming of one ambition for that long might not even know he's lying."

"There's only one question that I don't want to answer."

"What question?"

"If I were the surgeon, and I had to decide whether to do a bilateral on that girl, what would *I* have done?"

"What, Burt? Tell me."

"On a girl of twenty-two, under those conditions . . . *never!*"

"Then Craig was right."

"Of course he was. I just hope they don't ask me."

AFTER Harvey Prince concluded his talk with Burt Carlyle, he said, "I didn't expect any resistance from him. But he came around in the end. Ambition is a wonderful lubricant."

337

Prince laughed and held out his brandy glass. Rita poured him a large refill. In a victorious mood, he drank a stiff slug. His witness of consequence—Burt Carlyle—was now under control.

That confidence and the brandy had a synergistic effect. He leaned back expansively, holding the glass up to the light to study its golden color.

Suddenly he said, "They're not going to do it to me again! They're not!"

"Not going to do what?" Rita asked.

"Doesn't matter," he said, seeking to end the conversation.

She probed. "Darling, who are 'they'?"

"Wasn't 'they,' " he replied impatiently. "One man—jealous, resentful. Who ever heard of practicing surgery by statistics?"

He drained his brandy glass. "That's right!" he exploded. "Statistics! Because I was more successful than all the other men at the hospital, he accused me of doing unnecessary surgery. I laughed him off. Nobody paid any attention to him. Until he began spouting his damned statistics!"

He held out his glass. Rita reached for the decanter.

"Just because I did four times as many hysterectomies as any other man in the county does not mean they were unnecessary! But that's not the way they saw it. Of course, they were all competitors. Vultures, waiting to pounce on my practice if they could drive me out.

"My wife said, 'Why fight them? You can do as well anywhere you go.' I'll say one thing for Margaret, she stuck by me. Even offered to sell all the jewelry I'd bought her so I could afford to come here and set up practice again."

He smiled. "Silly girl had no idea of my investments. I needed her jewelry like the Arabs need another oil well. The important thing is, she offered. That's why, Rita, I can't ever . . ."

He realized, too late, that in his alcoholically expansive mood he had said too much. He was silent, wondering if Rita now understood fully that all his reassurances over the years had been lies.

Stunned, Rita said nothing for a moment. What pained her almost as much as his long-practiced deception was her realization that, even now, she had neither the courage nor the strength

to end things between them. She made every effort to conceal her pain and anger by remarking, "So that's why you came here eleven years ago?"

He admitted, "That's why."

"Funny," Rita said. "When you joined the hospital, everyone was so impressed. You, from such a fine hospital in the East, with such praise from your colleagues there."

"Those letters, all that 'praise'? Only written to get me to leave. They were protecting themselves. Their hospital. After all, if I made a public scandal, patients might start saying, 'If Prince has been doing that for nine years, what about the rest of the men on that staff?' So to get rid of me in a nice, quiet way, they gave me those magnificent letters."

Angrily he added, "Well, they're not going to do that to me again! At fifty-five a man can't pull up stakes and start somewhere else. So I am going to destroy that arrogant Pierson." He glanced at his wristwatch. It was just past midnight. "I'd better go. Margaret waits up for me."

He had gone. Rita Hallen sat alone, dwelling on Harvey's words. "That's why, Rita, I can't ever . . ."

She mustered all the things she should have said. Silently she accused: Liar! Fraud! All these years, inventing excuses, empty promises! I hate you. . . .

The tears started down her cheeks as she had to confess: I've always known. Tonight, when you said that terrible thing, why didn't I say, Get out! Out of my house! Out of my life!

And because she knew why, Rita Hallen put her face in her hands and wept. She hated him more than she had ever hated anyone. Until she realized you couldn't hate anyone that much without having loved him.

She fell asleep, as she so often did, alone, in tears.

Once Burton Carlyle was sworn in, Simmons turned the hearing over to Harvey Prince.

"Doctor," Prince began, "would you tell the panel what took place during Cynthia Horton's operation?"

Meticulously avoiding any opinion, Carlyle recited the facts.

"Doctor, that same morning in the OR, did I permit you to do a rather complicated operation?" Prince asked.

Puzzled at the question, Burt answered, "I performed an exenteration. Under your direction, of course."

"Did you do as much surgery in your second year of residency as in your third?"

"Of course not. Third-year men are expected to do more."

"Now, isn't it true that second-year men, eager and ambitious, sometimes feel that they're being deprived of the opportunity to do the more involved types of surgery?"

"I guess so," Burt admitted. "I felt that way last year."

"And Pierson was no different, was he? I mean, you must have heard him gripe about not being given enough surgery?"

"As you said, we all feel that way in our second year."

"Now, that day, I permitted you to do an exenteration. But Pierson was only permitted to do an exploratory. Isn't that so?"

"Yes," Burt agreed cautiously.

"Have you ever heard Pierson express the opinion that he was confident that he could do more complicated surgery?"

"If a surgeon hasn't got confidence, he ought not to approach the table," Burt said, thinking to defend Craig.

"Is there such a thing as having *too* much confidence?" Prince asked suddenly. "Might a man feel equipped to do cases in his second year that are beyond his ability and experience?"

"Dr. Pierson's surgical technique is excellent."

"His technique is not in question," Prince said a bit sharply. "Only his overreaching ambition. This young surgeon, feeling I was denying him opportunity for experience, resented me. And thus he decided to make outrageous charges against me! You do admit he felt deprived of opportunity?"

"There was nothing personal in that."

"Stop beating around the bush, Doctor," Prince said. "The point is, Pierson resented me. I wouldn't let him do surgery he felt entitled to do. That's what it comes down to. And it was especially marked that afternoon of the Horton case, because that morning I had chosen you, not him, to do the exenteration."

"I wouldn't say he was resentful that day," Burt pointed out.

"We'll let the panel decide that. Thank you, Doctor."

Burt Carlyle was tremendously relieved. Especially when Craig, realizing the pressure his friend was undergoing, sacrificed the opportunity to question him.

He had risen when Simmons said, "One moment, Doctor. Is there anything you'd like to add to your statement?"

Burt Carlyle hesitated and finally said, "No, sir."

"Then we thank you very much. You're excused."

Burt swiftly left the room without glancing at Craig Pierson or Kate Lindstrom.

THE remainder of the morning was given over to the testimony and slides of pathologist Sam Becker. At the end of his presentation, Simmons turned to Craig. "Do you have any questions?"

"Just one. Dr. Becker, when you sectioned Cynthia Horton's second ovary, what did you find?"

"It was clean—absolutely healthy," Becker replied.

Prince asked, "Dr. Becker, do you know the incidence of eventual involvement of the second ovary once one has been found to be malignant?"

"I've seen estimates of fifty percent," Becker admitted.

"So that since there was a finding here of a mucinous carcinoma, though borderline, it was good practice to remove that second ovary in order to save that girl's life."

"I can only say I found that second ovary to be perfectly healthy," Becker reiterated.

Becker was excused, and Simmons decided to take a break for lunch.

When the hearing reconvened, Kate did not reappear, nor was there any message from her.

Simmons said to Prince, "Doctor, do you have anything further to say?"

"I'm quite satisfied with the opportunity you've been kind enough to afford me," Prince said graciously.

"Dr. Pierson, do you have any witnesses to present?"

"No witnesses, sir. But I have scientific papers I'd like to present,

342

papers which prove the desirability of unilateral oophorectomy in cases such as this." He offered to the panel reprints of articles from several gynecological journals.

Fein accepted them, glanced at the titles and the summaries stating the conclusions of each paper. "I've read these before," Fein said, passing them to Simmons and Kearney.

"Is this the sum and substance of your case?" Simmons asked.

"That. And a statement," Craig responded.

"Before you make any statements, we have some questions to ask you," Simmons said. He drew from his portfolio a sheaf of typed pages. Craig wondered if those questions had been prepared by Harvey Prince.

"Doctor, how many oophorectomies have you scrubbed for?"

"I'd say ninety, a hundred," Craig responded.

"Ninety, a hundred," Simmons repeated, belittling Craig's experience. "Now, as to those which the path lab reported as being malignant on frozen section, how many resulted in bilateral ovarian excisions? Make an estimate. All? Most? Few? None?"

"I . . . I would say . . . most," Craig had to admit.

"So that a decision to do a bilateral is not unusual. Yet you're attacking Dr. Prince's actions." Simmons glanced at his two colleagues with an air of intolerance.

"There are two things different in this case!" Craig interjected. "First, the path report said borderline mucinous carcinoma in one ovary—*borderline!* Second, there was no palpable mass in her other ovary. Those two facts together said one thing to me—*caution. Give her a chance!* A chance to bear children! That's a precious right. It belongs to her!"

"Doctor," Simmons responded acerbically, "we are surgeons. Not fairy godmothers, in whose power it is to grant every wish. We have to make choices. Hard choices. As in this case."

Craig exploded. "In this case, the choice was not between life and the ability to bear children! The patient's life was not endangered. The tumor was *in situ*, completely contained. It was removed. We had every obligation to wait and see." Craig paused. "We didn't, and when the patient realized what she had become, she tried to kill herself."

There was a sudden hush in the room. Finally Simmons asked, "Doctor, explain that phrase, 'what she had become.'"

"A twenty-two-year-old menopausal woman deprived of the supplementary benefits of estrogen," Craig said.

"Are you blaming Dr. Prince for her thrombosis?"

"Only for the irreversibility of her condition."

"Tell me, Doctor," Simmons asked, "at the time the decision was made to perform a bilateral oophorectomy, did you point out to Dr. Prince what could result if the patient later suffered a thrombosis?"

"No," Craig admitted.

"Why not, if you seem so exercised about it now?"

"Because at the time . . ." Craig found himself entrapped.

"Isn't it because at the time no one could have predicted that a girl of twenty-two would suffer a thrombosis?"

"A thrombosis is always a postsurgical possibility."

"What would you estimate that possibility to be?"

"I'd say about five percent," Craig conceded.

"Aha!" Simmons exclaimed. "So what is at the crux of this issue is the following: Dr. Prince, at a vital point in the procedure, had to decide between two eventualities. A thrombosis with a less than five percent chance of occurring. And the spread of a malignancy which, as Dr. Becker pointed out earlier, has almost a fifty percent chance of occurring. He chose the odds that favored the patient. You disagreed with him. And that's why we're here now."

Craig bolted up from his chair, leaned toward his three judges. "You won't get away with this!"

"Doctor . . ." Simmons tried to override him.

Craig reached across and seized the papers he had submitted. "There was another choice. The procedure described in these new studies! The conservative alternative. Remove what is dangerous. But preserve what is healthy and life-giving."

He turned to face Prince. "A doctor's obligation is to administer the most helpful therapy with the least harmful effect on the patient. If what we do to a patient is such that when she discovers it she wants to commit suicide, then we have a great deal to answer for! And instead of using percentages to conceal the issue,

instead of doctors helping doctors to conceal mistakes, we should sit as judges of each other. We all make mistakes. But the way to prevent future mistakes is to vow never to repeat them!"

Craig felt cold sweat trickle down his cheek. It required all his effort to retain control and continue.

"We must remember that each patient is a special, singular being. Unless we treat all patients that way, perhaps we have no right to touch them at all!"

Kearney challenged sharply: "Are you saying that Dr. Prince would have been better advised not to do surgery at all?"

"Surgery? Of course. Butchery? No!"

All three panel members glared fiercely at Craig on the use of "butchery." But far from being silenced, he was outraged as he continued, "And the rest of you are equally guilty! You have made our science a medical Mafia, with the same code of honor! *Silence!* We do not inform on one another. I say it is time . . ."

Craig did not conclude but sank down into his chair, covering his damp face with his hands. There was an awesome stillness in the room. Finally Simmons cleared his throat and announced hoarsely, "I think the panel would like time alone for discussion."

Once the room was cleared, Fein spoke up first. "Too bad. Dedicated young man. Bright."

"Not bright enough to keep his mouth shut," Simmons said. "Using a word like 'butchery.'"

"Of course," Fein agreed. "I suppose we have to vote now. How do we do this?"

Simmons explained, "We announce our decision orally. Then each of us confirms it in writing."

Fein nodded, but could not avoid adding, "I'll always wonder what would have happened to that patient if Prince *had* adopted Pierson's recommendation."

The other two did not respond.

CRAIG, Prince, Ordway, and Deering were called back to the room. Craig could tell from the ominous silence that his future had been determined.

Simmons somberly declared, "We have come to our decision.

346

It is the unanimous consensus of this panel that Dr. Craig Pierson has been guilty of unprofessional conduct. He was insubordinate in the operating room. He was unethical in interfering in the post-operative care of a patient. We therefore conclude that Dr. Pierson's dismissal by State University Hospital is justified, and we affirm that action."

Clinton Ordway glanced compassionately at Craig Pierson, who stared straight ahead—realizing full well what Simmons' words meant for his career.

After Simmons' pronouncement, Prince said briskly, "I thank you gentlemen for your time and patience. And for your decision."

As Prince was rising from the table, there was a sharp knock at the door. Simmons called out, "Yes?"

The door opened slowly. Burt Carlyle peered into the room. "May I? There's something I feel compelled to say."

"It's too late. This hearing is over," Simmons announced.

Carlyle could glean the verdict from the look on Craig's face. "Maybe I can still change your minds."

Prince glared at Carlyle—a hostile warning. Simmons repeated, "The matter is closed."

The chief resident insisted, "It is not closed as far as I'm concerned. There was one question none of you asked. But you should have." He advanced toward the panel. "Why didn't any of you ask, 'Dr. Carlyle, you were the only other surgeon who scrubbed on that case. You were there when the path report came back. You heard the discussion. What would *you* have done under the circumstances?' I think that's a fair question."

Craig called out, "Burt, no! It won't do any good!"

But Carlyle continued, "The answer is, I would have made the same decision as Dr. Pierson. Give that girl every chance to bear children. I would not have deprived her of that, as one man did, who at the time was more interested in the stock market news his broker had just given him than in his patient!"

The look that passed between Harvey Prince and Burt Carlyle made it clear that the young resident had forfeited all chance of joining Prince's office.

Their backs to the rest of the room, the judges conferred in whispers. When they swung about, Simmons said, "Dr. Carlyle, we find nothing in your statement to alter our decision. But we thank you for coming forward."

Burt Carlyle turned and started slowly for the door.

"I think we can safely close this hearing," Simmons said.

CHAPTER TEN

DR. KATE Lindstrom sat in the modest waiting room of Dr. Leonard Stiehl while the gynecologist consulted with a patient. Kate had not informed his nurse of her mission, permitting her to assume that she was here as a new patient.

While she waited, Kate fingered a note that showed the wear of five hours of folding and unfolding. In a woman's handwriting, it stated: "Suggest you investigate Dr. Prince's background. Especially young doctors on service prior to his resigning." The note, unsigned, had arrived in Kate's interoffice mail.

It could be a hoax, Kate had feared. But desperation forced her to pursue this lead. Tracking down Dr. Stiehl had required a visit to Prince's previous hospital, where she had questioned the chief of the ob-gyn service, Dr. Charles Angelo.

"Didn't I see you here a few days ago, asking questions?" he demanded.

"Yes."

"Then what brings you back?" he asked. "I'm very busy."

"So am I," Kate responded. "A doctor's career is at stake. And I won't leave without the information I came for."

"And that is?"

"Eleven years ago Dr. Harvey Prince resigned from this hospital. He left a thriving practice to set up in a new place. Surely there must have been a reason. Some days ago I investigated his file. It contains many letters of recommendation from this hospital. I was assured the signatures on those letters are genuine."

"They are," Angelo confirmed.

"A man so highly regarded, so successful—why would he leave?"

Angelo turned his swivel chair and stared out the window. "As far as this hospital was aware, his record was perfect."

348

"Good recovery rate among his carcinoma patients?"

"Best in the hospital."

"Even among patients who actually *did* have cancer?"

Angelo swung slowly back to face Kate. "If you're hinting that his number of hysterectomies was a bit higher than the average, I guess that's true."

"A bit?" Kate challenged. "Is that why he was asked to leave?"

"I never said he was asked to leave," Angelo responded.

"Of course not," Kate replied, an edge of sarcasm in her tone. Out of her purse she drew the well-creased slip of paper and handed it to Dr. Angelo.

He scanned it swiftly. His eyes flicked from the page to Kate. "Just a bit of hospital gossip."

"If I had to guess," Kate said, "I'd say this was written out of some personal resentment against Dr. Prince. And while it is general in its accusation, it is specific in one regard: 'Especially young doctors on service prior to his resigning.' I want to know *which* young doctors," Kate demanded.

Angelo responded quickly, too quickly. "It was only one man, and—" He interrupted his outburst.

"That's all I want—the name of that one doctor," Kate said.

"How far do you mean to go with this?" Angelo asked.

"As far as I have to. As I said, a man's career is at stake."

Angelo scribbled a brief note. Before handing it to her, he warned, "Remember, I didn't give you this. Do what you have to, but keep this hospital out of it. Agreed?"

"I'll try," was all Kate would promise while reaching for the note. It read simply, "Leonard Stiehl. Middlebury."

Now SHE was in Dr. Stiehl's waiting room, fingering the anonymous note. Finally the nurse led her into the doctor's office.

Dr. Stiehl appeared to be in his early forties, with a lean, ruddy face. He was studying Kate's file. "When was the last time you had a complete gynecological checkup, Miss Lindstrom?"

"Three weeks ago."

He glanced up. "You want a second opinion? Who's your man?"

"Angelo. Charles Angelo."

349

Slowly Stiehl lowered the file and stared at her.

"He recommended I come and see you. He indicated that you could enlighten me about events, eleven years ago, surrounding the resignation of Dr. Harvey Prince."

Stiehl was thoughtful for a long moment. "What would you want to know? Provided that it didn't come from me."

"That's the first thing I want to know. Why Angelo, and now you, both say, I'll help you, but don't reveal it was me?"

"Not for the same reason," Stiehl said. "He's fighting to preserve the reputation of his department. I'm fighting to overcome six years when I couldn't get an appointment to any good hospital."

Stiehl rose from his chair and began to pace nervously. "How do you suppose I wound up in Middlebury? A small town. With a hospital far smaller than the ones I trained in."

He turned to face Kate. "Mind you, this town has been good to me. But I wanted to be on staff at a large teaching hospital. Do research. We don't have facilities for that here. But I keep in touch, follow all the latest literature. I do my best."

"But it isn't the same," Kate sympathized.

"It's too late to change that. There is a certain time in the life of a doctor when decisions he makes, or which are made for him, determine the rest of his career."

"What kind of decisions are 'made for him'?"

Stiehl turned away. "There's no avoiding it, I suppose."

"No chance," Kate said. Then she smiled. "You can say anything that comes into your mind. I'm a psychiatrist."

He faced her and smiled, relaxing for the first time. "The female psychiatrists I met during my training were all dark, thin, and appeared very neurotic. You're a refreshing change."

"Thank you," Kate said. "Now?" she persisted.

"About Prince." He began to relate in detail his long-ago conflict with Harvey Prince. Finally he concluded: "He had power and prestige, so I ended up with a reputation for being a trouble-maker. I had to go elsewhere to finish my residency. With a wife six months pregnant. And no money. But we managed. I couldn't get an affiliation with a large hospital, so I set up here. Maybe it was for the best. We've got a good life. Nice people."

But Kate could tell there was a hunger in the man that would never be satisfied. She was looking at Craig ten years from now.

"There's another doctor in the same kind of trouble," Kate said. She proceeded to tell him about the Horton case.

Stiehl said, "Fool! He should have kept his mouth shut!" In a moment he added, "Look who's giving advice." He smiled ironically. "I suppose you want me to do something about it?"

"I suspect it will be painful for you, but yes. Please!"

Stiehl stared off, pondering, muttering only once, "Not again!"

"They can't do anything to you this time," Kate consoled.

"Just living through it again will be bad enough."

DR. SIMMONS was slipping into his topcoat. The others too were about to leave when the boardroom phone rang.

Simmons answered with a brisk, "Yes?"

"Dr. Simmons? This is Dr. Lindstrom. I must ask you to hold the hearing open for another four hours. I'm bringing in a witness."

"We have rendered our decision," Simmons informed her curtly.

"You upheld Dr. Pierson's dismissal?" Kate asked.

"We had no choice," Simmons replied. "Sorry."

"Not nearly so sorry as you're going to be if you don't suspend your decision until you hear my witness."

"Young woman, are you threatening me?"

"Yes, Doctor. Unless you hear my witness, I am going to cause the biggest uproar you've ever faced in your long, distinguished career. I'll make it public that you are shielding and protecting a doctor who should have been barred from practice long ago."

"What?" Simmons exploded.

Kate Lindstrom continued coolly, "Do you want to handle this fairly? Or do you want all the publicity that will follow?"

"Doctor, I think your conduct is highly unethical. I shall report it to your superiors."

"Don't bother. I'll do that when I tell them the whole story," Kate replied firmly. She persisted. "Will you give me four hours? It might keep this out of the courts."

She sounded so contentious that Simmons was forced to take her warning seriously. "One moment." He drew Fein and Kearney aside, and after a whispered conversation he returned to the phone. "Four hours. No more!"

"Four hours," Kate agreed. "Meantime you might send for Dr. Prince's personnel file." She hung up.

THREE hours and forty-nine minutes later, Kate Lindstrom and Dr. Leonard Stiehl raced up the steps of State University Hospital. In the boardroom, the panel and all participants were waiting. On the table before Simmons lay the Prince file.

Prince termed the entire exercise an amusing but desperate ploy. But his smile turned to an angry glare when he saw Leonard Stiehl follow Kate Lindstrom into the room. Prince rose swiftly and shouted, "Dr. Lindstrom, if you brought this man to testify against me, I'll sue you. I'll have you kicked out of this hospital. And barred from practicing in this state! How dare you!"

Taken aback by Prince's outburst, Simmons gestured Kate and Stiehl to chairs. "Now, then," Simmons said, "this hearing is reopened." He turned to Stiehl. "You are the witness?"

"Yes, sir," Stiehl responded. "My name is—"

Prince interrupted. "Leonard Stiehl! Ask him why he's here. Ask him *where* he practices. Ask *why*. Ask him how his affiliation with General Hospital terminated!"

Simmons warned, "Harvey, please, we'll ask all those questions. And a good many more. Just relax. Now, Dr. Stiehl," Simmons asked, "what *are* you here for?"

"Dr. Lindstrom explained the case in detail. I'm here to state certain facts about Dr. Prince. It will be your duty to determine if they are accusations."

"That's the most benign description of slander I've ever heard," Prince accused. "I warn you, Stiehl, what happened last time will be nothing compared with what I'll do to you now!"

"Dr. Prince, they've never heard of you in Middlebury. And they think I'm a pretty fair country doctor. So you can't threaten me." He turned to Simmons. "This situation may be new to you, but it's familiar to me. Because the same thing that has happened to Pierson happened to me. I would like to relate the events."

"Proceed," Simmons said.

Stiehl began uneasily. "Dr. Prince is, I must say, the finest technician I've scrubbed with. Skillful. His incisions were cosmetic gems. *Except . . .*" He paused. "Except that he had a tendency to get carried away with his own skill. He worshipped technique to the exclusion of his patients total welfare. He seemed to court difficult surgery, dangerous surgery, to revel in the praise and envy of his colleagues."

"Envy is the answer!" Prince blurted out fiercely.

Stiehl continued, "I've had plenty of time to think about him in the past eleven years. Sleepless nights when I relived unfulfilled ambitions. What was it with Prince? Greed? Is that why all the unnecessary procedures? He charged the highest fees, had the most extensive practice of any attending at General.

"In the end I concluded that it was more personal than that. He was in love with his own ability. He needed praise, applause. He went into the OR each time feeling, I am going to give them a great show! And he did. And *overdid*. More than a few times. Perfectly healthy uteruses, ovaries that other surgeons would have hesitated to remove, he removed without a second thought.

"And when his judgment was questioned, he always had a ready response: 'My patients rarely come back with uterine cancer.' If you're content with statistics, that argument is valid. But those statistics fade before the personal disaster visited on a patient as a result of ruthless, if elegant, butchery."

Stiehl began to perspire. "I wasn't the only resident who noticed this tendency. I was simply the only one foolish enough to speak up. I went to my chief. He confessed he'd been troubled about Prince. By the tissue committee reports that steadily produced findings in Prince's cases: 'Lack of pathology demonstrated.' But how could he accuse Prince without accusing the hospital? And creating a scandal? The system tied his hands, shut his mouth.

"Well, I determined it wouldn't shut mine. So I collected all those tissue committee reports. I insisted a conference be called or I would make them public. A conference was called. Pathologists spoke up. Other residents who had scrubbed on Prince's cases. Staff men felt obligated to add their criticisms."

"Staff men!" Prince interjected. "Hired hands!"

"Dr. Prince, please." Simmons looked to Stiehl. "Continue."

"Talk of that meeting got around. Eventually the trustees sent for me. They listened to my evidence. Respectful. But silent. Then, in their collective wisdom, they decided that Dr. Prince should resign. That he be given a sheaf of recommendations so that he could affiliate with some other hospital, preferably out of the state."

"Didn't anyone question that?" Simmons asked.

"My chief. Because they forced him to sign one of those letters, he resigned in protest," Stiehl said.

"And you, Doctor?" Fein pursued.

"What usually happens to the bearer of bad tidings? I was professionally 'executed.' Because of my reputation as a troublemaker, I wasn't reappointed to my last year of residency."

There was total silence in the room. Simmons reached for the folder before him. "Do you mean to tell me that the letters in Dr. Prince's file are not completely truthful?"

"*Far* from truthful. They were written to protect the hospital against any possible libel suit by Prince and also from adverse publicity. Better to let him resign. Send him on his way with cheers. Let him practice his slaughter of innocents elsewhere."

Harvey Prince brought his fist down on the table, shouting, "I'm not going to sit here and listen to these lies! Those letters are from reputable men. Are you going to take the word of this . . . this country doctor . . . against men like those?"

Simmons handed the file to Stiehl. "Doctor, are you acquainted with the men who signed these letters?"

Stiehl examined the letters, commenting after each one. "Dr. Briscoe is dead now. And Silversmith. So is Harrison . . ."

Harvey Prince interposed, chuckling, "Very convenient. You come here accusing honorable men of writing dishonest letters. Then, challenged to prove your accusation, you say blandly, But they're all dead now!"

Kate Lindstrom leaned toward the panel and said, "I believe Dr. Prince made one error in his last statement."

Prince turned on her with a disparaging smile.

"He said the men who wrote those letters are all dead now. *Not quite true*," she said with great precision.

354

The smile froze on Prince's face. She went on, "Two men are still alive. And can explain how these letters were written. Dr. Angelo, the present chief of the department. And the chief who resigned."

She looked across the table at Prince. "If Dr. Prince would care to call them." She pushed a slip of paper across the table, face down. "Their phone numbers, Doctor."

Prince did not respond. Simmons leaned forward intently. "Harvey?"

"I wouldn't take Angelo's word!" Prince blurted out. "He was jealous of my practice! He'd say anything Stiehl asked him to!"

"And what about your old chief?" Kate Lindstrom pursued. "Why not call him and find out why he resigned?"

Simmons drummed his fingers on the table. "Harvey, do you wish to make those calls, or shall we?"

No longer smiling or confident, his face drained of color, Harvey Prince was forced to speak the most painful words he had ever had to utter. "There's no need. . . . I know what they'll both say."

He rose and, without a glance at anyone, slipped silently out of the room.

Once the door closed, Simmons beckoned to Kate to hand him the slip of paper. He turned it over, stared at it. "Only Angelo's phone number? What about the former chief?"

Kate smiled a small innocent smile as she said, "I took a chance that he was still alive. I guess Dr. Prince believed me."

Simmons had to stifle his own smile, but his eyes confirmed his admiration for her successful gamble.

"Now," he said, "I think this panel had better reconvene in private session and reconsider our decision."

KATE and Craig drove Dr. Stiehl to the airport. Before he boarded his plane, Kate said, "I hope it wasn't too difficult for you."

"Actually, it was good therapy. I've fought that battle with Prince almost every night for eleven years. I looked forward to the day when I could even the score. Now I must admit when I saw him slink out of that room, I felt sorry for him. He's going to relive that bitter moment for the rest of his life. Only he won't have the consolation I had. I was right. That made it bearable."

Craig suggested, "You know, Stiehl, many large hospitals would be happy to have a good experienced man on staff. I bet Ordway would jump at the chance. Shall I talk to him?"

Stiehl smiled. "Not on your life. When I sat facing that panel, with all the power they represented, I said, Thank God for Middlebury and my small hospital. Where I'm a physician, not a politician in a white coat. I wouldn't go back to that for all the money in the world." He laughed, a free and happy man again.

Kate threw her arms around him. "Thanks for everything."

"Believe me, it was a pleasure!" Stiehl declared, and started for the boarding gate.

On the way back to the city, Craig drove, Kate leaned against him. "What do *you* think?" she asked.

"I think we ought to get married right away."

"I meant, who do you think sent me that note?"

"Prince's wife. She finally got wind of his affair with Rita Hallen," Craig said. "Betrayed wives do that sort of thing."

"She couldn't just have got wind of it. Deep down, she's known all along."

"Would *you* know?" Craig asked, half joking.

"Don't ever test me," Kate warned.

"If she didn't just discover his affair, why would she write that note?" Craig asked. "And if not her, who?" Then his own deduction told him. "Rita Hallen?"

"Likely," Kate said.

"But why?"

"Frustration. Perhaps the realization that she's wasted her life in her affair with Prince."

Craig drove on, thoughtful. "Old Goldfingers. Still, I understand Stiehl's reaction. You have to feel a little sorry for him. To possess so much skill and betray it."

IN THE same room in which the panel had earlier voted to reinstate Dr. Craig Pierson, the board of trustees, Walter Deering, and Clinton Ordway were meeting to discuss the matter of Dr.

Harvey Prince. Bruce Miller, chairman of the trustees, presided.

"Madam and gentlemen, I almost feel I should disqualify myself. Because the patient in the case is the daughter of one of my law partners. Needless to say, I am outraged at what happened to her.

"However," Miller continued, "when I contemplate the legal effects, I must caution against any hasty or ill-advised action. There can be repercussions. A lawsuit by Prince for slander and libel. So discretion is strongly indicated."

Walter Deering observed, "We have to consider other practical effects. If we terminate Prince, we're assisting the Hortons if they decide to sue Prince for malpractice. They would undoubtedly include this hospital in such a suit. And if they won, our malpractice insurance would skyrocket!"

The one woman on the board, usually timid about expressing herself, spoke up from the far end of the table. "Mr. Deering, if we retain Dr. Prince, aren't we exposing ourselves to even more malpractice actions in the future?"

"Mrs. Young, I was only suggesting that we do this in an expeditious manner. We permit Dr. Prince to resign. We avoid making any statement that would jeopardize him professionally. After all, he's been good for this hospital. When you see the amount of money Dr. Prince has brought in, you can appreciate his value. Am I right, Ordway?"

Resentful of being enlisted in a conspiracy for which he had no heart, Ordway replied, "Dr. Prince has been responsible for substantial cash flow in the department, because his patients are admitted before it is necessary and linger on after it is indicated. I regret to say that I permitted this. But the Pierson affair has caused me to do some deep and painful thinking.

"It is because trustees in another hospital decided to turn Prince loose on an unsuspecting public that we are faced with the problem now. If we let him make a graceful exit, with another fistful of 'recommendations,' we'll be doing the same thing to some other hospital. To protect other young girls like Cynthia Horton, to protect our profession, I say we must treat with Dr. Prince in the way he deserves."

By the end of the meeting, it was unanimously voted by the

trustees that Dr. Harvey Prince have his hospital privileges revoked and his association terminated. That he be notified to that effect in a letter which would set forth in precise detail the reason for that action, including the dishonest letters of recommendation in his file.

The last was a cautionary step advised by chairman Miller, who said, "Dr. Prince wouldn't dare sue this hospital and make our letter part of his complaint."

Dr. Kate Lindstrom opened the door of her office. She was surprised to find Peter Tompkins waiting for her.

He explained, "You said to call after I had thought it over carefully. Instead of calling, I decided to come see you."

"I said call me if you think you can do it," Kate reminded him.

"I think I can make it work, but I need assurance," he confessed. "Do *you* think it's possible?"

"If there's understanding and compassion, yes."

"I'll need help."

"You'll have help. Mine. Dr. Pierson's. Things can be done to make your love most enjoyable and satisfying. But the most important is tenderness."

"Then will you ask her if you can treat me at the same time you're treating her?"

"It would be better if *you* asked her," Kate suggested. "I'm due to drop in on her this morning. Let's go up now."

On the psychiatric floor, she knocked gently at Cynthia's door.

"Yes?" the girl called listlessly.

Kate peered in. "You have a visitor." She opened the door wide enough for Cynthia to see.

"Pete?" she asked, tears welling in her eyes. "Oh, Pete!"

Kate said, "He has something important to ask you." She waited until Pete crossed the room, lifted Cynthia to her feet and embraced her. Then Kate silently closed the door and started down the hall, confident of Cynthia's answer, confident as well of their future together.

Of all the therapeutic agents in her specialty, Kate knew that the most effective healer was being wanted, being loved.

CRAIG PIERSON was examining a young woman who presented all the signs and symptoms of an ectopic pregnancy about to rupture. His beeper had been tormenting him for ten minutes, until he shut it off and turned his full attention to the patient.

He decided on immediate surgery, and was giving the nurse instructions when Burt Carlyle appeared in the doorway. Once the patient was being prepped, Craig was free to greet Carlyle.

"I never did have a chance to thank you, Burt. . . ."

"I didn't do that for you. I did it for me. No, I guess I did it for LuAnne. Why haven't you answered your beeper?"

"Was that you trying to raise me?" Craig said.

"Ordway. The board's decided. Prince has got to go. Without any nice speeches, complimentary letters, or bon voyage baskets. Out! Terminated!"

"Good," Craig said, deeply relieved.

"Ordway wants to see you," Burt said, smiling.

"I've got this emergency."

"It will only take a few minutes. And pretend you don't know about the decision. LuAnne was delighted too. She asked could you and Kate come for dinner tonight."

"Okay. We'll bring the wine," Craig said as he headed down the corridor.

Clinton Ordway was scanning a research paper when Craig Pierson entered his office. "You wanted me?"

Ordway looked up. "Oh, yes, come in, come in."

"I've got an emergency being prepped right now, sir."

"This won't take long. I guess Carlyle told you about the board's decision."

Craig was about to deny it when Ordway preempted him. "If Burt didn't tell you, how did you know I wanted to see you? You didn't answer your page."

Craig smiled and pleaded guilty.

"One thing Burt didn't tell you, because I didn't tell him. I am going to appoint you chief resident for your third year."

"Thank you, thank you very much."

"No thanks necessary. You're a good surgeon, on the way to becoming a better one. But that wasn't the only reason. You took a grave risk. And you did it in behalf of patients, and for the good of the profession. I like that. Because, frankly, it was something I would not have had the courage to do.

"Now," he said brusquely, "get along to your emergency."

CRAIG Pierson scrubbed in preparation for surgery. At the sink on his right was Burt Carlyle. On his left was Willis Blinn, who seemed to scrub harder than either of them. When Craig went into the operating room, he saw that his scrub nurse was Rita Hallen. Each sterile instrument was laid out in order. Her mask was in place, only her deep, discerning dark eyes were visible.

"Rita, I want to thank you," Craig whispered.

"What for?" she countered, turning away. Craig studied her. As if she felt his eyes, she turned back to look at him. She said nothing, but now somehow he was sure.

They were wheeling in the patient. Craig draped her body, leaving only her abdomen exposed. He held out his hand. Rita passed him a forceps at the end of which was a large cotton swab soaked in brown solution. He began to paint the field of the operation.

The Author
as Seen by the Artist

Drawing Henry Denker's portrait gave me the unique experience of meeting the author while in the midst of illustrating his book. I have to rank him not only as one of my favourite portrait subjects, but by his third sitting I felt I was coming to see an old friend.

In *Error of Judgment* I used the same techniques I had used in illustrating his earlier novel, *The Scofield Diagnosis* (also a Condensed Books selection). I chose professional actors who resembled the author's characters. Then, after they had read the scene to be depicted, I drew them acting out their roles in the proper settings.

Mr. Denker and I found we had much in common. Since he has written and directed plays, he, too, has been involved with actors and the visual arts. We shared ideas on the scenes in his novel best suited for illustration. We also agreed that the most creative hours to practise our crafts are between dawn and noon.

Perhaps best of all, I savour the memory of the way he saved the day when one of my actor-models failed to show up. Mr. Denker heroically left a very hot typewriter to pose for me in New York Hospital as one of his own characters. Like Alfred Hitchcock, he is hidden in two of the *Error of Judgment* illustrations for the reader to find. I might add that Mr. Denker turned out to be my very best actor!

KALAHARI

A CONDENSATION OF THE BOOK BY

Henry Kolarz

Illustrated by Jack McCarthy

Published by Wolfgang Krüger, Frankfurt

Translated from the German by Joachim Neugroschel

The diamonds, millions of pounds' worth, were hidden beneath a small stone cairn somewhere in the waterless wastes of the Kalahari desert.

Only one man knew their exact location. And he was on the run, both from the South African secret service and from the KGB.

This is his strange story—and the story of the young idealistic German, a voluntary service worker caught up quite by chance in potentially world-shaking events, who befriended him.

It is also, above all, a story of Africa, of its deserts and rivers, lakes and forests, and of the fascinating natural life that abounds there.

I

"Just give me a sign, Jan, and we'll turn off and head west."
The pilot lowered his voice so that only Jan Feuchtenbeiner, who
was sitting behind him, could make out what he was saying. "The
fuel will hold out till South America, and then we'll be on Easy
Street for the rest of our lives."

With a discreet sidelong glance, the pilot's eyes took in the two
aluminium suitcases, which were fettered to Feuchtenbeiner's
wrists with steel handcuffs and chains. It was one of the rules of
their game for Jan Feuchtenbeiner to ignore the implicit question,
whether the suitcases were filled with diamonds today, or just
pebbles, and for the pilot not to ask directly.

Both men knew that a discussion of this question, even as a
joke, would cost them their high-paying jobs—as pilot of the company's own Beechcraft King Air and as security head of the Orapa
Diamond Mine. The management of the De Beers Botswana
Mining Company didn't appreciate jokes about its security.

Feuchtenbeiner had stood the metal suitcases on the seats to his
right and left. In the Gaberones airport, he would hand the precious freight over to the security man of the central office and then
accompany it right to the vault in the administration building of
the holding company, the Anglo-American Corporation.

In the course of time, Feuchtenbeiner had stopped smiling at
the invariable and meticulous accuracy of the procedure. It was

365

irksome but unavoidable. No one in Gaberones knew whether this time Feuchtenbeiner's two aluminium cases for the vault of the Anglo-American contained the monthly output of Orapa or just one hundred and fifty pounds of pebbles. No one except Feuchtenbeiner and Bill Scranton, the general manager of Orapa.

Today the cargo was pebbles.

Feuchtenbeiner stretched out his legs and looked at his watch. In ninety minutes, they would land on the small airfield in Gaberones, the capital of the Republic of Botswana: a Land-Rover would have taken two days to drive the three hundred miles from the diamond town of Orapa to the metropolis. As they flew across the eastern edge of the Kalahari with its parched thorn bushes, a herd of antelopes fled from the noise of the engines in an ochre cloud of dust. It hadn't rained here for eight months.

A few minutes later, the pilot reached the fertile strip of land on the eastern outskirts of Botswana, along the railway line connecting Rhodesia and South Africa. Now he had only to follow the dead-straight track southwest to touch down in the capital.

The plane flew lower, and Feuchtenbeiner gazed down at Gaberones, one of the least known capital cities in the world. A housing development with 25,000 inhabitants, it had been conjured out of the bush thirteen years earlier in 1964. Now, in 1977, it was a precise rectangle consisting of a shopping precinct, a small government area, the president's palace, three dozen churches and a few thousand houses. An asphalt street framed the city on all four sides. Except for slums in the east, the bush began abruptly at these edges. Gaberones was not the navel of the world. God knows, but Feuchtenbeiner had learned how to adjust his needs for urban life to the local realities.

The pilot circled over the reservoir which supplied water to the city. Then he touched down on the runway. When the plane had taxied to a standstill, Piet and Balthasar, the security officers, drove right up to it in the Anglo-American armoured transport car. Balthasar, his machinegun at the ready, looked around before waving to Jan Feuchtenbeiner to come over. It was only then that the security head climbed out of the plane, the last man to leave it. With the metal suitcases under his arms, he ducked down as he negotiated the few yards to the armoured car at a run.

Ten minutes later, in Anglo-American's six-storey office building at the end of the precinct—the highest structure in Botswana—Feuchtenbeiner got a receipt for the cases from the security director, who carefully locked up the contents in the vault: seventy-nine sealed leather sacks containing 360,000 carats of worthless pebbles.

Feuchtenbeiner rubbed his swollen wrists. His mission was over now. Balthasar dropped him off at the Holiday Inn, and Feuchtenbeiner, breathing a sigh of relief, plunged into the antiseptic enclave of luxury and civilization: air conditioning and muted light behind dark glass, golf, tennis, a swimming pool; roulette and baccarat; a band and liveried waiters. Meggy, at the reception desk, wordlessly handed him the suitcase which was kept ready for him: toiletries, pyjamas, two shirts, a tropical suit, a tie, swimming trunks.

This time, he had a room with direct access to the garden and the swimming pool. There was still an hour to go until the restaurant opened. He swam a couple of lengths.

At seven p.m., wearing a linen jacket and a tie, he strode into the restaurant. By Botswana standards, the hotel was quite demanding about the costume of its guests. Any man trying to enter the restaurant, the bar, or the casino without a jacket and tie was turned away by the uniformed hotel staff.

In the muted artificial light of the dining room, Feuchtenbeiner couldn't find anyone he wanted to sit with. He nodded at a De Beers prospector, at a table near the band. There was also an English UN expert from the Okavango Delta, a Dutch geologist from Shell, tourists from South Africa, an Indian businessman from Durban, and—now, in 1977, particularly well-dressed—a few self-assured members of the black government of the republic. Feuchtenbeiner chose a table for one, ordered two martinis, South African smoked salmon, and a steak. The black head waiter smiled at him unreservedly. The staff here behaved differently from those in Johannesburg. No suppressed hatred, no servility towards the white guest.

After dinner, Feuchtenbeiner had a third martini at the bar.

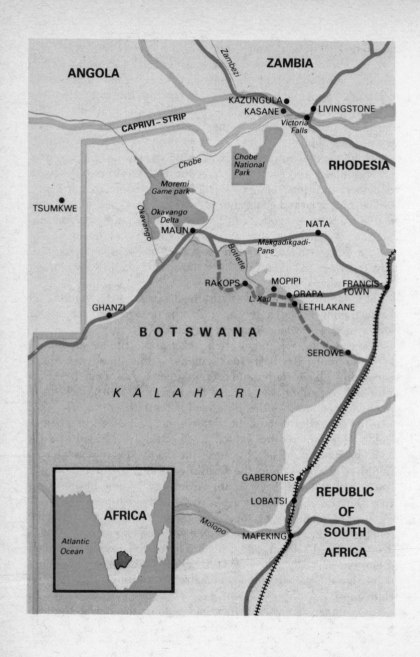

Back in Orapa, where he and June now lived in a standard prefab home, he would have buried himself in a newspaper with a drink, to avoid talking to his wife. He was fed up with her nagging and wailing about the monotonous life in the sterile diamond ghetto, about Orapa's rigid social hierarchy, the gossip about the same unchanging dozen people, the eternal bridge, squash and golf with the same partners. Everyone in Orapa envied Jan Feuchtenbeiner, because being head of security was the only job that allowed regular outings to Gaberones, a far more amusing place.

The South African finished his martini and ambled through the barred gate to the casino. It was still early; only three of the eight roulette tables were occupied. Feuchtenbeiner was no gambler. The only thing that attracted him to roulette was that it was illegal in South Africa. He was content to buy fifty rands' worth of chips and doggedly stake one after the other on number thirty-five. Nineteen-thirty-five was the year of his birth.

At the second table, the croupiers were changing: Sheila was handing over to Denise. Feuchtenbeiner pushed five ten-rand notes over to her, and she converted them silently into green chips, responding to his smile with friendly indifference. It was a mute, hopeless flirtation, which had been going on for about two years now.

Denise was the most attractive of the young girls the casino employed as croupiers. Feuchtenbeiner was self-critical enough to be realistic about his chances with her. He had at least seventeen pounds too much fat on his frame, his coarse skin was covered with freckles, the back of his neck was strewn with scars from boils, and his colourless eyelashes and eyebrows made his rough-hewn, ruddy face look almost like an albino's.

"Please place your bets."

Feuchtenbeiner shoved a chip to thirty-five. On the other side of the table, an African woman leaned over and dropped a yellow chip on his green chip. She didn't look like one of the black women who discreetly plied their trade here, always recognizable by their conspicuous make-up and their wigs of straight, full hair. She had the national peppercorn hairstyle: tiny knots of hair between dead-straight avenues with many crossings and with little barbed-wire braids that stuck out. She gazed at him probingly with her black eyes.

"Twenty-seven red." Denise cleared the playing area, pushed a winning pile towards an Indian, and dropped one chip into her empty glass. "For the staff, thank you. Please place your bets."

For a moment, the African woman's hand grazed his over thirty-five. He flinched. Her yellow chip covered his green chip and she smiled, as though begging his indulgence. There had been something like restrained tenderness in the touch of her delicate fingers. Was it intentional? He couldn't tell by her face. Spellbound, she followed the run of the ball, and when it finally came to rest, she emitted a high giggle of delight.

"Thirty-five black." Denise pushed a stack of chips over to each of them.

There was something like camaraderie, like adventurousness, in the African woman's look. Should he invite her to the bar? Feuchtenbeiner was always a bit awkward with women, and it had never before occurred to him to sleep with a black woman. He had heard that many white men dreamed about it, although hardly any of them dared to articulate this secret desire. Feuchtenbeiner himself had never had any such conflicts. Now, with a mixture of dismay and yearning, he noticed that an inner barrier had been torn down. For the first time in his life, he desired a black woman.

When he stole a look at the exit and her smile signalled agreement, Feuchtenbeiner pulled his key with the stamped room number from his pocket and placed it next to his little pile of chips. She nodded. His hands were wet when he exchanged his winnings for cash and left the casino. In his room, he drew the curtains and uncovered the bed.

He cooled his face with cold water, then opened the door and peered briefly into the empty hallway, sweating at the thought that somebody might observe the woman entering his room. The Holiday Inn was crawling with South African informers, disguised as tourists or businessmen. If he were an ordinary Boer, they might overlook an offence against the Apartheid laws, at least abroad. But for the head of security at the second biggest diamond mine in the world, there had to be different standards.

A few minutes later, there was a knock. After making sure the hall was still deserted, he pulled the African into his room. Her flowing walk was as graceful as a gazelle's. A crooked smile touched the corners of his mouth. "What's your name?"

"Dikeledi."

"What does that mean?" African first names always meant something.

"Tears."

He grinned. "Funny name for such a pretty girl."

She raised her head. "And you?"

"What about me?"

"Don't you have a name?"

"Jack Griffith."

"Are you from South Africa?"

"England. I've never seen you before in the casino, Dikeledi." He offered her a chair and a cigarette.

"I'd like to hear some music." Her English had almost no accent.

Feuchtenbeiner pressed the button of his room radio. Mantovani on tape, sugary mush. Dikeledi puffed silently on her cigarette. Then she stood up, put it out, and went into the bathroom.

While the water was gushing, Feuchtenbeiner switched off every light except the lamp by the window. The air conditioner hissed like an old VW. He flicked it off, poured himself a glass of iced water and undressed. When Dikeledi returned from the bathroom, she was naked. As she walked through the room with a scrutinizing look, turning up the music a bit and switching all the lamps back on, Feuchtenbeiner appreciatively studied her slender body. But Dikeledi's face expressed nothing but careful indifference. When they were in bed, she pushed the covers away. Then she became totally passive. And when it was over, in less than a minute, she promptly got up, vanished into the bathroom again, and left Feuchtenbeiner alone in bed. He got up and placed a two-rand note on the bureau in front of the mirror. The episode wasn't worth more.

When she came back from the bathroom, in her dress and with fresh make-up, she sat down at the mirror, pushed the banknote aside, and straightened out her braids, taking no notice of Feuchtenbeiner. It seemed to him that she was slightly amused. Feuchtenbeiner wasn't amused. He had been nice to her, tried to treat her almost like an equal, and this was all the thanks he got.

And when she left the room without saying goodbye, Feuchtenbeiner had a vague, creepy sense that the episode with this black hooker would cost him more than the two rands he had offered her.

THE DUMP CAR with the blasted fragments of ore trundled off, and Mogomotsi loosened his chinstrap. He had a headache. The air down here in the shaft at a depth of thirteen hundred feet tasted like warm, dirty water, even though the ventilator sucked out the poisonous dust and a fan steadily brought in fresh air all the way down to the bottom.

After seven months, Mogomotsi still hadn't got used to the work down here. One more hour, then his shift was over. "I have to go to the toilet."

"You already went once." The foreman looked at his watch. "Get back here in ten minutes."

They spoke mine pidgin, a mishmash of English, Afrikaans, and a dozen different Bantu languages that could be understood in all the mines between Kenya and South Africa.

Mogomotsi leaned his shovel against the wall of the shaft and found his way to the explosives room in the cone of light from his safety lamp. There old Chabalela crouched between the shelves like a hen squatting on golden eggs. He was known to be incorruptible, and the mine management, which usually didn't employ any blacks over forty, entrusted him with the supervision of the explosive supplies in this shaft.

Chabalela looked up amiably, opened the barred door and let Mogomotsi in.

"*Dumela.*" Mogomotsi offered the old man the normal greeting of the country. "*Otsogile*—how are you?"

"*Kitsogile.*" The old man nodded. "I woke up well."

Chabalela pointed to an enamel bowl, and Mogomotsi had a sip of the lukewarm tea. He liked the old man, and had accepted the mission only because they had assured him that it was necessary for the liberation of their brothers in Zimbabwe and that he alone was in a position to carry it out. Besides, if Mogomotsi followed his orders precisely, the old man would simply drop off into a deep, lovely dream for a couple of minutes and not remember anything afterwards.

While chatting with Chabalela about past wonderful times in their native village, Mogomotsi said, "I can't hear you so well. The ventilator's too noisy."

After the old man had switched off the ventilator, Mogomotsi pulled out a spraycan from his overalls and shot the contents into Chabalela's face. For a second, he opened his mouth in amazement. Then he collapsed on his chair, unconscious.

Mogomotsi moistened his handkerchief in the tea, and pressed it to his mouth and nose as he had been told. Then, with his free hand, he removed twenty sticks of dynamite from a shelf, replacing them with the same number of mock-up sticks, which he had brought along in his lunch box.

His hand trembled slightly, for he had been warned not to drop the highly explosive dynagel sticks. Before leaving, he switched the ventilator back on. Then he returned to his workplace.

The foreman looked at his watch again. "Do you call that ten minutes, Kaffir?"

Mogomotsi cowered. Don't start a fight with the foreman, the organization had told him. "Sorry, boss."

"What's wrong?" The mine captain, on his daily round of inspection, stepped up.

"That kaffir there! He was supposed to be back in ten minutes, and it took him eighteen."

The captain turned to Mogomotsi. "Get to work!"

Mogomotsi went back to shovelling ore into the dump car. The foreman was a vicious dog, worse than the white bosses, a Shona from Zimbabwe, and his skin was even blacker than Mogomotsi's. I'm fighting to free our brothers from white domination, and he calls me a kaffir, thought Mogomotsi.

An hour later, the mining cage heaved Mogomotsi and the men of his shift thirteen hundred feet aloft to the open air. Mogomotsi shed his overalls, showered, and dressed. His shirt was tattered, and there was a sleeve missing on the jacket. He needed new clothes, but he would have to ask an aunt to mend the old ones. Back in his village, things had been easier. He hadn't needed money there, or a jacket, or shoes. And when he had tended his father's cattle out in the bush, he had taken along a blanket and a sack of cornmeal and brewed his own beer. Then a friend had told him about the mines at Selebi-Pikwe. The South Africans, using American, English, and German money, had built a mining town in the middle of the bush. They had a cinema there, his friend had said, and supermarkets with wonderful things. No clay huts, real tin-roof houses, cars on real tarred roads, and everybody, black and white, with the same rights. Not like in South Africa.

So Mogomotsi had tied his belongings up in a blanket and thumbed a lift to Francistown. There a government truck had taken him to Selebi-Pikwe where Mogomotsi had found work for forty rands a month. In his village, this would have lasted a year. But here, the cents ran through his fingers like water. Everything that was free at home suddenly cost money. Six days a week, eight hours a day, he went underground and dumped ore fragments into a dump car—until one Monday morning his friends and he refused to descend. They called it a strike. A man from Francistown had come and told them that a white overseer got eight hundred rands a month, twenty times as much for work that was only half as hard. The next day, the president of Botswana gave a radio talk. He spoke of sympathy with the striking workers, but of the jobs that would be jeopardized if the foreign financiers lost patience and withdrew their money. He also spoke about Communist saboteurs, who wanted to take advantage of the mine's predicament, and finally, he promised to see to it that the lower-salary ranges were improved.

Next day, the management fired the twelve hundred striking workers and promptly rehired eight hundred of them, including Mogomotsi. The minimum pay stayed the same, but the management granted some improvements. Before his shift, each worker received a free bowl of tea and a slice of bread.

After the strike, Mogomotsi had talked to the man from Francistown, and the man had told him about the freedom struggle in Zimbabwe, which the whites called Rhodesia, and where, even

374

though there was only one white man there for every twenty-four Africans, the whites still ruled the land by themselves.

When Mogomotsi wanted to know why the twenty-four blacks didn't simply kick out the one white, the man from Francistown replied that the whites owned all the property, made the laws, and the police worked only for them.

It made him sad, said the man from Francistown, to see his black friends drudging here to increase the wealth of the whites. And he told Mogomotsi about the liberation army, the ZLA, and its commander-in-chief, Tutuma, whose goal was to reconquer Zimbabwe for the Africans. Did Mogomotsi perhaps feel like helping Chief Tutuma? For Tutuma was dependent on volunteers, men who were brave as lions, fast as gazelles, sly as serpents, and mute as tiger fish.

Mogomotsi was impressed by the man from Francistown. He would have liked to follow him back to town immediately. But the man said that Mogomotsi could be a lot more useful here in Selebi-Pikwe, for Tutuma desperately needed explosives. The next day, the man gave Mogomotsi twenty fake dynagel sticks and a spray can of knockout gas. Mogomotsi was proud of carrying out his mission all by himself. Tutuma would be satisfied with him when he handed the haul to the middleman tonight.

Back home, alone in his shack, he stared at the sticks of dynagel. They looked like sloppily-wrapped giant cigars. Mogomotsi counted them again. There were twenty-one. He must have grabbed one too many. Mogomotsi thought hard, and he decided to keep his little mistake from the man from Francistown. He hid the extra dynagel stick at the head of his sleeping pad, carefully stowed the other twenty in his supply pouch, and went to his rendezvous with the man from Francistown at the end of the big lawn with little holes and the little flags, where the whites gathered to play a game they called golf.

"Do you have the stuff?"

Mogomotsi opened his pouch, and the man from Francistown gingerly placed the dynagel sticks in a small case. He said, "Tutuma sends you his best wishes. He wants to meet you. Tomorrow you're coming with me."

Mogomotsi was radiant. "Where?"

The man from Francistown put a finger on his lips. "Mute as a tiger fish. Wait for me here tomorrow evening. *Sala sentle*—goodbye."

"*Tsamaja sentle.*"

On the way home, Mogomotsi was happy for the first time in many months. No more filthy work. He would be a free man; he could sleep in the bush like a real guerrilla, and maybe Tutuma would even give him a rifle.

Home again, Mogomotsi pocketed the remaining stick of dynamite and started off to Lorato's shack. He didn't want to leave the stick behind. It only dawned on him now that he should have asked the man from Francistown whether Tutuma couldn't also use a young girl.

It was already dark inside, so Mogomotsi crawled past her sleeping parents and shook her shoulder. "Come along," he whispered. "I have to tell you something."

Obediently, she went along to their favourite spot under a mopane tree. While they were making love, chastely and awkwardly as usual, he thought of how well her name fitted her. In Setswana *lorato* meant "love".

"I'm going away tomorrow, Lorato," he said. "I'm going to Tutuma in Zimbabwe."

Lorato giggled. "Really? You're not seventeen yet."

"Tutuma sent a man from Francistown to get me."

Lorato laughed. "Why are you trying to tease me? I like you even if you're not a hero."

"As soon as we've liberated Zimbabwe, we'll go there together and buy a lot of cattle."

She was still shaking with laughter. "Mogomotsi is a hero. He's gonna fight all the white people in Zimbabwe. And when he beats the white people there, he's gonna kick all the Boers out of South Africa."

"Stop acting so silly, Lorato." He pulled the stick of dynamite from his pocket. "Look—dynamite. I got it for Tutuma."

"Show-off!"

She grabbed the stick from him and threw it at the tree.

The flash could be seen from all over Selebi-Pikwe. When people came running up, all they could find next to the blasted mopane tree were the shredded bodies of two young people.

Thus Mogomotsi and Lorato were the first victims, even before the great battle for Rhodesia had begun.

THE ENVELOPE was white and had no return address. Feuchtenbeiner weighed it in his hand for a moment. "Who delivered this?"

"An errand boy," replied Meggy, the hotel receptionist.

At the breakfast table, Feuchtenbeiner slit the envelope open with the bread knife. It contained a set of colour photos. No sooner had he glanced at the topmost photo than he swiftly stuffed the others back into the envelope.

Leaving his breakfast he jumped up and ran back to his room, trying to tell himself that someone was indulging in a tasteless joke at his expense.

He shooed out the chambermaid and bolted the door. Then he spread the photos on the bed and studied each in turn. There were eight of them, a bit underexposed but sharp. They had been taken from the foot of the double bed and showed him and the kaffir girl from yesterday in all phases of their joyless sexual act.

Feuchtenbeiner took a deep breath. Now various things became clear to him. For instance why Dikeledi had pushed away the covers and switched on all the lights before crawling into bed.

Feuchtenbeiner tried to remove the mirror from the wall opposite. It was screwed on tight, probably transparent from the other side.

He ran out into the garden. The sliding glass door to the next room was open. The room was untenanted. The head of the double bed was against the wall of his room. Someone had hurriedly plastered up and painted over the hole in the wall, a hole as big as a fist. The paint was still fresh. Whoever it was hadn't felt it worthwhile going to a lot of trouble to hide the evidence.

Feuchtenbeiner picked up the receiver.

"Meggy, can you tell me who had the room next to me last night? Number twenty-three?"

"One moment, please, I'll check . . . . Room twenty-three was occupied by a Mr. January from Francistown. Is there anything wrong? Were you disturbed?"

"No, no. Just curious. Where can I find Mr. January now?"

"He checked out this morning."

"Does he often stop here?"

"I've never seen him here before."

Feuchtenbeiner hung up and went back to his room.

He tore the photos to shreds, dumped them into the lavatory bowl, and flushed. But he didn't give in to the illusion that he had flushed the entire matter away with these bits of evidence. When the telephone rang, he picked up the receiver calmly. Mr. January apparently didn't care to waste any time. At least, Feuchtenbeiner would now find out what he was up against. The soft accent told Feuchtenbeiner that the voice belonged to a black man.

"Have you read your mail today?"

Feuchtenbeiner tried to laugh. "I just looked at the pictures, Mr. January. Great shots. May I keep them?"

"By all means, Mr. Feuchtenbeiner."

"Could you also give me the negatives? I'd love to make a few more prints of them. For my collection."

"We can talk about it."

"Naturally, I'll take care of your expenses." Feuchtenbeiner bit his lower lip. Maybe he was jumping the gun. On no account could he make them think he cared one way or another. The man would then be happy with a couple of rand. These kaffirs were undemanding.

"I'm glad you don't resent my little joke, Mr. Feuchtenbeiner." The caller let a few seconds go by. "June must have a good sense of humour too."

The caller must have done his homework thoroughly. "My wife? She won't take this kind of thing too tragically."

"Good. I was worried she'd make a scene if I sent her a set of the photos."

"No way!"

"Then you certainly won't mind if Bill Scranton also gets a couple of prints."

The man even knew the name of the general manager of Orapa. Feuchtenbeiner wiped his damp palm on his trousers.

"It's not the moral issue," said Mr. January. "But a security head who can get lured so easily into a trap . . . . Do you believe he'd still be acceptable?"

Feuchtenbeiner pulled himself together for a feeble counter-attack. "You can go to prison for blackmail."

"But I don't want your money, Feuchtenbeiner."

"OK. You've had your fun. Now hand over those goddamn negatives and all the prints. The matter will remain just between us and we'll forget the whole thing."

"Fine. But not right away, Feuchtenbeiner. I think you owe me a little favour. It'll cost you merely one word."

"I don't understand."

"The word 'today'."

It was out at last: the very thing that Feuchtenbeiner had been afraid of. He reflected. Keep a clear head, don't let yourself be bluffed.

"You're wrong, January. I couldn't give you that information if I wanted to. I never know the date myself."

"Come, come, Feuchtenbeiner. Don't be so modest. Only you and the general manager know when the monthly output is flown to Gaberones. He tells you the day before the flight. Everybody in Orapa knows that."

"Even if that were so, knowing the day wouldn't help you. The security measures are perfect. De Beers is not a third-class super-market that you can rob with a pistol in your hand."

"Let me worry about that. All I want from you is the exact day. There's a castor-oil bush in your garden in Orapa. It has seven stalks. The day you find out that the next shipment to Gaberones will not have pebbles in the suitcases, you will snap one stalk. And to make doubly sure, switch the light in your kitchen on and off. Three short flashes in a row. At precisely one a.m. That's all you have to do."

"You'll never make it!" Feuchtenbeiner said. "The airfield in Orapa is guarded. So is the airfield in Gaberones. And our men are heavily armed."

"You'd do better to wish us success, Feuchtenbeiner. If we fail, then De Beers, Scranton, June, and the public prosecutor in Johannesburg are going to get illustrated mail."

Feuchtenbeiner yelled into the mouthpiece, "You haven't got a Chinaman's chance!"

"You're repeating yourself."

Feuchtenbeiner sat down on the bed. "Let's just assume you make it. What guarantee do I have?"

"My word. One day later, you'll find a sealed white envelope containing the negatives in your letterbox."

"The word of a blackmailer . . . ."

"The word of an African patriot, sir."

And before Feuchtenbeiner could answer, the caller hung up. The receiver slid out of Feuchtenbeiner's wet hand, and when he stood up, he felt he didn't have a dry garment on his body. He tore off his clothes and got under the shower. The cold water helped him collect his thoughts.

The blackmailer must be bluffing. No one would be able to haul him into a South African court for miscegenation in Botswana . . . But professionally, of course, he would be finished. The security head of the second-biggest diamond mine in the world had let himself be photographed in a compromising situation with a black girl.

He could, of course, confide in Bill Scranton. On the human level, Bill would forgive him. They would take their precautions, and they would smash the attack on the diamond shipment. But then, if copies of the photos popped up, Bill would have to report his security head's misdemeanour to the central office in Johannesburg or risk his own job.

If Bill was generous, he might give him six months' severance pay. But Jan Feuchtenbeiner would never get a comparable job anywhere in Africa. A security head susceptible to blackmail was intolerable. They wouldn't trust him as a night watchman. Feuchtenbeiner turned off the shower and dried himself. From any angle, he was trapped.

Wait. Maybe there was a way. It was highly uncertain, but he had to make sure that the insane attack in Orapa didn't come off.

II

The African felt the cold like snakebités in his toes as his feet, in sandals, trudged ankle-deep through the white, glittering snow from the runway to the clearance building. The Soviet consul who had given him his visa in Lusaka, the Zambian capital, had warned him about the Moscow winter; but Tutuma was still quite unprepared as far as his footwear was concerned.

The reception hall of Sheremetyevo Airport was badly heated, and Tutuma recalled the woollen cap that a thoughtful friend had handed him in Lusaka. He pulled it out of his coat pocket, tugged it down over both ears, and waited for the official from the foreign ministry who was supposed to call for him.

"Long live the African struggle for freedom!"

Tutuma whirled around. A Russian in a fur cap beamed at him, took him in his arms, and pressed hearty kisses on his cheeks. "I am Volodya. Did you have a good flight?" He spoke English without an accent, and smelled faintly of alcohol. "Your luggage?"

Tutuma pointed to a suitcase, and Volodya picked it up.

"Let's go." Outside, a driver sprang out of a Volga and stowed Tutuma's suitcase in the boot. After Volodya and his guest had settled in the back, the Russian leaned back and emitted a sympathetic sigh. "You must be tired. I'll take you to your hotel, and you can have a good rest. If you like, we'll go sightseeing in Moscow tonight."

During the forty-minute drive to the centre of the city, Volodya chatted about Africa, American imperialism, and the Moscow climate. Tutuma listened absentmindedly. He was more concerned about why the Soviet embassy counsellor in Lusaka had called upon him and invited him to Moscow. "You will meet a series of important persons," the diplomat had announced, "who can offer you very interesting suggestions."

At last, the Volga stopped. "This is the Intourist Hotel," said Volodya. He picked up Tutuma's case and carried it into the vestibule of the hotel. Tutuma followed him, somewhat taken aback that the white man insisted on carrying the case. To his surprise, the hotel room, with its impersonal furnishings, matched the Holiday Inn standard Tutuma knew from Bulawayo and Gaberones.

Volodya put down the case. "The foreign ministry wants you to feel comfortable. Would you care for a drink?"

"Tea, perhaps."

While they waited for room service, Tutuma freshened himself with a bath.

"'Tutuma' is a very melodic name," Volodya called from the bedroom through the half-open bathroom door.

"Among our people, it is customary to name children the way we feel when they come into the world. Happiness, gift, gratitude —but also sorrow, tears, loneliness."

"A lovely custom. And what does 'Tutuma' mean?"

The African came out of the bathroom. He was drying his body. "Have you ever seen a bush fire, Volodya?" Volodya shook his head. "It roars so loudly that you can't hear yourself think. The Setswana word for that is *tutuma*." He smiled. "I must have yelled terribly when I was a baby."

Volodya laughed. Tutuma had a gentle voice. "You must have exhausted your vocal powers as a child," he said.

The waiter had brought the tea and Volodya sensed that the reserve between them was melting. Glancing at Tutuma's still-naked torso, he said: "You have a smooth skin, Tutuma. Let me show you something." He unbuttoned his shirt and exposed his abdomen, which was covered with scar tissue. "It looks a mess, doesn't it? A German grenade splinter in the Battle of Kursk. It tore my guts to bits. The military surgeon sewed them up, but he tied the wrong ends. They had to cut my belly open again, separate the intestines, and stitch them together a second time." Volodya rebuttoned his shirt. "The tea is getting cold."

THE REPORT by Volodya Naumov, colonel in the KGB, chief of the African Relations Division, was marked: "Provisional".

"The recommendation of our office in Lusaka can be fully accepted within the framework of our present knowledge. The undersigned has determined in the first exploratory conversations

382

that Tutuma's training is sufficient for the prospective position. Tutuma studied law at the University of Salisbury. His English is excellent. He is highly intelligent and has a quick mind. In his political ideas, he is close to the African humanism of President Kaunda of Zambia; however, he seems open to Marxist-Leninist doctrines as well.

"Despite his age (he is only thirty-two), Tutuma possesses the necessary measure of dignity, charisma, and revolutionary energy. His position on the white rulers in Zimbabwe is uncompromisingly aggressive. As our agency in Lusaka reported, Tutuma is extremely popular with his people. Being the son of a chief, he can bank on unconditional support in his own Kalanga tribe."

General Korotkov put the report aside. "Is that all?"

"I only spent one evening with him," said Volodya.

"And you think it's worthwhile developing the man?"

"Absolutely, General."

"Fatherly feelings, eh? Sometimes I get the feeling that you can't always keep business and private life apart."

Volodya shrugged. "That's going too far. But I do like him."

"We don't need an adopted son in Zimbabwe; we need a man who's useful to us politically. Arrange a meal tonight. Tutuma, you, I, and the under-secretary of the foreign ministry." General Korotkov stood up. "And make sure that this Tutuma doesn't accidentally run into our guests from South Africa. We don't want all Africa to know that Tutuma is our man."

One hour later, in the park by the Moskva, General Alexander Korotkov met his equal-ranking colleague from South Africa, General Erik Van Zyl, who was travelling as an Australian business-man. The South African had insisted on meeting outdoors despite the piercing cold. The things he had to tell his Soviet colleague were not meant for hidden microphones, and tapes of the con-versation in the wrong hands would cost him his job as assistant chief of BOSS, the Bureau of State Security.

The salutations between the two generals were businesslike, with no bogus cordiality.

"I want to lay all my cards on the table," Van Zyl said. "There are groups in our country who believe that the Americans might sacrifice the Boers to a new black government—a strictly anti-Communist black government, of course. And that would not be in the Soviet interest."

"Perhaps. But you will not resent my saying that we do not exactly regard the present government in South Africa as furthering our interests."

Van Zyl ignored the sarcasm. "That need not always be true. Assuming the Soviet Union guaranteed the survival of the South African Republic under white rule, we would no longer need Rhodesia and South-West Africa as buffer states against the black terrorist movements. We would not object to your installing Marxist governments there."

"Zimbabwe is an independent country."

"Formally, yes. But you know as well as I do that Rhodesia would collapse in two weeks if we withdrew our support of Ian Smith."

"But our government might possibly be interested in a naval base on the Cape."

"That is negotiable. And we can talk about chromium too. If you get our chromium and the Rhodesian chromium as well, you will control almost all the chromium in the world."

The KGB general smiled. "Then Western cars would have to get along with less trimming."

The South African, too, smiled for the first time. This slippery Bolshevik was pretending not to know how indispensable chromium was for armaments.

"I shall transmit your proposals to the Politburo," Korotkov said. "We will convey the answer to you in Pretoria."

AFTER THE sixth toast, Tutuma had a queasy feeling in his stomach. His concentration was waning. But he felt warm around the heart. Never had white men enveloped him in so much cordiality.

Volodya had picked him up two hours ago, and they had walked across the street to the "Aragvi" on Pushkin Square, a Georgian restaurant. While Tutuma poked at the whitefish, the undersecretary pulled a photo out of his wallet and handed it across the table to the African. "My wife. The boy behind her is my eldest son. He's studying at the military academy."

"Do you have a family too, Tutuma?" asked Korotkov, as the waiter served roast chicken tabaki.

"I was married. My family was killed."

"By white Rhodesians?"

"By black Africans. The whites had penned them up in a 'protected village' as they call it. It's really an internment camp with a high barbed-wire fence and a six p.m. curfew. At night, black guerrillas got in and took the village chief away. Then they threw a hand grenade into the crowd and fled. We had twenty casualties, among them my wife and my little boy."

"Why do freedom fighters do things like that?" Volodya asked in the poignant silence.

"They weren't freedom fighters. They were black soldiers of the white army, mercenaries. They put them in civilian clothes. Right after the phony attack, white soldiers supposedly freed the chief. But they only shot in the air. The whole thing was a bloody sham. The villagers were supposed to think that the black freedom fighters are their enemies and that only the whites can protect them." Tutuma stared at his plate. "It was sheer murder, and I had to watch."

The under-secretary pushed his plate aside furiously. "How did you find out that it was a white plot?"

"I found a black soldier later who'd taken part in the massacre. He confessed. Before the massacre, I was about to take my bar exams. After the massacre, I went into the bush to build up a second guerrilla front in Botswana against the white Rhodesians. Our liberation army has 6,000 men. And we get more every day. What we lack are weapons, munitions, armoured cars."

Korotkov nodded. "And tanks. And instructors."

"Naturally we'll pay for everything," said Tutuma.

Korotkov raised his eyebrows. "Pay? We don't take money from friends. We will equip your freedom fighters. We can discuss the details later."

"We—my people and I," said Tutuma, "greatly appreciate your generous offer." How could he make it clear to the Russians that he didn't want to become dependent on them? "Nevertheless, I would prefer to pay."

The Russians fell silent.

"A gift from friends need not injure your pride," said Korotkov after a reflective pause. "But if you insist, then we could envisage a payment after the war. Naturally not in cash; you'll have greater need of money than the Soviet Union for building up your country. We're thinking of payment in kind. Natural resources, for instance."

"Gold?"

Korotkov waved it off. "That too. And chromium."

"Perhaps we could work out a treaty for your entire output," the under-secretary suggested, as if the thought had only just flashed into his mind. "Then you won't have to worry about finding other takers. Naturally, we'll pay the world market price."

"A little more," Korotkov threw in. "For every ton he delivers to us, our friend will get a bonus of—well, let's say ten per cent."

Foggy as his mind was, Tutuma had not failed to notice his hosts' close attention when the subject of chromium had come up. Why were they so keen on chromium that they even scorned gold?

The under-secretary smiled. "As head of government, you would naturally be entitled to a commission. That's quite normal."

Tutuma wiped his mouth in surprise. "I, head of government? There are other men with much older rights and more experience. I'm far too young."

"Your modesty does you credit, my friend. But our government has already decided in your favour."

Tutuma rubbed his chin. "I am not interested in money. And perhaps we ought to negotiate delivery contracts only when Zimbabwe is free. I hope you will not misunderstand if I consider it much better to pay for equipping our freedom army. And in advance."

The Russians smiled in pity. "Do you have any idea what that would cost?" asked Korotkov.

"Would ten or twelve million dollars be enough for the time being?"

386

Volodya almost choked on his chicken. Korotkov pulled himself together first. "That would certainly be a fine start."

"In rough diamonds. Eighty per cent industrial diamonds and twenty per cent gemstones. I will deliver between three hundred and four hundred thousand carats at thirty-five dollars per carat. That is a price between friends. You will mix the diamonds in with your own Siberian yields. And we will get weapons from you of an equal value."

Flabbergasted, Korotkov shook his head. "How can you get your hands on such a treasure trove, my friend?"

But not even another half dozen toasts could loosen Tutuma's tongue. He left the Russians with the disturbing impression that this young African from the bush had a lot more to him than they had expected. He was not to be corrupted, at least. Whether he could be manipulated—that remained to be seen.

Next day Korotkov and Volodya took leave of Tutuma at the airport. "Volodya will stay in contact with you," Korotkov said. "Send us the name of a liaison man through whom we can reach you. It is better if we don't communicate directly."

"How long will it take you to deliver?"

"Some time in February."

While the KGB general kissed the African on both cheeks, his eyes came to rest on a passenger who sat at the other end of the waiting room, leafing through an English newspaper. "Come, Tutuma." Korotkov pushed his guest through the door into the next room, which was reserved for KGB travellers. "We have time for a cup of tea."

Through the loudspeaker they heard in Russian and English: "Lufthansa announces the late arrival of Boeing 707 flight number 659 from Tokyo. The further flight to Frankfurt, scheduled departure at 17 hours and 45 minutes, will be delayed by about three hours."

As tea was brought, the general murmured to Volodya in Russian: "I thought he'd gone long ago. Three hours' delay! Did Tutuma notice anything?"

"No."

"And Van Zyl?"

"He didn't look up from his newspaper."

"Please excuse us, Tutuma." Korotkov was speaking English again. "It just struck us that your men have no experience with our weapons. We'll send along Cuban instructors."

Volodya embraced Tutuma. "Your flight is about to be announced. I hope that you have no trouble changing planes for Damascus and Lusaka."

GENERAL ERIK VAN ZYL absentmindedly took the boarding card from the ground stewardess. Ahead of him he had a three-hour flight to Frankfurt, where he would catch a plane for Johannesburg.

It would not be easy to recognize the man from a file photo, for all kaffirs looked alike to Van Zyl. Still, his memory had stored up a few characteristics. The dense mop of hair over the conspicuously high domed forehead. The Ho Chi Minh moustache with the dangling ends. The tarry complexion of the intelligent face. The casual light-green jeans, the orange sweater, and the lined trenchcoat. The man was rather short, and his shuffling walk would be unmistakable. He had worn a fashionable ivory ring on his little finger.

No one was as meticulous about questions of protocol as the Soviets. If the head of the KGB section for African affairs had personally taken the trouble of seeing a guest off at the airport with hugs and kisses, then there had to be more to it than merely a polite gesture.

III

The dust wrapped him like a fog, working its way into his lungs, eyes, nose, but the roughness of the barely-used road—a trail really—gave Dieter Hahn no chance to accelerate away from the cloud the wind whirled up from the tyres.

Like nearly all roads and paths in Botswana, this one was unnegotiable during the rainy season, even for vehicles with a cross-country gear and a four-wheel drive. But the last rain had fallen eight months ago, and there was still no sign of an end to

388

the dry spell. Setting out from Serowe, he could have used the all-weather road, which ran from Gaberones to Maun in a wide sweep through Francistown and Nata, but he didn't want to reach his destination along beaten paths. For one thing, he hoped to see big game along this short cut on the eastern edge of the Kalahari. But all he had spotted so far was a couple of baboons and antelopes.

The one-and-a-half-ton Ford truck he was supposed to drive to Maun was brand-new. Helmuth Dieckmann had requested it a year ago, and after a dozen applications the German Voluntary Service Overseas had finally approved it. Dieckmann needed it badly for the training farm of his youth brigade. The farm was a long way from Maun, and the produce that was grown there had to be transported to the market.

Bespectacled Dieter Hahn, just arrived from Germany with four other new volunteer workers, had offered to drive the truck the six hundred miles to Maun in the Okavango Delta. Work on his own project wasn't starting until March, and he wanted to use the eight weeks till then in getting to know the country where he would be spending the next two years.

So far, he was disappointed with Botswana, not so much with the country as with the people, who were either gently indolent or tried to mimic the few whites in the country. They were relaxed rather than aggressive, and they seemed free of the nationalist feelings of the Zambians and Tanzanians. A peaceful nation of shepherds and nomads, they had no bloody colonial past: they had never been worth exploiting. After eighty years as the British protectorate of Bechuanaland, the country had been granted independence by the unresisting British—an independence for which the people were unprepared.

It couldn't be much farther now to Lethlakane, but the radiator water was boiling, and Dieter didn't want to overstrain the new truck. He stopped, climbed out, gathered a few pieces of sun-bleached wood, piled them up, and started a fire. It blazed like tinder. He clambered into the back of the truck and filled a pot with water from one of the two plastic containers. After putting on water for tea, he washed the dust from his face, slit open a can of

South African sardines in tomato sauce, and cut a slice of bread from the loaf.

Dieter had lived with his parents until three months ago. He wasn't used to looking after himself, but he enjoyed the feeling of cutting the umbilical cord in this way. The patriarchal father, the over-attentive mother, the restrictions of Germany—all those things were far away, nothing compared with the task he had taken on here. After a long time, Dieter had finally sorted out his own life for himself.

After lunch, he slung the camera over his shoulder and strode through the elephant grass into the Kalahari. It would probably take a long time for his eyes to get used to the colours of the steppe. He was fatigued by the bleached-out grey of the dead branches, the wan yellow of the elephant grass, the dusty ochre of the parched earth. He sat down now in the grass and let the stillness work upon him, a perfect hush, such as he had never before experienced. A herd of zebras was grazing on the horizon, and an ostrich was strutting around him in a wide circle.

Dieter pushed his spectacles up on his forehead, peered through the camera view-finder, and adjusted the distance and the aperture. The grazing zebras were too far away for a decent photo, but he was standing downwind. If he was lucky, the herd would move towards him.

The ostrich had come closer. Dieter raised his camera and took a few snapshots of the bird, whose long neck towered out of its feathers like a snorkel. Now it was only twenty yards away. Its head was tiny, and swayed to the rhythm of the long strides.

Dieter concentrated on the zebras. The leader raised his head as though sensing danger, and Dieter ducked behind a hollow tree nearby. The ostrich crossed his view once more. The bird was only about twelve yards away now; it seemed to be orbiting round an invisible point near him. The next round brought it within five yards, and Dieter drew attention to himself with a low "ksh, ksh". The comical bird would drive away the zebras.

But the ostrich appeared to take no notice. The head gazed straight ahead, the tail see-sawed, the distance narrowed down by another twist; and gradually Dieter realized that he was at the centre of a spiral. When the ostrich started approaching him from behind, Dieter stepped to the other side of the tree trunk. The bird stopped, its head tipping towards the ground, as though ashamed of its curiosity.

"Well—what now?" said Dieter. In high spirits, he bowed slightly: "Allow me to introduce myself: Dieter Hahn."

The ostrich stood motionless, gazing into the ground—a grotesquely disproportionate creature, with its naked legs carrying a round, shiny black tangle of plumage. The ugliest part, Dieter felt, was the neck—a flesh-coloured tube, on which the tiny head perched, with a kind of goose-beak and brown eyes set far apart under lashes so unnaturally long that they looked glued on.

When Dieter stripped off his T-shirt and waved it to shoo the bird off, the zebras vanished. The ostrich flapped its stubby wings three or four times and opened its beak in an angry hiss. The scene brought back a long-forgotten incident in Dieter's childhood: the hissing of a gander that had painfully tweaked his calves in a barnyard. Only this gander seemed about ten times as big.

Dieter retreated one yard deeper into the drooping branches of the tree under which he had sought cover; he felt safe here, and waved his T-shirt more energetically. He hissed: "Ksh, ksh!"

The ostrich hopped up and down a few times, ruffled its feathers, fluttered its wings wildly, swayed its bare neck back and forth, and emitted a hoarse roar. Then it thrust its head through the branches and tried to peck at Dieter, who jerked back. When the bird discovered it was lunging into empty space its fury seemed to turn into hysteria. It pulled back its head and stamped its feet like an unruly child. Then it took up its old position, turning its head to the side, looking like a statue of helpless simplicity.

Dieter kept calm to avoid irritating the bird. He replaced his T-shirt. He was not exactly comfortable in his position, but he was convinced he could out-manoeuvre the ostrich. What could be going on in the bird's tiny head? Would it give up, or was it thinking out some new assault tactics?

The truce went on for about a quarter of an hour. At last the ostrich turned around and leisurely trotted away. Then, after twenty yards, it suddenly wheeled and made a frontal dash towards Dieter's tree. Before smashing into the branches, it screeched to a halt, stood perplexed for a couple of minutes, trotted back, and charged again.

The bird repeated this manoeuvre several times. When it appeared to realize that it couldn't take the enemy fortress this way, it tried a new tactic. It began to circle the tree, trotting faster and faster, obviously seeking a place to slip in.

Within the circle of branches, Dieter followed the ostrich's circles, making sure that the tree trunk remained between him and the bird. He glanced over his shoulder. If he could manage to reach the Ford before the ostrich, he could lock himself in the driver's cab and take off. But the truck was at least five hundred yards away. Dieter was a rather good middle-distance runner, but not even an Olympic winner could out-race an ostrich.

He decided to wait calmly; sooner or later, the ostrich would get hungry, lose patience, and amble away. After a while, the bird slowed down and flapped its wings listlessly a couple of times. Then it went back to laying siege. Dieter looked around for help, but he knew it was quite hopeless. In Serowe, he had been urged to take along enough water and to conserve petrol because only three cars a week, at most, drove along this remote trail. Little by little, the ostrich seemed to lose interest in him. It moved twenty yards off and began peacefully tugging at the grass with its beak.

What if he managed to climb the tree? Up in the crown, the ostrich couldn't do anything to him. To test the bird's attentiveness, Dieter cautiously stretched his arm aloft. As though waiting for this, the bird made a dash at the tree. This time, it tried to smash through the branches, and when it got stuck in the thicket, hopped furiously up and down, hissing and stamping, a caricature of an unspeakably ugly ballerina in a black tutu over monstrously long legs. At the sight of this eccentric choreography, Dieter had to struggle against overpowering mirth. But now it took the ostrich longer to calm down, and Dieter began to doubt that time was really working for him. He had to do something himself.

This archaic creature was his superior in strength and speed, and also in endurance, or so it seemed. No less than the beak,

Dieter feared the two gigantic toes on each foot, horned claws that could effortlessly rip open a man's abdomen. Dieter had nothing but his intelligence to fight with. What if he tried leaping from cover to cover until he reached the truck? The first goal that Dieter sighted was a bush nearer the truck. It was lower than the tree, but its dense twigs seemed to offer enough protection.

However, the ostrich could easily cut off Dieter's escape path. He had to try to lure the bird to the other side of the tree. Pulling off his T-shirt again, he crumpled it up, and threw it to the spot where he wanted the ostrich to go. The bird scurried over, grateful for an object to vent its fury on, trampled on the shirt and tore at it with its beak. Dieter seized the moment. Before the ostrich could see through his tactics, he had sprinted twenty yards. He heard the bird behind him, but he was sure his head start was enough.

At the bush, Dieter threw himself down and rolled under the bulky twigs. The ostrich slowed down in the last few yards and stood gazing at Dieter with a fatuous expression.

The twigs were as impenetrable as a barbed-wire entanglement. Dieter's bare arms and chest were ripped and blood oozed out, mixing with sweat into a brine that scalded the fresh welts on his skin. Dieter cursed softly. A thorn bush, of all things! He should have remembered that all the bushes here were brambly. That's what he'd been taught in Berlin, in the preparatory course given by the development aid service.

The bird stood immobile next to the bush, gazing sidelong into the distance. After half an hour, which seemed like a day to Dieter, it finally began orbiting the thorn bush, obviously inspecting it for places to penetrate.

To Dieter's right, where the twigs were somewhat less dense, the bird halted and thrust in a tentative foot. Dieter slammed it with a brambly switch. The ostrich reacted with a furious fluttering and hoarse roaring. Leaving a couple of feathers in the twigs, it circled the bush again, but at a wider radius.

Dieter's throat was already dry. If the ostrich didn't give up, he would gradually die of thirst in full view of the truck with its two forty-gallon water tanks. He must act now.

393

The next bush in the direction of the Ford was a bare hundred yards away. To reach it before the ostrich, he would need a head start of at least one third of the stretch. He waited until the bird was on the far side of the bush, then crept out from under the thorns and sprinted off. By the time the bird had scurried to the bush and then around it, Dieter had already covered sixty yards towards the next bush.

A final spurt, with the ominously approaching clopping of the ostrich, a dive through a narrow cleft into another brambly tangle, and—he had made it, for now. The ostrich began revolving around the new cover at an insane tempo, tail hopping, neck craning.

The new bush was smaller and thinner than the previous one, with two not wholly dense places. The bird did a sudden about-face and charged towards the first one. It slowed down in a whirl of dust and kicked its left foot at Dieter, missing him by inches as he rolled over to the other side of the bush. Damn it, that was close!

The ostrich ran around the thorn bush and tried the gap on the other side. Again Dieter hurled himself away, the thorns tearing fresh welts in his chest, back, and arms. Then the bird began to attack him through both gaps alternately, each charge widening the breaches a little, the legs getting closer; sinewy strings under a horny skin running into the two tremendous toes with black, hoof-like claws.

The first time the ostrich struck, tearing a gaping wound in his thigh, Dieter felt something like mortal panic. He was closed in now by an impenetrable tangle of thorns, while the ostrich attacked him with a bizarre leonine roaring, interspersed with the hissing and honking of a gander. A film of blood and sweat began to cover his spectacles. He took them off and rolled back and forth on the ground. Let anything happen, but not a direct hit! A full kick in the chest or belly, and he would be totally at the mercy of the bird.

Finally, the ostrich seemed to tire. It pulled out its foot and trotted around the bush again; apparently it was in no great hurry any more to kill its enemy. But it was clear to Dieter that he would not survive another hour in this trap. He had to run for his life to the truck.

For a moment, he thought he could make it; the ostrich lost one or two seconds in alarm before launching into pursuit. Dieter felt his legs getting heavier and his lungs about to burst, but he had only another hundred yards to go.

Then he stumbled. Instinctively, he curled up into a ball, shielding his head with his arms. The ostrich landed a full kick below the ribs, and Dieter lost his breath for a couple of seconds. But he staggered to his feet and managed to get both hands around the ostrich's neck and force it to the ground. The bird tipped over, lashing out. His beak opened, but what had sounded like a lion's roar was now more like a throttled croaking. Dieter felt the cartilaginous neck vertebrae under his fingers. With all his strength, he tried to wring them like a wet towel. The ostrich kicked desperately into empty air.

Suddenly, Dieter felt a dull cracking under his hands. Something had broken. The kicks became weaker and weaker, swinging to a halt like the pendulum of a clock that was running down. At that, Dieter's strength also ebbed. But his fingers still clutched the limp neck, and it was only when the ostrich no longer stirred that he let go and lay on the ground exhausted.

He thought of his father, the characteristic mild condescension in his eyes. He had always tacitly let his son feel that he considered him a weakling. Too bad he hadn't seen this struggle. His son had lived up to his demands, this time.

Half an hour later, he crawled to the truck on all fours, clambered into the back, and poured water over his head and upper body. He spilled most of it, feeling dizzy as he broke into a cold sweat. When he opened his eyes again, he found a black man eyeing him imperturbably.

"I killed it." The African didn't seem to understand English; he didn't bat an eye. "My glasses. I have to have my glasses." Dieter rolled off the back of the truck. He reeled towards the thorn bush, followed by the African. Near the dead ostrich, the man peered at Dieter sceptically.

"It attacked me." Dieter pointed to his wounds.

In the bush, Dieter found his glasses, the frames bent, but the lenses intact. "My camera must be over there," he said. They walked over to the tree where the fight had started.

The black man found the camera, studied it with interest, and handed it to Dieter. "He really did a nice job on you." Surprisingly, he spoke in perfect English. "You ought to see a doctor."

"How far is it to Lethlakane?"

"There's no doctor in Lethlakane, but there is a telephone. The doctor comes from Orapa. That's only twenty-five miles away."

"Then I'd rather drive straight to Orapa."

The African smiled. "They don't let anyone into Orapa without a pass." On their way back to the truck, they came to the dead ostrich. "He's a male," said the African. "He's got black plumage. Maybe you got too close to his nest. Or else he was a loner. If a male doesn't find a female, he gets very irritable. He attacks anyone entering his territory."

At the Ford, the African asked: "How did you get out here?"

"I'm a voluntary-aid worker from Germany and I'm supposed to drive this truck to Maun."

"Maun? Then you should have gone by way of Francistown."

"I thought this route would be more interesting."

"You were right."

"Do you need a lift?"

"Yes. But it's better if I do the driving."

An hour later, the first shacks of Lethlakane came into view. The African stopped. "You'll find white people there you can ask for help. Engineers. They're opening a new diamond mine."

"Are you coming along?"

The African took up his food pouch, climbed out wordlessly, and disappeared among the bushes. He didn't seem to be from this area. The Botswana usually had short hair that crinkled on their heads. This man's hair was thick and full.

Funny guy, thought Dieter. Won't let anyone approach him. Maybe he doesn't like me because I'm white. Still, I should have at least asked him his name.

But even if Tutuma had given him his name, it wouldn't have meant anything to Dieter.

IV

Although he had other worries at the moment, Jan Feuchtenbeiner was riled at being two games to five down. He had already lost the first set, four six. Bill Scranton knew how to keep the ball in play with a sure, undercut backhand until his opponent lost patience and chanced a risky forehand drive.

Changing sides, they met by the net, and Bill gave him an inquisitive sidelong glance. "You've played better, Jan. Your forehand is too uncontrolled."

Feuchtenbeiner dried his hands. His palms were so wet that his racket kept slipping, though it was still cool at this early time of day. The sun had risen only an hour ago. "I'm not hitting the ball squarely," he said.

"Or are you trying to let me win because I'm the boss?"

Feuchtenbeiner shook his head in annoyance. An absurd thought! For him there was no sport, only battle. Win or lose— nothing else counted.

Three minutes later, Scranton had won. Feuchtenbeiner shook his hand, growled a laborious "congratulations", and started away.

"One minute, Jan. Did I tell you you're flying a full shipment tomorrow?"

Feuchtenbeiner spun around: "Tomorrow?"

"Take off is at 1600 hours. This time it'll be almost 400,000 carats. So take someone along to help."

"I can manage alone, Bill," said Feuchtenbeiner.

The general manager blamed his security man's terseness on his defeat at tennis. "We all have bad days, Jan. Normally, you sweep me off the court."

They walked to the locker room and, after showering, Bill smiled: "Well? Cooled off? Sometimes I feel you'd rather bite your tongue off than admit your opponent was in fine form."

"OK, Bill. You were in fine form." Feuchtenbeiner would have preferred to smash his racket on Bill's head. For eighteen days now, he had been trying to forget, but now the day had come. Perhaps it still wasn't too late to confide in Bill. As they walked to their cars, he took a deep breath. "Does it really have to go tomorrow?"

"Do you mind?"

"Just a funny feeling . . . . A hunch something might happen."

"You've been a little nervous lately. What *can* happen? Apart from us, nobody knows that the pebbles will stay home tomorrow. And your security measures are one hundred per cent foolproof." Bill seemed a bit irritated. "So, OK?"

That terminated the discussion.

At home, Feuchtenbeiner was welcomed by June with over-done courtesy which did not bode well. Usually she began her day in grumpy silence, a woman who performed her household chores as reluctantly as her other wifely duties. She was too weak to rebel against her life in the bleakness of Orapa and too strong to come to terms with it, so she had been vegetating next to Jan for years, and her only way of getting her own back was through her resentful attitude.

Feuchtenbeiner couldn't quite understand her dissatisfaction. Didn't she have a respectable rank in Orapa's strict hierarchy? Didn't they live in a comfortable house? Didn't they have a black housekeeper, a cook, and a boy who took care of the garden?

No one prevented June from playing bridge, attending the teas given by the other management wives, making dates for squash or golf. The aeroplane from Gaberones flew in a new film twice a week. There was a supermarket, the most modern and best-stocked in the whole country. And finally, there was the all-weather road to Mopipi Lake, thirty-five miles away, an artificial lake that provided water for Orapa and where she could go swim-ming whenever she wanted to. So for a long time Feuchtenbeiner had regarded June's eternal bad moods as simply the whim of an ungrateful woman.

Next to his breakfast tea there was a note that consisted of only one word: "When?"

Mr. January was jogging Feuchtenbeiner's memory again: over the last eighteen days Feuchtenbeiner had felt his presence every-where in Orapa. A letter with no return address in his mailbox; a scrap of paper with a hand-written note under his napkin in the casino; another note in the breast pocket of his bush shirt in the locker room of the club. Just three days ago, Mr. January had called Feuchtenbeiner's secretary, leaving a message that sounded harmless only to outsiders: "The photographer called. He would like to know where he should send the pictures."

"I found this slip of paper under the windshield of the Range-Rover," June said casually. "At least she had enough taste not to sign her name. Is it Pieter's secretary?"

Feuchtenbeiner shrugged to indicate how ludicrous he found her suspicion. "Oh, get off my back."

A love affair in Orapa, of all places; a ghetto where each of the two hundred white men and eighty white women knew every step that everyone else took.

"How long has it been going on?"

"There *is* no woman, June. In my position—I'm not crazy, you know." Feuchtenbeiner pushed his half-eaten breakfast aside, and wiped his mouth. "I have to get to the office."

"Are you coming home for lunch?"

"I'm eating in the cafeteria."

"We still have to talk about it."

"Not now."

To hell with her goddamn jealousy. Out in the garden, as he passed the castor-oil bush, he snapped one stalk. The action had something irrevocable about it. It was the first of two signs the blackmailer had demanded. The second must wait until after midnight.

Feuchtenbeiner climbed into his Range-Rover and sped out to the road barrier at the eastern gate of Orapa. He had himself helped to work out the security measures for the town, and he set great store on checking that they were followed to the letter. Requests for visits were not approved without Feuchtenbeiner's express OK, and he restricted passes to guests from the central office in Johannesburg or to government officials from Botswana.

The diamond mine itself, with its airfield and its central block, Recovery House, were behind him in an inner security zone, separated by an electric fence from the homes and the social and athletic facilities of Orapa. For this area, there was a red pass,

399

which was practically never issued to outsiders. The outer security zone consisted of the small clean residential town and a zone of wild bushland running to the outer security fence, which was three miles away. Two barred gates at the east and west entrances to the road running through Orapa separated it from the outside world. De Beers's own security officers checked everyone coming in or going out of the two gates and were themselves responsible to Jan Feuchtenbeiner.

Jan climbed out at the eastern barrier and walked towards the black sergeant. "A lot of traffic today?"

"Hardly any, sir." The sergeant pointed to a sand-coloured Ford truck. "But there's a man here who won't go away."

The driver of the truck came closer, smiling. "The security officer won't let me drive through."

Since the man was white, Feuchtenbeiner forced himself to smile. "Do you have a pass?"

"Why? I only want to drive through."

"You'll have to drive around. This is the private property of the De Beers Mining Company. Where are you going?"

"I'm driving this Ford to Maun." Dieter Hahn pulled out his passport. "I'm a German voluntary worker."

Feuchtenbeiner threw a casual glance at the passport and handed it back. "Sorry, Mr. Hahn." Without another word, Feuchtenbeiner climbed into his Range-Rover and drove off.

The trivial meeting had scarcely lasted three minutes. Later on, when this German volunteer suddenly became important to him, Feuchtenbeiner could only vaguely remember his face.

Jan drove back to town as fast as possible. From far away, the rock dump by the mine, with its smoothed-off side walls and flat roof, looked like a pyramid shaped by a child's hands. The dump was at least a hundred and fifty feet high and a kind of visual symbol of Orapa; smashed rock fragments, after they had been pulverized and ground twice, sifted, washed, X-rayed on a conveyor belt, rewashed and sorted, a dozen times in all, and moved as a greyish-brown mush on the last of the four conveyor belts into Recovery House, onto six tables where black sorters picked the tiny diamonds out of the rubbish with tweezers.

Feuchtenbeiner got out at Recovery House. At the electronically-secured gate of the fence surrounding it, Laurens was waiting. It was eleven thirty a.m., and the inspection of the inner sanctum was part of Feuchtenbeiner's daily routine. Laurens had to watch over the entrances to the windowless vault, where the spoils of each mining day were gathered and deposited in the safe until they were flown to Gaberones.

Laurens unlocked the steel door to the vault; a black colleague then opened the second lock. This additional safety measure was based on the assumption that a white man would never join forces with a black.

Before passing the X-ray lock to the vault room, Laurens and Feuchtenbeiner sent the black away. Then Laurens worked the combination of the safe. It was almost full of diamonds, roughly sorted into gems and industrial stones and sealed in soft leather pouches. 400,000 carats, to be sold at an average of forty-one dollars per carat at the London Diamond Exchange—if they ever reached London.

Laurens eyed him. "What's wrong? Don't you feel good?"

Feuchtenbeiner turned away. "I need a cool beer."

FEUCHTENBEINER spent the evening at home, barely speaking. When June started her jealous nagging again, he pleaded a headache to escape her. When, half an hour after midnight, she followed him into the bedroom, Feuchtenbeiner pretended he was asleep.

Soon he heard June's regular breathing in the other bed. He got out of bed, slipped from the bedroom, and groped through the darkness of the house. The moon shed a feeble light through the kitchen window. The luminous dial of the alarm clock showed four minutes to one.

Feuchtenbeiner perched on a stool and peered out of the window. Somewhere outside, someone was lurking for his signal. Assuming the theft worked—what guarantee did he have that he'd really get the photos and the negatives? What good was a blackmailer's word anyway?

It was one o'clock now. He had to make up his mind. He

groped for the switch and turned on the ceiling light, put it out, turned it on again, and then a third time.

Now it was done. He couldn't go back.

THE BLEEP from the walkie-talkie startled Tutuma out of his sleep. He pressed the speaking button.

"I'm on the western side, by the Rysana Pan."

"He gave the second signal. The patrol passed the western gate twenty minutes ago."

"I'm coming."

Before getting under way, Tutuma checked the packaging of the twenty dynamite sticks. They were inside the food pouch, and he had made a tight knot in its top to protect the dynamite against moisture. The coming rainy season was already fore-shadowed by hot, sticky nights, and dew lay on the elephant grass of the Kalahari. Tutuma gingerly put the sticks back into the pouch and marched eastward.

An hour later, the outer fence cutting Orapa off from the wilderness loomed up in the dark. Tutuma pulled a small pair of cutters from his overalls and snipped through the wire close to the ground. After crawling through the hole in the fence, he stuffed some bramble twigs into the gap. It was a makeshift camouflage, but it would be enough for one day. Sooner or later, they'd dis-cover the hole anyway.

He still had three miles to go to Orapa, through a bush-covered no-man's-land. But soon the silhouettes of the first houses stood out against the dawn.

So far, it wasn't much more than a Boy Scout manoeuvre. The dangerous part of the adventure still lay ahead. On the outskirts of the golf course, Tutuma lay down under a bush and waited for dawn. This day, he thought, would decide the war for Zimbabwe.

AFTER a sleepless night, Feuchtenbeiner felt lousy. The office day had started with a call from the general manager. His after-noon take-off would be two hours late. Gaberones couldn't issue a landing permit before seven p.m. because the president of Botswana was expected to fly in from Johannesburg at five thirty.

402

For Feuchtenbeiner the two hours were like a gift, a temporary reprieve.

The jangle of the telephone startled him out of his brooding. Even before picking up the receiver, he knew who was at the other end.

"Are you alone in your office, Feuchtenbeiner?" It was the voice of Mr. January.

"Yes."

"The take-off—when is it precisely?"

"At six p.m. Listen, Mr. January, assuming someone wants to hijack the transport to Gaberones . . . . Even if it came off, and the hijackers got away. . . . It would make no sense. They would never be able to fence the goods."

"You really think so?"

"Did you ever hear of the CSO in London? The Central Selling Organization? It belongs to De Beers and Anglo-American, and both those companies belong to Harry Oppenheimer, who also owns the mine in Orapa. If a smuggler or a thief wants to sell diamonds anywhere in the world, he has to deal with the CSO. Oppenheimer has the world monopoly, from extracting to polishing, without a gap, do you understand? Anyone who tried to sell a large amount of rough diamonds would be tracked down instantly. And there's no black market. Especially not for 400,000 carats." Feuchtenbeiner waited for a reaction. "Hello, are you still there?"

"Keep talking."

"That's why there's nothing more hopeless in the world than robbing De Beers. And what do you want with stolen diamonds that are just as unsellable as—well, say—the Mona Lisa Do you understand me?"

"I understand you very well. You said six p.m., right?"

"Mr. January, the Gaberones airport will be crawling with policemen. The president's coming back from South Africa. It won't work!"

"That would be too bad, Feuchtenbeiner. Too bad for you."

Feuchtenbeiner sweated.

The countdown had begun.

AT FIVE TWENTY-EIGHT P.M., at Recovery House, he signed a receipt for eighty-seven pouches of diamonds. Laurens was the third man to find out about the shipment, but only now, at the last moment. Even though Feuchtenbeiner presented the authorization document signed by the general manager, Laurens called Bill Scranton to make sure it was all right. Feuchtenbeiner himself had introduced this double-check measure four years ago. Then Laurens helped him load the two aluminium suitcases, which together weighed a good one hundred and eighty pounds.

The Range-Rover had to drive them almost nine hundred yards to the airstrip. The Beechcraft King Air plane stood outside, unattended except for a black mechanic who was tinkering with an engine.

The pilot hadn't arrived. Feuchtenbeiner was sure that the hijacking would take place either in the Gaberones Airport or during the two-mile drive from the airport to the Anglo-American Building. Probably during the unloading on the airfield.

As far as Feuchtenbeiner could judge, the attack couldn't succeed. He would have no choice but to shoot, and he was an excellent marksman. Everybody in Orapa knew that. A bad shot would look odd . . . . But on the other hand, he had to let the hijackers escape. They must have accomplices, who would get even by sending the photos to Bill Scranton if they did not escape. He might claim that the handcuffs manacling him to the cases kept him from firing. But what about the pilot? And Piet and Balthasar, the security officers in Gaberones—they were armed too.

Laurens climbed into the cockpit with him, heaved the two cases onto the seats behind the pilot's, and locked the chains of Feuchtenbeiner's handcuffs. Until Gaberones, there was no way he could get rid of the burden: apart from Laurens, only Piet and Balthasar had keys for the handcuffs. Anyone who wanted to steal the two cases en route would have to kidnap Jan Feuchtenbeiner as well. He tried to make himself as comfortable as possible between the cases.

Ten minutes later, the pilot arrived. "The president landed five minutes ago. Gaberones is cleared for traffic." He climbed in. "Everything OK? I'm closing the entrance hatch."

The black mechanic stuck his head in through the hatch. "Wait. There's another passenger coming."

"But there's no one else on the list today."

Another black man came out from behind the mechanic's car. He was also in overalls. He had a toolbox under his arm and a pouch slung over his shoulder. As he reached the plane, he dipped into the pouch and pulled out a sand-coloured stick that looked like a giant cigar. "I'm flying along." And when the pilot groped for his Luger, the black man added softly: "Don't! Do you see what I have in my hand? Dynamite. And I have nineteen more sticks in my pouch."

The pilot shrank back and the mechanic and Tutuma vaulted through the hatch into the plane.

"My friend will collect your weapons. Start the engines and get going."

While the mechanic bolted the hatch and gathered in the pistols, the pilot looked frantically at Feuchtenbeiner who only nodded: "Do what he says."

Then Feuchtenbeiner turned to the black man with the dynamite. "Where do you want to go?"

"Angola—Serpa Pinto. Nothing will happen to you if you follow my instructions."

The mechanic sat down next to the pilot, never taking his eyes off the instrument panel. "Fly south, as always. I can read the instruments."

Tutuma took the seat behind Feuchtenbeiner. "Tell the pilot what effect the dynagel has when it's dropped."

"But you'll be blown up too," said the pilot.

Tutuma gazed reflectively at the stick in his hand. "Would you like to take the risk?"

"Do what they say," Feuchtenbeiner repeated.

The pilot fussed over the instrument panel. "I have to check the instruments first. Besides, I don't have a landing permit for Angola."

The mechanic sprang from his seat and pushed down a lever. "The radio! He switched it on!"

"Oh," said the pilot, "I didn't even notice."

Tutuma grabbed the pilot by his collar and held the dynagel stick ominously under his nose. "That was your first and last trick. You will now fly due south. Later, when we're out of sight from the airport, you will turn and fly northwest. Get going!"

The pilot obeyed. He raised the Beechcraft into the air, and after five minutes, he made a wide loop to northwest. Tutuma looked at Feuchtenbeiner. "Stay calm. We are patriots, not criminals. We hold to our agreements, whether they are made in the air or at the Holiday Inn."

Feuchtenbeiner got the hint. The man wanted to let him know that he was ready to return the photograph negatives, assuming that Feuchtenbeiner made sure the plan went off without a hitch. Now that he was no longer dealing with a phantom, but with an enemy in the flesh, his tension gradually waned. He even felt something like gratitude.

BILL SCRANTON was doing his lengths in the management swimming pool when he was urgently summoned to the phone. Laurens was on the line: "Ground control's caught snatches of a conversation on the King Air's radio. It sounded like the plane was being hijacked to Angola."

"Do you know any details?"

"No, only that they were talking about Angola."

"Keep it a secret for now, Laurens. And get me Johannesburg, please."

Scranton didn't stop to get dressed. A few seconds later, he had a board member of De Beers on the radio telephone, and the man instantly put him through to the central commando of the company's security force.

Johannesburg had plans for all possibilities. Less than five minutes later, the air force had made its preparations. Fifteen minutes after the alarm sounded, Mirage fighters zoomed into the sky from Mafeking in the south, right by the Botswana border; from Pietsburg in the east; and from Tsumkwe, the desert strip in South-West Africa, which had been expanded into a military airfield after the troubles in Ovamboland. The head start of the slower King Air wasn't important. The Beechcraft would need

406

more than an hour to fly the 250 miles from Orapa to the Angolan border.

Time enough to cut off its path.

AT FIRST, Tutuma thought it was a storm. But within seconds, the distant booming of thunder swelled into an ear-shattering roar. The King Air rocked in a compression wave. The pilot flipped on the radio. A voice croaked: "Turn due west and follow us."

Tutuma stared out of the window. The final rays of the sun glowed on the fuselage of a Mirage and on the pilot's white helmet.

"Switch that radio off!" The pilot obeyed. "How long till Angola?"

"At least fifty minutes." The pilot tried to sound matter-of-fact. "Those are Mirage fighters. They've got rockets, and they're at least eight times as fast as we are. Look—three more are coming. You don't have a prayer."

"Fly lower and stay just above the ground," said Tutuma. "It'll be dark soon."

"That won't help you. They've got radar."

The Mirages formed into a new approach. A new compression wave shook the cabin like an earthquake.

"Do you want to kill us all?" shouted Feuchtenbeiner.

Tutuma reached under his seat, where he had stowed the tool box. He opened the top and groped around until he felt his steel shears. He applied the shears to the chain round Feuchtenbeiner's wrists. At first, they left only feeble notches, but Tutuma pressed the handles again with all his strength, and at the third try, the steel cracked open. One suitcase was free. The slicing went faster with the second chain.

Tutuma tapped the mechanic's shoulder. "We're bailing out."

The mechanic shook his head. He seemed paralysed with fear. "I can't."

"You've got to!" Tutuma turned to the pilot. "Where are the parachutes?"

The pilot wordlessly pointed under the empty seats in the row behind them. Feuchtenbeiner got up and helped Tutuma into a parachute. Tutuma handed over his pouch. "Hold it tight. But be

407

careful. It's a wonder the things haven't exploded yet with all this rocking and swaying." He pulled the mechanic from his seat. "Come on, Moses; it's easy."

The mechanic stubbornly shook his head. "I can't jump."

"Do you want them to torture you?"

"I still can't." The mechanic dropped on the floor and lay there like a rock.

"Then at least kill yourself." Tutuma threw Feuchtenbeiner's gun over to the mechanic. He used his shears to smash the pilot's radio. Then he dragged the two aluminium cases to the rear section and unbolted the hatch. The blast of air almost knocked him over. He clung to the side of the hatch and kicked the two cases out, one after the other, and jumped after them. He felt a jerk as the parachute opened. Overhead, he could hear the roar of the Mirage fighters. Had they noticed his jump? He peered down and tried to concentrate on the moment of impact. Here in the Kalahari there were no tall trees in which his parachute could get entangled, but there were man-high thorn bushes.

A moment later, he struck the ground. He felt a violent pain in his left ankle and lay still until the pain eased a bit. Then he pulled himself to his feet, took off the harness, folded the parachute, and buried it in the soft, peaty soil with his hands. He could see no bush, no blade of grass in the surrounding desert.

He rubbed his ankle. It was probably only twisted, for the pain had gone down a bit. He'd be all right tomorrow, after a rest, and it made no sense to look for the two cases in the gathering dusk. He lay down on the ground. It was springy, soft and dry, and still reflected something of the heat of the day.

The King Air couldn't be heard any more; only the faint growl of the jet fighters in the distance. Maybe it would have been better to blow up the plane. He should at least have shot Moses; he realized now that it had been foolish to leave the mechanic. If Moses fell into the hands of the South Africans, he'd be a danger to the Zimbabwe Liberation Army, the ZLA. And the South Africans would murder him eventually anyway, certainly in a far more lingering manner.

No matter where he was, Tutuma had the gift of going to sleep

whenever he wanted to, so he made use of the hours until sunrise. He would need all his strength during the next few days, if he was to bring his mission to a successful conclusion.

V

For the rest of the flight, Feuchtenbeiner took charge of the King Air. The black mechanic let him take his weapons and frisk him without resistance: he seemed helpless without his leader. Feuchtenbeiner poked him. "What's your name?"

The black man remained silent. Feuchtenbeiner grabbed him by the overalls and hauled back for a punch.

The pilot turned around. "Forget it! His name is Moses. He's been working on the airfield for three months. You can give him the third degree when we're on the ground."

The Mirages zoomed past them, back and forth, like a pack of dogs driving a sheep into a fold. "Where are they steering us?"

"Southwest. Windhoek probably, I don't know. The border's seventy miles away."

A Mirage roared past them. Feuchtenbeiner tried to wave to the pilot that everything was OK.

Feuchtenbeiner grabbed Moses by the collar. "What's the other man's name?"

Finally, Moses said: "Kgosi."

"What does the name mean?"

"Chief."

"And what's his real name?"

"Kgosi."

"How long have you known him?"

"A couple of hours. He only came today. Through the fence."

The pilot rubbed the back of his neck. "I just can't figure out why they wanted to hijack the Beechcraft today of all days. I've never asked you before. You don't have to make a secret of it now."

"I can only tell you this much: They weren't after the plane."

The pilot nodded. "Then they must have got a tip. I wouldn't like to be in your shoes, Jan," he said.

410

TOWARDS MORNING, when the cold crept up from the ground into his feet and hands, Tutuma awoke. The sun hadn't risen. He had no blanket, no compass, no water or food, only his thin overalls. He should have been in Serpa Pinto by now, deep inside friendly Angola. The diamonds were to have been handed to a Soviet courier in Luanda.

Tutuma jumped up. The diamonds!

The King Air had been flying northwest. He had only to strike off towards the dawn and then veer a little to the right.

When it was lighter, he started out to hunt for the cases. The pain in his left ankle had waned. The South African police must have been alerted long ago. They would send out planes and choppers to hunt for him, and as soon as they determined his approximate whereabouts, they would put hounds on his trail.

Tutuma peered around. No tree, no bush, not even savannah grass to hide in. And his footsteps no longer bounced off the peaty soil; he was walking on a rock-hard salt crust covered with a layer of fine dust, until recently the bottom of a vast lake.

Half an hour later, he came upon one of the two cases. The metal skin reflected the rays of the sun like a mirror. It had burst open when it crashed on the ground, and the leather pouches lay scattered in a radius of ten yards.

Tutuma gathered them together, tugged one of them open, and peered inside. Yellowish-grey grit; each stone barely larger than a coarse grain of sand. Cautiously, Tutuma bit into one of the grains. A piece of tooth enamel broke off. Industrial diamonds. So Feuchtenbeiner hadn't lied. Tutuma put the pouches back into the battered case and locked it as best he could. He would not be able to drag the cases along, for in the sunshine they would be visible to even a distant aeroplane.

A hundred yards farther north, Tutuma found the second case and not far away a small patch of peaty soil in the salt crust. With his hands, he dug out a hole large enough for both cases. The second case had a couple of dents, but had not burst open like the other. Tutuma buried both cases, collected two dozen fist-sized rocks, and placed them like a loose wall around the hiding place. Recognizable only to an insider, the rocks formed the approximate outline of Zimbabwe with the characteristic horn in the west.

When he was done, Tutuma marched off towards the north. He had done about 8,000 paces in a kind of endurance run, when suddenly, far to the east, he spotted a cloud of dust moving slowly towards him.

DIETER HAHN had rolled up the window of his truck to keep from swallowing any more of the dust whirled up by the tyres. He wiped his face with the back of his hand. Actually, he should have delayed his trip. The white doctor who had come to Lethlakane from Orapa had given him a tetanus shot and prescribed rest so that he could recover from the bruises and gashes he'd got from the ostrich. The wound where the bird had clawed him looked particularly bad. But after a day, Dieter had felt strong enough to drive on.

When he had rounded Mopipi Dam, the road had turned into an ill-defined track on which he couldn't go more than twelve miles an hour. But now the ground was as hard as macadam, and for the past fifteen minutes he had managed almost to double that speed.

The African up ahead was squatting by the edge of the track. He raised a tired hand. Dieter braked to a halt and rolled down the window. "Haven't we met before?"

"Yes, two days ago." Tutuma smiled. "After you wrung the ostrich's neck."

"Of course; it's you. Why did you disappear so quickly in Lethlakane? I couldn't even thank you properly."

Tutuma ignored the question. "Where are we now exactly?"

"You ought to know better than I do." Dieter took the map and climbed out. "A few miles back I drove past a lake. But there's no lake shown there on the map."

"That was Mopipi Dam. It's only four years old. The Botletle used to flow into Lake Xau, but the Orapa people diverted it into the Mopipi depression and laid a pipeline to supply water for Orapa."

"So now we're on the bottom of what was once Lake Xau?"

412

Tutuma nodded. "There used to be flamingoes here. Now it's just a salt waste." He picked up some stones and formed a kind of signpost pointing to the south, where he had bailed out. Then with no further word of explanation he climbed in next to the driver's seat. "You're still going to Maun?" Dieter nodded. "Have you seen anyone so far?"

"Only an African with a couple of goats."

"No Land-Rover or helicopter?"

Surprised, Dieter shook his head. He pulled out a can of Fanta. "Are you thirsty?"

"Thanks." Tutuma unsealed the lukewarm can and emptied it at one draught. "Can we get started?"

It was only now that Dieter realized the African had invited himself along. That was probably normal in a country without public transport. The black man seemed educated, and not only because he spoke English so well.

A few miles later, Dieter broke his silence. "Do you know anything about cars?"

"Not much. Why?"

Dieter pointed to Tutuma's overalls. "At first, I thought you were a mechanic." Tutuma ignored the sly question.

Suddenly, the Ford lurched so violently that Dieter almost banged his head on the roof. "Springhaases," said Tutuma. "They build warrens. You have to drive around them slowly. Otherwise the axle could break."

The salt steppe, devoid of vegetation, had now turned into a dry savannah with meagre thorn bushes, burrs, and sparse, yellowish-brown grass. When they came to a fork in the trail, the African said: "Follow the track to the left. The right goes to the village."

Dieter stayed on the left. Obviously the man was in a hurry. Dieter was now exceedingly curious about his nameless passenger. He had been standing in overalls on the dried-out bottom of a lake and hadn't even known where he was. He had no water, no food, yet he could hardly have lost his way. And the Africans whom Dieter had met up till now always wore their hearts on their sleeves, while this one was taciturn. Something was wrong here.

413

Eventually, the African broke the silence: "Europeans who come here generally visit the Victoria Falls." It sounded like a question.

"I've only been in Africa a week. I'm a development volunteer. My name is Dieter. In seven weeks, I'm supposed to take charge of a brigade in Ghanzi. If I have time before then, I definitely want to go to Zimbabwe and see the Falls."

"Why don't you call Zimbabwe Rhodesia as all the whites do?"

"Zimbabwe is the African name. It is an African country."

The African nodded in agreement, but stayed as reserved as ever. "I'm hungry," he said finally.

Dieter drove the truck into the bush, parking in the shade of a tall acacia.

The African gathered wood while Dieter set up his kettle. The parched wood burned without smoke, like tinder. Dieter filled the kettle from his plastic water container, took out some teabags and two enamel mugs and made tea. His wholemeal bread was so dry it crumbled when he sliced it.

The African was staring hard at a cloud of dust approaching from the west. Then Dieter saw it too. "Who's that?"

"Whoever it is, he's going to stop and speak to you. That's customary here. I have an important request: Don't mention me." Before Dieter could say anything, he quickly added: "And don't ask any questions right now." The African took his mug and crept behind a nearby tree.

A few minutes later, the cloud of dust proved to be a land-cruiser of the Botswana police. A sergeant in neat shorts and a khaki bush shirt greeted Dieter. "*Dumela morena.*"

Dieter raised a friendly hand. "*Dumela.*"

"Where are you coming from?"

"Gaberones. I'm supposed to drive this Ford to Maun. On behalf of the ministry for youth and education."

"It's not so easy to find the road to Maun. Are you alone?"

Dieter nodded.

"I've got a map. It shows the highway."

"Highway!" The amused sergeant puffed out his cheeks. "It's a dried-out river bed. If you break down, you may have to spend

414

weeks waiting for help. When you get to Maun, you ought to report to the police. Goodbye. *Sala sentle.*"

"*Tsamja sentle.*" Dieter was glad he could use one of the few phrases of Setswana he had learned in Germany.

When the landcruiser had vanished, the African came out from behind his tree. He sized Dieter up with a long stare. Then he said softly: "You just helped me. Why?"

Dieter didn't reply immediately. He needed time himself to puzzle out his motive. "Maybe I sensed you needed help. Maybe I just didn't want to lose you again right away. As a partner, I mean. It would be fun to drive with you for a while."

"You come from Germany. You're white. A white man does nothing that he can't profit from."

"Naturally I want to profit from you." Dieter smiled. "I came to Africa to learn, and I hope you can help me understand a few things better. You see: I'm just as egotistical as all the other whites. Some more tea?"

The African held out the mug. "We can certainly travel a while together."

"Where are you going?"

"I don't know yet."

"You must have some sort of destination."

The African seemed to be mulling something over as he sipped tea and wolfed down a can of corned beef. After a bit, he asked: "What side are you on politically?"

"I volunteered for the overseas service because I wanted to help the people of Botswana out of their economic encirclement by South Africa."

"You've really taken something on." There was no telling whether the African meant it ironically.

"I heard that there are too few places at higher institutions for students who finish elementary school. They can learn some sort of craft in my brigade—masonry or carpentry or farming, so Botswana can produce more at home rather than import everything from South Africa or Rhodesia. Does that satisfy you?"

The African nodded. "Fine, you want to help the people of Botswana. Would you help me too? Me personally?"

"You mean: Would I help you hide from the police?"

"For instance."

"I would help a victim of persecution, but not a criminal. Besides, I didn't have the impression they were looking for you."

"It might happen very soon. I'm a political refugee from Zimbabwe."

"Why should they hunt for you here? Botswana is on the side of the black independence movement."

"You know very little about the reality in southern Africa. Just look at the map. Botswana is surrounded by hostile governments. In the north and west, Namibia, which the South Africans completely control. In the south, South Africa itself. And in the east, Zimbabwe, which is ruled by the racist Ian Smith. There's only one railway from Botswana to the South African docks, and that line belongs to the white Rhodesians. If Vorster and Smith agree to cut Botswana off from the outside world, all they have to do is blockade the roads and the track. In a few weeks, Botswana would be ruined."

"You have a ferry across the Zambezi in the north."

"Both banks are within shooting range of the Rhodesians. You won't get anything out of Zambia if the whites don't want you to. Botswana is an independent republic on parole. The South Africans have their fingers in everything: the mining industry, the economy, the authorities. Now do you understand why I can't trust the Botswana police?"

"Are you really that important to the South Africans?"

"Soon I'm going to be the most-wanted man in southern Africa." Something in the African's voice convinced Dieter that the man wasn't showing off. The African pointed to his overalls. "Do you have anything else I could wear?".

Dieter got his suitcase from the back of the truck and handed the African a pair of corduroy jeans and a blue T-shirt. The shirt fitted him, and though the jeans were too large, the African threw his crumpled-up overalls into a bush.

"My name is Tutuma," he said. "It would be better if I weren't seen in Maun."

"You can lie under the blanket in the back of the truck."

416

"How much of a hurry are you in to get there?"

"Not much."

"I'm afraid they'll be hunting for me everywhere, except perhaps deep in the Kalahari. No one ever goes there."

"Ka-la-ha-ri." Dieter spoke the word with relish. A yen for adventure flashed in his eyes. "The word doesn't sound bad. Like a lot of sand and a lot of adventure."

VI

From the air, the place looked vaguely like a gold-mining settlement. In the moonlight, Feuchtenbeiner could make out eight Quonset huts, a radar station, and an airstrip with a wind cone, now dangling slackly. The pilot landed the King Air shortly after eight p.m., and the Mirage fighters touched down quickly one after the other.

Feuchtenbeiner met the airfield commander, a uniformed major, and briefly put him in the picture. The major vanished inside one of the huts to get further instructions via radio telephone from the air force commander-in-chief.

He came back five minutes later. "I'm to fly you to Pretoria. The mechanic, too."

The pilot was impatiently stretching his legs. "Where are we anyway?"

"At Tsumkwe Airbase in South-West Africa," the major replied tersely.

Tsumkwe, near the borders of Angola and Botswana, had been secretly built by the South Africans when Angola became independent.

Feuchtenbeiner and his prisoner were escorted to an aircraft which would take them to Pretoria. The King Air pilot had been told to wait until the next day and then head back to Orapa. He was warned to keep the incident top secret. Meanwhile, Orapa had radioed the tower in Gaberones that the King Air had a defective motor and would not be landing there after all.

That evening, the national security board met in Pretoria.

Because the situation was so delicate, it was decided to keep the incident under tight wraps; to outsiders, everything would seem normal. Business as usual.

AROUND TWO a.m., the aircraft carrying Feuchtenbeiner and Moses landed at Pretoria's military airport. A Mercedes was waiting on the runway, and a taciturn chauffeur drove Feuchtenbeiner and the prisoner out into the country for over an hour.

Feuchtenbeiner was surprised. He had been ready for endless conferences with high-ranking officers from the security police headquarters. Instead, he found himself in a farmhouse, with an almost domestic atmosphere—an open fire burning in an expensively furnished living room, and three men casually dressed in lumberjack shirts. One of them led Moses away. A second man, of about sixty, sat on one side, not saying a word. The third man, obviously the highest in rank, introduced him: "This is Heinz."

The leader's handshake felt to Feuchtenbeiner like a vice. "Glad to meet you." But the cool gaze from the man's piercing eyes made his words an empty formula. "The government has decided that the investigation is to be kept unofficial. There *was* no incident in Orapa. Please remember that. My office has taken charge of the case. I am General Van Zyl of the Bureau of State Security." He offered Feuchtenbeiner a chair. "What we need first of all, Jan, is a detailed oral report. We can take your written statement later on."

Feuchtenbeiner rubbed the sweat off the back of his neck. They must have switched on a hidden tape recorder. He made an effort to describe the assault as precisely as possible. Van Zyl listened closely, without interrupting. Heinz took occasional notes.

When Feuchtenbeiner was done, Van Zyl asked: "And you saw no possibility of overpowering the men?"

"The leader seemed resolute about using the dynamite."

"But how could the hijackers have known that you were flying to Gaberones with 400,000 carats yesterday, of all days?"

"I think it was a coincidence," said Feuchtenbeiner. "They probably thought that the cases contained diamonds on every flight to Gaberones."

Van Zyl exchanged an expressionless glance with Heinz. "To me the thing looks like it was set up by an organization. The man sneaking into the security zone unnoticed, the dynamite, Angola as the destination. Those were no kaffirs snatching an old lady's handbag in the street. They were trained terrorists. Frankly, I'm amazed at your judgment of the situation. For me, it's as clear as day that the hijackers got a tip."

Feuchtenbeiner tried to get himself out of the situation as inconspicuously as possible. "I'm only a security official with no strategic training. Naturally, you have a better grasp of things."

Van Zyl smiled thinly. "As far as I'm informed, only the general manager and you knew about the shipment."

"And Laurens Hafner."

"Who is that?"

"The security man in charge of Recovery House."

Feuchtenbeiner saw that Heinz was writing down the name.

"When did Hafner find out about it?"

"When I picked up the eighty-seven pouches in the vault. He handed them over to me, and I signed the receipt. Exactly according to regulations. I think it was five twenty-eight p.m."

"Half an hour before take-off." Van Zyl thought for a few seconds. His forehead wrinkled but quickly smoothed out again. "To prepare a coup like this, one would need more time."

"The whole thing didn't have to come from Orapa, you know," Jan said. "At Anglo-American in Gaberones someone may have known about the shipment. And at the top level of the company in Johannesburg, too."

"We'll check into that," said Van Zyl. "Did you ever talk about the shipment with anybody? Your wife maybe?"

"I know the regulations. I helped to make them. My wife doesn't have a clue that yesterday's flight wasn't empty."

Van Zyl seemed satisfied with this for the moment. "This Moses. Did you check his background before he was hired?"

"Of course. He's been a mechanic on the airfield for three months now."

"And you gave the man complete security clearance?"

"We've got almost 2,000 blacks in Orapa. I don't have all of

419

them at my fingertips. I'd need to send for the files first. By the way, I've just thought of something: they've probably noticed Moses's absence in Orapa. How are we supposed to explain it if the incident is to be kept under cover?"

"Everything's being taken care of. Moses's absence has been explained, and Bill Scranton's been let in on the secret. Incidentally—what do you think of Scranton?"

"I don't presume to express any opinion about Mr. Scranton," Feuchtenbeiner replied stiffly.

"When security aspects are involved, you most certainly must presume to express your opinion."

"Nevertheless, I'd rather not. He's a friend of mine: we play tennis every morning . . . . But who can really look into another man's heart?" He thought that he had wriggled out of it skilfully.

Van Zyl switched on the ceiling light and walked over to a table with a map of Botswana lying on it. "I would like you to show me where you think the terrorist leader bailed out with the two cases."

Feuchtenbeiner deliberated. "It was getting dark, and I don't know for sure how long we'd been flying. Maybe half an hour or so." He tapped his forefinger on an area some ninety miles north of the bail-out point. He had to make absolutely sure that they didn't get their man: the terrorist must know about the photos.

"Are you sure it wasn't farther west?"

"It must have been roughly here. Over the Makgadikgadi Pans."

Van Zyl looked annoyed. "In your pilot's opinion, the man must have jumped out approximately here." He made a circle, with Lake Xau at the centre. "There's only a salt desert there in a radius of over one hundred miles."

"Things were a little hectic, you know. Maybe I'm wrong. Or the pilot's wrong. Both of us were so glad the man had jumped out, that we didn't pay too much attention to our position."

"It doesn't matter. We'll get him. Do you know his name?"

Feuchtenbeiner shook his head. "All I know is that he calls himself Kgosi. In Setswana, the word means 'chief'. I'd never seen his face before."

"Then describe him for us."

"About thirty, not more than five feet eight, khaki overalls.

420

Pitch-black skin, very high forehead. He made an educated impression. Spoke English with no trace of an accent. What else . . . . ? Yes, a Ho Chi Minh moustache with drooping ends."

Van Zyl held his breath for an instant. "Was he possibly wearing an ivory ring on his little finger?"

"He had nothing on except his overalls and sandals. I didn't see any ring. Do you have a particular suspect in mind?"

Van Zyl shrugged. "Just an idea." He stood up. "It's four o'clock already. You ought to sleep a few hours before flying back to Orapa tomorrow. A couple of our men are going to accompany you. There's a guest room prepared for you upstairs."

That night, no one on the farm got any rest. Certainly not Feuchtenbeiner, who kept recapitulating his interrogation to make sure he hadn't slipped up on any detail.

Not Moses either, who had refused to reveal his and Kgosi's true identities during his first interrogation. He insisted on his impossible story that Kgosi, previously unknown to him, had hired him only a couple of hours before the assault.

Not Van Zyl and Heinz, who worked out a temporary strategy on the basis of the meagre facts. Four BOSS agents were to fly to Orapa, where they would take charge of tracking down Kgosi. They would be "security inspectors from De Beers", routinely checking the facilities at Orapa.

After breakfast, Van Zyl visited Moses. "My colleagues believe that you got involved in this affair more or less by chance," he said jovially. "I agree with them. You've done something foolish, Moses, but let's forget about it. Of course, we have to have a statement, and it would be best if you wrote it yourself. Just describe your participation in the assault and promise that you will never do anything like that again. Once all the formalities are taken care of, we'll release you."

Moses stared at him incredulously and asked: "You're letting me go?"

Van Zyl laughed. "We're not the monsters that Communist propaganda makes us out to be."

"How can I write a statement . . . . ? I only had three years of English at school."

422

"Just write it in your own tribal language. In your own words, and as detailed as possible. Take your time."

After an agent brought him a ballpoint pen and paper, Moses eagerly got to work. He figured it couldn't hurt to make his account official. Tutuma certainly wouldn't have anything against that. And if this white man believed he could pull one over on him, he was mistaken. Moses only had to stick to his story.

Outside, Van Zyl said to the agents who had questioned Moses: "As soon as he's finished his statement, bring it to me and put him through the wringer again. But this time properly. I need at least his full name, his home address, and complete details on his family."

WHEN THE SUN was no longer so high in the heavens, the white man opened his umbrella, crept out of the shadow of the water tank, and slunk closer to the wire fence. He had the same name as genuine white men—Monna Sweu, which means "white man" in Setswana. But he was not a real white man. A missionary who was teaching Monna Sweu a little English had called him an "albino". But he had not told him where the "Albino" tribe lived.

All the same, Monna Sweu was glad he finally knew what nation he belonged to. His father had claimed he was not a Bamangwato; the women had whispered that his mother had gotten him from the spirit of a dead white man. He had gone looking for the Albino tribe, but the police caught him secretly milking a villager's goat and locked him up in the Rakops prison camp. Monna Sweu had felt just fine there, with regular meals of millipap. But then the police chief set him free again, allowing him to stay outside the prison fence, where he camped in the shade of the water tank.

One day, a white trader gave him money to buy a goat, and then before he left Rakops, he asked Monna Sweu to do something for him. As soon as anything new happened in Rakops, Monna Sweu was to report it by radio telephone to a man in Francistown—no matter how insignificant it seemed.

No place in Rakops seemed more suitable for this assignment than the fence around the prison camp, for if anything happened

423

or if a stranger wandered into the village the police were the first to find out. And so he squatted under his umbrella, day in, day out, never moving from his spot except to report his observations to Francistown or to lie down with his goat for the night by the dried-out river bed.

Now Monna Sweu peered into the camp to catch what the new foreigner was talking about with the police chief. Two hours ago, the foreigner had come here to Rakops from the east in his truck. Since his arrival, he had been speaking English to the captain, who kept gesticulating and shaking his head.

The foreigner had a beard, his skin was freckled, his hair was smooth, his lips narrow, and his eyes pale. He wore spectacles, a pair of blue trousers with shiny buttons, and a checked shirt. He was a real white man. How did they ever manage to keep their skin from glowing like fire when it was exposed to the sun?

Now a wind had come up, carrying the conversation between the police chief and the foreigner more clearly across to Monna Sweu. "This is absolutely crazy, Mr. Hahn," he heard the police chief say. "Just last year, three tourists drove into the Kalahari in a Land-Rover. They broke down, and all we found, weeks later, were their gnawed skeletons."

"I only want to drive a short way in," said the foreigner. "The Ford is new, and besides, I've got a compass."

"You don't need a compass, Mr. Hahn, you need a guide. There are no roads in the Kalahari and no people, and the next village to the west is three hundred and fifty miles away. I'll send a policeman with you."

"Thank you very much, captain. But I can manage."

Before the police chief angrily turned away, he said: "At least, fill up your petrol and water tanks. That way you may extend your life by a couple of days."

The foreigner drove the Ford up to the big water tank and a policeman attached a hose to the tap, letting water flow into the half-empty plastic reserve tanks tied to the back of the truck. After the policeman had filled the petrol tank (the barrel of petrol in the truck was *still* full), the foreigner drove out along the dry bed of the Botletle river.

ALL DAY LONG, planes and helicopters had circled over the Makgadikgadi Pans, without discovering the slightest trace of life on the whitish-grey salt crust, which had dried out here generations ago. Without water, the escaping hijacker could have survived only a few hours in this blazing-hot desert, where millions of salt crystals reflected the rays of the sun. Since Anglo-American planned to exploit the rich deposits of sodium carbonate and potash in the pans, Orapa said they were doing geological reconnaissance. When the first day after the assault wore by unprofitably, Van Zyl ordered the flights to be extended further south and west, all the way to Rakops and the northern rim of the Kalahari.

Meanwhile, an artist had drawn an identikit portrait of the hijacker based on information from the pilot and Feuchtenbeiner. BOSS distributed copies to all its agents and informers in Botswana. Van Zyl's most efficient interrogation specialists had been grilling Moses all day long, though Moses cited the general's promise to release him after getting his handwritten statement and taking care of the formalities.

It wasn't until afternoon that he owned up to being an officer in the ZLA, the Zimbabwe Liberation Army, and demanded that his gaolers adhere to the Geneva Convention. At this, Van Zyl took personal charge of the questioning again. He pointed out to Moses that an imprisoned officer need only give his name, rank, and home address.

After some wavering, the prisoner said that his name was Moses Nkala, that he was a first lieutenant in the ZLA, and that he lived in Plumtree, a small Rhodesian town on the Botswana border.

General Van Zyl asked his colleagues in Rhodesia's Special Branch II for confirmation. Late evening brought a reply by telephone from Salisbury: a Moses Nkala was registered in Plumtree, but was employed as an aeroplane mechanic in Botswana. He was married to a teacher named Naledi. He had never appeared to be politically inclined or criminal.

Van Zyl looked at Moses's handwritten statement. It was written in Ndebele. Next, he sent for the head of Department VI (National Evaluation, Investigation, and Special Studies). He handed him the statement and the text for a letter.

"I would like this letter to be translated into Ndebele; not literally, but in terms of the meaning. The important thing is to make sure the handwriting, grammar, diction, and spelling coincide with those in this statement. Can your lab do it?" The head of Department VI said it was child's play for his trained graphologists and language experts.

That evening Van Zyl received, via Francistown, a message from Monna Sweu. But it seemed unimportant. After all, he was looking for a black man, probably carrying two suitcases, not a white adventurer.

Then Van Zyl asked Department V (Staff and Administration) to send him a member of the Matabele tribe who was a loyal agent to BOSS. Towards morning, he got him. His name was Edson Mojo, twenty-seven years old, single, and a migrant worker who had done an excellent job as an informer and *agent provocateur* in Soweto, the African suburb of Johannesburg.

Shortly before midnight, after instructing Mojo, Van Zyl went to bed with the soothing feeling that God had given him a plan for warding off one of the most dangerous assaults yet on the reigning order in Africa's southern region.

BOSS AGENT Roger Niehoujs and his three colleagues were welcomed in Orapa with the same enthusiasm that management would have shown to unannounced tax agents. But since they presented a written order from De Beers in Johannesburg to inspect the security facilities, Orapa had to acquiesce. The only ones who knew the real reason for the BOSS visit were Feuchtenbeiner, who had flown in with them, and General Manager Scranton. The pilot of the hijacked King Air, now returned from Tsumkwe, prudently said nothing, sticking to the official version that Feuchtenbeiner and he had had a routine flight to Gaberones.

The irksome visitors from Johannesburg had some questions for the executive manager. Who was informed about the exact times of the monthly diamond shipments to Gaberones. Who had access to the Red security zone? Who was allowed to work in the airport? And who were Feuchtenbeiner's friends?

Roger Niehoujs was going through the staff file with Feuchtenbeiner after lunch when the pilot of a search plane radioed that he had sighted a truck in the northern Kalahari. But there was no way an aircraft could land on that terrain. Niehoujs took down the exact position: forty-five miles west-southwest of Rakops. Then he called the airfield: "Tell the pilot to get the chopper ready. We're taking off in ten minutes."

"I'll get my elephant gun," said Feuchtenbeiner.

"There's no room in the chopper for you."

"If we squeeze together, it'll work."

"You don't understand. I have orders to take no one along."

"That may hold for outsiders, but not for me. I'm in charge of security in Orapa—"

"You're wrong, Jan," Niehoujs interrupted. "BOSS is now in charge." He left him standing there and drove to the airfield.

An hour later, the helicopter had reached the area. The pilot pointed to a grey dot slowly ploughing through the yellow elephant grass. When they had flown down to one hundred and fifty feet, they saw it was a truck. Two blacks were sitting on the roof.

The pilot carefully touched down. The rotor blades whirled, the man-high elephant grass lay down invitingly. A couple of zebras grazing nearby galloped away.

The pilot and Niehoujs released the safety catches on their machineguns. The truck stopped and the driver clambered out and jumped into the grass. "Dr. Livingstone, I presume?" With a grin he shook hands with the pilot and a taken-aback Niehoujs.

"I'm Jim Rockwell. That's my wife Linda in the truck, and this man . . . ." He pointed to a little white man with a thick, black beard, a long shock of curls which he had partly tamed with a red headband, a bulbous nose, and black friendly eyes. He looked like one of Disney's Seven Dwarfs. "This man," Rockwell said, "we caught en route. He seems to be an indigenous inhabitant of the Kalahari. You can shake hands with him. He won't bite."

"I'm Bob," said the dwarf in purest West-Coast American. "Would you like a cup of tea?"

Niehoujs blinked impatiently. "Who are the blacks up there?"

"The quiet man up there is Click-Clack." Jim clicked twice.

"Click-Clack?"

"Something like that. Our guide. A Bushman. He only speaks the Bushman dialect. And the other guy is Dits. He translates Click-Clack's words for us."

The two blacks in no way resembled the wanted portrait that had been drawn of the hijacker. Niehoujs pulled the drawing out of his breast pocket. "Have you run into this man?"

Jim took the picture. "Nice-looking guy. If we bump into him, any message?"

Niehoujs gruffly tore the drawing out of his hand. "What are you doing here anyway?" he yelled.

"Looking for Bushmen—what else? We're archaeologists. Americans." Jim turned indignantly to Linda. "Here I am, happy as a child at finally seeing a human being after three weeks. And then—would you have guessed . . . cops!" Ignoring the visitors, he and Linda unlocked the Datsun truck and lifted out a goat, which began to graze.

Since there was nothing else to do, Niehoujs and the pilot flew off, and after a brief rest, the Americans drove on. The trail to Rakops, unused for years, was almost indiscernible. They relied on the compass, and especially on the tips from the Bushman, who seemed to know every bush in this wilderness. As soon as they deviated as much as an inch from the route to Rakops, Click-Clack slammed the palm of his hand on the roof of the driver's cab, and brought them back to the right direction.

Towards evening, after they'd stopped to eat, Click-Clack elbowed Dits, emitting a few clicks, and Dits said, "He says we're getting visitors."

Now the Americans, too, heard the distant singing of an engine, moving laboriously across the steppe in low gear. Then Dieter's sand-coloured Ford broke through a thicket to the east, like a buffalo, and halted sixty feet away.

Dieter waved: "Hello!"

"Hi!" Jim replied.

They strode towards each other like two dogs about to sniff one another. Jim drew himself up to his full six feet three. If he had been equipped with a tail, he would have stuck it straight up into the air.

"Are you a policeman, tax official, child molester, pop singer, or Boer?"

Dieter laughed. "My name is Dieter Hahn and I'm German."

Jim grinned. "Don't worry. I even know a few nice Japanese."

Linda came hurrying over. "Jim doesn't mean it. He thinks he's being funny."

"Are you on a pleasure drive, Dieter?" asked Jim.

"Sort of. I'm an overseas volunteer, but I don't have to get to my project for a few weeks." Dieter hesitated. Then he called over to the Ford: "Tutuma, come out! These people are OK!"

Tutuma crawled out from under a blanket and climbed down from the back of the truck.

"The South Africans are after him," said Dieter.

Dits, who was stoking the fire with Click-Clack, put his hand to his chest in a gesture halfway between horror and reverence.

Tutuma glared reproachfully at Dieter. "You're too reckless."

"You don't have to hide from these people."

"They're white." Before greeting them, Tutuma exchanged a few words in Setswana with Dits. Then he appeared a shade more relaxed. "So you're scholars?"

"Archaeologists. We're looking for Bushmen, not ruins."

Tutuma made a face. "You're looking for Massarwa? Why?"

"Supposedly they live the way our ancestors lived in the Stone Age. We think it's a fascinating task for scientists to investigate the people who still live in full harmony with nature."

"Massarwa have no place in modern Africa. They learn nothing, and they don't want to learn. They're useless."

Bob came up grouchily kneading his beard. "It's still not settled who can learn from whom here. In any case, I don't know of any other people who could exist under the living conditions that Bushmen have in the Kalahari."

"Jackals can survive in the Kalahari too."

"But Bushmen aren't jackals, they're human beings. Africans like you," Dieter put in. "And you drove them out into the desert, where no man can challenge their tiny right to life. The way the Boers drove you out."

"You're not going to compare us to these savages, are you?"

429

"You call them savages, and the Boers call you savages. I'm against all racism. Even yours."

"You're a romantic, like many white men who come here to teach us how we ought to live. But what do you know about Africa? You've only been here for ten days. We don't need tutors from the United States or Europe. We want to live the way *we* think we should. If you absolutely have to help us, then give us weapons. We can do without your ideologies. Do you know who my favourite is among all the white self-styled Samaritans? The Soviets. They have no colonial past to overcome. They see the human being in us and not the consumer." Tutuma thought back to Volodya's warmth, and the way he had shown him his war scars, and the weapons the Russians had wanted to force upon him as a gift.

"The hell with politics!" called Linda. "Soup's on!" It was a nourishing stew of potatoes, paprika and corned beef, and afterwards there was a mug of Nescafé, powdered milk, and sugar.

Dieter lay on his back, folding his arms under his head. He began to form the glittering sequins on the velvet cloth of the African sky into ever-changing figures. He felt at one with nature. He had never thought about happiness, and at this moment he discovered something that millions of people had discovered before him: there was no such thing as happiness, there were only happy minutes, and this was one.

Later, Jim poured handfuls of corn kernels into the scrubbed-out pot. The kernels exploded into fluffy popcorn, and everyone but Click-Clack helped themselves.

"He's been with us for three weeks now," said Bob. "But he won't let any of us get close to him. He's got a special kind of dignity, even though he's been domesticated for a long time. A black cattlebreeder gave him to us for the expedition. He works all year long for a blanket, plus a bit of cornmush and a handful of tobacco every day. There's no cheaper labour than a Bushman."

Click-Clack peered over at them with his clear antelope eyes, which revealed neither friendship nor distrust. He wore some rags of tanned animal hide. His skin seemed loose, one size too large, like the skin of a young dog.

430

"When they bag some game after weeks of fasting," said Bob, "they stuff their tummies until the skin gets tight and smooth. No one can eat as much at one sitting as a Bushman. You ought to see them at the end of the rainy season, which is rich in game. They look like tiny barrels. Then they live all winter on the fat they've stored up."

The Bushman's small body was athletically proportioned, with finely modelled hands and feet. His face, with its tiny, pointed ears and slanted eyes over high cheekbones, had a definitely Mongolian cast.

"Have you met any wild Bushmen during your expedition?" Dieter asked.

Bob tugged at his beard in annoyance. "We've had bad luck. Three weeks and not one Bushman. Either they avoided us, or we didn't get deep enough into the Kalahari. We came at the wrong season, anyway. The damned elephant grass is ripe; thousands of seeds got caught in the radiator of our Datsun and when it clogged up, the engine overheated. Three or four times a day we had to take out the grill, scrub it with a wire brush, rinse it with our precious drinking water, and blast it with our air pump. What a drag, man! On some days, we didn't even do twenty miles. How about you guys?"

"We only started this morning in Rakops. Around noon, we stopped the truck because of the air search and put brambles and savannah grass over the roof so they couldn't spot it."

"They were after you all right," Jim growled. "They stopped us and stuck a picture of Tutuma right under our noses."

Tutuma looked up in alarm. "A picture?"

"It was an identikit drawing. I recognized Tutuma as soon as I saw him. What did you do anyway? Rip off some chickens?"

"It's political," said Dieter.

"They used to hunt us for our politics too, and beat us up because we were against the war in Vietnam. Today everyone knows we were right."

Outwardly, Jim looked as trustworthy as a bandit in a spaghetti Western, with his adventurously dented floppy hat, his tattered jeans, his grey T-shirt, and his full beard, which gave off dust like a mop at every vehement turn of his head. But his eyes revealed humanity and a sense of humour. "Don't worry, Tutuma," he said. "We won't rat on you. Even if it's just because we don't like cops. I just thought of something. We're driving back tomorrow to our base camp near Nata. Why don't we take Tutuma along?"

Tutuma reflected for a few seconds. "It's still too dangerous for me. I can't take the chance of being among people."

"How long do you want to stay here?"

"A few days. Maybe a week."

"Are you prepared for that? Do you have enough water?"

"I think so," said Dieter.

"Do you have food?" asked Linda, practical as ever. After brushing her teeth, she had wet a rag in the water left in the enamel mug and used it to wipe some of the dust from her round face. A few freckles appeared.

"We'll think about it more carefully tomorrow," Jim decided. "In any event, we can give you Lizzy."

Linda glared at him indignantly. "You want to give them Lizzy? They can have anything they like from us, but they're not going to slaughter Lizzy."

"That's sentimental nonsense, Linda," said Jim. "It's why we took her along, after all."

"Who the hell is Lizzy?" asked Dieter.

Bob pointed to the tethered goat. "Our live dairy."

Linda withdrew to pitch one of the tents.

"Where do you sleep?" Jim wanted to know.

"I have my own sleeping bag. Your Peace Corps people in Gaberones gave me some baggage for their volunteers in Maun. It included a sleeping bag. Tutuma used it last night."

"My tent's big enough for three," said Bob.

Jim snuffed the remnants of the fire with sand while Dieter helped Bob to put up the second tent. Each man had a cup of water to wash in before they crept into their sleeping bags.

Dieter lay down outside in the warm sand, and Click-Clack, as usual, kept at a distance.

A lion roared close by, and somewhere hyenas began a grisly fugue. Lizzy emitted a thin, anxious bleating.

NEXT MORNING, Jim and Bob gave Dieter half their provisions, half their portable medicine case, and some tobacco. "If you run into any Bushmen," Jim said, "it might come in handy."

Dieter promised to visit the Americans in their base camp near Nata as soon as the coast was clear. Finally, Jim told them: "Many people have died in the Kalahari. Without a guide, you'll be a banquet for the vultures. We'd like to give you Click-Clack. He'll bring you out alive."

"Oh, and Lizzy," Jim went on. "I spoke to Linda, and she agrees that Lizzy would be in good hands with you after all."

Bob had untied the goat and now pressed the loose end of the rope into Tutuma's hand.

When they climbed into their grey Datsun truck, Linda cast a tearful look of farewell at the goat, which was indifferently chewing her cud. Then she shot a pleading glance at Dieter. "But you can only eat Lizzy if you're *really* about to starve to death."

Then, with Jim, Bob and Linda in the cab and Dits on the roof, the Datsun broke its way through the brambles and vanished in a cloud of dust.

Dieter and Tutuma gazed silently after them for a while. Click-Clack squatted on the earth, passive as always, and Lizzy turned back to the grass with a miserable bleating.

VII

Shortly before four p.m., the Rhodesian Railways train lumbered into Plumtree station.

Edson Mojo and Johan Vermaak were the only passengers leaving the train in Plumtree, Vermaak from a comfortable first-class compartment, Mojo from the fourth class. En route, both of them, the black agent and his white operations officer, had strictly observed General Van Zyl's instructions to avoid any contact with one another.

Plumtree didn't seem like a place that could offer much entertainment. A tarmac road with bleak houses, two service stations, a general store, a haberdasher's with dusty window decorations, a post office, a police station, and, at the end of the street, a boarding school, guarded by soldiers, for the children of white farmers.

While Vermaak turned towards the only hotel, a hundred yards away, Mojo trudged off with his bundle in search of a lift to the protected village for blacks. Outside Plumtree, he was picked up by a truck filled with black farmhands. From six p.m. till six a.m., the blacks were locked up in the village—a protection, according to Rhodesian authorities, against terrorist assaults. These villages, with their temporary huts of clay and elephant grass were surrounded by high fences and watch towers. All activities, even worship and schooling, took place inside the fence. And anyone found outside the camp after six p.m. risked being gunned down by a white sentry. A truck took the men to the corn harvest on the surrounding farms every morning and then drove them back to the protected village every evening.

The white guards at the entrance gate asked Mojo no questions, simply waving him through when he flashed his forged ID card. It identified him as a migrant labourer travelling home from the South African gold mines.

It was child's play for Mojo to find Moses's wife, Naledi Nkala. The young teacher was very popular in the protected village, and anyone could show him the way. Mojo found her outside her round clay hut at the centre of the village, where, surrounded by children, she was listening to music from a transistor radio.

"My name is Edson Mojo. Send the children away. I have a message from Moses for you."

When the children were gone, they stepped into the hut, and Mojo pulled a folded note from his pouch. "Read this, Naledi."

Naledi read the note half-aloud. It was written in Ndebele. "The bearer of this message has my trust. Something has gone wrong. As soon as I can get away, I'll be in touch with you. For the moment, I have to stay hidden. It is important that the bearer of this message transmit something from me to my friends. Please show him the way. Long live the freedom of Zimbabwe. Your M."

She put the paper in the fire. Worry, doubt and relief alternated in her face. "It's his handwriting, and his spelling mistakes," she said finally. "Where is Moses hiding out?"

434

"In Angola. I met him in Balundaland, on the Zaire border. He can't get away. The South Africans are after him. But I have to transmit something to his friends. It's urgent."

A crease appeared on her brow. She had a flat broad face with alert black eyes. "Why can't you tell *me?* I'm his wife."

"He only gave me the letter for you."

"Was he alone?"

"Yes."

"There was no friend with him? A man with a high forehead?"

"He told me about a friend, but I didn't see the friend. He called him Kgosi and spoke about some cases and an aeroplane which had landed in the wrong place."

"And where is Kgosi?"

"If I understood correctly, he vanished with the cases. I can't reveal anything more."

Naledi sprang up. "Wait here." She hurried off, returning ten minutes later with an older Matabele.

The Matabele made no effort to hide his suspicion. Without introducing himself, he began cross-examining Mojo. "Did you know Moses beforehand?"

"No. I met him by chance. He accosted me. He looked harassed, as if he were being hunted."

"How come Moses decided to trust you?"

"I'm an ANC member in Soweto. I can't say any more." Mojo opened his shirt and bared his chest. Four baboon teeth dangled from an elephant hair that he wore around his neck.

The Matabele smiled in relief and bared his chest in turn. He wore the same kind of amulet, the secret sign of the ANC, the African National Congress. He embraced Mojo.

Naledi, too, calmed down. "Excuse my distrust, Edson," she said. "The letter seemed so . . . odd. It's Moses's handwriting and his diction too. But Moses is a loving husband." She looked aside in confusion. "So far no letter of his has ever failed to mention that he loves my eyes because they are as gentle as a gazelle's."

Mojo was primed for some such objection. "He was afraid they'd catch me en route and find the letter. That's why there are no words and no salutation to reveal the addressee."

435

"That makes good sense," said the Matabele. "But let's be done with this hide-and-seek, brother. What really happened to Moses?"

"I have already said he was escaping. He confided something else to me, but I can only tell that to his chief."

"I don't quite understand," said the Matabele. "The chief was with him in Angola."

"Do you mean the man he called Kgosi?"

"Yes. Kgosi is Tutuma."

Mojo knew he was getting to the heart of the matter now. "So Tutuma is the man with whom he hijacked the Orapa aeroplane."

"Yes," replied the Matabele impatiently. "Didn't he tell you why Tutuma wasn't with him?"

"He told me." Mojo scratched his head indecisively. "But I can only report it personally to his chief, and to no one else."

"He must have meant January," said Naledi. "You'll have to go to Botswana tomorrow, to Francistown. I'll give you a message for January. That's his code name. His real name is something else. January is the second man in our movement, a sort of chief of staff."

"When does the train leave for Francistown?"

"You can't take the train. You've got to walk across the border . . . with the others."

"What others? Who else is coming along?"

"About twenty kids from my school. I'll put them in your safe-keeping." And when he looked at her, baffled, she said: "The kids want to fight at Tutuma's side. I'm only taking the older ones. Whenever I can find a reliable escort, I send recruits to Botswana."

"Where should I deliver the children?"

"To January. He'll take them to the training camp in Botswana. In the bush."

"Does the Botswana government allow this?"

"This is no action for which we can ask permission from any government."

The next day, Naledi left the protected village with eighteen schoolchildren—fourteen boys and four girls between thirteen and seventeen—for practical botany instruction, she explained to

436

the white guard. Mojo joined them at the appointed place, beyond the guard's range of vision. After a two-hour hike through the bush, Naledi handed him a small sack of cornflour. "In case you're hungry on the way. We're in Botswana now. You've got another thirty miles or so till Francistown." She pointed. "Just follow the railway line."

Before heading back to the village, she turned around once more. "Take good care of the children. They are going to war."

FOR A DAY and a half, Feuchtenbeiner had secretly combed the bottom of dried-out Lake Xau for the hijacker. Without success. Yet he was convinced that he had been hunting in the right area. Before starting out in Orapa yesterday morning, supposedly for a hunting holiday in Moremi Game Park, he had made a thorough calculation once again. All the data—the air time from Orapa till the hijacker bailed out, the flight speed, and the course—kept producing the same result: namely, that only an area of at most fifty square kilometres was possible. And how far can a man on foot carry one hundred and seventy pounds of baggage?

Now Feuchtenbeiner had pitched his tent, and sat thinking. There was, of course, the trail from Orapa to Rakops. An accomplice could have been waiting for the man in a car . . . . But the hijacker had wanted to steer the plane to Angola. The sudden appearance of the Mirage fighters had been unforeseen, and also the parachute jump. It made more sense to surmise that the diamond robber had hitched a ride in a car soon after bailing out. A car going to Rakops.

He shut his eyes to concentrate better. There had been someone heading for Rakops. At the eastern gate of Orapa, he remembered a German worker volunteer in a sand-coloured truck who had asked for a pass because he didn't feel like taking the bumpy road that went around the town.

The first person Feuchtenbeiner spoke to next morning in Rakops was the albino. Monna Sweu sat as usual with his goat by the fence of the police camp, in the long shadow cast by the water tank in the evening.

Feuchtenbeiner brought his Range-Rover to a halt and climbed

437

out. "Is there anything like a hotel or a bar around here?" Monna Sweu shook his head. "Where can I find out if a friend of mine is here?"

"I can tell you. If stranger come, he drive by here."

"A black man with a high forehead?"

"No strange black man here. But big bird, make noise and whistle, with two white men." The albino whirled his arms over his head like a helicopter. "Make wind, and wind make much dust. Not find white man with truck."

Feuchtenbeiner raised his head. "What colour was the truck?"

"Colour like sand."

"Did the man drive into the Kalahari alone?"

"Police chief yell bad because dangerous alone. But Dits come later in a grey truck. Dits say white man not alone. Dits see black man with white man in lorry in Kalahari."

Feuchtenbeiner forced himself to keep calm. "Where did he see them?"

The albino pointed to the southwest. "Sunday Pans."

Feuchtenbeiner strode to his Range-Rover and pulled out a pile of maps. He searched for a while. Then his forefinger stopped on some very small type at a point west-southwest of Rakops.

"Did you hear where they wanted to go?"

The albino shook his head. Feuchtenbeiner gave him a cigarette. He returned to the Range-Rover, and ten minutes later he had left the last huts of Rakops behind.

He had no time to lose. If the hijacker fell into the hands of the BOSS agents, they would make him talk.

Feuchtenbeiner stroked the smooth, cold barrel of his elephant gun with affection. He would need a steady hand.

ALL DAY LONG, Dieter and Tutuma took spells at the wheel. There were long stretches of the desert where springhaases had dug so many holes that the Bushman, his eyes fixed to the ground, had to run on ahead; and still the truck rumbled into a hole from time to time. The shock jolted the men from their seats so abruptly that they banged their heads against the roof. In the back, Lizzie swayed and bleated in annoyance.

438

Hour after hour, Click-Clack ran on ahead like a hound, with long strides, his body bent forward. Dieter wondered how long it would take him to collapse in exhaustion, but Click-Clack showed no sign of fatigue.

The deeper they drove into the Kalahari, the sparser the vegetation. The mopane trees with their leathery twin leaves had long since vanished. The bushes reached only to the radiator base. Many of them were parched, leafless, bizarre; greyish-white branches with vicious thorns that ripped deep scratches in the skin. Even the savannah grass was lower here; the bumpers pressed it down before the fine seeds could whirl into the radiator. The water remained just under boiling, even though the engine had been in low gear for hours now.

All at once, Click-Clack came to an abrupt standstill, and turned his head in all directions like a wild animal that has caught a scent. His nostrils flared, and Dieter read something like disquiet in his slanting eyes. Then he wheeled around and pointed back. The grass behind them was burning. A small, low flame, barely visible in the blazing sun, crept slowly towards them like a fuse.

Dieter and Tutuma sprang out of the truck and, together with Click-Clack, stamped out the fire. Fifty yards farther back, another tiny flame tongued its way up a dead thorn bush. Dieter grabbed a blanket from the truck and smothered it.

"We're lucky," Tutuma snorted after they had trampled down the glowing trail. "If we'd noticed it any later, it would have spread into a bush fire." He bent over and followed the trail of charred grass two hundred yards back. "It started here. It was our exhaust. A spark ignited a dry blade of grass. Luckily there was no wind, otherwise the whole area would be burning now."

"And so would we, with that barrel of petrol."

Tutuma nodded. "Should we take a break?"

Ten minutes later, Dieter was listlessly chewing the doughy bread they had bought in Rakops. It was quite palatable with sardines in tomato sauce, hot tea, and fresh goat's milk. Click-Clack had only a mug of tea with lots of sugar.

"They're crazy about honey and sugar," said Tutuma. "But I bet Click-Clack has never seen a fish in his life."

"I'll open a can of corned beef for him."

But Click-Clack struck off into the bushes. After a quarter of an hour, he returned with an armful of plants that had yellow nodules, about the size of golfballs, on their stalks. He tore off the foliage and put the nodules in the hot sand near the remains of the campfire.

Then he tore a long tendril out of the ground and picked its bulbous pods until he had gathered enough for a meal. He peeled the thumb-sized beans from the pods and added them to the nodules. They took a long time to cook. Meanwhile, his impassive eyes swept around, finally fixing on a bush. He leaped up and broke off a flexible rod. Next he scurried about, hunting for a sturdy stick among the dead branches, then squatted next to a springhaas warren. With the switch he poked into the sandhole.

What occurred next took place so fast that Dieter could only guess what had happened. Suddenly, a blood-spattered bundle of fur lay next to the hole. Click-Clack had killed a springhaas with a smooth, sure blow on the head. A second springhaas flashed out of the warren. Screeching fearfully, taking huge kangaroo leaps, it loped away on its long hind legs.

The one Click-Clack had bagged was a full-grown animal, its thickset body about a yard long, and its bushy tail at least that long. The front paws were disproportionately short, with powerful nails. It looked like a cross between a beaver, a rat, and a kangaroo. Dieter handed Click-Clack his pocketknife. In a few short moments the Bushman had skilfully skinned and gutted the animal.

They grilled the meat on an iron skewer, given them by Jim. It tasted as tender and juicy as lamb. The tubers tasted neutral, almost insipid; the beans something like roasted pistachios. Click-Clack devoted himself to his food with typical Bushman enthusiasm, smacking his lips.

A light breeze had come up, and Dieter gazed in fascination at a column of dust that whirled across the steppe at high speed. The vortex was not much higher than the head of a man, and it moved in a zigzag. Eventually it collapsed, only to be resurrected a hundred yards farther on.

"A Matswana has died," said Tutuma. "His soul can find no rest."

"That's a nice superstition."

"You call it superstition, but for us it's reality."

Dieter looked up in surprise. "Do you really believe it?"

"I wish I still could." Tutuma's voice sounded even softer than usual. "The white professors at the University of Salisbury drove it out of me. It's as though along with the superstition—as you call it—they took away a piece of my African identity. Took it away for good." His eyes clung to the vortex, which was dissolving into nothing.

"I studied law, British law. There's no room in it for anything irrational, for anything that can't be proven with logic. You Europeans have never understood us, you haven't even bothered to make an attempt. What do you know about our languages? About our religion? About our very essence? What we laugh at or admire? We Africans could have given you so much, you civilized people with your crippled senses."

"That's why I came here—to learn."

"I'm not saying you don't mean well, Dieter. But you're a hundred years too late. What are you after here now? You lost your access to the souls of the people long ago. I studied at Cambridge one summer as a guest of the British government, and I learned plenty there about your civilization. Students once took me along to what they called 'group therapy'. With primal screams and touching and all that pseudo-psychological nonsense. They were looking for a little human warmth, a little physical contact with others who were just as stunted.

"Take your old people's homes. Can you imagine what an impression they make on Africans? Fine, the rooms are clean, there's lots of food. But you've buried your parents alive there. You make them feel their uselessness. Any African feels lucky to have his parents living with him. He knows he's indebted to them because he profits from their wisdom. There is no family that wouldn't share its bread with a relative, however useless or lazy he might be."

During the monologue, Dieter had been about to retort several

441

times, but he sensed the feebleness of his arguments. Perplexed, he poked around in the dying embers.

It had turned dark, and the Bushman had burped in contentment and stretched out on a bed of savannah grass. His quiet snoring added a soothing accompaniment to the serenade of the Kalahari, and the wild dogs carried its melody that night.

Dieter brought the sleeping bags from the truck, and Tutuma put out the embers with sand. They indulged in the luxury of a bowl of water to wash with and then they burrowed into a hollow in the sand which was still warm from the sun.

VIII

Dikeledi looked up from her typewriter, where she was typing out a contract for a rented car. She must have noticed the ANC amulet, the elephant hair and baboon teeth on the visitor's chest, but she emitted only a terse: "Sir?"

"Naledi sent me," said Edson Mojo. "I'm supposed to deliver the children here. The only travel bureau in Francistown with a Hertz Rent-A-Car agency, I was told. I'm supposed to meet Mr. January."

Dikeledi's black eyes scrutinized the stranger as if through a barbed-wire fence of suspicion and reserve. "Sorry, sir, but there's no Mr. January working here," she said. "But if you insist, I'll ask my boss, Mr. Badubi." She stood up, opened the door, and spoke into a tiny office. "A Mr. . . . . what was your name, sir?"

"Mojo. Edson Mojo from Plumtree."

An African of about thirty-five came into the small store from the office, walked up to Mojo, and shook his hand. "What can I do for you?"

Mojo pulled a crumpled note from his chest pouch and handed it to Badubi, who glanced at the note and nodded. "Lock up the shop," he said to Dikeledi. "Naledi writes that they examined this man in Plumtree. He's one of us, and he's bringing eighteen new recruits." Then he turned back to Mojo. "Please excuse us, brother. Francistown is full of spies and *provocateurs.*"

"The kids are waiting at the depot," said Mojo. "We had a strenuous hike from Plumtree. They are soaked to the skin."

Without waiting for her boss to say anything, Dikeledi left the office. "She'll take care of the kids," said Badubi. "We'll take them in for the night, and then tomorrow morning I'll drive them out to the training camp. We'll go to my place now. You must be hungry." Badubi put a sign saying "Closed" on the door and locked up. "Do you know Francistown?"

"No."

"The English built the town a century ago when they found gold along the Tati River. Then they discovered diamonds in Kimberley, so they shut down the mines here and the whole white pack moved on to Transvaal. That ended the brief flowering of Francistown."

On first sight, Francistown didn't look like a ghost town. In the square, Mazazuru women, dressed in dazzling white, hawked potatoes, corn, tomatoes and honeydews. A small boy tugged at Mojo's trouser leg. "Gimme five cents." He came from the other side of the tracks, where the town ended and the slums began with shacks of clay, corrugated iron and cardboard. At the railway station, hundreds of Matswanas with their bundles were waiting for the uncertain arrival of the next train.

Badubi was apparently part of the town's establishment. The rare whites they met greeted him with no trace of patronage, and Badubi waved back. In his faultlessly-ironed khaki suit with a gaudy tie, its knot as big as a fist, and his perforated white leather shoes, he looked vaguely like a character from *Porgy and Bess*. He headed towards a fairly new Jaguar Mark 10. "I know it looks flashy," he said. "But it's crucial to look like a well-to-do business-man. In the eyes of whites, you see, no man with money can be a revolutionary."

Badubi lived in a comfortable wooden house, colonial style, with white columns, and a wrought-iron balustrade around a veranda, in the shade of a tamarisk tree with salmon-red blossoms. He mixed a drink of oily orange syrup, water, gin, and ice. "Dikeledi'll fix something to eat later on. But tell me why Naledi sent you, rather than a man from the protected village?"

Mojo told the story he had already given Naledi: his secret assignment in Angola, his encounter with Moses and the message that Moses had given him for his wife. "He told me something else, and made it clear to me that I shouldn't convey the message to anybody but his leaders. Naledi thinks he could only have meant Mr. January. Where do I find this Mr. January?"

"Mr. January is my code name. You have a message for me?"

"It's about Orapa."

"Orapa?" January's cheek muscles tensed.

Mojo sensed that the conversation had reached a critical point. "First, everything there went according to plan. Moses and Tutuma hijacked the plane, kept the pilot and the security man, Feuchtenbeiner, in check with their dynamite sticks, and forced them to head towards Serpa Pinto in Angola. After they crossed the border, Tutuma suddenly redirected the plane and made it land on an airfield right by the Zaire frontier."

"What?" January gaped at him, uncomprehending. He had told the Russians to go to Serpa Pinto for the diamonds.

"Moses says that Tutuma is a traitor. A thief. He drove Feuchtenbeiner and the pilot away after landing, and then he told Moses he had no intention of delivering the two cases. He wanted to share the diamonds with Moses and escape to Zaire. Moses refused. Then Tutuma threatened him with a pistol and vanished. Eastwards. Later, Moses saw that the aeroplane had flown back to Botswana with the two whites."

Mojo had rehearsed this story over and over again until he knew it by heart. General Van Zyl had warned him not to deviate one iota from this text and to brush off all questions about further details by saying he hadn't learned any more from Moses.

January was silent. He obviously needed time to digest the shock. "Something's fishy," he said finally. "Tutuma never gave a damn about money. He lived for only one goal: to free Zimbabwe from the whites. You can't be that mistaken about a friend." He started brooding again. "Why to Zaire . . . ? Mobutu's working with South Africa, and Oppenheimer's people from the Central Selling Organization are all over Zaire. How can Tutuma get rid of even one diamond there?"

"I don't know anything about diamonds," said Mojo. "I'm only the messenger."

Dikeledi came home. "The children are lodged." She noticed January's perplexed look. "Is something wrong?"

While January told the girl the news, Mojo excused himself, saying the ANC in Soweto was waiting for his call. January told him there was a telephone in the Grand Hotel.

In the hotel bar, Mojo threaded his way through a motley company of refugees, informers, white deserters and black guerrillas from Rhodesia, native businessmen and farmers, to the telephone booth. After a dozen wrong connections he finally reached the Plumtree Hotel, where his superior officer Johan Vermaak was staying. Vermaak was more than satisfied. He announced he would hop on the next train for Francistown.

Mojo spent the night in January's house after a futile attempt at comforting the despondent host and the weeping girl—both of them broken-hearted at the loss of their leader and the diamonds. Then, shortly after sunrise, January and Mojo loaded the children on a truck. January wore tattered corduroy trousers and a checked lumberjack shirt.

On the road to Maun, just outside Sebina, January turned north, crossing the Shashe River at a shallow place, and then drove another three hours through the roadless bush. During the last few miles, they were escorted by a herd of baboons, who had a screeching contest with the gleeful children. Then, without warning, in the midst of the wilderness, a huge cornfield emerged, inside a corral of dried thorn bushes to keep out wild animals. January announced: "We're almost there."

In the heart of the yellow cornfield, Mojo discerned a green spot. "Marijuana," January explained. "Corn doesn't bring in enough money to finance the camp. We only sell it to whites; it turns revolutionaries into dreamers. The only thing we're worried about is planes spotting our camp from the air. But as long as Botswana has no army or air force of its own . . . ."

The first open huts came into view, poles supporting roofs of elephant grass. January stopped outside the biggest hut. Mojo jumped down and slammed down the ramp.

"I've got eighteen new recruits," January said to a trainer. "Take care of them."

The trainer walked off with the children to assign them to their huts. January turned to Mojo: "We've got enough recruits in our camps to win the war. Tutuma built up the camps; he's a brilliant organizer. How can I tell the children that their idol is a thief and a traitor? If our action in Orapa had worked, we'd have enough Sam 7 rockets in a few weeks to build up a second front on the southwestern border of Zimbabwe. Our friends in Zambia are only waiting to march in from the north. With our troops in the east, on the Mozambique border, we'll have the whites cornered from three sides. The Rhodesians are fanatical fighters, but they don't have enough soldiers to put up a resistance on three fronts."

"Will you send these kids out with knives against the enemy?"

"We'll get the weapons sooner or later, don't worry. But without a leader, any revolution will collapse." He put a pleading hand on Mojo's shoulder. "Only Moses, Dikeledi, and you and I know about Tutuma's betrayal. No one else must know. At least for now."

GENERAL KOROTKOV pushed a file across the table to Volodya Naumov. Volodya glanced through the paper. "Excuse me, General, but I don't understand this. What's happened to Tutuma?"

"I don't understand it either," said Korotkov icily. "You know the foreign ministry intended to make Tutuma prime minister of Zimbabwe . . . afterwards. That makes this affair somewhat delicate. I had relied on your research and your knowledge of human nature."

"You met the man yourself, General. You were highly impressed by him. And you explicitly supported my recommendation."

Korotkov shook his head. "That's not the issue now. I want you to go abroad as soon as possible. Your passport and background details are here. Your name is James Pritchard, you come from Liverpool. Memorize your biography and then destroy it. You know the procedure."

"I haven't been abroad for a long time. Why can't this be done by one of our people in Zambia?"

"Because you are the only one who has any kind of personal relationship with Tutuma. You're something like a father figure to him. Personal trust is of the essence here."

"I know you don't care to hear it, General, but I like him."

"Fine with me, so long as you don't lose sight of your duties. The documents division has prepared everything. You'll have the complete wardrobe and baggage of an upper-middle-class Englishman. Traveller's cheques and a plane ticket are waiting for you in London at the Aeroflot counter. Take-off on Zambian Air Lines for Lusaka is tomorrow. There you'll change to Air Botswana for Francistown. You can get a visa at the Botswana airport."

"The day after tomorrow . . . ? I would have preferred to polish up my English first. What is this Mr. Pritchard doing in Botswana?"

"He's a tourist. He wants to get away from the British winter, get to know Africa. The authorities in Botswana aren't especially alert, and they won't tread on an Englishman's corns; they were a British protectorate far too long for that. The real problem will be to find Tutuma. Supposedly, he bailed out over the Makgadikgadi Pans, but he's vanished without a trace. His deputy, Mr. January, is claiming that Tutuma got hold of the diamonds, but has to stay hidden until the dust settles. January promises that he'll deliver the diamonds to us soon, and he's pressing us to arm his troops meanwhile. Tutuma, he says, will come back in time to take command. At least that's what we got from our agent in BOSS. This version may be true, because the Orapa plane did not arrive in Serpa Pinto. Or else—"

"The South Africans captured Tutuma and want us to believe he's still at liberty."

"And if they interrogated him, they know by now that a freighter with Soviet war material is en route to Beira, and that the cargo is to be transported from Mozambique to Zambia. At the right moment, the South Africans can electrify the world with a scoop: the Soviet government planned a diamond robbery and is trading weapons for the loot. You can imagine what consequences this would have. Both Tutuma's movement and we ourselves would be out of the running in Africa for years. Do you know what that would mean for the Soviet Union?"

"The USA would continue to have access to the Rhodesian chromium deposits."

"And without chromium, there is no Western armaments industry. We've got enough in Siberia; we even sell our excess to the Americans. But ninety-four per cent of Western chromium deposits are in South Africa and Zimbabwe. If we get our hands on them, we'll have the world monopoly. Then we can dictate disarmament conditions to the American government."

The general banged the table. "It's a unique political opportunity, Colonel. And that's why we need Tutuma. If he's still alive. I'd like you to feel this deputy out. January seems to be the only one who is in contact with Tutuma. I'd start with him. He runs the travel agency in Francistown."

DIETER awoke feeling free and adventurous, as on every other morning in the Kalahari. He rolled out of his sleeping bag and stretched towards the rising sun. The sand with which he had put out the campfire last night, he found was still warm. A thin wisp of smoke curled up from a charred piece of wood. The goat lay close by, chewing her cud and gaping at Dieter with unfathomable amber eyes as he turned to his morning toilet.

The Bushman had taken off on one of his morning expeditions. Dieter gathered wood, fanned the fire, put on the cast-iron pot of water and got out marmalade and the dry, rusk-like bread called zwieback. Tutuma was still in his sleeping bag.

"Hey, Tutuma! I'm in favour of racial equality, but that doesn't mean that blacks can exploit the labour of the whites!" Dieter walked over to him. Tutuma lay stockstill. His eyes were wide open; thick sweat beaded his forehead.

Worried, Dieter bent over. "Are you running a temperature?"

Not a muscle stirred in Tutuma's ashen face, but there was something like a fervent warning in his eyes, and Dieter sensed that the man was scared to death. Dieter peered around for some predatory animal, but aside from Click-Clack, who was just returning, he saw nothing. The Bushman stopped short, froze in mid-motion and then moved forward slowly and soundlessly, placing one foot after the other on the ground.

It was obvious that Click-Clack knew what was frightening Tutuma. Finally, the Bushman bent over, very slowly, and his right hand groped cautiously along the sand until it grasped a stick. His eyes never turned from Tutuma. With equal caution, he raised the stick aloft.

Suddenly, a snake's head came out of the sleeping bag, right next to Tutuma's left cheek. It darted its tongue in and out; its cold eyes stared out between olive-coloured scales. It inched out slowly, and twisted across Tutuma's chest down to the ground. Then, light and agile, it slithered away.

Click-Clack dropped his club, and Tutuma's head fell to the side. He lay there for a while before creeping out of his sleeping bag, his naked body drenched with sweat. He tried to speak, but all he could produce was a dry croak. Dieter got him some water.

After drinking, Tutuma said: "It was a black mamba. It must have crawled in while I was asleep. Snakes love heat. I felt something stir near my hand. If I'd made the slightest move, it would have bitten me on the spot." He shook himself. "I was scared you'd startle it. Black mambas have a diabolical nerve poison which paralyses the respiratory muscles. I once had to watch a man choke to death in just a few minutes after he was bitten."

Tutuma fell silent. He wouldn't touch any food. Unmoved, Click-Clack lapped the marmalade straight out of the pot. Dieter gave him a handful of tobacco, and he stuffed it into his pipe. He lit it in the embers and puffed with relish.

Meanwhile, Dieter milked the goat. Tutuma caught the milk in his enamel mug, and offered some to Dieter, who refused. He still wasn't used to the sharp taste of goat's milk. They loaded their equipment, Tutuma got behind the wheel, and they drove off.

"A funny guy, that Bushman," said Dieter.

"Dits told me Click-Clack isn't totally wild or totally tame. In the winter, he wanders around the farms, and in the summer, he vanishes to hunt with his people. Wild Bushmen are nomadic. They do nothing but hunt and collect plants. But the few thousands who roam the Kalahari all year round are getting fewer and fewer. You see, the news has spread to even the most remote tribes that there's water on the farms even during the dry spell,

449

and livestock that they can drive off at night. All Bushmen are thieves."

"Maybe it's because they don't have the concept of property."

Since starting off they had been driving at walking pace, because they were once again moving through an area of spring-haases. Click-Clack trotted ahead, making signs whenever his sharp eyes spotted a warren. But he kept halting more and more often, craning his neck and lifting his nose as though trying to catch a scent. Finally he motioned to Dieter to stop. He climbed up on the roof of the cabin and peered forward. Whatever he saw seemed to agitate him terribly.

Dieter and Tutuma joined him on the roof. The Bushman pointed, emitting excited clicks, and then ran on ahead. But the others could make out only a delicate haze of dust. Dieter fished out a pair of binoculars, had a look, and handed them to Tutuma.

"Looks like a herd of impalas," said Tutuma. "And a couple of ostriches farther on. They seem to be moving towards us."

Click-Clack was already half a mile away from the truck. Then he stopped, turning his head to one side. Now the impalas could be seen clearly through the binoculars, and behind them the ungainly bodies of ostriches, drawing closer to them.

"There are five!" said Tutuma. "If I didn't know they were ostriches, I'd swear they were stalking the impalas like hunters."

"An ostrich is capable of anything," growled Dieter, remembering the one he had fought to the death a few days back.

The procession had now come so close that he could observe the ostriches with his naked eye. Spreading out in a semicircle and always with the wind behind them, they were now less than fifty yards from the herd. Suddenly, a fat buck sank to his knees, as though struck by an invisible blow. A doe collapsed almost simultaneously. The herd scattered, galloping off in long bounds and vanishing in a cloud of dust on the skyline.

The ostriches went through an inexplicable metamorphosis. They straightened up, ran towards the wounded impalas, and tore off their own necks and wings, which were suddenly transformed into human arms. Now Dieter saw that the long necks were really barbed spears with primitively painted ostrich heads on top.

"Those are human beings!" shouted Dieter. He started the engine.

"Wait! Let Click-Clack talk to them. They're young Bushmen."

The five Bushmen stripped off their ostrich skins. Bows and quivers full of arrows came out from under the plumage. Click-Clack started talking to them, and after an excited palaver, obviously managed to convince the Bushmen that the Ford and its occupants were harmless. He beckoned to Dieter and Tutuma.

"Drive slowly, so that they don't get scared," Tutuma advised Dieter. "Most savage Bushmen have never seen a car."

But they were far from showing fear. When the Ford came within twenty yards of them, the little men were so amazed that they fell on their backs, rolled in the sand, and burst into screeching laughter. Then excitedly clicking and clacking, they fingered the Ford. One of them tried to climb into the cabin.

"They're wild about metal things," Tutuma said. "If you don't watch out, they'll have the truck dismantled in half an hour."

Dieter remembered the bag of tobacco that Bob and Jim had given them for bartering, and soon the five Bushmen and Click-Clack were stuffing their pipes. Dieter envied them the relaxed way they stared at him, casually, without inhibitions. At that moment, he wished for nothing so much as to be able to talk with the naked little men in their own clicking and clacking language. Their skin was walnut-coloured, under a layer of ashes, dust and plant juice which shielded them against the sun. Despite their youth, their faces were wrinkled like those of old men. Dieter felt he had at least some feeble perception of their harsh lives, always exposed to a blazing sun that dried out their bodies like prunes. A life cycle of thirst, hunger, and brief periods of stuffing their guts.

"Would they be insulted if I looked at their weapons?"

Tutuma shrugged, so Dieter smiled at the Bushmen inquiringly and bent down to examine a spear. It consisted of a straight stick with a sharpened bone point tied to it with sisal fibres. The arrows, in a quiver of hollowed wood, were constructed in the same way. When Dieter started to run his finger over a sticky arrow tip, a Bushman snatched the arrow from him and held it behind his back.

451

"Are you trying to kill yourself?" Tutuma shouted at Dieter. "If you scratched your finger, you'd never get up again."

"Can I ask them if they want a lift? I'd like to find out more about them."

Tutuma made a face. "They stink, and they steal like magpies. Don't get involved."

"I got involved with you."

"Then let's go." Tutuma sullenly climbed into the Ford. Click-Clack, as though guessing Dieter's wish, started a long discussion with the Bushmen. He seemed to convince them, for they lugged their weapons, pouches and game into the back of the truck. Click-Clack pointed out the direction, they clambered aboard, and Tutuma stepped on the accelerator.

An hour later, Click-Clack banged loudly on the roof. Tutuma braked to a halt, the Bushmen sprang down and dashed off to a thorn bush, digging up sand with their hands until three ostrich eggs came into view. Holes stuffed with grass had been bored into the shells. The Bushmen uncorked the eggs and drank, making sure not to spill a drop of the precious contents.

"They've got water stores hidden all over the bush," Tutuma explained.

One of the Bushmen brought Dieter and Tutuma an egg and offered them a drink. Dieter took one, then climbed into the back of the truck and refilled the egg with water from the plastic tank while the Bushmen watched in delight. With this present, he seemed to have won their full trust. Once again, there was a long palaver between Click-Clack and five old Bushmen. It ended with a gesticulated invitation to Dieter and Tutuma to accompany them to their camp—but without the Ford.

Dieter had qualms about simply leaving the truck, but ultimately his curiosity got the better of him. To square his conscience, he locked everything of any value in the driver's cabin and protected the tyres with newspaper and cardboard. He took only the bare necessities along: a toothbrush, a blanket, powdered milk, instant coffee, some corned beef, a canteen of water, the compass, and a Swiss army knife his mother had given him. At last, the tiny procession got under way, the Bushmen taking the

452

lead. Then Dieter, glancing around, noticed the goat staring after them from the back of the truck.

"We forgot Lizzy!" he shouted, and ran back to get her.

A FEW HUNDRED YARDS outside Rakops, the trail vanished and Feuchtenbeiner had to rely on his compass. Late that afternoon, he knew he was still on the right course: under an acacia, he found three empty corned-beef tins and the charred remnants of a fire. He studied the map and the aerial shots. He was about two miles from the Sunday Pans. The albino hadn't lied, and the black with Dieter had to be the skyjacker. Why else would Dieter have tried to make the Rakops police chief think he was driving into the Kalahari alone?

The meeting of the two must have been pure chance, since the bail-out over the Kalahari had not been part of the original plan. Feuchtenbeiner couldn't figure out why a white man should pick up a criminal, especially a black, and help him escape. However it had come about, though, the important thing now was to silence both of them for ever.

It made no sense driving on tonight. After Feuchtenbeiner had eaten, he dropped into a brief, heavy sleep, and then before sunrise, he leaped up briskly. He indulged only in a cup of instant coffee and a couple of rusks before starting out on the trail left by the German only forty-eight hours ago. Forty-eight hours wasn't much of a head start against a veteran game hunter like Feuchtenbeiner. It took trampled elephant grass several days to straighten up again.

That very afternoon, Feuchtenbeiner came upon the remnants of a second bivouac. The reeking skin and bones by a dead fire were those of a springhaas. He found some embers in the warm ashes, and hurried on. He halted his pursuit at sundown, but he felt he had gained a lot of ground. If things kept going this smoothly, he would have the two of them within sight the next morning, and then two shots would free him.

That night, he could barely sleep. Next day, around noon, he discovered a camping place covered with many small prints of human feet. Bushmen had gone hunting here and started a fire:

the ashes were still hot. And tyre marks revealed that from here the truck had headed in a different direction, from west to south.

Feuchtenbeiner drove on. After a while he sighted the truck in the distance. He parked under the cover of an acacia and gazed through his binoculars. The Ford was standing between two parched thorn bushes, abandoned. A breakdown? Had they gone hunting? Feuchtenbeiner got out, released the safety catch on his elephant gun, and stalked up to the truck.

The sand around the Ford was trampled by small naked Bushmen feet, with in between the prints of two pairs of sneakers. It didn't look like a struggle, more like a joint march to the southwest. The truck door was locked, but the back was accessible. They had left their baggage there, so they were probably returning very soon. Feuchtenbeiner saw at first glance that the two aluminium cases of diamonds were not there.

He climbed into the back of the truck, turned the tap of the plastic tank and let the water run out into the back of the truck and down into the sand. When all of it had drained out, he felt better. The kaffir wouldn't get off with an easy shot in the head. A couple of hours of thirst and panic would teach him that you can't make a fool of Jan Feuchtenbeiner and get away with it.

He returned to his Range-Rover, drove it back a few hundred yards behind a hill, and lay down to wait.

IX

The Bushman camp was so smoothly integrated into its natural surroundings that Dieter noticed it only when he was a hundred yards away. The huts were light and portable: four poles shoved into the ground and loosely covered with woven grass and bushwork as a shield against the sun.

The inhabitants of the small settlement took the arrival of the strangers with a mixture of equanimity and curiosity. They showed most interest in the game. The five hunters, Click-Clack, two old men, and four Bushwomen skinned the animals, using the sharpened shoulderblade of an eland. Then the Bushmen gutted

454

the impalas, taking care not to let anything go to waste—lungs, entrails, head. They removed the sinews from the loins and cleaned them, to use for their bows later on. They sucked the raw marrow, a special delicacy for Bushmen, from the bones, and while the men roasted the meat over the fire, three of the women began curing the skins to make clothes.

One Bushman had collected the blood of the impalas in a turtle shell and passed it around to the others. The men looked as if they hadn't had a square meal for a long time. The eldest was coughing. He was scrawny and his skin was crumpled, his buttocks wrinkled and droopy, his eyes dull and tired after a lifetime of deprivation.

Dieter looked around the camp. In front of a hut, a young Bushwoman had a wooden mortar, in which she was pounding the seeds of a *tsama*, the Kalahari's wild watermelon, into meal. She was naked except for a tattered loincloth knotted together above her navel. Her sole adornment was a string of beads made from ostrich eggshell fragments, filed smooth and drilled. She had a delicate body, with a finely chiselled face under a stringy mushroom of hair, and very small ears and nose. She emanated dignity and grace.

Dieter asked Tutuma where the children were.

"Very few survive," replied Tutuma. "During the drought, the women are barren anyway, and if a woman conceives in the rainy season and then bears in the dry season, the other women take the baby away right after its birth and kill it." He spoke softly, deeply moved. "In the dry season, a child would jeopardize the survival of the entire tribe."

One of the hunters, gesticulating, invited the two strangers to the feast. It began with a kind of hors d'oeuvre: thin, black strips of an indefinable origin.

"They look like dried worms, but they taste like smoked sprats." Dieter took another.

Tutuma smiled. "They're caterpillars."

"Don't be funny!"

"I swear! The guts are squeezed out, and the caterpillar cooked and dried. They're considered a great delicacy." Dieter choked.

455

"Swallow it," Tutuma ordered. "You wouldn't want to hurt our hosts' feelings."

When the roast antelope was cooked, the Bushmen sliced off pieces, smacking their lips but unhurried, ungreedy, even as hungry as they were. The two antelopes provided enough meat to fill everyone. The men removed a remaining haunch from the skeleton and one of them put it down in front of the older man's hut. Then the women broke into a song, while the men clapped their hands to the rhythm. It was an infinitely melancholy song, with many stanzas, accompanied by a kind of harp with four gut strings in a strangely wild, mournful melody.

The old man stared into the fire with dead eyes even after the others had entered their own huts, and then slumped down with his head on his chest. Dieter and Tutuma made a bed out of grass, and while Tutuma drowsed off, Dieter stared at the sky, over-whelmed by this confrontation with the Stone Age, this hopeless, primitive struggle for survival in a ruthlessly harsh world. The Bushmen had once populated all of southern Africa. But in the course of centuries, they had been pushed back by Bántu tribes and white colonizers into the bleak Kalahari, where they managed to keep alive thanks to their skill as hunters and their unique familiarity with wild plants. These talents weren't needed on Botswana farms, so they remained beggars and pariahs.

Dieter was not willing to accept this. He nudged Tutuma. "Why wouldn't it be possible to create a reservation for the Bush-men and prepare them for a new way of life?"

Tutuma yawned sullenly. "You want to settle Bushmen here? But they're nomads."

"Do you see any other way to help them?"

"Attempts have been made to teach them to be farmers and stockbreeders, but they refuse to be domesticated. And a leap directly from the Stone Age to a modern agricultural society? No one's ever done it."

As far as Tutuma was concerned, the subject was closed.

When Dieter awoke in the morning, the Bushmen seemed to be breaking camp. Their spears, bows and arrows were already in the hide pouches slung around their waists. The women brought over water-filled ostrich eggs in nets of sisal fibres. Their creased skin was smooth now and their wrinkled buttocks swollen with fat which they would draw on for days, perhaps weeks. As they moved off unceremoniously, without saying goodbye, Click-Clack turned away from them and sat down next to Dieter like an obedient dog.

"The old man," said Dieter. "They've forgotten him."

The old man was staring stoically at his people as they drew away. Tutuma lowered his voice to a whisper. "He's got TB. They've left him behind to die."

"If we take him along he might be saved."

Tutuma held Dieter back by his shirt. "We don't have the right to interfere with the natural course of things. He's dying according to the laws of Bushmen. They've done everything they could to ease his death."

The old man's hand groped for the two ostrich eggs filled with water that would keep him from dying of thirst for a while. The impala haunch would keep him from starvation for the time being. A bow and a quiver of poisoned arrows leaned against the hut. As long as his strength permitted, he could keep hyenas and jackals at bay. Dieter stood up queasily. "Let's get out of here."

On his way back to the truck he didn't turn his head.

CLICK-CLACK, leading the way with Lizzie on a rope, brought them back to the Ford in less than three hours. After Dieter took the things that had been locked up in the cabin and stowed them in the back of the truck again, he decided to fill his empty canteen. But the plastic tank yielded no more water. The other tank also sounded hollow when he struck it with the flat of his hand.

"Tutuma!"

Together they lifted the two forty-gallon tanks. Only a small amount of water was left in the bottom of the cannisters.

"Three quarts at the most," Tutuma whispered.

"The taps are turned on. Somebody let the water run out."

"The farewell present of the Bushmen," said Tutuma. "We shouldn't have left the truck unguarded."

"Our Bushmen weren't malicious."

457

"Can you suggest someone else?"

Click-Clack had realized what had happened. He crouched down and began scooping up the wet sand under the truck. Tutuma shovelled it into a spread-out plastic sheet. Dieter poured the remainder of clean water from one tank into the other. Then they heaved the plastic sheet with the moist sand into the back of the truck, forced one end into a spout, and let water drip into one of the empty tanks, obtaining at most two quarts of dirty brown water.

But then Click-Clack went behind a bush and came back carrying three ostrich eggs.

"The Bushmen's cache!" shouted Dieter. Gingerly he removed the grass stopper from the upper end of the ostrich eggs and poured about ten quarts of water into the other plastic tank. "We'll use the dirty water for the radiator. If we're lucky, we'll make it back to Rakops."

Tutuma shook his head. "Leave me here with a little water and a couple of tins of corned beef."

"What are you talking about?"

"I'm not going to Rakops. It is crawling with informers."

"We'll do what we did on the way here. You'll stay down by the river, and I'll drive into the village alone."

"Bob, Jim and Linda and their interpreter have already been in Rakops."

"They've kept mum. I'd bet all our drinking water on that."

"I'm not worried about my own life. But if I don't come back alive, our movement will fall apart."

After a pause, Dieter said: "Leaving you here like the old Bushman is simply out of the question. So—what do you suggest?"

"We could head north to the road from Francistown to Maun. That's three or four days from here."

"With ten quarts of water?"

"I have to get across the border to Angola or Zambia."

It took Dieter a while to make Click-Clack realize, with the aid of much gesticulating, that they wanted to turn north and not northeast, where there was water. Ten minutes later, with the compass by the driving seat, they were off.

458

WHEN FEUCHTENBEINER AWOKE, the sun had circled around the Range-Rover, in whose shade he had lain down, and was shining straight into his face. He looked at his watch. One p.m. He jumped up. He had meant to sleep for an hour at the most. Now he regretted giving in to his leaden fatigue after an almost sleepless night. He reached for his binoculars and elephant gun, climbed up the small incline, and peered at the place where he had tracked down the truck. The Ford was gone.

Feuchtenbeiner loaded his belongings into the Range-Rover and drove to the spot. The tyre marks of the Ford pointed north. Either the German and the kaffir had both lost their sense of direction, or they had changed their minds for some reason.

Feuchtenbeiner was not dissatisfied. The track of the tyres was still fresh, so they couldn't be too far away—an hour, two hours, no matter. The only thing that annoyed him was missing the moment of their return: he had looked forward to seeing the terrorist's face at the sight of the empty water tanks. He washed, made some instant coffee with lukewarm water, and swallowed a couple of salt tablets before leisurely beginning his pursuit.

IN THIS AREA, the Kalahari was red. It was as if all the rust of the world had been brought together, finely ground, and stored here. Even the bright parts of Lizzy's shaggy white and brown fur were tinged with it.

The dry river bed they were following was full of stones and red sand, and the cabin was stifling. Dieter lowered the window on his side, and in minutes the seat was covered with red dust. The red dust crept into every fold in Dieter's face, and powdered Tutuma's black skin.

Click-Clack had run ahead so far that they had lost sight of him, but around a turn in the river bed he suddenly reappeared, kneeling in a little dell, digging the ground excitedly with his hands.

Dieter and Tutuma got out. From his pouch Click-Clack pulled out a hollow rod they had not seen him use before. It was as thick as a thumb and three feet long. He made a hole in the sand with one hand; when it was as deep as his arm, he wrapped dry grass around the lower end of the tube, pushed it into the sand and

459

packed the sand around it. He got the three empty ostrich eggs from the back of the truck and placed them in the sand next to the tube. He pulled a second tube out of his pouch, thinner and shorter than the first, and stuck one end into the ostrich egg and the other into a corner of his mouth. Then he took the end of the first tube in his mouth and began sucking. His cheeks hollowed; the whites of his eyes turned red.

For minutes, nothing happened. Then suddenly a burst of clear water squirted from the corner of his mouth and ran down the second staff into the ostrich egg. When it was full, Dieter quickly replaced it with the second one.

Right after that, the source dried up. Breathing heavily, Click-Clack rolled over on his side. Dieter helped him to his feet and supported him as he reeled back to the truck and lay down in the shade between the wheels.

Dieter and Tutuma took advantage of the break to make tea, and serve pilchards, zwieback and goat's milk. Click-Clack refused the pilchards, but ate the cornmush Dieter cooked for him, and then greedily slurped up a whole jar of orange marmalade. The food seemed to restore his strength and although Dieter invited him into the truck, the Bushman preferred to run again, in an indefatigable jog, a couple of yards ahead of the Ford.

FOR A MAN who knew his way around the bush, the pursuit of the Ford was child's play. As long as the bushes were low, the nimble Range-Rover was superior to any truck. Jan Feuchtenbeiner orientated himself by the red cloud of haze on the horizon, and made sure he kept back far enough not to enter their field of vision. Shortly before sundown, the dust cloud collapsed, a sure sign that they had stopped and were setting up camp for the night. Feuchtenbeiner turned and drove back half a mile, where he also prepared for the night.

Before starting off on foot, he cleaned the barrel of the elephant gun carefully and polished the lenses of his binoculars. Then he strode off in an arc. He wanted to approach their camp from the west, against the wind, as he had always done when stalking big game.

Half an hour later, he spotted the Ford by the river bed. He sneaked up till he was about two hundred yards away, then lay down on his belly in the sand and gazed calmly at the camp of the two fugitives.

The German was opening a tin, and the kaffir collecting wood. He was wearing corduroy jeans now and a T-shirt. When he straightened up, Feuchtenbeiner saw his face, the face of the hijacker whom Moses had called Kgosi. A hot wave of fury surged up in him, but he resisted the temptation to gun the man down on the spot. The distance was too great and he had left the sniper-scope in his Range-Rover.

Feuchtenbeiner crept backwards on all fours. When he was out of sight of the two men, he straightened up and marched back to the Range-Rover. The sniperscope lay in a leather case behind the driver's seat. He mounted it on the elephant gun. The sun had gone down, but before total darkness set in, the moon came up. It was a full moon, with just enough light for him to find his way back to his observation post. He would only need two bullets. He was a first-class marksman with first-class equipment.

THE JACKALS launched into their night song. Tutuma chewed on a dry rusk. The two men had very little appetite.

Tutuma stared at Click-Clack, who was holding his nose up like a scenting dog. "He's got something," said Dieter. "He's never been this fidgety."

"It must be the jackals." Tutuma yawned. "Put out the fire before you go to bed. We have to get an early start tomorrow morning, or we won't make it with the little water we have."

They hadn't talked about the sabotage of their water since that morning, but Dieter sensed why Tutuma had insisted on a small fire this time, just big enough to heat water for coffee, but too small to lure unwelcome guests.

The fire sank into a tiny heap of embers, casting a red glow on Dieter's face. Sitting there, with his face towards Feuchtenbeiner, he offered an excellent target. But Feuchtenbeiner put down his gun. First the kaffir, then the other. A thorn bush blocked his view of the African, and he bellied a few yards to the right. The

461

kaffir was sitting by the fire with his back to him. He had taken off his T-shirt and jeans. He was probably going to bed.

Feuchtenbeiner dried his hands with a Kleenex. His target was at most thirty-five yards away. He pulled the trigger. It was a smooth, clean shot in the head. The kaffir fell forward with his face in the embers.

After a terrified moment, the German sprang up, pulled the

kaffir's torso out of the fire and bent over him. He offered an excellent target, and Feuchtenbeiner's finger felt the trigger, but a barrier suddenly sprang up in him. After all, the man was white.

Besides, the German could hardly be dangerous to him as a witness. The black had most likely told him nothing about his actions, and the little he might know could hardly do any damage —even if he ever made his way out of the Kalahari without a guide and without water. Feuchtenbeiner let the elephant gun sink. Without looking back, he dashed to his Range-Rover, started the motor and drove off.

What Dieter held in his arms was no longer a head, but a shapeless mush of blood, brain and bone splinters. From an unreal distance, he heard a shout: "Get out of the light!" Then Tutuma grabbed his arm. "Get away from the fire!"

As the African pulled him deeper into the darkness, Dieter crumpled up and vomited. He dropped into a bush. The thorns scratched his face. When Tutuma yanked him up and slapped his face, Dieter struggled to his feet and reeled after Tutuma. "They've shot Click-Clack!" He was crying.

Dieter had no idea of how long he stumbled through the darkness, holding his friend's hand. At some point, Tutuma pushed him to the ground and flung himself down next to him. For a while, they lay there motionless, listening. Then, somewhere far off, a soft rumble became audible.

"They're driving away," whispered Tutuma. The rumble became fainter and fainter until the darkness sucked it up.

"Who could do a thing like that?" whispered Dieter. "Shooting a harmless Bushman . . . ."

"It was meant for me. They wanted to gun down both of us, one after the other."

Dieter gaped at him. "Who?"

"BOSS."

"Click-Clack sensed it," Dieter said after a pause. "He kept running around nervously. But he couldn't tell us."

"Keep quiet!" Tutuma raised his head and listened into the darkness. He kept his eyes on the area around the burned-down fire, and when nothing stirred for half an hour, he stood up. "Come on," he said.

"Are you sure they're gone?"

"I don't know."

"If they're still here, they'll gun you down."

"You, too, Dieter. I'm sorry I got you into this."

"It's all right."

Tutuma put a hand on his shoulder. "We've waited long enough.

Now we must get the hell out of here as fast as possible."

"On foot?"

"In the Ford."

"What about Click-Clack?" Tutuma shrugged. Dieter protested, "We can't just let him lie there like that!"

"What do you suggest? A Christian burial with a salute by the South Africans?"

"I'm sorry, Tutuma. I just can't deal with the situation."

"The jackals would grub him out soon enough anyway."

The fire had burned down almost totally. Dieter and Tutuma flung their belongings in the back of the Ford. Dieter avoided looking at Click-Clack's body.

"*You* drive," he said. "I'm wiped out."

Tutuma switched into the cross-country gear. "I'll drive without a light for the time being. Watch the compass carefully."

NEXT MORNING, a wind spout rose out of the ground, whirling along next to the Ford like a top. "He's still with us," murmured Dieter. "The Bushman's spirit . . . ."

Tutuma didn't reply. He stared ahead with tired eyes. "Do you feel better?" he finally asked, but Dieter only shrugged.

In their headlong flight, they had taken a breakneck drive through the night, following the compass, rolling down thorn bushes in their way, jolting over the springhaas burrows. Dieter felt utterly exhausted. His battered hip-bones ached, his head was bruised from banging against the roof. But no pursuer could be seen, and suddenly everything seemed to Dieter as unreal as a dream. Only the bloodstains on his clothes reminded him of reality.

A flickering haze had settled over the desert and the air seemed unusually heavy, charged with electricity. In the west, a white cloud emerged. Soon other clouds joined it, turning grey. Within a few minutes, they had covered half the sky, drawing a black curtain over the sun. Tutuma stepped on the brakes, and with stiff legs they jumped down and stretched their numb limbs. It was the first time they'd stopped in twelve hours.

The first heavy raindrops bounced off the parched ground,

breaking up like quicksilver in the dust. Thousands of new ones joined them, and now the earth began sucking them up greedily, like a blotter.

"Get the tanks!" cried Tutuma.

Dieter dashed to the truck and dragged the tanks from the back. He unscrewed them and put them under the cascade pouring out of the back of the Ford. As they slowly filled up, he pulled off his blood-smeared clothes and stood naked, stretching his arms high and devoutly facing the rain that scoured away the horror of the previous night. Tutuma had also stripped, and his shining body reminded Dieter of a statue in polished ebony.

"Now you understand why we call our currency 'pula'," Tutuma said. "The word expresses all our riches. It means 'rain'."

The rain brought a drop in the temperature, and they fled back into the cabin of the truck. After an hour, it stopped as suddenly as it had come. When they climbed out again, they sank into red, slimy mud up to their ankles. Water had gathered in the truck and Lizzy was dripping wet. She stank horribly. The sleeping bags and knapsack were soaked through. Dieter untied the knapsack. All he could do was wring out the contents and spread them out to dry. "Now we've got nothing to change into," he said.

So they sat naked in the truck. The engine started instantly, but the wheels merely spun in the soft red mud.

"Switch off the engine," said Tutuma. "It's a waste of petrol."

Dieter looked out of the window. "Do you think they're after us again?"

"Maybe. If they are, they're stuck in the mud, just like us."

X

When Jan Feuchtenbeiner arrived in Gaberones, he looked worn out. After the shot finishing off the hijacker, he had driven back to Orapa nonstop—all through the night and the whole of the next day. He had finally arrived late in the afternoon. First, he went to his office, where his secretary told him that he had had another call from the photographer in Gaberones. The man had asked her to tell her boss that he would meet him in Gaberones on

466

Saturday. He would hand him the photos in the cinema, during the evening show.

This Mr. January was getting more uppity. It was sheer madness ringing Jan up in his office, for BOSS had bugged all the phones since the hijacking. The King Air had taken off for Gaberones a couple of hours ago, so Feuchtenbeiner was forced to drive the Range-Rover to Francistown and to take the train from there to Gaberones. He let no one see him at home, much as he yearned for a bath, a shave, and fresh clothes. He preferred to avoid June's questions.

In Gaberones he rented a room in the Hotel President, diagonally across from the cinema. No one seemed bothered by his seedy appearance. The sight of men coming straight from the bush was an every-day occurrence here.

An hour later, freshly washed, he sat on the hotel terrace, devouring a boiled halibut. It was his first real meal in four days.

Half an hour before the beginning of the show, Feuchtenbeiner walked across the street and bought two half-pula tickets for the stalls, where the whites mixed with the black upper class. He sat down in the second seat of the last row, reserving the seat next to him with a copy of the *Botswana Daily News.* The house was almost full, and no one noticed when, after the lights faded, an African silently took the corner seat. As Feuchtenbeiner instinctively reached for his Luger, January placed a gun in the white man's ribs.

"Look straight ahead, Feuchtenbeiner."

The man who belonged to January's voice was not very tall. He wore a light-coloured suit and sunglasses. Feuchtenbeiner could make out nothing else at this moment.

Feuchtenbeiner cleared his throat. "Do you have the photos?"

"First I want to find out more from you."

"There's not much to tell. The pilot didn't switch off the radio, and when your Moses noticed it, it was too late."

"Where's Moses?"

"The Mirages forced us to fly to South-West Africa. From there, they took Moses to Pretoria. BOSS took over the investigation."

Feuchtenbeiner saw that the African was flabbergasted.

"BOSS?" he finally asked.

"I couldn't help it. I wasn't trying to trick you."

"What happened to the second man?"

"He bailed out with a parachute, somewhere over Lake Xau. He threw the cases out beforehand."

Face to face with Feuchtenbeiner, January didn't seem as sure of himself as on the telephone. "Did he say anything about Zaire?"

"Zaire? He wanted to go to Angola, to Serpa Pinto. But then those goddamn Mirages butted in."

"Feuchtenbeiner, it's suicidal to tell me a fairy tale."

"I swear to you, January, it wasn't my fault. Can I have the photos now?"

January reached into his breast pocket, pulled out a white envelope, and handed it over. Feuchtenbeiner opened the envelope and counted. There were eight photos. In the darkness, he couldn't see whether they were the right photos. He stretched out his hand. "And now the negatives."

"Not until we have the diamonds," said January. "That was always the agreement—surely you remember."

Feuchtenbeiner forced himself to keep calm. "What are you planning to do with them?"

"Nothing. Assuming you haven't tried to pull anything on me."

"I should've known. Blackmailers never stick to the rules."

"A war is no tennis match." January used the roar of the audience, now vociferously taking sides in a karate fight on the screen, to sneak out through a side exit.

VOLODYA NAUMOV had envisioned something better from a grand hotel in the West. The telephone in his room wasn't working, the hot-water tap yielded only an asthmatic groan. When he opened the bed, bedbugs scurried across the greyish-white linen.

An hour ago, he had signed the hotel's guestbook as "Mr. James Pritchard, Liverpool." At fifty-five, Volodya felt too old for this kind of work, with the masquerading, the conspiratorial meetings, the agent hocus-pocus. And he was having trouble with the change in climate. He had taken off from Moscow in a crisp frost; the sultriness in Francistown was like a hot, wet cloth.

It comforted Volodya that the restaurant looked fairly decent, with white tablecloths and cordial black waiters. He had been shown to a seat at a table with a white man, obviously a Boer, who introduced himself as Johan Vermaak.

"Have you only just arrived, Mr. Pritchard?"

"Does it show?" Volodya smiled apologetically. "Just one hour ago by Zambian Airlines from Lusaka."

"What's brought you to this god-forsaken town?"

"Well, I've always wanted to see an old gold-mining town."

"There's not much to see here now. If you really want to see something, you ought to go to South Africa."

And while Vermaak lauded the tourist attractions of his home-land, Volodya poked listlessly at his smoked salmon. To the right of his navel, the old scars were aching. He begged off when Vermaak invited him for a drink at the bar, pleading a digestive disturbance, which wasn't too much of a lie. The Boer didn't seem particularly disappointed. Basically, he wasn't interested in this dull Englishman.

Yet they would have had a lot to talk about, for they were in Francistown for the very same reason.

THE BRIEF NOTE was scribbled in English: "January from Gaberones back. Thursday new shippmen recrutes from skool Rhodesia."

January folded the note, reinserted it in the transparent plastic pouch and replaced the pouch under the rock beside the log road to Gaberones where he had found it. Edson Mojo had not been very cautious when hiding the message for his contact. A friend of January's, who had been assigned to watch Mojo, had informed January, who raced to the spot in his Jaguar.

"Hide behind the tree and see who picks up the note," he ordered the friend, before driving back to town.

So Mojo was a traitor. Feuchtenbeiner's story was correct, and Mojo's version a pack of lies. In January's first burst of fury, he thought of liquidating the traitor who had worn the ANC amulet. But then he wondered if it wouldn't be smarter to fight the enemy with his own weapons. He would use Mojo for a while to pass false information to the South Africans. First, he would have to move the training camp, with which Mojo was now familiar, close the travel agency, and temporarily put off any further shipments of recruits from Zimbabwe.

It would take a few days to attend to these matters. Then he would set up new headquarters in some other camp in the bush. Once the Soviet weapons had arrived, he wouldn't need camouflage anyway. BOSS had found out so much about his organization that all he could do was to seize the bull by the horns.

They couldn't count on Tutuma any more. Maybe he'd broken his neck when he'd bailed out over the Kalahari. Or the South Africans had nabbed him. Well, they would just have to get along without him. The threads began to come together. Sooner or later, the soldiers would get used to him as their commander.

Admittedly, Tutuma was popular, and he was a man of integrity. But in strategy, January was at least his equal. And if he won a reputation as the man who had driven the whites out of the country, then he would eventually grow into the job of statesman, capable of ruling a liberated Zimbabwe.

A white man was waiting on the terrace at his home.

"Hello, Mr. Badubi," he said.

January recoiled. The white man doffed his boater cordially. "I would like to book a passage to Manila." That was the password to be used by the Russian who, as they had been notified, would come from Lusaka.

January walked back to his Jaguar. "Hop in. I'll show you the town." Then he remembered the response to the password: "In Manila, the vanilla stalks grow on trees."

The Russian's impassive face lit up with a smile. "My name is James Pritchard."

"Excuse me for not asking you into the house."

"That was prudent of you. There are no eavesdroppers in a car."

"You probably want to find out from me where the diamonds are, Mr. Pritchard."

"Oh, the diamonds." The Russian waved the diamonds off. "No, we're worried about Tutuma."

"Tutuma is OK. He's hiding out in the bush. The Boers are after him, as you can imagine. He ordered me to receive the weapons and start the war of liberation from inside Botswana. Our people are impatient, you know. Once the war has begun, Tutuma will join us. With the diamonds, of course."

Pritchard didn't seem very excited by this idea. "I would have preferred speaking with him beforehand."

"Impossible! That's much too dangerous for all of us." January drove around a cow in the middle of the road. "Unfortunately, the action did not go as planned."

"I'd like to know the details."

January told him Feuchtenbeiner's version of the affair, the Mirage fighters and Tutuma's bail-out. "Reliable friends assisted him," he said darkly. And he let things stand with that hint, though Pritchard asked insistently for further details.

After dropping the Russian off near his hotel, January located the friend he had left beside the log road. He learned that Mojo's note had been fished out by Johan Vermaak, a travelling salesman from South Africa. Now he knew Mojo was a traitor for sure.

FEUCHTENBEINER'S Range-Rover screeched to a halt in the square in front of the casino in Orapa. He stuck his head out of the window. The first acquaintance to cross his path after his return was BOSS agent Roger Niehoujs, of all people. He informed Feuchtenbeiner that the man they were after was named Tutuma, but that this hadn't helped them any further.

Feuchtenbeiner rubbed the back of his neck. "You know, Niehoujs, I think he must have died long ago."

Niehoujs blinked grouchily. "You think so?"

"Well, if you haven't tracked him down by now . . . ."

"Funny. Yesterday a plane scared off a swarm of vultures out there in the desert. I flew over right away in a chopper. Just a skeleton, picked clean."

"Did he have the cases with the diamonds?"

"What's a Bushman supposed to be doing with diamonds?"

"So it wasn't Tutuma?" These treacherous outbreaks of sweat could cost him his head some day.

"I told you. It was a Bushman. The skeleton was at most five feet four, and wore only a leather loincloth and a pouch. The odd thing was that the man hadn't died of thirst. A shot in the head. Are you going to be in the casino later on?"

Feuchtenbeiner gazed flabbergasted at the BOSS agent. It took him a while to digest this turn of events. Where could a second kaffir have come from? If he had killed the wrong man, he was even worse off than before. Tutuma would inform January about the murder attempt and the photos might be in the mine manager's letterbox by tomorrow morning. But yesterday at the cinema, January had obviously not known anything about the assault on Tutuma, or he would have reacted differently.

Feuchtenbeiner still had a chance. The German had wanted to drive the truck to Maun. Maun was on the route to Angola, and Angola was the destination that Tutuma had named in the plane. So it was quite possible that the two were still together.

This time Jan would get the right man.

THE FACT THAT January had asked him to collect his mail made Mojo both proud and unhappy. Proud of being trusted, unhappy at having to abuse this trust. At the post office, he presented a notification slip. "I'm supposed to pick up a package for Mr. Badubi. He doesn't have time to come for it."

The clerk fished out a package, and Mojo signed a receipt. The package was somewhat smaller than a shoebox. Mojo glanced at the return address: Embassy of the USSR in the Republic of Zambia. It was postmarked "Lusaka".

Mojo slipped the package under his arm and ran the three blocks to the bookshop safe house. The proprietor, an Indian, was alone in the shop. With a terse movement of his head, he indicated that someone was waiting for Mojo in the back room. Mojo stepped inside and waited until Vermaak, who was busy cleaning his nails, looked up. At last the Boer asked: "What is it?"

"I have important news, Mr. Vermaak. January told me that he wants to disband the freedom movement and the training camps in the bush. He has learned that the Russian weapons will not be delivered. Without weapons and without Tutuma, it makes no

472

sense to him to continue trying for the liberation of Zimbabwe."

"What's that package?"

"It's for January. From the Soviet embassy in Lusaka."

"Hand it over." Vermaak turned and twisted the package with keen curiosity, holding it to his ear and shaking it. Then he opened his penknife.

"Careful! January mustn't see that we opened it."

Gingerly, Vermaak loosened the knots with the tip of the blade, before undoing the string.

Right after the explosion, the Indian dashed into the back room. He trod on glass fragments and plaster. The air reeked of singed flesh. When the clouds of dust settled, the Indian saw a torn-off head on the floor, the Boer's head. A yard away he discovered the bloody body of Edson Mojo.

THE KALAHARI had turned green overnight. Leaves sprouted from the parched wood of the thorn bushes. The earth swallowed the masses of water and then hardened again, forming a weave of cracks and crevices.

Compared with the axle-breaking tracks on which he had been forced to drive during the past week, the road from Francistown to Maun seemed like a motorway to Dieter. The surface was compressed clay and stones, and it was relatively even. They reached the road that morning, after driving for an hour over the rock-hard Makgadikgadi Pans. Dieter planned to stop in Nata first, to give Lizzie back to the American archaeologists. Tutuma, not wanting to be seen, crept under the blanket in the back of the truck.

For Botswana, the traffic on the road was heavy: a car drove past them almost every hour.

In Gweta, a village of some thirty clay huts, Dieter bought two cans or orangeade. Then he strode over to a whitewashed booth. In front of the booth, an old African was sitting behind an antediluvian camera.

The old man gave him a toothless grin. "Photo, *Monna?* One pula."

Amused, Dieter nodded, and the old man put him in front of a battered cardboard wall on which a lion was painted. The old

473

man's head vanished under a black cloth, and one minute later the photo was taken. Dieter handed the old man a pula note and wrote down his boss Helmuth Dieckmann's address in Maun. Then he walked back to the truck, shooing out some African hitchhikers, pulled back the blanket, and handed Tutuma the orangeade. "Did anyone see you?" he asked.

"Yes."

"Were you recognized?"

Tutuma pulled down the seal of the can. "I hope not."

It had started raining again, and the wheels could barely grip the muddy road. Towards evening, they reached Nata, a large collection of clay huts. An African boy showed them the way to the river, where, to their surprise, Bob, Jim and Linda had pitched their camp.

In an open dugout sheltered by reeds, Bob was banging away at a typewriter. Linda stood in the water with her jeans rolled up, washing the cast-iron cauldron, and Jim lay cursing underneath the Datsun. Bob was first to spot the visitor. He came running from the dugout and embraced Dieter. Then he ran to the Datsun: "Jim! We've got company!"

Jim crawled out from under the truck, oil-stained. "Dieter! So the Kalahari's coughed you up again!"

Now Linda came up from the river. "Where's Lizzy? Did you eat her?" Dieter pointed at the goat, which stood in the back of the Ford, exhibiting no trace of joy at seeing her friends again.

"What about Tutuma?" asked Jim.

"They almost caught him." Tutuma emerged from under the blanket. He listened in silence as Dieter told the Americans the mysterious tale of Click-Clack's murder. "I'm sorry to spoil your evening with the story."

"You're damn right you've spoiled our evening," Jim said furiously.

After dinner, which they ate silently at a tin table under a large umbrella acacia, Bob said that the director of the German voluntary service back in Gaberones was worried. "Maybe you ought to call him, Dieter. It's not really fair to keep your people guessing so long."

Dieter embarrassedly polished his glasses. "Is there a telephone in Nata?"

"Yeah. Sometimes you can even get a call through."

"I'm driving to Francistown tomorrow," said Bob. "I have to do some shopping and send the report on our Bushman expedition to the university. I can tell Gaberones for you."

"That's nice of you. You can have Lizzy back for that. And as for your research—maybe we can contribute a few details."

He told them about their encounter with the Bushmen. It became a long night. Bob, Jim and Linda squeezed every last detail out of him.

Next morning, Tutuma asked for a ballpoint pen and a sheet of paper. He covered the paper with coded writing and gave it to Bob. "Can you do something for me in Francistown?" He described the way to January's travel agency. "The man's name is Badubi. I rely on your not letting this get into the wrong hands."

Bob glanced at the note. "Is this the first draft of a declaration of independence for Zimbabwe? What does it say?"

"That's a matter which concerns only Badubi and myself," Tutuma said, turning his palms upward.

IN HIS DEPARTMENT, Erik Van Zyl was considered a man without passions, aside from his predilection for jigsaw puzzles. The general had two cupboards full of puzzles, including a Japanese one with 13,944 pieces. And he preened himself on having never given up on any puzzle, no matter how complicated it might be.

For five days now, Van Zyl had been playing with a different sort of puzzle. And the fact that it still wasn't solved was due, he felt, to his not yet having all the pieces. Most of them so far had been supplied by the Matabele, Edson Mojo. From Mojo's superior, Johan Vermaak, Van Zyl knew that a guerrilla organization was behind the assault on the diamond shipment. Its leader, Tutuma, was still a fugitive. His lieutenant was named Teko Badubi, alias Mr. January.

It was regrettable that they would now have to do without Vermaak and Edson Mojo. The fact that it had been Van Zyl's own men who had killed them was one of those breakdowns that occur however careful secret-service planning may be. Who could have foreseen that, contrary to custom, January wouldn't pick up and open his own mail this time?

Van Zyl had had qualms about getting rid of January while BOSS was still receiving information about his plans via Mojo. But now time was of the essence. January was warned. He would react by going underground, disbanding or moving his training camp in the bush.

For the time being, Van Zyl could add no new pieces to this corner of the puzzle. But two new pieces had come from Gweta. The photographer had informed the BOSS resident in Francistown that an African had detected a man concealed under a blanket in the back of a sand-coloured Ford truck, and the description had been very similar to Tutuma's identikit. The truck belonged to one Dieter Hahn. A photo showing Hahn with a cardboard lion had also been sent along by the informer, with the number of a post-office box in Maun where he was to send the picture "c/o Helmuth Dieckmann". Evidently another German overseas volunteer. If the man in the truck really was Tutuma, then the German would lead them to the guerrilla leader and the missing diamonds.

There was one more piece, but Van Zyl wasn't sure whether or not it fitted into his puzzle: Jan Feuchtenbeiner. Orapa had notified Van Zyl that the head of security had no sooner come back from his hunting trip than he had gone on the road again. This time to the Okavango Delta, near Maun, allegedly to hunt crocodiles. Van Zyl would have liked to know what kind of crocodiles Feuchtenbeiner was after. Maybe one of them was black? Another spoor leading to Maun. Van Zyl decided to send three of his men there, led by his best agent, Niehoujs.

LATE THAT AFTERNOON, Dieter and Tutuma reached the Botletle River. The downpour had turned the shallow trickle into a raging brown torrent. "The road from Francistown to Maun should have a ford here," Tutuma said. "We must wait until the water has subsided, but I have to get across the border as fast as possible."

Dieter looked at him dubiously. "Why so much fuss over one man? The South Africans are risking protests and diplomatic complications, chasing you across a foreign country like this. I'm involved now, so I want to know who you are."

"I'm the leader of a guerrilla army in Zimbabwe."

"Do you have anything else on your record?"

Tutuma hesitated. "The whites make their laws to solidify their rule. And we act by our own laws."

"You're being evasive, Tutuma. You don't trust me because I'm white. I've risked quite a bit for you. For instance, my life. I want to know what I'm doing all this for, goddammit!"

"Why are you yelling?"

"Because I dropped everything in Germany to come and help you Africans. Because I want to try to make up a little for what the whites have done to you. I had a good job teaching in Germany and a girl friend I'm very fond of. By the time I get back, she'll have some other guy."

"Why are you telling me all this?"

"So that you'll understand how important this is for me."

Tutuma sighed. "We're waging war, and it's best that you keep out of it. It's not your war."

When they had drunk their tea and wolfed down their stew of corned beef and tinned corn, they took their sleeping bags behind a cluster of thorn bushes. The danger they had overcome had made Dieter feel closer to Tutuma. It irritated him that the African still kept his aloofness. Was it because of the history of his people, forced to see an oppressor and exploiter in every white? Dieter wondered whether he had done the right thing in coming here. He would have liked to ask Tutuma's opinion, but he was afraid of another rebuff.

"You're really taking this well," he heard Tutuma say. "It's not easy for a European who's never been in the bush."

"When I was a kid, I was a pretty good athlete. My father sent me to the playing fields. I was supposed to learn that you have to torture yourself to succeed at anything. Maybe my father expected more of me than I could give."

"We Africans believe that age brings wisdom," said Tutuma. "But age also corrupts. Conformity is an insidious poison. My father was a conformist. As the village elder he had a lot of influence on our tribe. When the whites got richer and richer and we stayed poor, he regarded it as God's will, which we had to bear with humility. No wonder the whites paid him a good salary and gave his son a good education." Tutuma's voice was even softer than normal, as always when something affected him very deeply. "Whites are capable of anything to defend their privileges. And we're capable of anything to fight for our rights."

"Anything? Even war?"

Tutuma folded his arms behind his head and stared into the heavens. "Has there ever been revolutionary change in history without violence?"

THE DAY after the attempt on his life, January had driven out to the bush to disband the camp and distribute the recruits over other camps. Bob's surprise visit had not fitted in with his plans. A few days earlier, he would have been happy at a sign of life from Tutuma. But the way things were going now, Tutuma's handwritten message confused him more than it delighted him. In Kalanga language and in code, it confirmed what January had already found out from Feuchtenbeiner about the Orapa operation. Tutuma also wrote that he was en route to Angola both because things were too hot for him in Botswana, and because he had to see the Russians in Serpa Pinto. If January wanted to send him any messages, he could still reach him for a few days by contacting Dieter Hahn, a German volunteer in Maun.

After reading the note, January burned it. Why did Tutuma have to interfere now that things were going so well without him? The assassination attempt had changed everything. Who even mentioned Tutuma now? It was he, January, whom the South Africans wanted to blow up, so he had grown in importance; and there was no room for two leaders. January was the one in command of the troops. And if you've got the army, you've got the power.

THE NEXT DAY, January invited Tutuma's girl for a drive in his Jaguar. Getting out at Shashe Dam, he said: "It's good to have someone you can confide in fully. You don't feel so alone then."

478

"Do you have problems, Teko?" Dikeledi asked.

"It's hard when you've been fooled about a friend."

"Tutuma?"

"I really didn't mean to talk about him."

"You've always shared your problems with me, Teko."

They walked silently for a while. Then they sat down under a mopane tree. January took a rock and hurled it furiously into the water. "He used us for his own ends, you and me. And now he's impudent enough to send us a messenger with a note." Dikeledi looked at him wide-eyed. "That American who visited me yesterday. He brought a note from Tutuma."

"Show it to me."

"I burned it. I was furious. In the note, he says he parachuted out over the Kalahari and he had to hide the two cases with the diamonds."

"So then he's not in Zaire?"

"He's come back to Botswana because he's made a date with a buyer from De Beers' Central Selling Organization. He couldn't find a buyer in Zaire. Only the CSO can take such a huge amount. De Beers will pay a fraction of the real value; let's say a million dollars. And Tutuma will settle down somewhere and lead the life of a white gentleman."

"How do you know about the million dollars and the buyer?"

"My agent in Maun told me. The buyer's waiting there now for Tutuma and the diamonds."

"Are you sure he's telling the truth?"

January nodded sadly. "There's too much evidence. The buyer in Maun, Mojo's treachery, the fact that De Beers is still keeping the skyjacking a secret. Tutuma wants to keep us in the dark as he always has. And do you know what the most arrogant thing of all is? I'm supposed to meet him. He probably wants to pump me about our plans so that he can give them away to the South Africans. Maybe that's part of their bargain."

January gave Dikeledi a little time to digest this. At last, perplexed and depressed, she asked: "Well, what are we going to do now?"

"He thinks he's cunning, but we're more cunning than he is.

You will go to him. I'll tell you what to say to him." He hesitated.
"Only—Tutuma speaks with a thousand tongues. He learned that
at the university from the whites. He'll wrap you in a new web of
lies. Promise me one thing, Dikeledi. Whatever he tells you, you
mustn't believe a word of it. Just keep your mind on your mission."

"What mission?"

"You've got to try to lure the secret out of him. The hiding
place of the diamonds."

"Why should he tell me?"

January softly stroked her thigh. "He likes you." Dikeledi's face
froze. She pulled away and stood up.

"It's not easy for me either, Dikeledi. But we need the
diamonds. Otherwise we can't pay for the weapons."

Dikeledi turned back to him. "And once I get it out of him?"

"Then use this." From a pocket of his bush shirt, he produced a
piece of bamboo reed as long as a little finger. The end was
sharpened to a point. From the other pocket, he pulled out an
innocent-looking little phial.

"What's that?"

"It's very simple. You dip the bamboo tip into the phial and
scratch him while he's asleep. He'll barely notice. Maybe he won't
even wake up . . . . He really deserves a harder death."

Dikeledi flinched. "I can't, Teko."

"I'm asking a lot of you, maybe too much for a woman." He
gazed at her, long and pleadingly. "He's with a German called
Dieter Hahn. Do it for our people, Dikeledi."

XI

At last the Ford reached Maun. Dieter offered to put Tutuma up
in the house of a fellow volunteer, but Tutuma refused. Now that
they had come to the Okavango Delta he preferred to hide out on
one of the islands—he felt safer far from human beings. So Dieter
hired a boat, and went out with him.

The boat struggled northward against the powerful current,
chugging loudly. Tutuma looked hard at the banks. He still hadn't

480

found an island that appealed to him. The UN biologists estimated that there were about ten thousand islands in the Okavango Delta, of which perhaps a dozen were inhabited. The delta waters came down from Angola by way of the Okavango River. In Botswana, they broke up into thousands of rivers, lagoons, canals and tributaries, wandering through an area almost the size of Holland.

During the first few miles along the edge of the delta, Dieter and Tutuma had run into the occasional hunter or fisherman. Later, they had turned off, into the Boro River, one of the few half-negotiable streams. It led straight into a confusing labyrinth of tributaries and lagoons.

Cranes indignantly rose into the air above the river, and from the shore. Dieter heard the scolding of a herd of baboons. A hippopotamus gazed towards them, and indignantly flapped its ears. At last, Tutuma felt they had found a suitable island for a hideout. Dieter switched off the engine and headed towards it. Tutuma leaped into the shallow water and pushed the boat across a carpet of white and blue waterlilies into the belt of reeds.

On shore, Dieter was surprised to be standing on an island about four acres in size. A distinctive group of palms loomed on the far side. When he was about to investigate the place, the African held him back. "Let's stay near the boat. There are crocodiles and hippopotamuses. I'd feel better if I had a rifle on me."

Dieter helped Tutuma gather papyrus leaves, which the African used to prepare a bed. Then they went to look for dry wood.

At the first prick in the back of his neck, Dieter knew that it couldn't be a mosquito. Mosquito bites itched, but this felt like a red-hot needle. He slapped the spot and squashed an insect which looked vaguely like a horsefly. Then a whole swarm attacked him. The weird thing was that they couldn't be heard. They simply dropped silently from the trees. Soon Dieter's yellow T-shirt showed red spots. But most of the flies seemed to have a strange preference for his jeans, which were soon covered with them, biting through. Desperate for help, he called to Tutuma.

"Take your jeans off and jump into the water," the African shouted.

Dieter stripped off the jeans, and as soon as he dived into the crystal-clear water, the flies left him in peace. "Why didn't they attack you?" he yelled. "Don't they like blacks?"

Tutuma laughed. "It's your jeans. Tsetse flies love blue."

Because of the flies under the trees, they lit their fire in a clearing. "It'll be dark soon," Tutuma murmured. "They don't come out at night." He listened to a fine whirring. "But replacements are coming. Mosquitoes."

"Sleeping sickness or malaria. Some choice."

Dieter was tired, hungry, and in a foul mood. He had been looking forward to Helmuth Dieckmann's place. Maun even had electric light, and Helmuth's house probably had a flush toilet and a bath.

Tutuma gave him an encouraging look. "We'll have fresh fish tonight." He pulled a burning stick out of the fire and held it over the water like a torch. Instantly, a swarm of cichlids gathered. Tutuma struck the water hard a few times and hauled out half a dozen dazed fish.

It was a monosyllabic meal. Ever since Click-Clack had been shot before his eyes, Dieter hadn't been able to stand the nights out of doors. And noises in the swamp were even stranger, more varied, more threatening, than in the Kalahari.

From the figtree, he heard a soft smacking of lips: maybe it was a bat, eating fruit. An owl swept overhead on quiet wings. Buffaloes stamped on a neighbouring island, and nearby an animal broke through the bushes. A muted plop occasionally accompanied the chant of the crickets—a fish leaping out of the water to snap at an insect. And over everything lay the unchanging noise of the toads.

The next morning, Dieter was in a hurry to get away. He promised Tutuma to come back as soon as possible with a mosquito net, a bush knife, and provisions.

"Why do you want to be here, anyway, in this swamp?" Dieter asked. "I thought you were heading for Angola."

"I'm waiting for news. An African is going to come to you in Maun and ask about me. Bring him back here."

"How can I tell if it's the right one?"

"If he mentions the name January, you can trust him."

When Dieter switched on the engine, the African put his hand on Dieter's shoulder. "You've done a lot for me, Dieter. This is the last favour I'll ask of you."

HELMUTH DIECKMANN lay on the floor in front of a wardrobe. He had a homemade fly-swatter in his hand.

"I'm Dieter. I've brought the truck."

Helmuth's free hand waved uncertainly. "Sit down somewhere." He tried to peer under the wardrobe, his long, thick beard sweeping the floor. "C'mon out, you bastard!" he said.

A cockroach shot out from under the other end of the wardrobe. Helmuth lifted the swatter—and missed. The cockroach escaped through the crack in the door.

Disappointed, Helmuth stood up and held out his hand to Dieter. "I was expecting you a week ago." Helmuth was twenty-nine but appeared ten years older. Dust flakes hung in his beard, and he peered at his guest from behind thick horn-rimmed glasses. But he inspired confidence. Dieter liked him at first sight.

"I took a detour through Orapa and Rakops."

Helmuth trudged to the refrigerator in the kitchen and mixed a jug of squash. "How long are you staying?"

"I don't know. I want to have a look at your volunteer brigade, because I'm supposed to start my own in Ghanzi."

While Dieter got his stuff from the back of the Ford, Helmuth examined the truck delightedly. He needed it for his brigade's farm, an hour's drive from Maun at the edge of the Okavango swamp. His pupils had learned how to plant beans, corn, cabbage, onions and tomatoes on the farm. Helmuth could sell his brigade's produce at a profit in Maun, where there was always a shortage of fresh vegetables, but until now there had been no means of transport. He had only a small Honda motorcycle, part of the standard equipment for German volunteers.

Helmuth locked the Ford and went into the house. A roof over their heads was all that the government was supposed to offer the white voluntary workers. The furniture in the living room—three chairs covered with artificial leather plus a couch of sorts, a rickety wardrobe and a table—were all rough-hewn products of

Helmuth's carpentry brigade. Candle stubs were stuck everywhere, and sand ground underfoot.

Helmuth cracked a couple of eggs into a pan and produced a kind of scrambly mixture. "I'm no great chef," he excused himself. "But it's the fault of the eggs too. They are Rhodesian rejects and edible only when they're fried. Now I'm planning to raise poultry myself."

They discussed his farm. Finally Helmuth put away his plate and glanced at his watch. "I've got to go. The board of governors is meeting."

Helmuth took the truck and gave Dieter his Honda, and after washing and unpacking, Dieter set out to have a look at Maun. He found a clean store run by two English women and priced a mosquito net. It cost five pulas, so he crossed the street to a Barclay's Bank.

The African teller was involved in a conversation with a white man, probably a big-game hunter from South Africa. When Dieter stepped up to the window, he moved back a few paces. Dieter had seen the man somewhere; the expressionless eyes in the coarse face, the red hair and colourless eyebrows. Probably in Gaberones. Dieter thrust the pula notes into his coat pocket, cashed his cheque and went back to the shop.

Luckily, Feuchtenbeiner thought, the German hadn't recognized him. He had probably long since forgotten the brief meeting at the eastern gate of Orapa. All the better. Sooner or later, the young man would unwittingly lead him to Tutuma.

Feuchtenbeiner looked out of the bank window until Dieter had roared off on his Honda; then, in the store, he learned that the German had bought a bush knife and a mosquito net. A mosquito net? The windows in the houses of the whites were covered with screens. You only needed nets out in the delta. And you could only reach the delta in the motorboats that Tony Graham rented out at Island Safari Lodge.

In less than forty minutes, the Range-Rover brought Feuchtenbeiner to the thatch-roofed lodge. Yes, said Mrs. Graham. A German had rented a motorboat yesterday and returned it this morning. He had gone out alone, refusing the native guide she had offered him. He had probably wanted to save the guide's fee. There was no other explanation for such folly.

To Jan Feuchtenbeiner, there *was* another explanation. Tutuma would have been waiting a short way down the river bank.

NEXT MORNING, when Dieter started off on the Honda, an African woman stopped him in front of the house. She was, at most, twenty and she carried a Zambian Airlines bag. "I'm looking for Mr. Dieter Hahn," she said.

She had nothing of the submissive attitude that many African women have towards men, especially white men, and when she gave him a self-confident smile, Dieter noticed her extraordinary beauty. Her graceful body was sheathed in a light-green calico frock; her skin had a velvety shimmer and was the colour of coffee with just a few drops of milk. Dieter looked at her in surprise. "Me?"

"Mr. January sent me." She looked around cautiously. "My name is Dikeledi. I would like to talk to you. Alone."

"Why don't we go for a drive?"

He stepped into the house, and got Helmuth's crash helmet. It came down to her nose. He drove through the village with the girl on the pillion seat and stopped a few hundred yards behind the bridge, where the tarmac ended and the sandy lane to Francistown began. They removed their helmets, walked on a bit, and settled near a thorn bush away from the road. The girl's presence made Dieter feel self-conscious. For weeks now, he hadn't been near a woman, except for Linda, and Dikeledi exuded a strange blend of the erotic and the vulnerable.

He caught himself staring unabashedly at her. Dikeledi broke the silence. "Tutuma usually doesn't like whites. But he trusts you." And in response to his questioning look, she added: "That's what he wrote in the letter that Bob brought us."

"Tutuma is my friend." He would have liked to say why that was, but he couldn't think of a plausible explanation. "He was standing on the road from Orapa to Rakops. He wanted to hitch a ride, and I took him along."

Dikeledi was surprised. "Are you sure that's what happened?"

Dieter laughed. "Of course. It was about ten days ago. He was standing there in overalls, without any baggage—"

"Ten days ago?" she interrupted. A steep, thoughtful crease appeared above her nose. "In the Kalahari?"

"Didn't he even tell you that in his letter?"

"And you didn't come with him from the north? From Zaire?"

"He didn't say anything about Zaire. Only that he wanted to get to Angola."

"Dieter, will you swear by God that you're telling me the truth?" There was a probing, almost pleading look in her eyes.

"I swear."

"Ten days ago, between Orapa and Rakops?"

"To be exact, two days earlier." He told the girl about the fleeting encounter with Tutuma after the fight with the ostrich; about running into him later; about the trip through the Kalahari, and Bob, Jim and Linda, and the Bushmen, and the shot which was meant for Tutuma but had hit Click-Clack.

Dikeledi never took her eyes off him, and when he was done she said simply: "I believe you."

"There's no reason why I should lie to you."

"Then someone else has been lying." A shadow of bitterness darkened her beautiful face, but Dieter felt that he could not ask her to explain this sudden change of mood. "I must think about this," she said. Dieter watched her as she drew figures in the sand.

"Dikelédi," he asked. "How do you feel about Tutuma?"

She reflected for a few moments, and her reply was enigmatic: "Differently from what I felt half an hour ago."

"Is he your—friend?"

"Tutuma is the friend of all people in Zimbabwe." She chewed on a blade of grass and gazed at the road, the Honda. "I'd like you to take me to him. Immediately."

"But first I have to get something for him," Dieter said. They drove back to Helmuth's house. "Wait. I'll be right back."

Dieter fetched the mosquito net, some canned meat, and the bush knife. Before leaving, he scribbled a note for Helmuth. "Taking the Honda to the delta. Don't know if I'll be back for supper. Dieter."

486

DIETER could tell by the distinctive group of palms that he had found the right island. He switched off the motor, jumped out of the boat, and pulled it deeper into the reeds.

During the ride from Island Safari Lodge to Tutuma's hideout, Dikeledi had gazed at the river with awe. She had never seen as much water in all her twenty years as in these two hours, and she was afraid that the boat might capsize, for she couldn't swim. From time to time, she looked up nervously at a single-engine plane flying low over the Boro. It vanished on the skyline and then circled back. Dieter calmed her fears. He said that scientists stationed at Maun were investigating the delta for the FAO, the World Food Organization.

When Dikeledi climbed out of the boat, Dieter took her by the hand, pulled her ashore, and ran to the place where he had left Tutuma. No one was there. Where the campfire had been, they found nothing but a pile of ashes, some charred wood, gnawed fishbones, and empty cans. Dieter called Tutuma's name, not too loudly. Baboons fled with shrieks, and nearby a hippopotamus crashed through a thicket and plunged into the water, panting angrily.

Dikeledi stared at the charred pieces of wood near the ashes. Suddenly she ran over and bent down. "Look at the arrangement, Dieter! Don't you recognize it?" He shrugged, perplexed. "It's in the shape of Zimbabwe: the horn points to the east. Tutuma wanted to give us a sign." She followed the lengthened tip of the horn to an empty corned-beef can, lifted it, and peered inside. "He's left us a message."

He ran over to her. "Show me."

Together they read the message, which was written in English on a piece of paper: "There are leopards here. Look for me two islands farther downstream. Watch for smoke signals."

"Leopards!" Shuddering, Dikeledi dashed back to the water, running so fast that Dieter could barely keep up with her. They waded out to the boat and shoved it from the reeds into the stream.

The din of the motor shredded the silence like an explosion, and a surprising current pulled them out to the southeast. If Tutuma was any sort of swimmer, he had only to drift with the current to reach the next island. The island after that seemed to be about a mile and a half downstream.

A thick carpet of clover-like drifting plants covered the water, and the open cups of water lilies added touches of white and blue to this green velvet. The boat crept towards a point of land which narrowed the river down to a width of some eight yards.

A man stepped out of the papyrus thicket on the point and motioned to them to stop. When Dieter didn't obey promptly, the man raised his elephant gun and shot. Inches in front of the bow, the bullet smashed a hole in the green carpet of plants.

Dieter switched off the motor. "Have you gone nuts?" he shouted.

The man's face was shadowed by a visored cap, but Dieter recognized him by his movements. He turned to Dikeledi: "Don't worry. It's only a big-game hunter. I saw him yesterday in Maun, at the bank." In the reeds Dieter saw a mocoro, a primitive dug-out, in which the man had evidently paddled here.

"You didn't have to be so trigger-happy," said Dieter. "We would have taken you along."

The man ignored Dieter. "Where is he?" he said to Dikeledi. But Dikeledi was staring at the man with an expression that Dieter had not seen on her face: hatred, fear and disgust. Mutely she pointed to the island they had left a few minutes ago.

"Take me to him at once." The man pushed up the visor of his cap, sized Dieter up from head to foot, and then glared at Dikeledi again. Apparently he was convinced that Dieter couldn't have a weapon concealed beneath his shorts and T-shirt. He pointed to Dikeledi's flight bag: "Empty it out!" She pulled open the zip, turned the bag inside out, and poured the contents on the floor of the motorboat. The man nodded in satisfaction. "Get back to the stern. I had enough of your tricks in that hotel."

Dikeledi gathered the contents of her bag together, then sat down next to Dieter on the bench by the outboard motor, nestling against him. Dieter recalled the aeroplane that had curved over them earlier and reproached himself for not realizing that the South Africans were still after Tutuma.

488

Carefully, the Boer stepped into the water. With his finger on the trigger of his gun, his eyes glued to his prisoners, he waded to the boat. He would be vulnerable for one moment: the moment he needed to clamber over the side. But Dieter didn't think this out. He was wondering about the hotel the Boer had mentioned.

"You're not smart enough for any tricks, Hahn. I can shoot you with one hand," the man said. He pushed the bow down and pulled himself up in one motion. For an instant, he had trouble keeping his balance, and the gun in his free hand pointed straight up. But before Dieter could take advantage of the moment, the Boer had his body and his gun under control again. The opportunity was gone. Now all three were on board.

Since the man's appearance, Dikeledi hadn't spoken a word. Now her expression suddenly changed. A mysterious peace settled on her face. She kept her eyes half-shut and chewed on a reed she had taken from her flight bag. But her body trembled and Dieter felt the tension that leaped from her into his own body.

The man trained his gun on Dieter's chest. "Switch on the motor."

"And then?"

"To Tutuma."

The girl next to Dieter stopped breathing. For an instant, she sat there woodenly. Then her body jerked and came out of its paralysis. The reed dropped from her mouth.

The man winced and slapped his left cheek with his palm. "Goddamn flies!" He gazed at the blood on his hand. "Does Tutuma have any weapons on . . ." He broke off in mid-sentence, reaching for his throat. His hands trembled, and the gun slipped away.

Then Jan Feuchtenbeiner felt a cold sweat break out of all his pores, and paralysis cut off one part of his body after the other; first his arms, then his hands, then an iron ring around his chest, around his lips, his legs, and finally his feet. When the deadly spasm reached his respiratory muscles, Jan was still fully conscious, and his last thought was about the eight photos which would now be worthless to the blackmailer. He felt a vague sensation of triumph before he melted into eternal night.

The massive body swayed slowly to the side and hung, halfway over the bow, in the water. The boat tipped, rocked, and turned in a circle. Dieter sprang up and reached for Feuchtenbeiner.

"Leave him there!" screamed Dikeledi. She gave the body a final shove and it glided slackly into the water, floating along on its back next to the boat. Then she yanked Dieter back with a strength that he would never have believed her delicate body capable of. The expression of wild hatred in her face terrified him. "He was a pig. He's dead. He didn't deserve any better. He would have killed all three of us."

"But you can't just let him drift like that."

"He's dead."

Dieter tried to think straight. Within a few days, this was the second man to die, suddenly and inexplicably, right before his eyes. "I have to take him to Maun."

"Do you want to be arrested for murder?"

"You can testify that I had nothing to do with it. And I you."

"I'm not going to the police with you. You can't force me."

Maybe she was right. How could he make a simple-minded Botswana policeman believe that this man, who had emerged in the swamp and threatened them with his gun, had suddenly dropped dead, as though struck by lightning? "But how could it have happened?"

"If I hadn't killed him, he would have killed us."

"*You?*"

She picked up the reed that had fallen from her mouth. "With this. I put a piece of bamboo into it and blew it into his face with all my strength."

And there was actually a finger-long bamboo reed under the seat, where the stranger had been sitting. Dieter picked it up.

"Careful!" Dikeledi said. "It's sharp as a needle." She opened the small phial January had given her. It was filled wiith a brown paste. "I dipped the point in here. He didn't notice because he was watching my face, not my hands." Gingerly she closed the box and put it back in her bag. "It's Bushman poison."

Dikeledi peered across the river. The current was carrying Feuchtenbeiner's body swiftly downstream.

Dieter felt afraid of this girl. "You knew that man!"

"He's our enemy."

"He hated you, didn't he? A South African secret agent would have acted differently. Cooler. But this man had a very private hatred for you. He mentioned a hotel. Why?"

"Ask Tutuma!" Dikeledi avoided his eyes. She shook herself in quiet disgust and switched on the motor. Then she sat down at the rudder and steered the boat downstream, to the island where they thought Tutuma would be waiting.

XII

Tutuma must have heard the motor long before. When the boat came towards the island, he stepped out of the papyrus thicket and waved at them. Then shouted in surprise: "Dikeledi!"

She laughed. "I hope you're not disappointed."

He waded towards them. "It was lonely here," he said. He embraced Dieter and the girl with warmth.

"January can't come himself," Dikeledi blurted out breathlessly. "A lot has happened. I'll tell you everything."

"Dikeledi killed a man," Dieter said. "A few minutes ago. With a bamboo dart."

"It was Feuchtenbeiner," she said. Still breathless, she told him what had happened during the past hour.

"He was a killer," Tutuma said pensively. "I'm sure that he shot Click-Clack."

"Is he one of the BOSS men?"

Tutuma shrugged. "Maybe."

"Then the others can't be too far away."

"We're safe here for the time being." Tutuma pulled the boat into the high reeds until it couldn't be seen from the river. "I found fresh leopard tracks on our island, so I came here. I built a raft." He pointed to a primitive raft behind a cluster of trees: papyrus plants held together in a makeshift way by ropes of plaited grass. "Did you bring the bush knife?" Dieter handed it to him, along with the tins of food and the mosquito net.

There had been rain in the air for a long time, and now it suddenly poured down. Tutuma pulled his visitors into a refuge with a roof of papyrus leaves. Dikeledi sat down by Tutuma and they started speaking Kalanga together. It was an earnest, urgent conversation and Dieter felt excluded.

If Dikeledi had any doubts left about Tutuma's sincerity, this conversation removed them. His account confirmed what she had found out from Dieter and she was infinitely relieved. January had evidently been fed misinformation to force a wedge into the movement. The misunderstanding was cleared up. There should never again be a falling-out between the two leaders. That was why it would be unwise to tell Tutuma about January's plan to have her murder him. Later on, all three of them would laugh about it: President Tutuma, his Foreign Minister January, and Dikeledi, their confidante.

Whose confidante? Whom did she really belong to?

The question confused her. She brushed it aside for the moment. She belonged to the independence movement. She would tell Tutuma only about what would not drive the two men apart: the abortive attempt on January's life, and that January had joined the soldiers in the bush.

"Couldn't you speak English for a change?" Dieter grumbled.

"We didn't mean to be rude," said Tutuma, "but we have a problem that we've got to solve. Here, the South Africans will track us down sooner or later. We've got to get away at once. Feuchtenbeiner's body is drifting downstream. It'll wash up at Island Safari Lodge or in Maun."

"You wanted to go to Angola, anyway."

"Yes, but now there's a problem. The Caprivi Strip lies between the Okavango Delta and Angola. It belongs to South-West Africa, which means that the South African army has the territory under control. It's well-patrolled, and I couldn't get through alone. But if an armed commando squad infiltrated from Zambia and waited for me on the shore of the Chobe, they could get me through and ferry me across the Zambezi to Zambia."

Dieter smiled sceptically. "Zambia won't risk a military involvement with South Africa just to get one man out."

492

"Not officially. But I have influential friends there."

"Do they know where you're hiding?"

"That's the problem, Dieter. I have to get word to them."

"Can't Dikeledi—?"

"She's too well known. She has no more chance of making it across the border than I do."

"And your friend in Francistown?"

"He's hiding in the bush." Tutuma tugged nervously at his moustache. "There's a flight from Maun to Gaberones three times a week, and one from Gaberones to Lusaka, in Zambia. You could get word to Lusaka in a day or two."

"No, Tutuma."

It wasn't the refusal, it was the rude tone that seemed to astonish Tutuma. "Didn't you say you were my friend?"

"There's a limit to any friendship. You know I'm for the independence movement. But playing courier in a war . . . . I'm a development-aid volunteer, not a guerrilla."

"But my life depends on it. Now that we've got rid of Feuchtenbeiner, BOSS will be panting at my heels. Botswana is a mousetrap for me."

"I could go back to Maun with Dikeledi. From there, she could telephone to Lusaka."

"That won't work." Tutuma waved it off. "The radio telephone is tapped."

"Wait a moment!" Dieter leaped up excitedly. "There's a German volunteer in Maun named Sigi. He's a ham radio operator. He sits at his set every night and talks to other hams all over the world."

"Do you think he'd do it for us?"

"Sure!"

"We have to encode the message," said Dikeledi.

Dieter looked at her in surprise. "Do you know anything about it?"

Tutuma smiled. "She's the radio expert in our organization."

When Dikeledi and Tutuma switched back to Kalanga to discuss the text, Dieter felt left out again. He was annoyed that they used him, the outsider, when they needed his help, but never took him into their confidence. And it irritated him that he didn't know any more about Tutuma's function than on the day they had met.

He was even more puzzled by Dikeledi. She sat on the ground, jotting letters and numbers on a sheet of paper. Now there was nothing left of her apparent need for protection. When she had finished, she handed the paper to Dieter. The message on it consisted of the letters CQ ZAMBIA 9J1AX and long columns of numerals in groups of five.

"Is this a specific code?"

She nodded. "The key is an African proverb."

"What's the proverb?"

When Dikeledi hesitated, Tutuma said, "Where elephants fight, the grass suffers."

Dieter folded the note carefully and put it in his pocket. The thought of perhaps never seeing Tutuma and this beautiful girl again made Dieter feel melancholy.

Could he visit Tutuma later when everything was over? Dieter tried to imagine him in a splendid general's uniform, flanked by bodyguards. Kenyatta, Bokassa, Mobutu, and others—hadn't they all started out like Tutuma?

"You can count on me," he said. And he added emphatically: "But it's my last favour."

"Your last but one," Tutuma corrected. "When my friends get the message, they'll send a man to you. You'll bring him to me."

"Here? To this island?"

"No. We're not safe here any more. I have friends among the Bayeis who live here. They will get us out in a mocoro. The new hiding place will be on the banks of the Chobe. We can be there in three days. A monkey bread tree between Kasane and the Kazungula ferry. I'll describe it to you precisely. Just wait for me there; I'll be there every day at sundown. But be careful: you might be followed."

Dieter irresolutely scratched his head. "I'd rather you had someone else do that. And besides, how am I to recognize your friend from Lusaka?"

"He'll identify himself with the proverb: 'Where elephants fight, the grass suffers.'"

494

THE REPORTS from the agents in Botswana had been pouring in since yesterday. No one in the decoding room had time for lunch, and even Erik Van Zyl went without his meal.

Unfortunately, the strategy of using Feuchtenbeiner to lead Niehoujs and his men to Tutuma's hiding place had been only partly successful. Yesterday in Maun, around noon, Feuchtenbeiner had suddenly chartered a single-engine Piper Aztec. That had seemed to bring Niehoujs closer to his goal than ever before. Feuchtenbeiner had flashed his pilot's licence and insisted on flying the machine alone. Agents in the delta had reported that he had landed the aircraft on Chief's Island. There he had rented a mocoro and paddled off towards Bobo Island.

A short time earlier, that German volunteer had been sighted in the delta. He had gone up the Boro River in a rented motorboat, together with a black woman, whose description matched that of Dikeledi, January's colleague in Francistown. This morning, Dieter Hahn had returned the motorboat to Island Safari Lodge and then gone back to Maun alone. Feuchtenbeiner hadn't returned to Chief's Island, and Dikeledi, too, had remained in the delta.

At the crack of dawn, Niehoujs had ordered a dozen mocoro men who knew the area to conduct a discreet search in the chaotic maze of islands, lagoons and streams between Chief's Island and Bobo Island. The search had not yet turned up anything, but Van Zyl was certain that Tutuma must be hiding on one of the islands. As long as the other three participants in the delta meeting couldn't be found, there was only one whom BOSS could stick to: Dieter Hahn. Yet how could they get at him in Maun?

The best thing, Van Zyl's adviser Heinz proposed, would be to use a black.

"Niehoujs has to keep out," he said. "The last thing we need is a diplomatic incident with West Germany."

"You mean we should let blacks do it?"

"There's a bar in Maun: Riley's. A couple of kaffirs grab him when he comes out at night, and they take him into the delta or the bush and grill him. Our way of asking polite questions loosens every tongue. And after that—well, so many things happen in Africa. People vanish in the bush and never come out again."

SIGI WAS a car mechanic in the government's central transportation organization. He was supposedly the only man in Maun that no one had ever fought with. His obsession was his radio transmitter, which he sometimes worked all night, talking with other hams. When Dieter dropped in on him, Sigi told him that a ham in Berlin was transmitting the latest soccer scores. Sigi came from Berlin. As Dieter stood in the doorway, Berlin began signing off: ". . . . Have to QRT. XYL is waiting with dinner. So long and best 73. DL6KJ of A2BZV signing off. Over."

"Did your team lose?"

Sigi turned his head. "Yeah, that too. You want a squash?" He got syrup, water and glasses.

"I didn't understand any of that jargon. QRT, XYL, 73 . . ."

"It's very simple." Sigi clued Dieter in with an expert's indulgence. "QRT means to sign off. XYL is short for ex-young lady—his girlfriend. 73 means 'greetings'. Those numbers at the end that sound like car licences are his and my operating numbers."

Sigi launched into a lecture on his NCX-5 transceiver, his three-element directional antenna TH3MK 2, and his 14-megahertz frequency, until Dieter's head swam.

Finally, Dieter managed to get to the point. "Listen, Sigi—I'd like you to send a message for me. To Zambia." He pulled Tutuma's note from his pouch, carefully smoothed it out, and handed it over. "Could you do that for me?"

Sigi read it and shoved it aside in disgust. He glared at Dieter. "Espionage, huh?"

"What do you mean?"

"It's in code. Numbers in groups of five. Even a blind man could see it. Who's it for?"

"For a friend. A very good friend."

"A black friend?" Dieter nodded. "Man, you're really freaking out. Coded messages to rebel organizations! What does it say?"

"Will you do it without asking? It will cost my friend his life if you don't send it."

"But it's illegal, Dieter. It's illegal anywhere in the world. And all these ham transmissions are bugged."

"Here in the bush, too?"

496

"Well, maybe they're not all that careful out here. And if it's against South Africa . . . . You say it's important?"

Dieter nodded. "But I don't want you to risk your licence."

"I'm not stupid!" Sigi finished his signal, took the note and switched on his set. "Where in Zambia?"

"Lusaka."

"That's northeast." He fiddled with the dial until the directional antenna pointed northeast. Then he called into the hand mike: "CQ ZAMBIA, CQ ZAMBIA. This is A2BZV calling. A2BZV receiving. Over." With his head at an angle, he listened to the roaring in his receiver. After a couple of seconds, a squawky, slightly warped voice came out. "Hello, A2BZV, hello, A2BZV. This is 9J1AX. I'm getting you fine. Please go on. Over."

Sigi pressed the button. "Hello, my name is Sigi. My QTH is Maun. I can receive you here with five and eight till nine. I need some replacement parts for my five-ton Bedford. Can you order them for me! I'll transmit the order numbers . . . ."

After reading off the columns of numbers, he took a deep breath. "I hope you got it. I'm switching to reception. Over."

"This is 9J1AX," replied the squawky voice. "I received everything precisely and I'll try to get the parts for you. Talk to you tomorrow, same time, same frequency. Back to reception. So long and best 73. 9J1AX QRT with A2BZV. Over."

Sigi switched off and leaned back contentedly. "Well?"

"Terrific, Sigi. Really!"

"That'll cost you a beer at Riley's."

DIETER spent the following day with Helmuth and the farm brigade. That evening, Sigi brought a message he had received from 9J1AX in Zambia: "To Sigi, A2BZV. Passed on orders, trying to fill them. Here is a list of the parts we have in stock now. Please jot them down . . . ." A long series of numbers followed.

Dieter took the note and tucked it into his pocket. Sigi asked no more questions, but he told Dieter to make it clear to his friends that he would not be transmitting or receiving any more coded texts. The whole thing made him queasy. He was seriously afraid of losing his licence.

VOLODYA left his room in the Grand Hotel only when he had no other choice. He did his tour every morning. First he checked Mr. January's travel bureau to see whether the "Closed" sign still hung on the door. Then a glance at the closed shutters convinced him that Mr. January's white wooden house was also deserted.

January had said goodbye to Volodya three days ago. He had said that he had to inspect his troops in the secret bush camps, but that he'd be back in Francistown right away. Then he'd vanished without a trace.

Volodya had never felt so superfluous in his job. He took three cans of Fanta up to his room, lay down on the bed, played the Karpov/Petrosyan match on his pocket chess set, and switched on the transistor radio. Radio Botswana broadcast in Setswana. Radio Bulawayo in Rhodesia broadcast in English. The air conditioner was on the blink. Volodya felt worn out. He was homesick for a crisp winter's day in Moscow.

In the old days, Volodya had felt he was part of the Soviet élite, despising the bureaucrats in the central office behind the thick walls of the Lubyanka. Now he had become a bureaucrat himself. Evaluating reports; putting files together which usually vanished in the archives unread. Volodya had lost his idealism. He had been fighting fits of depression with the thought of his coming retirement. He wanted to settle in the Crimea and go back to what he'd stopped doing thirty-five years ago: growing strawberries. Then they could leave him alone. . . .

It wasn't good having so much time for thinking. Volodya pressed out his ballpoint pen and took out a rolled-up tissue paper with his numerical code. Then he switched his transistor to the short-wave frequency on which Lusaka was broadcasting. He glanced at his watch. Four minutes to go. The message came promptly every morning at nine thirty.

This time, it was more detailed than usual. It took Volodya almost an hour to decode the groups of numbers. The decoded text was an order from the central office. Volodya was to get to Maun on the double and contact a German volunteer there. His name was Dieter Hahn and he would take him to Tutuma who was waiting for him on the Chobe, at a spot where he wanted to cross over with Volodya's help. A civilian commando would meet Volodya and Tutuma on the opposite bank and accompany them through the Caprivi Strip to Zambia. Volodya would get details of the action in the next few days. Over.

Volodya burned the message in the ashtray and flushed it down the toilet. At last things were moving.

DIETER had been playing with some black children outside Helmuth's house. So the stranger must have been watching him for some time from the shade of a mopane tree before he stepped out and ambled towards him. "Are you Mr. Hahn? Dieter Hahn?"

"Why?" Dieter couldn't see the man's eyes. They were shadowed by the brim of the straw hat.

The stranger sized him up and down. Then he said: "I'm British. I've come from Zambia. James Pritchard. That name won't mean anything to you. Perhaps an African proverb would be more useful. 'Where elephants fight, the grass suffers.'"

Dieter was flabbergasted. He had taken the stranger for a South African agent. "Frankly, I was expecting a black."

"We received a radio message. Now I'm here."

"Who sent you?"

"Hasn't Tutuma informed you?"

Dieter preferred not to answer.

"Can't we stop playing cat and mouse?" Mr. Pritchard suggested. "After all, I did give you the password."

"You mentioned a radio message. What did it say?"

"Tutuma asked for help. He wants to cross the Chobe into Zambia, around Kasane. And now I'm here, and instead of taking me to Tutuma, you're asking questions as though you didn't understand."

"Excuse me, Mr. Pritchard," Dieter began. "I wanted to make sure you weren't on the other side." He pulled the note that Sigi had handed him out of his pocket. "Lusaka has answered in the meantime."

"May I have a look?" Volodya glanced at the columns of numbers. "I don't know the code, but I'm sure that Lusaka has approved of Tutuma's plan and is assuring him of support. At least, that's what my instructions say. When can we get going?"

"Do you have a Land-Rover or something like it?"

"My Landcruiser. But it's ready for the junkyard. I wouldn't want to drive it two hundred miles through the bush to Kasane."

"Wait till this afternoon, Mr. Pritchard. Maybe I know of a second possibility."

But Helmuth said, "You're out of your mind: after two years of pleading, I finally got a truck. I didn't much like your joy-riding through the Kalahari with black rebels. If we start getting mixed up in domestic politics, they'll kick us all out. All the projects that are absolutely crucial to Botswana's survival. You've got no right to do that."

Dieter had never seen his good-natured countryman so furious.

So he turned again to Sigi. And Sigi had an idea. The next day, a Bedford belonging to the provincial government was driving to Kasane. For two pulas per passenger, the African chauffeur was willing to take Mr. Hahn and Mr. Pritchard to the Botswana border, along a seldom-used road that ran straight through Chobe National Park.

GENERAL ALEXANDER KOROTKOV, the head of the KGB division for African affairs, entered Botswana on a diplomatic passport. A chauffeur called for him at the airport in Gaberones and drove him to the Soviet embassy. The next morning, Korotkov started off in a rented VW for the meeting place near the border town of Lobatsi, fifty miles away.

The South Africans had insisted on vetting him, so the general drove the last few miles along the tarmac road to the border alone. From the checkpoint to the actual border, visible from far away through double barbed-wire, there lay a stretch of no-man's-land. This area was filled with concrete blocks, and the car had to zigzag slowly through them.

At a gate in a cattle fence, a few hundred yards before the border, Korotkov stopped as agreed, opened it, and drove a short distance along a bumpy side road, past an old steam engine. When the manganese mine there had shut down years ago, it had been left, like the housing for the workers, and a prefab office building.

As agreed, General Erik Van Zyl had likewise come alone. He stepped out of the shade of the buildings and shook hands.

"I would never have dreamed that we would meet again this soon," said Korotkov. He looked grumpy. "Not a cosy place."

"I don't exactly have fond memories of that cold park in Moscow," said Van Zyl. "You didn't tell me that Tutuma was there, too. Too bad, I would have liked to meet him."

"Excuse me—what did you say this man's name was?"

Van Zyl laughed. "Now really, you brought him to the airport yourself. Have you forgotten? I saw you together."

"You must be confusing two different men," growled Korotkov, slightly irritated. "When two people talk about a third person whom neither of them knows, nothing much can come of it. I suggest we change the subject."

"OK. Let's go back to our conversation in Moscow. We discussed the topic thoroughly then. A division of our spheres of interest in southern Africa. We took the first step, and it would be good if you took a step towards us. Pretoria is waiting for proof of your good intentions—a definite gesture."

"For instance?"

Van Zyl paced up and down. "My government is somewhat irritated at the contradictory behaviour of your organization. On the one hand, we are having what I hope is a serious discussion about peaceful collaboration. On the other hand, you are conspiring with a man like Tutuma. This has greatly hindered the efforts of the group I represent. Let us call them the doves. I do not see now how we can prevent the hawks from disavowing the Soviet Union at our next international press conference."

Korotkov grinned sceptically.

"We have Tutuma's accomplice in custody," Van Zyl went on. "An African named Moses Nkala. The hawks would like to present him to the international press. He will state that he and Tutuma robbed the diamond mine of Orapa under orders from the Soviet government."

"Your Moses can't state that because it's a dirty lie."

"We could present a witness to corroborate his statement: the pilot of the hijacked aeroplane. We could present a photograph of

Orapa's head of security, Jan Feuchtenbeiner. More precisely: a photograph of his corpse. It washed up yesterday in the Okavango Delta. Would you be interested in the name of the murderer?"

"You didn't drag me all the way here from Moscow to give me a cops-and-robbers story!"

"Tutuma, the man whom the Soviet Union wants to install as head of government in Zimbabwe, is a thief and murderer. There should still be some morals left, even in politics, don't you think?"

"Let's leave morality out of this. I do not know any Tutuma. And if this man really did rob your diamond mine and shoot a security officer, then it happened without the knowledge or approval of the Soviet government."

"So you would leave Tutuma to us?"

"I think I have expressed myself clearly enough. I do not know this Tutuma."

"Let's assume we intercepted a coded radio message that was transmitted from Maun. Let's also assume we know the recipient, who lives in Lusaka. His call number is 9J1AX."

"You seem to be implying that we are in contact with this Tutuma. Why in the world should we hand the man over to you?"

"You sacrifice a piece, which has become worthless for you anyway. But you gain a better position in the overall strategic concept."

"You mean that in that case you would not gamble your long-range goal of an arrangement with the Soviet Union just for the sake of a short-term propaganda coup? You would not present him at an international press conference in order to defame the Soviet Union's policies in Africa?"

"No sensible chess player bothers with a pawn if it risks the loss of his queen."

"Are you hoping for a draw?"

"A fair draw would help us both and harm neither of us."

Two hours later, in Gaberones, General Korotkov composed a radio message. A courier flew to Lusaka, where the text was ciphered in the embassy code department and transmitted to James Pritchard's hotel. BOSS likewise changed its plans. Niehoujs in Maun received orders that there was no point for the time being in kidnapping Dieter Hahn.

502

ALL DAY LONG, they never said a word to one another. Volodya sat with pinched lips next to the black driver of the Bedford, staring grouchily at the tremendous zebra herds that galloped along in front of the truck. He felt a cutting pain beneath his operation scar. Nearly every half hour, he tapped the driver, who stopped the truck while he climbed out and vanished behind a bush. Dieter was too absorbed in his own thoughts to feel sorry for the Englishman. He had spent a bad night, his body often drenched with sweat. Now a feeling of indifference had grown up between him and the outside world. He recalled the stings of the tsetse flies in the delta and was afraid of sleeping sickness.

At Kasane, the driver dropped his two passengers in the middle of the village. On the terrace of the Chobe Safari Lodge, Dieter found Dr. Keiser, a fellow German who had taken over the public health centre here six months ago. "You don't look so good, Herr Hahn," he said.

"I got bitten by tsetse flies a couple of days ago," said Dieter. "And now I feel like hell."

"Fever, fatigue, trouble concentrating, diarrhoea?"

"My friend Mr. Pritchard is the one with the runs."

Dr. Keiser led the two sick men into his bush hospital. Taking samples of their blood, he vanished into his lab. "You have a very ordinary colic, Mr. Pritchard," he told Volodya when he returned. "Oatmeal, charcoal tablets, broth, black tea, salt tablets, and three days in bed." Then he returned to Dieter. "Were you bitten by a tick recently?"

"Yes, in the back of my knee." Dieter pulled up the leg of his jeans and showed the doctor the still-visible swelling.

"It's a clear case of South African tick fever." The doctor gave him a small bag of tablets. "Two pills four times a day, and stay in bed for three days. You men can get a two-bed ward here, with daily consultation."

"Tick fever? Is that dangerous?"

"You'll have forgotten all about it in three days."

"Thank you so much, doctor," said Volodya. "It's too bad we can't accept your offer. We're only passing through and we're in something of a hurry."

Dr. Keiser seemed seriously disappointed. "I was so delighted to see some new faces here. You're the first Europeans to make it through here in four weeks."

Dieter would have liked to stay, but he was too apathetic to argue with Pritchard, who insisted on travelling on. Tutuma would be waiting down by the shore of the Chobe at sunset, and the sun would be going down within an hour. When Dieter asked the doctor if he could borrow his Land-Rover, the doctor didn't ask many questions.

There was only one passable road leading out of Kasane to the Kazungula ferry. Dieter followed Tutuma's directions to the meeting place. Because of the nearby river, the vegetation on both sides of the road was luxuriant, almost impenetrable, but five miles outside Kasane, Dieter found the lane that Tutuma had described. It led off the road through jungle, down to the river. By the bank, they saw the placid monkey bread tree under which he was supposed to wait for Tutuma.

Dieter parked the Land-Rover two hundred yards farther on and walked back. A couple of hippopotamuses swam indolently in the water, but the fluttering of their ears betrayed their disquiet.

They found a mocoro waiting with two paddles. Abruptly, with almost no transition, night descended, as though someone had zipped a black curtain across the world. They hadn't heard Tutuma coming but suddenly he stood with them. "Volodya!" he said, stunned. "Did you come here especially from Moscow?"

Volodya hugged the African and kissed him on both cheeks. "Everything is ready, Tutuma," he said with a warning glance at Dieter. "But don't ask any questions now."

After Tutuma had hugged Dieter too, he pulled the two newcomers into a reed-covered shelter. Dieter recognized Dikeledi's slender silhouette. She went to nestle against Tutuma's shoulder, smiling at Dieter. Her eyes and teeth shimmered, radiant points in the darkness.

"She's afraid of the dark," said Tutuma. "And we mustn't light any fire here."

"I'll take you across tomorrow," said Volodya. "Two hours before daybreak. Our people will be waiting on the other bank."

504

Dikeledi touched Dieter's hand. "It's hot!" she said.

"I've got tick fever." Dieter had taken in the impressions of the day through a haze. Nevertheless, he couldn't get rid of a queasy feeling that something was wrong. Hadn't Tutuma called the Englishman "Volodya", and hadn't he used the word "Moscow"? What kind of a conspiracy had he stumbled into—sucker that he was?

Pritchard glanced impatiently at the luminous dial of his watch. "I have to go back to the Land-Rover and get my stuff."

"Wait, Mr. Pritchard," Dieter said. "I'll come along."

"Just tell me what to bring you." He sounded definite.

"Bring me my blanket and sleeping bag," said Dieter.

When Pritchard vanished into the darkness, Dieter turned to Tutuma. "Why didn't he want to have me around?"

"He probably wants to catch a radio message. They still have some things to work out. Like the exact point of crossing."

"A radio message? Who from?" Tutuma pointed wordlessly across the river. "Who's over there? The Russians?"

"Why don't you take a nap for a couple of hours, Dieter?"

"He told me his name was James Pritchard. But Volodya is a Russian name."

Tutuma was silent. Then he said: "No one else will help us."

"So the message that I radioed for you in Maun didn't go to your independence movement. It went to the Russians." It was a statement of fact, not a question.

"All we get from the others is fine words. But what we need is weapons."

"You lied to me from the very beginning."

"We're at war, and you're white."

"Don't you make any distinctions among whites?"

"It wasn't we Africans who put up the barrier between black and white."

A bitter, sobering feeling rose in Dieter. He got to his feet and shook hands with his friend. "Lots of luck, Tutuma. Now you probably don't need me any more."

Tutuma took his hand and held it tight. "You can't go yet."

"Are you afraid I'll rat on you?"

Tutuma hesitated. "It's because of Volodya. He wouldn't like it. He doesn't want to run any risks."

"Do *you* at least believe I wouldn't do it?"

"Yes."

"So do I," said Dikeledi.

Nevertheless, Tutuma still clutched Dieter's hand.

"When will you let me go?"

Tutuma loosened his hold. "As soon as we start to cross the river. Two hours before sunrise."

Dieter heard Volodya coming back. He seemed disgruntled.

"Is something wrong?" asked Tutuma.

"Everything's fine," mumbled the Russian. "Two hours before sunrise. Right here." He took a blanket under his arm and trudged off without another word.

Tutuma stared after him. "What's wrong with him?"

"Stomach ache," explained Dieter, picking up his sleeping bag and carrying it off. He undressed at the foot of the monkey bread tree, unrolled the sleeping bag, and snuggled into it.

Dieter wanted to be alone with his disappointment. Tutuma had used him from the very first moment when he stood in his overalls by the trail in the Kalahari. He had needed a chauffeur, not a friend, and Dieter had been taken in. But he mustn't feel sorry for himself: it was his own fault, he was too trusting. By the time Click-Clack was murdered, he should have sensed that a game was being played without his knowing the rules. Instead, he had let himself be used as a go-between, to transmit a coded message to the Russians and finally even to bring one of their agents here. And he had involved others; like Sigi, who had risked his CB licence. And Dieter had even gambled the truck that Helmuth's brigade so desperately needed, and with that, all the German aid in that part of Botswana.

This would never have happened to Sigi or Helmuth. They were adults, and being an adult meant being cautious and conforming, and using common sense. "It's time you finally grew up," his father had always sermonized.

But if he had refused to help that fugitive in the Kalahari three weeks ago, Tutuma would have been shot down long since . . . .

506

Dieter shuddered at the notion of what the world would look like if it were only populated by adults.

Now the adventure was over, the stress and the great game. And all that Dieter had left was a stale, sober feeling. In a couple of days, his humdrum routine as a volunteer would begin. And he would sit in Riley's bar, like all the others, and listen to stories. Except that he could not tell *his* tale.

LONG BEFORE daybreak, the first signal light flashed from the opposite bank. It was followed by two more. Volodya looked at the luminous dial of his watch. Twelve minutes after three. He moved up close to the water and answered the signal with his torch.

Tutuma crouched on the ground like a cat. The river was at most 1,500 feet wide at this point, the current weak, the sky overcast. Conditions were ideal. Volodya and he and Dikeledi wouldn't need more than twenty minutes to reach the opposite bank. There they would be greeted by a squad of Zambian volunteers who had sneaked in one by one the previous night. The Zambian border was fifteen miles away from here. The soldiers would get them as far as the Zambezi river and then, so Volodya had told him, across it to safety. Slowly Tutuma slid the mocoro into the water. Dikeledi got in first, then the Russian, finally Tutuma himself. He pushed the dugout away from the bank, dipped one paddle into the water and gave Dikeledi the other.

On the shore, Tutuma could hear the engine of the Land-Rover start up. Tutuma glanced back, hardly longer than a second: "He could at least have said goodbye!"

"He can't do any harm," Volodya said. He listened to the waning hum of the engine.

Since receiving the latest radio message, Volodya had seemed surly. His eyes were fixed on the opposite bank as they drew closer and closer. Although Dr. Keiser had stuffed him full of tablets, the pains were more violent than ever. Volodya didn't have the strength to fight against a wave of self-pity. Why did they have to choose him for this filthy job? After all, General Korotkov had accused Volodya often enough of not always separating duty and private feelings. Why the hell hadn't they left him out of this business as in the past whenever an individual had to be dealt with harshly? Betraying friends was not part of his duty. The KGB had specialists for that sort of thing.

"Does it hurt?" asked Tutuma softly.

Volodya pressed his hands on his abdomen. He trusts me, damn it! He thinks he can still free his people, build something. I thought the same way when I was thirty.

The pain crashed like a wave over Volodya, knocking him breathless for several moments. He couched his head on the moist black wood. Tutuma stopped paddling and bent over the Russian. He said something in Kalanga to Dikeledi. She put down her paddle and felt Volodya's forehead.

"Turn back," the Russian barely squeezed out.

"Just a few more minutes, Volodya. Then we'll be there."

"I've put faith behind me. But you still believe in what you're doing."

"Just lie quietly. We're almost there."

"But you ought to have a chance." Volodya propped himself up. "You'll never reach Zambia, Tutuma. It's a trap."

"What is he saying?" asked Dikeledi.

"He's delirious. He's got a fever."

"I've never been so lucid in my life, Tutuma. You think your friends are waiting for us. *Nye chuya!* Not on your life! It's the South Africans!"

"But the radio message!"

"That's when I found out." Volodya grabbed Tutuma's T-shirt. "Stop asking questions. Turn back!"

Tutuma still hesitated. "Why did you send us across in the first place?"

"Orders. My people have made a deal with the Boers. They don't need you any more."

"Turn around!" Dikeledi was pleading now. "Quickly!"

Tutuma turned the mocoro around and paddled back. "I should've known you can't trust a white man!" he murmured.

He turned his head. On the other shore, there were shouts in Afrikaans. Spotlights blazed up, shone across the river surface, thrust white fingers towards the dugout, clutched it in their beams.

The roar of motorboats behind a tongue of land began to shred the silence. Then they shot ominously towards the mocoro. Their headlights made them look like one-eyed crocodiles.

Volodya held up his hand in front of his dazzled eyes. Now, he regretted giving in to his moment of weakness. He cringed on the floor of the rocking canoe. Dikeledi and Tutuma smashed the paddles into the churning water. They were nearly at the bank.

Bullets lashed the water. The water splashed into their faces. The first motorboat was only 150 feet behind them when the mocoro rammed against the bank. Tutuma and Dikeledi dropped the paddles and leaped ashore. By the time the first motorboat reached the bank, the jungle had already swallowed them up. For a while, the floodlights chased along the shore. They tried to penetrate the thicket, blocked by the dark wall of leaves.

Men with machineguns glanced at Volodya and ran on past him into the thorny jungle. He remained alone on shore for a while, hearing yells from farther and farther away. Then he pulled himself up, crept on all fours to the monkey bread tree, and banged his head against the hard bark five or six times, until blood gushed down his forehead, as if he had been beaten up by the young African. It doesn't even hurt, he thought, as he crawled back to the canoe.

A FEW MILES downstream, at the point where the Chobe and the Zambezi come together, four countries meet. Border guards heard the shots, and since nobody knew what the shooting was all about, the South-West Africans, Rhodesians, Zambians and Botswanans launched into an exchange of gunfire. This developed into a short, nervous skirmish with no casualties. Accordingly, the newspapers found nothing worth mentioning.

But in the hospital in Kasane, Dieter heard about the incident the next day. Things like that often happened here, said Dr. Keiser. It didn't mean a thing.

Recovering from tick fever, Dieter Hahn set out for Ghanzi to help the Africans in his own way and to pursue his dream of helping the Bushmen. He is still shadowed by BOSS today.

Colonel Volodya Naumov, upon returning to Moscow, was

severely reprimanded for lacking alertness during his assignment in Botswana. Such an experienced officer should not have been so easily overpowered by Tutuma and Dikeledi, said the KGB, sending him into early retirement.

BOSS was irritated too. For Erik Van Zyl had refused to accept the statement of his Soviet colleagues that the coup on the Chobe had failed because of a sick KGB agent. So the hawks in BOSS got the upper hand again. Further overtures to the Soviet Union were taboo.

There has been no reliable information on Moses Nkala. A prisoner who escaped from the penal colony at Robben Island claims he recognized Moses there in an exercise area set aside for prisoners in solitary confinement.

Tutuma and Dikeledi managed to get to South-West Africa, hiding out temporarily with the black freedom fighters of SWAPO. Tutuma, using a new *nom de guerre*, tried later to build up an independence movement in Zambia, but without Soviet arms neither January nor he had any chance of success. That night on the Chobe, the diamonds had lost any meaning for him. Without the Russians, he would never have found a buyer for them anyhow.

De Beers has long since got over the loss of 400,000 carats at a conservatively estimated value of twelve million dollars. The Central Selling Organization simply raised the world market price for diamonds by fifteen per cent.